English 5–11

English is central to the primary-school curriculum and successfully mastering the basics has a significant influence on pupils' ability to learn and achieve their future goals.

Now fully updated, *English 5–11* provides comprehensive, up-to-date and creative guidance on teaching English in the primary school. Each chapter provides the busy teacher with indispensable advice and guidance, as well as opportunities to reflect upon current practice in the classroom. Key areas covered include:

- language and literacy development;
- grammar, punctuation and spelling;
- talk for learning;
- systematic synthetic phonics;
- fiction, poetry and non-fiction;
- drama and creativity;
- teaching in a multilingual classroom;
- ICT and assessment.

This second edition reflects changes in government policy and gives greater attention to systematic synthetic phonics, assessment, drama and talk for writing, and is closely related to the changing curriculum for primary English.

The highly experienced author team are former literacy advisors and have frontline teaching, school-management and teacher-training experience. This book will be an invaluable resource for all trainee and practising teachers interested in teaching English in an accessible, contemporary and dynamic way.

David Waugh is Director of Primary PGCE and Course Leader for Primary English at the University of Durham, UK.

Wendy Jolliffe is Head of Teacher Education and Head of Scarborough School of Education at the University of Hull, UK.

The *5–11* series combines academic rigor with practical classroom experience in a tried and tested approach which has proved indispensible to both trainee PGCE students and to practicing teachers. Bringing the best and latest research knowledge to core subject areas, this series addresses the key issues surrounding the teaching of these subjects in the primary curriculum. The series aims to stay up to date by reflecting changes in government policy and is closely related to the changing curriculum for the primary core subjects.

Each book contains lesson planning guidance and methods to develop pupils' understanding as well as offering creative and innovative ways to teach subjects in the primary classroom.

Titles in this series include:

Physical Education 5–11, Jonathan Doherty

History 5–11, Hilary Cooper

Modern Foreign Languages 5–11, Jane Jones and Simon Coffey

English 5–11, David Waugh and Wendy Jolliffe

English 5–11

A guide for teachers

Second edition

David Waugh and Wendy Jolliffe

Routledge
Taylor & Francis Group

LONDON AND NEW YORK

Second edition published 2013
by Routledge
2 Park Square, Milton Park, Abingdon, Oxon OX14 4RN

Simultaneously published in the USA and Canada
by Routledge
711 Third Avenue, New York, NY 10017

Routledge is an imprint of the Taylor & Francis Group, an informa business

First edition published by Routledge 2007

British Library Cataloguing in Publication Data
A catalogue record for this book is available from the British Library

Library of Congress Cataloging in Publication Data
Waugh, David.
    English 5-11 : a guide for teachers / David Waugh, Wendy Jolliffe. -- 2nd ed.
    p. cm.
    ISBN 978-0-415-69971-6 (hardback) -- ISBN 978-0-415-69973-0 (paperback) --
    ISBN 978-0-203-13541-9 (ebook) 1. Language arts (Primary)--Great Britain. 2.
    English language--Study and teaching (Primary)--Great Britain. I. Jolliffe, Wendy.
    II. Title.
    LB1576.W29 2012
    372.6--dc23
    2012022394

ISBN: 978-0-415-69971-6 (hbk)
ISBN: 978-0-415-69973-0 (pbk)
ISBN: 978-0-203-13541-9 (ebk)

Typeset in Bembo Std and Helvetica Neue LT Pro
by Saxon Graphics Ltd, Derby

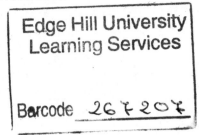

MIX
Paper from
responsible sources
FSC
www.fsc.org   FSC® C004839

Printed and bound in Great Britain by the MPG Books Group

Contents

Acknowledgements   vii

Introduction   1

1   The pedagogy of teaching English in the primary school   4

2   Classroom management in English   15

3   Creative approaches to teaching literacy   24

4   Understanding language and literacy development   44

5   Knowledge about language: grammar and punctuation   66

6   Talking to learn   84

7   Teaching and learning reading   105

8   Fiction and poetry   137

9   Reading and writing for information   158

10 Learning and teaching in a multilingual classroom   179

11 Developing children's writing   192

12 Spelling   212

13 Using technology to enhance the learning and teaching of English   230

14 Drama   248

15 Planning for English   263

16 Assessment for learning of English   289

Conclusions   309

References   311
Index   324

Acknowledgements

The authors would like to thank the following for their contributions to this book:

Claire Head for contributing Chapter 10, 'Learning and teaching in a multilingual classroom'. Claire is a lecturer in Primary English at the Faculty of Education at the University of Hull.

John Bennett and Richard English for contributing Chapter 13, 'Using technology to enhance the learning and teaching of English'. John is a former headteacher and now a lecturer in Primary English at the Faculty of Education at the University of Hull. Richard is a senior lecturer and PGCE Primary Programme Director at the Faculty of Education at the University of Hull. He has also worked as a consultant for the National Strategies.

Claire Hostick, a former pupil of David Waugh at Mount Pleasant C of E School, Market Weighton, for her kind permission to use samples of her writing 'The Fog'.

Introduction

The first edition of this book, English 3–11, was written at a time when the Primary National Strategy, which had evolved from the National Literacy Strategy, had introduced the Primary Framework in 2006. Some schools saw this framework as a replacement for the National Curriculum for English, although the latter has remained in place. Since then, there have been announcements about a new National Curriculum for England and Wales to be introduced in 2014 and a draft curriculum has been produced.

Since the 2008 edition, the National Strategies, for which both of us worked for two years, has disappeared, leaving a vacuum for some teachers who made considerable use of its many resources. Alexander (2010) has suggested that this will allow teachers to follow a *repertoire* rather than a *recipe*, and will afford them greater freedom to plan creatively. However, many teachers will still wish to use the resources, some of which are still available via an archived website at the time of writing, and many schools continue to use resources such as the *Letters and Sounds* phonics programme and *Support for Spelling*, its successor for Key Stage 2. However, the demise of the National Strategies has provided an opportunity for educational publishers to fill a void, and new teachers are increasingly faced with a huge range of schemes, programmes and innovative web-based resources, which they may not have explored during their training courses. This makes it all the more important that resources and teaching approaches are considered carefully and critically within the context of a reflective approach to what works well for the children we teach.

Teaching English for children aged five to eleven is a challenge, not only because an ability to read, write and speak English is central to success across the curriculum but also because, since English is such a central part of the curriculum, it is a matter for constant debate. And, when this debate is informed by concerns about standards of literacy, politicians become particularly interested and seek ways to address perceived problems. Hence the repeated modifications to the English curriculum and the regular changes in emphasis on the way in which teachers are expected to teach. There appears to be little doubt that the new curriculum for English in England and Wales will place a strong emphasis upon teaching reading through systematic synthetic phonics, and it is also likely to include an increased emphasis upon grammar, punctuation, spelling and handwriting. There are hints that the curriculum may be rather less prescriptive than its predecessors and, while it may permit more scope for innovative teaching, might also provide licence for some teachers to avoid aspects of English teaching that hold limited appeal for *them* but are essential for their pupils' development.

This book should be read in the context of the changes described above. While we accept that most readers will be involved with primary education in Britain, given that that is the context in which we work, and that the changes described will be especially relevant to them, we hope that we have written the book in such a way that it will have a broader appeal. It is intended to provide guidance on how to teach the curriculum as it is currently constituted, but we hope that it will also promote discussion and reflection upon practice based upon a review of relevant research. Anyone entering the teaching profession in the twenty-first century needs to be flexible enough to incorporate change and to adapt their teaching when the curriculum is revised. Teachers also need to be able to understand why changes come about and to ensure that they are able to justify their methods to parents and pupils, as well as to themselves. We hope that this book will provide a starting point for such reflection and that many of the activities within it will encourage teachers to think about their practice.

In Chapter 1, the pedagogy of teaching English is discussed, with key elements of knowledge, decision-making and teachers' actions explored. Chapter 2 takes the pedagogical theme further by looking at classroom management, and discussing practical strategies for improving it. One of the most welcome changes to English-teaching in recent years has been a return to focusing on creativity and enjoyment, and this theme is the subject of Chapter 3.

In Chapter 4, we examine language and literacy development, discussing the role of play, literacy at home and environmental print, as well as looking at early reading and writing and the development of language skills. Chapter 5 examines the knowledge about language that teachers need to acquire if they are to deliver the curriculum successfully, and provides practical ideas for classroom activities to develop children's linguistic understanding.

Teachers have welcomed the higher profile given to speaking and listening in the Primary National Strategy, and Chapter 6 explores the importance of developing and managing talk, and the value of drama and cooperative learning strategies. It is particularly important to ensure an understanding of the importance of speaking and listening for teachers as the draft National Curriculum for English gives only scant mention to it and thus there is a danger its central role in teaching literacy could be diminished. Chapter 7 focuses on the teaching and learning of reading and examines different approaches while offering practical advice on teaching phonics within a comprehensive programme. The content of this chapter reflects the changing approaches to teaching reading and provides both theoretical underpinnings to set the current debate in context and practical ideas for the classroom.

Chapter 8, 'Fiction and poetry', not only discusses the value of literature in the classroom but also provides examples of stories and poems that can be used both to entertain and to engage children's interest in the genres. Chapter 9 looks at non-fiction texts and at strategies for developing children's understanding of information texts.

In Chapter 10, written by Claire Head, there is a particular focus on children who have English as an additional language (EAL). The strategies designed to support them have wider implications for the ways in which we help others who face the challenge of developing language and literacy skills.

The development of children's writing is the theme of Chapter 11, and here again there are many practical ideas for work in the classroom, as well as a discussion about positive approaches to writing and the development of independent writing. Spelling and strategies for learning to spell in a language that is often irregular and phonically inconsistent are the focus of Chapter 12, and there are opportunities for readers to test their own spelling understanding and develop their own spelling abilities.

Chapter 13, written by John Bennett and Richard English, explores the use of ICT in teaching and learning in English, offering advice and tips on resources for making the most of what is available. This chapter has been radically rewritten (as with so much of the first edition), as a result of recent changes and technological developments. Chapter 14 is an addition to the first edition and focuses on drama, an aspect of the curriculum sadly neglected in many schools in the past. In Chapter 15, we look at planning for English and, in particular, at what might constitute good practice. The final chapter, on assessment for learning, complements the planning chapter in that it explores building assessment into curriculum planning, as well as the characteristics of assessment for learning, and involving pupils in the assessment process. There is also discussion about the assessment of reading, writing, speaking and listening.

At the beginning of each chapter we set out the chapter's purpose, and we summarise key points at the end. Every chapter has activities designed to encourage discussion and reflection; these may often be undertaken independently but most will best be done cooperatively with fellow professionals.

We hope that anyone reading this book will find it thought-provoking as well as practical, and that it will lead to readers reflecting upon their own practice and discussing the value of different approaches to teaching English from five to eleven.

David Waugh
Wendy Jolliffe
2012

1

The pedagogy of teaching English in the primary school

Purpose of this chapter

This chapter aims to:

- look at the nature of pedagogy and examine what the term means;
- explore the knowledge that teachers need to teach effectively;
- look at teachers' decision-making and how this is informed by their knowledge;
- examine how teachers' actions are influenced by their knowledge and by the decisions they make;
- look at the qualities needed to teach English effectively in the primary school.

What is pedagogy?

Pedagogy is defined by the *Oxford English Dictionary* as 'the science of teaching'. Alexander (2000: 540) states: 'Pedagogy encompasses the performance of teaching together with the theories, beliefs, policies and controversies that inform and shape it'. However, not many teachers use the term. Hayes (2000) discusses those experienced teachers who maintain that teaching is a practical activity and that the theoretical study of teaching in higher education is irrelevant once one enters the classroom. However, he counters that:

> Those who are charged with the difficult and demanding task of educating our children and young people must be clear about what they are doing, why they are doing it, and how they will know if it is successful.
>
> (Hayes 2000: 20)

To be effective as a teacher one needs to think about what one does and why. In this chapter, the three important elements identified by Kyriacou (1991: 5) will be used to focus discussion:

- *Knowledge:* comprising the teacher's knowledge about the subject, pupils, curriculum, teaching methods, the influence on teaching and learning of other factors, and knowledge about one's teaching skills.

- *Decision-making:* comprising the thinking and decision-making which occurs before, during and after a lesson, concerning how best to achieve the educational outcomes intended.

- *Action:* comprising the overt behaviour by teachers undertaken to foster pupil learning.

We will see how the three key skills apply generally and then specifically in the teaching of English. We will see that knowledge is essential if decision-making is to be informed and effective, and that the decisions that teachers make affect the actions they take and in turn affect the ways in which children learn.

Knowledge needed by teachers

Teachers need different types of knowledge to enable them to teach effectively.

Knowledge of the curriculum

Fox (2005) uses the term 'pedagogical content' knowledge to represent 'subject matter knowledge centred on classroom tasks, activities and explanations' and states that it includes knowledge of the following:

- representation of facts, concepts and methods in the subject, using metaphors and analogies to connect with more general knowledge;

- tasks that are productive for learning, including the relevant resources, their organization, and health and safety issues;

- examples of key ideas, rules and problems which link the particular to the general and thus promote understanding;

- students and their existing levels of understanding and skill in the subject, including common misconceptions and errors;

- how understanding in the subject typically advances from one level to another;

- productive locations for out-of-school work;

- knowledge of research that supports teaching and learning in the subject.

(Fox 2005: 257)

It is important to realise that pedagogical content knowledge is constantly changing, just as do the pupils we teach change each year, leading effective and reflective teachers to constantly review their practice.

The curriculum for English in English schools has gone through several incarnations since the inception of the National Curriculum for English in 1990 (DES 1990). While there are many common features, there have also been changes of emphasis that have demanded that teachers examine their own subject knowledge before planning schemes of work for their pupils. For example, an increasing emphasis in government documents upon the teaching of phonics culminated in the Primary National Strategy, which placed the teaching of systematic synthetic phonics at the heart of the teaching of reading (DfES 2006b).

The teaching of phonics is discussed in detail in Chapter 7, and so the mechanics will not be explored in depth here. However, as a teacher, you need to ensure that you understand the terminology relating to phonics teaching and that you are able to teach children how to use phonic knowledge to decode unfamiliar words. Remember that not all experienced teachers received adequate training in the teaching of phonics, particularly before 1990, when some training courses virtually ignored phonics in favour of less structured approaches to reading. It is by no means certain, therefore, that you will see good practice in your school, and you may find that you have a more sophisticated understanding of phonics than some of the teachers with whom you work. For a basic knowledge of phonics teaching and learning see Jolliffe (2006) and for more details see Jolliffe and Waugh with Carss (2012).

Another aspect of the curriculum that may challenge teachers is the growing emphasis on ICT, with the 2006 Literacy Framework including many activities related to film and computers, interactive whiteboards, children's writing and so on (see Chapter 13, on using ICT and English).

The levels of subject knowledge required to teach children about language are now considerably greater than many of us acquired during our secondary schooling, and even during teacher training. Chapter 5, on 'Knowledge about language', explores ways of teaching about language through meaningful activities, but many people may initially be confused by much of the terminology that appears there and in the Primary Strategy. Many students arrive at initial teacher education courses thinking that mathematics and science will be the most challenging subjects but quickly discover that English, a subject they had previously felt confident about (after all, they can read, write, speak and listen), is their greatest weakness.

Among student teachers' main concerns are:

- understanding the parts of speech and their functions;
- understanding punctuation, especially possessive apostrophes;
- understanding linguistic terminology;
- understanding how to teach reading.

Fortunately, each of these areas can be taught and learned so that the overwhelming majority of primary teachers begin their first job quite confident about them. However, with several other subjects to understand, as well as class management (the major concern of most trainees), training and induction-year programmes have become increasingly intensive. One would hope that, by the time the children who were educated through the Literacy Framework and National Strategies reach higher education, teacher trainers will need to give far less attention to explaining the first three items in the bullet list, which, on the whole, remain constant. As for the fourth item, teaching reading, this highly important part of the curriculum is a matter for constant debate and frequent changes of emphasis. Even those teachers described by Hayes (2000) who argue that teaching is a purely practical profession must find out about the latest theories on reading and consider adapting their teaching accordingly, if only because a failure to do so might be damaging if Ofsted comes calling.

Knowledge of pupils

Knowledge for the teacher is not restricted to the curriculum. It is vital that you know and understand your pupils and are able to differentiate your teaching to meet their needs. Also, you should assess pupils' progress in informal, semi-structured and formal ways, not only because teachers need to plan for progression but also because children, parents and colleagues will want to know how the children are progressing too. Information about children can be acquired from other teachers but must be kept up-to-date and modified as children progress.

Then there are children's special needs, which must be identified and acted upon. Good teachers will know a range of strategies for supporting pupils and will regularly seek professional development to increase their understanding of the needs of children with English as an additional language (EAL), various physical disabilities or learning difficulties such as dyslexia and dyspraxia. Where children in their classes receive external learning support, teachers will ensure that they know what this support entails and learn how it may be linked to how they work with the children in class.

Teachers also need to be aware of children's changing interests and that, by sometimes relating teaching and learning to children's hobbies and interests, teachers may be able to engage them, hold their attention and provide stimuli for discussion.

Knowledge of factors that affect teaching and learning

The classroom environment will impinge upon the way in which teachers teach and children learn, and this will be discussed in relation to language in the section on decision-making. However, besides understanding the features of a language-friendly classroom, teachers also need to be aware of the impact that the weather and classroom ventilation and temperature can have. Experienced teachers tend to be alert to the effects of the physical environment and even anticipate these and modify their teaching accordingly, especially on windy days (notorious for affecting pupil behaviour!) and days when children are kept inside all day due to bad weather. Attempting a lesson that requires lengthy periods of sitting still when children have been inactive can be very challenging, and teachers often modify tasks to make them more active and vigorous in such circumstances, perhaps using drama or debate.

Knowledge of how to teach the curriculum

Besides understanding the content of the curriculum, the needs of their pupils and the environmental factors that may affect their pupils' learning, teachers need to be aware of current thinking on how to teach the curriculum. We will explore this further in later chapters, but at this stage we will focus on some of the knowledge teachers need to acquire. For example, it is important to keep up to date on the latest government initiatives and to be aware of key pieces of educational research. While most teachers do not have time to read academic journals and government documents, they can find concise reports and reviews in the *Times Educational Supplement* on Friday and *Guardian Education* on Tuesday. Without an understanding of what is actually being said, teachers are as susceptible as the rest of the population to tabloid press misinterpretations and may find it difficult to justify their teaching methods when questioned by parents.

Knowledge of one's own teaching skills

Central to professional development is self-knowledge and an ability to reflect upon one's teaching and pupils' learning. Reflection and self-evaluation are key elements of teaching placements during initial teacher training programmes, with trainees usually having to write lesson evaluations or reflective diaries. Teachers are helped to reflect during training via frequent observation and written and oral feedback, with strengths and weaknesses highlighted and targets being set.

While teaching observation is now a part of teachers' professional development, it is seldom as intense or as frequent as during training. Thus, teachers who wish to develop their teaching skills need to invite constructive criticism from respected colleagues on their teaching style, mannerisms, resources used, classroom organisation and class management. This interaction should not be something to fear but should form part of a continuing professional dialogue.

ACTIVITY: REFLECTING ON YOUR TEACHING OF ENGLISH

- What do you do well?
- What could you do better?
- What do you really struggle with?
- What could you do to improve your teaching of English?

The way in which your knowledge affects your teaching can be compared with the way in which professional snooker players play a shot. In deciding which ball to aim for, snooker players draw upon past experience of the consequences of similar shots, an understanding of angles and where the balls are likely to end up after the shot, as well as considering the bigger picture and the next shots they will play. They also use prior knowledge to determine how to strike the ball to give it back spin or power. Experienced snooker stars make many of these decisions almost subconsciously because their knowledge base is so great that they can sum up their next move very quickly. Skilled teachers, too, often act instinctively, making hundreds of decisions every day about resources to use, ways of conveying information, classroom organisation, responses to children's questions, and questions to ask. Most of these decisions will be made quickly and will be based upon knowledge and experience. At other times, teachers have the luxury of being able to plan independently or with colleagues, reflect upon past lessons and observe how others work. Good teachers tend to make an increasingly high percentage of their decisions instinctively but still take time to reflect and plan, just as good snooker players build up their knowledge by practising.

In the next section we will look at decision-making, focusing in particular upon decisions that teachers can make about the environment in which they and their pupils work.

Decision-making

Wragg (1997: 94) stated that 'decisions about how pupils should learn and how teachers should teach need to reflect both purpose and context'. He went on to illustrate this point with examples:

When teachers are telling a story to a class of 5-year-olds, it is usually best sense to read the story to the whole class, rather than individually to each of 30 or more children. By contrast, if 30 people aged from 17 to 70 want to learn to drive, then they will expect individual practice in actually driving a car, not a mass lecture on the function of the clutch. Anyone wanting to sing in a quartet will need three like-minded people. Matching what is desirable to what is feasible is part of the art of teaching effectively.

(Wragg 1997: 94)

In exploring the kinds of decision-making that teachers of English engage in, we will look first at the nature of the classroom and then at planning for teaching, before examining ways in which teachers might reflect upon their teaching in order to improve and develop it.

Creating a classroom environment for language

At the heart of good English teaching is the environment in which teaching and learning takes place. Some classrooms are rich in language and opportunities for language. Walls are not only redolent with brightly coloured displays, including pictures and objects for children to discuss, but also adorned with pieces of text, lists of useful words and examples of children's writing that can be read by the class and by visitors. There may, especially for younger children, be an area in which role-play activities are focused on, say, a shop, café, house or train. There will be language games, newspapers, books, timetables and advertisements, as well as, perhaps, football league tables, interesting lists and facts about topics that interest children.

As children move through the school, they will find that the language stimuli in their classrooms change and increasingly cater for their different needs and interests. It is part of the teachers' decision-making process to ensure that they create an appropriately stimulating environment for their pupils that conveys the idea that language, both written and spoken, is valuable and to be celebrated.

Many of the children we teach will come from clean, tidy, well-decorated homes in which there are many stimulating things with which to play. They may have video recorders, computers, music systems, iPods, iPads, DVDs and electronic games. By contrast, the classroom can appear dull and uninviting. However, the provision of an attractive and linguistically stimulating classroom does not necessarily involve the inclusion of large amounts of sophisticated electrical equipment. Nevertheless, there are times when equipment such as an interactive whiteboard can provide almost instant access to a wealth of material that could never be so readily available using printed texts.

The language-friendly classroom will include a range of stimuli both written and aural and the presence of tactile displays that children are encouraged to discuss. It will also provide opportunities for children to use language and explore its possibilities within a secure setting. In Key Stage 1 classrooms, in particular, the presence of structured contexts for play may lead to variations on the traditional home corner. Ross (1992) suggested that such contexts should reflect some of the children's experiences outside school and asserted that children are aware of a wide range of environments and places, particularly through television, and that they will use these naturally in play. Ross (1992) also suggested the following variations on the home corner, each of which may be created with a minimum of resources:

SHOPS	TRANSPORT	HEALTH SERVICES	WORKPLACES
supermarket	buses	surgery	bakery
shoe shop	station	hospital	café
clothes shop	trains	veterinary surgery	building site
post office	airport	optician	

To this list might be added pizza restaurants, fast food shops, cars, lorries, dental surgeries, offices and factories. Within these, children might be presented with different scenarios and invited to adopt the roles of a variety of people. There might also be opportunities for reading and writing – for example, using menus in a restaurant, taking customers' orders, making tickets or writing prescriptions or recipes.

The organisation of the furniture in a classroom can affect the possibilities for language development. Tann (1991) maintained that, although in many classrooms children are seated in groups around a table or cluster of desks, research had shown that 90 per cent of teachers never used collaborative group work. However, this figure may have changed since 1991, particularly as the Primary National Strategy (DfES 2006b) increased the emphasis on speaking and listening, and it is hoped that this has led to an increase in collaborative work. Seating arrangements in a classroom affect communication, even if this occurs in a way that the teacher does not intend. When children sit in groups, they have eye contact with all the others in the group, which may lead to greater interaction between them. Teachers who wish to reduce the level of talk in their classrooms often introduce alternative seating arrangements such as rows and horseshoes. These, too, may promote conversation, but this may be limited to pairs and trios (see McNamara and Waugh 1993). Teachers should consider the nature of the interaction that they wish to foster when arranging the furniture in their classrooms, and be flexible in changing. Such decision-making may well involve seeking the views of classroom assistants and the children themselves.

Teachers need to decide how they want children to enter the classroom and what they will find when they get there. There may, for example, be written guidance on what the children should do, with instructions for the first task of the day written on the board. The drawers and cupboards may be labelled so that children can find things easily without constant reference to the teacher. This should not only develop reading skills but also encourage independence and free the teacher to concentrate on teaching rather than managing resources.

The teacher in a language-friendly classroom will take on many roles and will make almost subconscious decisions about these. The teacher may act as a writer or reader to provide a *model* for pupils, and may be an *audience* for their ideas and an *arbitrator* when disputes arise in discussions. The teacher may provide *stimuli* for language activities and *initiate* and *facilitate* their development. The teacher will also be a *source of information* and direct teaching of language skills as well as being an *assessor* and *recorder* of children's progress.

The language-friendly classroom is more than an attractively adorned room filled with words and literature. It is an interactive environment in which teachers play a leading role in fostering the development of pupils' language skills through extensive use of the resources that they provide and that they encourage the children to bring to school. It is also an environment in which teachers constantly evaluate and assess what is happening and make decisions about what will happen next.

ACTIVITY: EXAMINING A CLASSROOM'S FEATURES

Think about a classroom you have worked in or are currently working in and answer the questions below:

- Are books attractively displayed and changed regularly?
- Are instructions provided in writing as well as orally?
- Is extensive use made of labelling so that children can find things independently?
- Are children encouraged to share *ownership* of the classroom?
- Are displays of writing a regular feature?
- Are displays interactive?
- Are ICT resources readily available and well used?
- Are writing and reading areas provided?
- Are words discussed with the children regularly?
- Are children's interests taken into account when reading materials are selected?
- Is teaching style and the teacher's role adapted to different circumstances?
- How are adults other than teachers involved?

Planning and preparation

Chapter 15, on planning, gives details of how to plan effectively for English, but a chapter on pedagogy would be incomplete without highlighting the need for careful preparation and planning, which takes into account:

- the abilities of the children;
- the resources available;
- the environment in which the lesson is to take place;
- ways of extending the most able children and engaging those that are less able.

Planning should be based upon realistic goals that children can reasonably achieve and that they can identify and relate to. It should also be done in conjunction with colleagues teaching the same year groups where possible, and should involve teaching assistants, who have a key role to play in classrooms and whose expertise should be recognised and drawn upon.

One aspect of lesson planning that is often neglected by inexperienced teachers, who otherwise tend to plan in great detail, is deciding how to introduce a lesson. A lesson's opening is crucial to children's attitudes to it, and it is vital that teachers show that they are enthusiastic about the lesson and that they share this enthusiasm with their pupils. Good lessons might begin with an activity, a DVD, a clip from YouTube, a piece of music, a visual aid or a reading from a text. They will also probably include:

- reference to previous lessons;
- differentiated questioning to involve everyone;
- use of children's prior knowledge;
- sharing of learning objectives;
- involvement of pupils.

Actions

If our knowledge helps to inform our decision-making, then both will determine how we teach and how we are perceived by our pupils, their parents and our colleagues. Before we examine teachers' actions in more detail, look at the following activity.

ACTIVITY: REMEMBERING YOUR OWN FAVOURITE TEACHER

Think back to your own schooldays, either primary or secondary.

- Who was your favourite teacher?
- What qualities did this teacher have that you appreciated?
- Did you work better and learn more with this teacher than with others?

When asked similar questions at interviews for teacher training courses, candidates tend to refer to strictness but fairness, enthusiasm, sense of humour and knowledge of pupils. Some talk of lively, outgoing teachers while others mention quiet, calm ones who never raised their voices.

There is no recipe for the perfect teacher, but, without enthusiasm for the subjects and children, teachers are unlikely to be successful or remembered fondly. Teachers' actions profoundly affect children's perceptions of subjects and of learning. We will now turn to ways in which their knowledge, decision-making and actions can impact upon the teaching of English in the primary school.

Qualities needed to teach English effectively

The Primary National Strategy cited three pedagogic approaches – *direct*, *inductive* and *exploratory* – and teachers will make decisions about which is appropriate when (DfES 2006b). Let us look at these approaches in the context of English.

Direct

The direct approach is often used when the purpose is to acquire new skills. Typically, this is the mode employed in whole-class literacy work and includes shared reading and writing, and teaching and learning about word- and sentence-level features. This might be followed by individual or group work in which children are able to demonstrate that they have acquired the skills and knowledge taught.

Inductive

Inductive approaches are designed to develop a concept or process and involve the teacher setting up a structured activity that has directed steps. For example, children might be given a list of words and their plurals and be asked to work out a spelling rule for making words ending with 'y' plural (see Chapter 12, on spelling).

Exploratory

The exploratory approach enables children to consolidate or refine their skills and understanding and might involve children in testing a hypothesis set up by the teacher – for example, 'Sentences cannot begin with "Because".' Children could then look for examples in texts and attempt to write their own before drawing conclusions. Because children may arrive at misconceptions, teachers should complete such activities with a plenary session in which conclusions are shared.

The cooperative learning strategies discussed in Chapter 6 ('Talking to learn') underpin a pedagogic approach that provides opportunities for children to interact and learn together. Such strategies are ideal for exploratory work, and can be linked to both direct and inductive approaches.

Teachers can draw upon a knowledge of different pedagogic strategies when teaching English, but what constitutes 'good literacy teaching'? Towards the end of this chapter an activity focuses on the things effective teachers of English do and invites you to consider the extent to which you possess these qualities. However, before looking at the activity, we will examine the qualities of good literacy teaching identified in the Primary National Strategy (DfES 2006b: 19). The Primary National Strategy referred to lively, engaging teaching with 'a carefully planned blend of approaches' with children being 'challenged to think'. There will be both support for children and independence when necessary. Rather than arguing for a brisk pace (as its predecessor, the National Literacy Strategy, did), the Primary National Strategy maintained that in good literacy teaching 'the pitch and pace of the work is sensitive to the rate at which children learn'. The increased emphasis on speaking and listening is reflected in the assertion that 'the strong interdependence between speaking, listening, reading and writing should underpin planning and provision for learning' (DfES 2006b: 19).

The final paragraph is worth quoting in full since it neatly sums up the themes that run through this chapter:

> Leading children's learning requires a broad repertoire of teaching and organisational approaches. There are lessons where the emphasis is on techniques and the teaching is quite directive: there are lessons where the directing is less evident and teachers use carefully chosen activities and well-directed questioning. Good literacy teaching requires a good knowledge of the subject; an understanding of the progression in the curriculum being taught and recognition that some teaching approaches are better suited to promote particular learning and outcomes.
>
> (DfES 2006b: 19)

In addition, we would argue that good teachers see a bigger picture – they make links between aspects of lessons (see Medwell *et al.* 1998) and they see teaching and learning in a wider context, including across the curriculum as well as within a subject. At the level of a literacy lesson, this means making clear links between text-, sentence- and word-level work, rather than treating these as discrete units. In phonics teaching, for example, the Rose Report (DfES 2006a: 39) found that the best practice 'took advantage of opportunities to reinforce aspects of phonic knowledge and skills throughout the curriculum'.

ACTIVITY: ANALYSING EFFECTIVE TEACHERS OF ENGLISH

Wray *et al.* (2002) identified the following features of effective teachers of English:

- make explicit the purpose of teaching and how this contributes to making meaning;
- centre much of teaching around shared texts;
- teach aspects of writing and reading in a systematic way;
- have strong philosophies about teaching literacy;
- have well-developed systems for monitoring progress;
- have extensive knowledge about literacy;
- undergo regular in-service training.

Think about yourself as a teacher of English and rate yourself on a scale of one to ten for each of the items above. Discuss your self-assessment with a colleague and talk about ways in which you could improve in those areas in which you scored the least well.

Key points

- To teach effectively, teachers need to reflect upon their practice and understand why they do what they do.
- A key element of pedagogy is knowledge, and this includes knowledge of the curriculum, of pupils, of factors that affect teaching and learning, of how to teach the curriculum and of one's own teaching skills.
- Teachers' knowledge influences their decision-making and influences the ways in which they organise their teaching and their classroom.
- The way in which teachers act affects the way in which their pupils learn and their pupils' perceptions of them.
- There are identifiable qualities in good teaching of which teachers need to be aware.

Further reading

Jolliffe, W. and Waugh, D. with Carss, A. (2012) *Teaching Systematic Synthetic Phonics in Primary Schools*. London: Sage.

Lambirth, A. (2005) *Primary English Reflective Reader*. Exeter: Learning Matters.

Wray, D. (2006) *Teaching Literacy across the Primary Curriculum*. Exeter: Learning Matters.

2

Classroom management in English

This could be heaven or this could be hell.

The Eagles, Hotel California

Purpose of this chapter

This chapter aims to:

■ explore ideal scenarios for teaching English;

■ enable the reader to reflect on classroom management and consider the effects of different approaches;

■ examine classroom management in specific English-teaching situations, including reading sessions, writing sessions and class discussions;

■ provide practical ideas for successful class management.

Ideal scenarios for teaching English

Classroom management can be a preoccupation for both inexperienced and experienced teachers. Teachers often complain that they spend hours preparing lessons only to have them spoilt by the behaviour of some children. W.C. Fields once said that one should 'never work with children or animals'. Both can be unpredictable and difficult to work with. However, both can also be trained and a great source of pleasure!

A Primary National Strategy training pack (DfES 2004a: 22) suggested that literacy-training-course participants should consider – in teaching terms – what might be an 'ideal scenario' by trying to imagine the perfect literacy lesson with their class. They should think about what they and the children would be doing and what they would see. This is a worthwhile exercise, as it focuses consideration of classroom-management strategies on to a subject area with which we are all familiar, rather than upon classroom management in general. It enables us to relate class management to the activities that make up a typical literacy lesson and to consider how these can be organised so that lessons are not disrupted and are productive. As Hayes (2003: 159) has argued, 'The key to dealing with misbehaviour is to try to prevent it from happening in the first place'. This involves anticipating where problems might arise and planning lessons so that potential trouble spots are identified and strategies put in place to avoid them.

One teacher trainee's experience

A third-year teacher trainee was asked to write about how her literacy lesson would ideally run:

I collected my Y3 class from the playground where they were lining up at the end of morning break. They were rather fussy but as soon as I mentioned Lottie, the heroine of our story, they sprang to attention and walked sensibly into school. I could hear some of them discussing the story as they hung up coats and changed shoes.

In the classroom, everyone sat quietly on the carpet eagerly anticipating the next episode. Lottie had been kidnapped but had escaped from her captors and was on the run in the countryside at night. When we had last read the story she had been startled by a noise and I had stopped the story before the end of the chapter so that there would be a cliff-hanger and something to look forward to finding out about in the next lesson. Today, we were going to hear the rest of the chapter and then a little of the next before the children worked in pairs to continue the story in their own versions. But first I was going to do some shared writing and a short drama activity to give them ideas.

The children were really attentive when I read the next part of the story and left them on another cliff-hanger. I asked them to discuss in pairs what might happen next and then asked some to tell the class what they had decided. They came up with some really interesting suggestions and when Kyle suggested Lottie would be killed it was interesting to hear the others, very logically, counter that we were only half way through the story so it was unlikely the main character would be killed off now, if at all!

I asked the pairs to work together to dramatise the events they had suggested and they did this really well, even if it was a little noisy. I'm glad I decided to let them spread around the classroom to do this, as the space on the carpet would have been too restricting. We then took some of the children's ideas and wrote two sentences on the board based on these. I explained that this was just one version and that everyone needed to work in pairs to write their own next episode. The children were really enthusiastic about this and I was glad that I'd got them to have pencils, pens, paper etc. ready on their tables before break so that they could get on with their writing straight away.

As they wrote, I moved around the room providing encouragement and drawing attention to good work and even reading some aloud to the class. Every time I did this it seemed to spur everyone else on and lots of children asked if I would read their work. What was really pleasing was that talk was almost exclusively task-related and children were really focused on the activity.

After about 35 minutes I asked the children to return to the carpet one table at a time and said I'd choose people who were sitting sensibly to read their stories aloud. I could have chosen virtually anyone, so well-behaved were the children. We finished the lesson with me reading the next two pages of the story so that the children could compare their ideas with those in the story. Some clearly thought their versions were better!

Many children wanted to stay in at lunchtime to continue their stories so I promised to come back to the classroom early after lunch so that they could.

ACTIVITY: ANALYSING A LITERACY LESSON

Consider the following elements of the ideal lesson described above:

- At which stages in the lesson did potential trouble-spots occur?
- Which classroom management techniques did the trainee teacher deploy?
- What alternative strategies could she have used?
- What effect did the content of the lesson have upon the children's behaviour?

What seems to be clear from the trainee teacher's description of her lesson is that she has picked up useful techniques from other teachers in order to avoid the kind of minor disruption that makes teaching and learning less enjoyable for teachers and pupils. She has also planned carefully and has prepared the children for the lesson in such a way that they anticipated it eagerly. The Elton Report (DES and WO 1989) maintained that 80 per cent of disruption in schools was directly attributable to weak organisation, planning and teaching. A little thought in advance about what might go wrong may help to avoid problems.

Effective classroom management

Central to effective classroom management is the creation of an environment in which children and teachers feel comfortable and confident that they can work without distraction. Morris (2001: 136) maintains that 'An unkempt, untidy room sets the stage for students to develop the same kind of behaviour.' In other words, the way in which the teacher presents the classroom will influence the way in which the children behave within it. It is also important that, as Pohan (2003: 317) states, 'The general room arrangement (e.g. furniture, materials) and procedures for moving about the classroom help to achieve physical safety.'

Part of creating the right ambience for working involves the teacher in making it clear to children what they will be doing and why, and what they will learn as a result. As Pollard (2002) has argued, it is vital to:

> Introduce and interest children in the planned activities, to provide them with a clear indication of the learning objectives for the session, a clear understanding of what they are expected to do, and to structure the activity in practical, organisational terms.
>
> (Pollard 2002: 246)

When teaching literacy and numeracy, teachers usually share objectives with their pupils at the beginning of lessons and then revisit these during the plenary session. If this is done, children are able to feel a sense of achievement and can be made aware of where individual lessons fit in a wider scheme of learning. It was interesting to note that the trainee teacher whose lesson was described earlier did not introduce her objectives at the beginning of the lesson but did so after the children had seen the text they were to study. However, she made a point of enabling the children to see what they had achieved and what they had still to achieve during the plenary.

Many of the rudiments of successful classroom management for English are the same as those for other subjects. To most experienced teachers, the use of these strategies is second nature; they deploy them without having to plan or analyse. However, inexperienced teachers should set out the strategies that will be used in some detail in lesson planning, and discuss them before and after teaching with more-experienced colleagues.

Managing literacy lessons

Table 2.1 sets out some of the possible problem areas within a typical literacy lesson and provides strategies that could be used to ensure that the lesson runs smoothly. Consider the strategies offered and try to add ideas of your own. Think about a class you teach or have taught, and decide whether the strategies would work with the children or whether they would need to be modified, adapted or changed. Consider, too, which of the strategies the trainee teacher's lesson included.

Literacy lessons often run to a tight schedule and demand that children are attentive and on task at all times. There is a high degree of direct teaching and discussion and it is important that time is not wasted on trivial classroom-management issues. Careful planning that takes into account potential management difficulties will be rewarded.

Children may be expected to work in different ways at different stages of a literacy lesson. At the beginning, they may be listening, speaking to the whole class or to small groups, or reading aloud. They may be asked to write ideas on a mini-whiteboard and share these with the class, or they may be engaged in drama or role play or other forms of presentation. Later, they can be asked to work independently or with partners, or be involved in guided group work with an adult. Finally, they may be asked to present their work to the class or to a group. These stages will vary from day to day, according to the nature of the lessons. This may lead to class-management issues, especially if children are uncertain about procedures and unsure about what is expected of them. It is important, therefore, that they feel that the teacher is in control of the structure of the lesson and has anticipated potential problems. It is vital too that the teacher's expectations are made clear and that children understand these. Cowley (2002) recommends the strategy of *explain, repeat, explain*:

> Explain: tell the class what you want them to do; repeat: choose a student and ask the child to repeat what you just said. ... By hearing the students' interpretation, you may find out that they did not actually understand the instructions you gave; explain: repeat the instructions again in your own words, clarifying any areas of uncertainty, and then ask: 'Is there anyone who's not sure what we're going to do?'
>
> (Cowley 2002: 44)

Or, as many experienced teachers would have it: 'Tell them, then tell them what you told them, then ask them to tell you what you told them!'

TABLE 2.1 Problem areas and strategies for class management

Children's entry to the classroom	■ Tell them before they come in what they should do. ■ Look for those who do the right thing and praise or reward them. ■ Make your expectations clear. ■ Devise routines.
Movement to carpeted area (if applicable)	■ Provide some 'special' chairs for the most sensible children. ■ Move a few children at a time. ■ Praise those who are sensible. ■ Explain what you expect. ■ Make sure that children have everything they will need for group work ready.
Beginning the lesson	■ Tell the children what they will learn. ■ Make the lesson sound as if it is going to be interesting: show your own enthusiasm for it. ■ Use visual aids. ■ Insist upon attentiveness from everyone. ■ Make sure that everyone can see and hear you.
Shared reading	■ Make sure that the text is clearly visible to everyone. ■ Discuss the text and its presentation before reading it. ■ Involve the children as much as possible. ■ Use a pointer so that you do not obscure the text.
Word- and text-level work	■ Children may have become restless and fidgety by this stage: ask them to stand up for a moment. ■ Look for opportunities to bring some to the front of the class. ■ Use visual aids.
Group work	■ Make sure that children know what they will be doing. ■ Send them to places a few at a time. ■ Praise those who get on with work quickly. ■ Make sure they know what you will be doing and know not to disturb you. ■ Make a quick tour of the classroom to ensure that everyone is on task, before going to your group. ■ Sit in a position that allows you to scan the whole class. ■ Occasionally show that you are aware of what other groups are doing. ■ Remind children of how much time they have left.
Plenary session	■ Discuss the way in which the children have worked and praise good practice. ■ Give children opportunities to talk about what they have achieved. ■ Provide positive feedback on their work. ■ Talk about the ways in which the work will be followed up. ■ End the session calmly and dismiss the class a few at a time.

The following sections look more closely at key aspects of English lessons and examine potential problems and possible solutions.

Managing reading sessions: independent, hearing readers, shared, guided, group

A constant problem for teachers is managing to hear children read while ensuring that the rest of the class remains on task and does not become disruptive. This was especially true when teachers frequently tended to hear individual children reading, but it is also a problem when conducting guided reading sessions with groups during literacy lessons. The strategies below may enable teachers to create an appropriate atmosphere and allow them to devote attention to those children with whom they are working while making it possible for others to be gainfully occupied:

- Always sit in a position that allows you to scan the whole class from time to time.
- Occasionally make it clear that you are aware of what children are doing.
- Praise those who are getting on quietly.
- Resist the temptation to leave your group to help others.
- Try to create a climate of independence in which children are praised for having a go at solving problems without constant recourse to the teacher.

Managing writing sessions: extended, paired

Although some older primary pupils are able to concentrate on writing for long periods, it is generally unreasonable to expect that all can do this. Skilful teachers recognise the signs of children becoming restless and intervene quickly. They try to break the lesson up occasionally and use the opportunity to focus children's attention on the task and to share good work and good ideas. (See also the sections on shared, guided and independent writing in Chapter 11.) The following suggestions may be helpful in planning for successful classroom management in writing sessions:

- Discuss the 'rules for writing' with children at the beginning of the lesson and ask for their suggestions. Note these on the board and use them as a reference point when infringements occur.
- Occasionally write something yourself, and make the point that you need peace and quiet to be able to do so.
- Allot a writing partner to each child and ensure that the pairs sit near to each other.
- Look for opportunities during extended writing for partners to read each other's work and offer constructive criticism to each other.
- Rather than repeatedly telling children that they are too noisy, stop them to discuss common problems, make teaching points and read aloud good work. This has the effect of quietening them down but achieves it in a more positive and task-related way than constant rebukes.
- Be explicit about the level of noise that is acceptable. This is much easier for children to relate to than being told they are 'too noisy'. For example, you could say that no one should be able to hear what they are saying except the person whom they are addressing, or that no one from another table should be able to hear their conversation. You may also want to insist that any talk is task-related.

■ Try to catch children being good. Look for opportunities to praise those who are doing the right thing and draw the rest of the class's attention to this.

■ Go to the children who have problems rather than having them queuing at your desk. Tell them that they must not simply sit doing nothing with their hand in the air but should carry on with the parts of the work that they can do and wait for you to help them with any insurmountable difficulties.

■ Avoid the 'word conga'! Probably the greatest source of disruption to any writing lesson is the child's spelling dictionary. Do not allow children to pursue you with these, creating a long line behind you as you move around the classroom. Insist that they try out spellings and that they check that they do not already have the word they need in their books.

■ If you discover that several children are experiencing similar problems, stop the class and use these to make a teaching point, perhaps writing words that cause spelling problems on the board.

■ Encourage children to use dictionaries and other reference materials as a first rather than a last resort.

Managing class discussions

Class discussions often occur at the beginnings of lessons and can set the tone for the rest of the lesson. It is, therefore, vital that they are orderly yet productive and lively. The problems most frequently encountered include the following:

■ children calling out or not taking turns to speak;

■ children showing a lack of interest;

■ minor irritations caused by children sitting too close together or being uncomfortable;

■ dominance of discussions by a few people (sometimes including the teacher);

■ restlessness brought on by lengthy periods of sitting on the floor (this is especially so after a long assembly or hymn practice or a wet playtime).

The solutions to the problems are simple but can be difficult to deploy where inexperienced teachers lack the confidence to assert themselves. Children are generally very forgiving and accept rebukes and reprimands as part of daily life. It is important that the teacher makes clear the type of conduct that is acceptable and sticks to it. When asked to define rules for class discussions, children usually make up the same ones that teachers wish them to adhere to, and most accept that transgressions deserve to be reprimanded. Skilful teachers are able to do this in a positive way without upsetting children or creating a negative atmosphere. Some of the strategies for successful discussions may appear obvious:

■ Insist that children put up their hands and wait to be invited to speak.

■ Try to involve everyone in discussions and avoid allowing a minority to dominate.

■ Differentiate questions so that everyone is capable of answering something.

■ Ensure that there is sufficient space for everyone to sit in comfort and provide a limited number of chairs for those who behave especially sensibly.

■ Ensure that everyone can see and be seen by you.

■ Avoid lengthy discussions if children are restless after a long assembly or wet playtime.

- Use visual aids to stimulate interest and try to involve children physically by asking them to hold things or write on the board.

- Maintain order in discussions by asking questions and varying your voice level and tone. Avoid using 'Shhh', which is ineffective and gives the impression that you are struggling. Dropping to a whisper can be especially effective!

- When children transgress the rules, try to criticise their behaviour rather than the children themselves.

- If everyone seems desperate to contribute but you simply do not have time to allow this, ask children to tell their neighbours their views and then invite a few children to say what the key points were.

- Devise a signal that children know and understand in order to gain their attention. In cooperative learning, the teacher raises her hand and as children notice this they stop what they are doing and raise a hand too. The class quietens in a few seconds and the teacher does not need to raise her voice to gain their attention. This also has the advantage that children can finish the sentence they were saying rather than stopping abruptly.

Successful strategies for class management

Most elements of successful classroom management are common-sensical and seem obvious when one observes a skilled teacher at work. However, if you are faced with thirty or more children when you are not confident about the subject matter and are having difficulty remembering the sequence of the lesson – and in addition the children are restless after a long, indoor lunch break – sustaining order and creating a working atmosphere can seem very difficult. The key to success is to watch experienced teachers and learn what does and does not work for them and then adapt successful strategies to suit your own personality and situation. There is no definitive, correct way to manage a class well. Some people achieve success by being loud and assertive while others are very quiet and calm and convey their calmness to the children. What is certain is that every teacher experiences some problems at some time and all can recall the lessons from hell as well as those that were heavenly!

ACTIVITY: DEALING WITH CLASSROOM MANAGEMENT PROBLEMS

How would you deal with each of the following? Discuss your ideas with a partner or small group.

- Your class includes four children whose behaviour is a problem when they are asked to move from one part of the classroom to another during lessons.
- During class discussions, some children tend to dominate and most children don't listen when others are making contributions.
- It is difficult to keep the rest of the class on task when you work with a group on guided work.
- Although you often manage to enthuse children about independent work during introductions to literacy lessons, it often takes them a long time to settle down to work.
- You find it difficult to sustain children's enthusiasm during plenary sessions.

Key points

- Many behaviour problems can be avoided if we consider class management when planning lessons and anticipate potential difficulties, and if we organise our classrooms well.
- It is worthwhile considering what our ideal scenario for a lesson might be before we teach, as this may inform our planning and help us to anticipate difficulties.
- There are many simple, practical ideas that can be used to improve class management.

Further reading

Behaviour2Learn website: www.behaviour2learn.co.uk.
Burnett, C. and Myers, J. (2004) *Teaching English 3–11*. London: Continuum.
Wragg, E.C. (1993) *Class Management*. London: Routledge.

3

Creative approaches to teaching literacy

Purpose of this chapter

This chapter aims to:

- examine the concept of creativity;
- look at changes in developing creativity in education;
- discuss the impact of multimodal texts, including the moving image;
- look at the role of popular culture in promoting literacy development;
- present examples of creative approaches to teaching literacy and their impact across the primary age range.

Creativity and literacy

The first question to clarify is: what is creativity? Research conducted at Manchester Metropolitan, Bath Spa and Goldsmiths Universities in 2004 (Davies *et al.* 2004) that examined teacher trainees' views of creativity revealed a real lack of understanding of 'creativity' consisting of a narrow arts-based view. The research showed that these views could, however, be challenged through exploring definitions and observations in school and then beginning to teach with, and for, creativity.

One of the problems with creativity is that the concept is ethereal. As Fisher states:

> Years of research has [sic] gone into trying to specify what creativity is, but despite all the checklists, models and tests, researchers admit that we do not know how fully to explain the creative power of the brain.
>
> (Fisher 2004: 7)

ACTIVITY: DEFINING CREATIVITY

Review the statements below and discuss with colleagues what the key ingredients of 'creativity' consist of:

- '[t]he ability to solve problems and fashion products and to raise new questions' (Gardner 1997; see also Fisher 2002);
- '[a] state of mind in which all our intelligences are working together' (Lucas 2001; see also Fisher 2002);
- '[i]maginative processes with outcomes that are original and of value' (Robinson 2001; see also Fisher 2002);
- '[a]n act that produces effective surprise' (Bruner, cited by Nickerson 1999; see also Fisher 2002).

Principles of creativity

Fisher (2004) argues that the processes that underpin creativity also underpin the evolution of life, namely generation, variation and originality. In essence, creativity is 'making, forming or bringing something into being' (Fisher 2004: 8). There are in effect three key interlinked principles concerned in the concept of creativity:

- generating ideas, outputs, etc.;
- differentiating: varying of products;
- being original: as an individual, group or community.

There have been many attempts to define the term 'creativity'. Csikszentmihalyi (1996) advanced the idea that it is not an individual attribute but a product of a person with the interaction of a specific situation or stimulus. Csikszentmihalyi (1992) also developed the concept of 'flow', where, during creative activity in a state of total absorption and mental challenge, many people experience their greatest joy.

Creativity can, therefore, improve an individual's emotional state of mind and quality of life. Fisher states:

> Creativity is developed through intellectual engagement, purpose, energy and interaction tension with others. These positive, creative attributes are essential to citizens living in any increasingly complex, changing and challenging social environment and essential for teachers in schools.
>
> (Fisher 2004: 11)

It is also important to value what Craft (2002) calls 'the creativity of everyday life' or 'little "c" creativity', otherwise many of us may feel inadequate and lacking in achieving 'sublime' creativity (Cropley 2001). Einstein or Picasso we may not be, but in myriad ways we can be creative or support creativity in others.

Jones and Wyse (2004: 5) summarise creativity as something that is 'novel, created with understanding of the field and valued as creative by observers'. Perhaps the final word should be the definition by a ten-year-old (Georgie Eccles) cited in Fisher (2004: 6):

'Creativity is not just art. It is thinking deeply and having original thoughts about something.'

Creativity in education

Creativity has increasingly become a focus in education, with government and national policy promoting it. Perhaps the clearest example was the Excellence and Enjoyment initiative produced by the National Strategies, which aimed to 'enrich the learning experience amongst other things and make learning vivid and real' (DfES 2003a: 29). While this contained many useful resources and interesting examples of 'creative' approaches, many critics (e.g. Jones and Wyse 2004) found developing a creative approach to the teaching of literacy something of an oxymoron in an environment of heavily prescriptive government strategy.

Craft sees three 'waves' of creativity in education and suggests that in the last twenty or more years there has been a 'global revolution' (2005: 7) in the place of creativity, so that it has become a core aspect of education. The first wave was in the 1960s and largely occurred as a result of the Plowden report (CACE 1967). At the heart of this report was the recommendation that children learn by discovery and take an active part in their learning within an integrated (not subject-based) curriculum. While this report has much to recommend it and is worth revisiting, it did not fully explore the concept of creativity and largely associated it with play. The two are not synonymous, as not all play is creative. The Plowden report also led to a backlash on the curriculum by successive UK governments who felt that schools had too much autonomy and too little accountability. This culminated in the introduction of the National Curriculum in 1988.

In the late 1990s there was a resurgence of interest in creativity that Craft (2005) describes as the second wave. During this time there were several major initiatives. The first was a report by the National Advisory Committee on Creative and Cultural Education (NACCCE 1999). This proposed 'democratic creativity', the concept that everyone can be creative in different ways, provided they have the right conditions and opportunities to develop knowledge and skills as the foundation to creativity. A further stimulus was the inclusion of creative development as an Early Learning Goal in the Early Years Foundation Stage curriculum in 2000 (DfEE 2000). This has promoted creative expression within art, craft, design, dramatic play and so on, but it has also led to a categorisation of creativity within certain domains of learning. A series of other government reports, including Ofsted (2003) and the previously mentioned Excellence and Enjoyment (DfES 2003a), all helped to stimulate further interest in creativity. Two government-funded bodies also made significant strides; one, Creative Partnerships, supported such moves as an artist in residence in schools and early years' settings, while the other was the work of the Qualifications and Curriculum Authority (QCA) and the creativity CPD (continuing professional development) materials (QCA 2005), which are explored in more detail below.

The third wave Craft (2005) sees as the move to going beyond seeing creativity as something that is special to instead seeing it as something that is ordinary and everyday, so that (as Craft maintains) it has changed emphasis to *ordinary creativity rather than genius* and is thus achievable by everyone in myriad ways. This wave sees creativity as a core aspect of education that is not the preserve of the arts: instead it permeates every human endeavour.

Developing creativity in children

There are several ways that teachers can develop creativity in pupils:

- fostering curiosity and exploration;
- encouraging risk-taking;
- having high expectations about pupils' diverse talents and abilities and enhancing their self-image;
- providing choice and independence;
- giving time and responsibility for creative activity;
- encouraging collaboration with others.

The QCA materials *Creativity: find it, promote it* (QCA 2005) provide information and case-study examples in order to encourage teachers to promote pupils' creativity. These materials can, despite of the demise of the QCA, still be found at http://teachfind.com/qcda/creativity-find-it-promote-it?current_search=Creativity%3A%20find%20it%2C%20promote%20it. Over three years, this project investigated how teachers can promote pupils' creativity across all National Curriculum subjects at Key Stages 1, 2 and 3. It found that, by making small changes to their existing planning and practice, teachers can promote pupils' creativity, which can:

- improve pupils' self-esteem, motivation and achievement;
- develop skills for adult life;
- develop the talent of the individual.

Teachers found that, when they actively planned for and responded to pupils' creative ideas and actions, pupils became more curious to discover things for themselves, were open to new ideas and were keen to explore those ideas with the teacher and others. Promoting creativity is thus a powerful way of engaging pupils with their learning.

Examples of creativity across the curriculum

The Excellence and Enjoyment (DfES 2004b) materials cite creative thinking as a key aspect that can 'enable pupils to generate and extend ideas, to suggest hypotheses, to apply imagination, and to look for alternative innovative outcomes' (DfES 2004b: 22). It also cites some indicators of creative thinking. Children may demonstrate that they can:

- generate imaginative ideas in response to stimuli;
- discover and make connections through play and experimentation;
- explore and experiment with resources and materials;
- ask *why, how, what if* or unusual questions;
- try alternatives or different approaches;
- look at and think about things differently and from other points of view;
- respond to ideas, tasks and problems in surprising ways;
- apply imaginative thinking to achieve an objective;

- make connections and see relationships;
- reflect critically on ideas, actions and outcomes.

Examples of working creativity across the curriculum in literacy are cited in *Excellence and Enjoyment: learning to learn* (DfES 2004d), which are worth reviewing as a starting point for other cross-curricular work in school.

The changing face of literacy

Literacy in the twenty-first century presents a very different picture from the text-based concept traditionally associated with reading and writing. We need to start by understanding that children are from a very young age driven to make meaning from the many forms of stimulus around them. Kress (1997) describes how a young child comments on a father's deliberate attempt to shape a piece of toast by taking careful bites: 'You made it like a crocodile.' Children develop their own meanings and do this in a multiplicity of modes, means and materials: 'Children act multi-modally' (Kress 1997, cited in Grainger 2004: 75). This, helped by a rich environment of print, supports children's paths into literacy. Central to this is what Dyson (2001) describes as a 'patchwork quilt' of children's literacy development with a range of home and cultural influences. It is unfortunate that, as Kress (1997) notes, young children's imaginative drive is not always supported; he states:

> The brain's capacity for translation from one mode into another is not seen as a quality to be fostered. If it were, the imaginative capacity of humans in western culture would be entirely different.
>
> (Kress 1997, cited in Grainger 2004: 82)

Multimodal texts

Bearne's work on 'multimodal texts' describes how we need to redefine 'literacy' to include combinations of modes, with not just words and images but also moving images and sound (Bearne *et al.* 2004). The Essex Writing Project (2003) found it important to challenge and redefine teachers' perceptions of texts and concluded that by so doing we can bring about significant improvement in children's literacy skills, particularly boys' writing.

Multimodal texts combine word, image and often sound and have been made possible through digital technology. This has increased the number of screen-based texts: 3D animations, websites, DVDs, videogames, hyper-textual narratives, chat sites, email, virtual-reality representations, and so on. Numerous books and magazine texts use image, word, layout and typography, which echo screen-based technology.

Reading on screen involves a different process. Hyperlinks enable readers to flit from one text to another through links, developing their own pathways. The key point is that reading is not linear and readers choose routes and their own sequence. There have been many examples of this approach that use a 'choose your own adventure' model. This genre of books became popular because it requires the reader to interact, to choose a pathway and explore different possibilities. Using this approach, on-screen interactive texts have been developed (e.g. *Jack's Choice* developed by the Primary National Strategy – available as part of the Social and Emotional Aspects of Learning (SEAL) materials in the National Archives site). This powerfully shows not only the different ways in which the text can be read but also the engagement and interaction that such text stimulates when readers are invited to choose from different routes presented on the screen or change the outcome by making choices for the main character at key points.

The reading of on-screen text therefore

- engages the reader in a very active (dynamic) way;
- requires the *orchestration* of information from non-linear, multimodal sources;
- facilitates focus on some key aspects of text (sequence and structure, author/character perspective, etc.);
- extends reading into the *new literacy* of the ICT medium.

Creating on-screen text is also different from creating written text in several key ways. As Hannon (2000) comments, the production of graphics to aid such text has, in the past, been difficult for ordinary writers, but this is now being changed by software packages. Creating on-screen texts therefore

- brings the content and structure of writing into a new and very dynamic relationship;
- involves strong elements of design as well as language and style considerations;
- requires particularly careful consideration of the potential readers, and how and why they will access the content;
- extends writing into the 'new literacy' of the ICT medium, facilitating multimodal communication.

Email and text messaging

The way we create texts for email or as text messages contrasts with other forms of writing, and can be productive to explore in the classroom. The often-criticised use of shortened language in text messaging, which can lead to children not knowing conventional spelling, can be analysed. A dictionary of correct spellings and text messaging formats can be developed, or text messages can be translated into conventional format. Other possible activities can involve devising rules for the use of mobile phones on buses and trains, or stories about mysterious text messages appearing. One of the clear advantages of the popularity of text messaging, which many children engage in, is that it encourages children to create text – to be writers, even in an abbreviated form. Email is becoming less popular with children: instead, the more interactive world of instant messaging and Facebook has much more appeal. A number of websites aim to support children's creative literacy development in new and innovative ways. The need for e-safety in using such websites is clear, however; as Evans (2004) shows, children are fervent users of new technologies and these practices are influencing and changing the nature of literacy.

Another popular social networking system – Twitter – can be used productively in the classroom. Such Web 2.0 applications are becoming increasingly prominent because of the way they have transformed how people engage with literacy (Davies and Merchant 2009). Twitter is a micro-blogging service that allows users to 'tweet' and document snapshots using a maximum of 140 characters. One teacher describes how he uses Twitter in the classroom in a range of ways (Waller 2009: 2): 'We use Twitter in class to provide snapshots of our work and reflect on learning. ... It also provides children with reading and writing for a real purpose and audience as well as bringing the world into our classroom.'

Using visual texts: picture books

Picture books, a more traditional form in the classroom, are a common part of the repertoire of young children, and their value is often underestimated. They provide a powerful introduction to reading through the many outstanding examples of the attraction of the visual image. Indeed, many adult readers experience the draw and select books because of the attractive cover or illustrations. Merchant and Thomas (1999: 2) describe picture books as an 'art-form through which authors and illustrators communicate what concerns them and how they reflect on the experience of childhood'. These books are 'characterised by the dynamic relationship between print and visual image' (Merchant and Thomas 1999: 2). It is this relationship and the multiple layers of meaning that can be created through this medium that make picture books valuable for young and old alike.

ACTIVITY: ANALYSING HOW PICTURE BOOKS CONTRIBUTE TO CHILDREN'S UNDERSTANDING

For this activity, you will need access to a range of picture books. Some texts are given below, or see the list of suggested authors at the end of this chapter on page 43. Look at the following ways in which picture books support children's understanding of text and find examples that match. Notice, as you do, the meaning created from the interplay of pictures and text.

- They introduce us to narrative in pictures and written text.
- They introduce different types of text in interesting ways; for example, the use of the letter in *Dear Greenpeace* (Simon James), the links to children's comics in Colin McNaughton's work and the visual symbolism in Anthony Browne's work.
- They help in understanding different cultures, as in *Handa's Surprise* (Eileen Browne) and *Amazing Grace* (Mary Hoffman).
- They develop closer and critical readings of images, as in *Each Peach Pear Plum* (Janet and Allan Ahlberg).
- They support intertextuality (with implicit and explicit references to other texts), as in *The Jolly Postman* (Janet and Allan Ahlberg).

Some outstanding examples of this genre, by authors such as Janet and Allan Ahlberg, Anthony Browne, John Burningham, Pat Hutchins and Maurice Sendak, not only provide a clear incentive for young children to develop a love of reading but also can support a deeper layer of meaning for older children (e.g. *The Highwayman* by Alfred Noyes, illustrated by Charles Keeping). *Rosie's Walk* by Pat Hutchins is a prime example of the power of this genre for young children. It uses only thirty-two words, but it is what the text does not say and the pictures do that is significant.

Anthony Browne (1998) made the following comment about creating picture books that demonstrates the link with other multimodal texts:

Making a picture book, for me, is not like writing a story then painting some pictures … No, it is more like planning a film, where each page is a scene that includes both words and images inextricably linked. What excites me is working out the rhythm of the story and seeing how much it is told by the pictures, how much by the words, and how much by the gap between the two.

(Browne 1998: 194)

Arizpe and Styles (2002) investigated how children aged from four to eleven years actually read pictures, and showed how, in addition to providing access to a story that would otherwise be denied younger or less competent readers, the visual image can be better than spoken or written language in evoking an affective response. The project found that children were very good at analysing the visual features of texts and, when aided by teachers in discussing the texts and pictures, were thereby given the opportunity to operate at a higher cognitive level. Reader-response theory (Rosenblatt 1978) also shows the importance of children making personal connections in reading to actively engage in texts and draw on their own experiences.

Supporting children's understanding of picture books

To support children, begin from the understanding that a good picture book is multilayered and may be used for a variety of readings at different levels. The use of shared reading can scaffold children's learning. How this is done is important, primarily to ensure that the joy of the text is not lost. At times this will include extended reading aloud without deconstructing the text. It should also enable children to respond in an open and unstructured way. With picture books it will involve the close examination of visual elements and their interplay with the written text, supporting children's ability to 'read' the images.

Guided reading allows the teacher to explore the text with a small group and focus on particular elements. This allows the opportunity for pupils to practise skills that they have learned in shared reading and for the teacher to support individuals or groups. In addition, it is important that children are given the opportunity to read a range of picture books independently and with a partner. The use of 'storysacks' or 'storybags' can promote the use of picture books still further, incorporating props, characters, audio tapes and games. This can provide opportunities for pupils to really inhabit the text and further their understanding.

Moving image: film, television and video

Picture books illustrate the power of the visual image to aid our enjoyment and understanding of texts. The moving image is a development of this. Using it in class also ensures that we are relating to children's home experiences. It appears that most children watch television for a considerable amount of time. BBC Health reports that the research firm BMRB (a public body research company) estimates young people in the UK aged between eleven and fifteen spend, on average, fifty-two hours a week in front of a screen (BBC 2012). However, a far smaller proportion of the population visits the theatre, opera or ballet. We thus need to recognise children's 'cultural capital' (Bourdieu 1977); that is, the cultural experiences and contexts that are familiar to children and that Bourdieu feels may impact on social mobility.

One popular media form that has been shown to have clear educational benefits is film. The British Film Institute (BFI) has provided a range of resources for use in primary schools to support the effective use of film. Its teaching guide *Look Again!* (BFI 2003) is available online and contains some key arguments for building moving-image education into the learning experiences of primary pupils. These can be summarised as:

- *The necessity for active learning.* Using the moving image can involve children because it is familiar. Starting with what they know and building on this can support a deeper level of understanding.

- *Linking home and school.* This helps to form a bridge through the use of familiar moving-image texts. For pupils with English as an additional language, work with moving images can be central to developing understanding.

- *Deepening the understanding of the nature of texts.* Film can aid the understanding of all texts and their role in creating our culture. It can also develop higher-order skills such as inference.

- *Creativity and the moving image.* Use of the moving image supports the need to provide rich and varied contexts for learning and can help pupils to develop ICT skills by producing their own media texts.

- *Understanding culture and society.* Moving-image media have a unique capacity for the development of cultural understanding; for example, by watching films set in different cultures.

Resources from the British Film Institute for Key Stages 1 (*Starting Stories 1* and *2*) and 2 (*Story Shorts 1* and *2*), consisting of short video clips of about five minutes and accompanying lesson ideas, have demonstrated the impact of using film to develop literacy skills. One teacher involved in the pilot work commented: 'I have been more surprised by the children's reactions to the films than anything else I have ever seen' (cited in Jones and Wyse 2004: 14). Here the film *Growing* stimulated 'the strongest poetry ever written by children'. It is also possible to download free resources from the BFI website. For other useful resources, see the list of websites at the end of this chapter, on page 42.

The Film Education Working group (FEWG 1999) outlined a curriculum framework for work on the moving image consisting of:

- stage 1 – access to a range of films with opportunities for discussion, using film language;

- stage 2 – progression to deconstructing complex narratives.

This framework also stresses the importance of giving children the opportunity to produce media texts such as video diaries, watching and analysing reports (e.g. weather) and filming their own. These can provide rich opportunities for oral and literacy work as children plan and write scripts.

Teaching techniques when using moving images

When using film, various techniques need to be taught to broaden children's understanding. The British Film Institute cites eight basic techniques to help understand the codes and conventions of the moving image. The first three concentrate on the language of the moving image and help pupils to see that everything in a moving image contributes to the overall meaning.

- *Freeze frame*: pause the film and use focused questions.
- *Sound and image*: examine the sound and image separately.
- *Spot the shots*: after viewing a short sequence, ask children to guess the number of shots, then view the sequence again and mark each change in shot, examining the transitions and timings.

The next two deal with the way the moving images are produced:

- *Top and tail*: show the title sequence and then use one of the three techniques above to help pupils to identify the genre.
- *Attracting audiences*: examine merchandising or promotional material.

The next three techniques help to explore ways of recognising the conventions of moving-image texts:

- *Genre*: what happens next? Show short clip of a recognised genre (e.g. western, sci-fi, soap opera) and ask pupils to make predictions about how a scene will end.
- *Generic translations*: translate a moving image into a print genre.
- *Simulation/production*: place pupils in pairs or groups and ask them to act as producers and create plans for a particular film.

Vocabulary for analysing films

Analysing film requires knowledge of film language. Six elements (three Ss and three Cs) are recommended by the British Film Institute for exploring and interrogating a film text:

- story;
- setting;
- sound;
- colour;
- character;
- camera.

Many of these are self-explanatory; however, the use of camera requires clarification. In film the camera acts as a *narrator*, leading the viewing through the story. Different types of camera shots fulfil different purposes:

- extreme close up: for moments of high drama;
- close up: for detail;
- medium or mid shot: to give a sense of what the character looks like and of setting/ action;
- long shot: for an overview of location and/or action;
- point of view: narrative perspective;

- zoom: change in the size of the subject;
- pan: moving horizontally left to right or vice versa;
- tilt: moving up or down.

Moving images and literacy

A popular misconception is that watching films does not support the development of literacy skills. However, research has shown how, used effectively and employing some of the techniques above, film, television and video can be incredibly empowering (Robinson 1997; Mackey 1999; Marsh and Hallett 1999). As the BFI (2003: 15) comments in *Look Again!*, 'Children who are able to draw on connections and parallels between film and print are more likely to become confident and critical readers across different media, including print.'

Moving images can support literacy development in the following ways:

- illustrating genres or types of story;
- motivating children to read related printed texts;
- supporting the concept of narrative, which is key in linking print and moving-image media;
- developing sequencing skills;
- offering great depth for literacy work based around character and setting;
- enhancing oral skills through linked retelling, storytelling and drama;
- extending children's vocabulary;
- enabling children to compare and contrast narratives across media, thus developing their critical skills;
- enabling children to more fully understand the moving image by analysing it, giving them tools to shape their writing.

Short film clips can easily be incorporated within most literacy lessons. The power of the visual image to support creative approaches to literacy teaching can easily be demonstrated. Activities could include using soap operas; for example, watching an extract with the sound removed and then asking children to create their own dialogue. Marsh and Millard (2000) show how children often tap into their cultural capital of television and mix genres. They cite one child's mix of fairy stories and soap operas in which couples indulge in premarital sex:

> One upon a time there was an old woman and a princess and one day the princess found a prince and they made love and one day they got married and lived happily ever after and the princess had a baby.
>
> (Marsh and Millard 2000: 158)

Incorporating children's television experiences with literacy work can also impact on home–school links. Marsh and Millard (2000) cite the example of the television programme *Who Wants to Be a Millionaire?*, which has a more general appeal compared with other quiz shows such as *University Challenge*. In one school, a teacher asked the children to write three questions each for a class version of the quiz. This produced an astonishing level of involvement by parents, who became engaged in researching and writing questions. These were then put into a class booklet and a class quiz was held at the end of term, which engaged the children and created a community in a literacy experience.

ACTIVITY: INCORPORATING THE MOVING IMAGE INTO A LITERACY LESSON

Download a film clip from the web resources recommended on page 42. Then choose one aspect from the three Ss and three Cs (such as camera) and see how it impacts on the story.

- Work with a colleague to discuss how to incorporate this exercise within a literacy lesson.
- How could you build on this to support a unit of work?

Digital animation

Stop-motion animation is an engaging activity through which pupils may consolidate their understanding of a process, theme, topic or piece of text such as a story, scene or poem. It is an enjoyable activity, and uses ICT to engage and motivate pupils and develop a range of skills. The technique uses a physically manipulated object that appears to move on its own. A well-known example is *Wallace and Gromit*. Such figures are made from moulded material or clay, which can have movable joints and can be displayed in different positions. A series of freeze frames is then created and photographs taken of the figure(s) in selected positions and against backdrops/sets. The photographs of each frame are loaded onto the computer; then, using movie-maker software, the films are created and sounds and effects can be added.

The benefits of using such techniques have been shown to be significant and Mayer and Morina (2002: 91) concluded that multimedia presentations (such as narrated animation) are more likely to lead to meaningful learning than single-medium presentations. They also found that students learn more deeply from animation and narration than from narration alone (2002: 93). In relation to literacy, such animation can help to bring storytelling to life. It gives pupils opportunities to work together cooperatively to produce plans using storyboards and to produce scripts of dialogue and action. An excellent example of stop-motion animation produced by young children can be found on YouTube ('Yellow Wellies': www.youtube.com/watch?v=jGY7xT7qy1M). For useful guidance on producing stop-motion animations see: www.filmeducation.org/staffroom/film_in_the_classroom/animation/stop_motion.php.

Popular culture

It is vital to tap into the rich experiences that children bring to the classroom. We can utilise these to act as a stimulus to engage with a range of literacy practices. Dyson (2000: 362) describes the assortment of children's popular cultural texts as a 'tote bag' of 'symbolic material gleaned from the myriad of voices around them'. We need to make use of this *bag*, not 'shut out the noise of society at work'.

Marsh and Millard (2000: 51) ask: 'How many children living in high-rise flats in inner-city areas of poverty visit garden centres?' Too often teachers set up role-play areas in a

Foundation Stage setting without such considerations. In contrast, one teacher explored what existed in the local area and then set up a fish-and-chip shop in the nursery.

A range of examples is explored below.

Computer games

The proliferation of computer games in many homes would seem an odd starting point for literacy, and yet it can be productively utilised. It has a strong appeal for boys, encouraging activity: 'Video games are better than books 'cos you can be player in games and you just have to read books' (Livingstone and Bovill 1999: 17). They can help to develop a range of skills, for example by

- improving hand–eye coordination;
- improving processing visual information from a number of sources;
- developing problem-solving skills;
- improving concentration;
- developing understanding of narrative.

Computer games can be utilised in school through

- collecting data for class surveys;
- providing discussion points;
- designing own games;
- developing characterisation;
- making comic strips of computer-games characters.

Critics of computer games cite the tendency for issues of race to be inadequately addressed, as well as the violence that is frequently depicted. Such issues could form the focus for literacy work and discussion to encourage a critical response by children. Research conducted by Apperley and Beavis (2011: 141) explored a framework to support games-based literacy pedagogy that 'enriches understandings of contemporary texts and literacies, expands repertoires of practice and engages students in the lively exploration of the rich and complex world of digital games and cultures'.

Comics: an inferior medium?

Comics have traditionally received scant attention from educationalists, except to generally decry their use. However, attitudes have changed since the 1950s, when the author recalls that her demands for a comic were answered by being allowed to read the *Children's Newspaper*. Marsh and Millard (2000: 101) sum up this attitude: 'There is something about the combination of cartoon images and racy colloquial language that distresses a significant proportion of adults.'

Educationalists have in the past argued that children deserve better material than comics (Wertham 1953). Features such as the language, which often seems to be coarse or show a lack of respect (e.g. Bart Simpson's 'Eat my shorts'), are cited. Another factor concerns the misconception that drawings with relatively few words indicate a correlation with deficient literacy. However, Bromley (2000) has demonstrated that comics can help in critical knowledge of how texts work via their use of jokes and understanding of multilayering and intertextuality. Millard and Marsh's (2001) project of creating a home–school comic library in two Sheffield schools showed an enthusiastic response, and children found it motivating. The most popular aspect was the library's interactive nature and the inclusion of puzzles and games. One outcome was increased communal reading experiences with families. Comics were also integrated into school work with shared reading and writing. Activities such as cutting up versions of comic strips to sequence can support a range of literacy skills such as recognising the complication in a story, developing understanding of character, and learning how to use puns, alliteration and onomatopoeia.

Toys and media characters

A key aspect of popular culture for young children is the proliferation of toys and associated artefacts that are linked to computer games, films or fast food chains. Despite the commercial interests that undoubtedly make substantial profits from such crazes, the benefits of tapping into children's cultural capital should not be ignored. Where such items can be used to motivate, excite and engage children, teachers are justified in employing them.

How can they be used? Ideas include:

- Superheroes can be used in role play (e.g. Superman and Batman, Buzz Lightyear and space travel, Spiderman's climbing wall, Gladiators' gym).
- Toys can be used as starting points for various literacy activities (e.g. writing a letter/email/text to Spiderman).
- Collections or current crazes (historically, Dinky Toys, trolls, gonks, beanie babies, Tamagotchis, Pokémon, etc.) can be used to write narrative histories of collectors' crazes. Collectors' websites can be consulted. Children can write descriptions, list features or create instructions on how to look after the toys.
- Toys can be used for literacy (e.g. by providing Star Wars figures for children to construct a storyboard, first arranging the figures and taking photographs and then using these to write stories).

Popular music

> What Bart Simpson, Madonna, M.C. Hammer, or New Kids on the Block have to say about the world is far more important to youth than the social and moral lessons teachers extract from literacy or other school experiences.
>
> (Luke and Roe 1993: 115)

Again, popular music relates to children's common experiences and motivates them to engage with literacy. The world of popular music is, as Marsh and Millard (2000: 165) state, 'inescapable'. Very young children learn lyrics to pop songs and enjoy singing them. Sharing enjoyment of such music can transcend cultural boundaries, and more recently musical forms have shown an element of crossover with rap, hip-hop and bhangra. Concerns over the sexual overtones and the violent and sometimes misogynistic content of some of the lyrics of these songs are undoubtedly justified. However, with careful selection and thought, pop music can be utilised effectively, for example by:

- using rap to support engagement in poetry;
- using karaoke to support children's reading (one study used this effectively with children with reading difficulties);
- carrying out surveys of popular artists or songs;
- compiling 'golden oldie' charts that incorporate parents' and grandparents' views;
- analysing lyrics.

Advantages of including popular culture

By including popular culture when teaching literacy, we are clearly relating to children's everyday experiences:

- It is meaningful: in literacy it is essential if school practices are to be seen as meaningful reflections of home experiences.
- It is motivational: studies (Dyson 2000; Marsh and Millard 2000) show that inclusion of popular cultural texts into the literacy curriculum has increased motivation.
- It can introduce children to a more recognised canon of literary texts through engagement with familiar popular television and film programmes and other media.
- It can be a useful means of developing critical literacy skills.

ACTIVITY: USING POPULAR CULTURE

Working in a group of four, each select an area of popular culture to investigate (comics, computer games, toys or pop music). Plan an activity or series of activities for use in the classroom with an age group you are familiar with. Now share your ideas with the group and see whether you can combine the different forms of popular culture in creative ways.

After planning – and, if possible, after carrying out the activity with children – consider:

- How did this motivate the children?
- Did it promote good opportunities for talk?
- Did it support their growing vocabulary?

Creative approaches to teaching literacy

This section provides a diverse range of creative approaches to teaching literacy. As you read each one, note what is innovative and motivational and how creative responses are fostered.

Linking drama and writing: a research example

Research carried out by the Centre for Language in Primary Education (Barrs 2000) looked at the link between the quality of what children read and the quality of what they write. Working with Year 5 pupils and exploring the difference between oral and written storytelling, one of the project's main findings was the effect on children's writing of doing the writing as a result of acting out in role. The pupils began work on a text with a drama workshop. This delayed the introduction of the text itself until the fictional world and the themes of the story had been prefigured through drama. Barrs (2000: 56) states: 'This had a big impact on the children, who seemed to relate much more closely and personally to this text because they had already "lived through" some of the events and situations.'

Barrs (2000) reported that the writing was almost universally well done, with children filling in a range of detail and also developing a real sense of authorial *voice*. One example is based on *Fire, Bed and Bone*, an historical text about the Peasants' Revolt by Henrietta Branford (1997), where a child writes as Humble the Cat:

> I am a creature of very different worlds.
>
> I know where the dormice nest in the oat fields. I know valleys that have deep blue rivers with the silver fish.
>
> I know the house and the warmest place in front of the fire. I know where the rats play at the back of the house. I know the tops of the tall pine trees. I know where the plumpest birds nest. I know the comfiest branch.
>
> (Barrs 2000: 58)

This project, Raising Boys' Achievements in Writing, found similar results to that of Barrs (2000). Teaching units were designed to raise boys' engagement, motivation and achievement in writing, using either visual stimuli (integrated technologies – video, DVD and other computer texts) or drama and other speaking and listening activities (UKLA and PNS 2004). The project found very positive results:

- The importance of planning longer units of work, typically three-week blocks, was found to be significant.

- The impact of speaking and listening being employed to scaffold children's learning, particularly linked to the use of drama, was found to be important. One teacher stated: 'I've realised that the drama needs to match the writing in order to get the maximum from both.'

- Integrating visual approaches was another significant feature, with the most success showing how the use of varied media was woven into the teacher's planning. This integration of film, DVD, still images or pupils' own drawings into units of work, and an ongoing use of stimuli including music and video alongside books for both fiction and non-fiction writing, made one teacher comment:

> I have seen the difference that using film makes to motivating and involving boys and I will work to make sure it is part of my practice ... the 'wow factor' works as the films are so much part of what my children know, they are starting from a stronger knowledge base.
>
> (UKLA and PNS 2004: 36)

Linking performing arts to children's literacy development

Airs *et al.* (2004) described studying war through drama and using a range of media to promote responses. These included photographs, re-enacting everyday scenes, sound (air-raid sirens), music, movement, freeze-framing and thought-tracking. From this the children created scores of music to depict the scene and, using photographs, they worked in groups to describe the war. Having worked on issues around evacuation, children wrote letters home in role that demonstrated the power of this method of teaching.

Using drama imaginatively

The following example used *Where the Wild Things Are* by Maurice Sendak (Colleen Johnson, cited in Fisher and Williams 2004: 62). A Year 2 class had been reading the story of Max, who is sent to bed without any supper as a punishment for his misbehaviour. From his room he embarks on a journey to a different land where the wild things live. Later, Max befriends huge scary monsters and becomes their king, but finally goes home. When he returns to his bedroom he finds his supper; it is still hot and time appears to have stood still.

Using drama strategies, the teacher re-enacted scenes from the story, such as the first time Max saw the monsters. She divided the class into two and asked the second group to choose a monster from the pictures in the text. She instructed them to make themselves into a 'wild thing' and, after moving in role, on the signal, they froze. The other group (as Max) wandered around the still images, the teacher joining them speaking her thoughts aloud and encouraging the children to do the same: 'I'm terrified!', 'They'll kill me with their spiky teeth!', 'Is this a nightmare?' and so on. The teacher then froze this group, asking the children to remember their facial expressions. The 'wild things' group was then unfrozen so the children could look at the images of Max. The groups were then swapped over and in each case the children could describe the expressions they saw and speculated on what Max might do next. Out of role, the children were asked to think of a time they had been frightened. Further work on different scenes in the story took place, and, having really inhabited the setting and characters, the children could attempt a range of activities, such as writing a script of the story or a diary of Max's feelings (see Chapter 14, on Drama, for further ideas).

Responding to a work of art

In another example, a painting was used as a stimulus (Andrew Green, cited in Fisher and Williams 2004: 49) with a Year 6 class (other stimuli could be a map, object, piece of music, photograph, etc.). The class collectively (in small groups) and individually considered the picture (*Evening Thoughts* by Robert Herdman, National Gallery of Scotland) and were asked to focus on the expression, clothing, background and likely emotional state of the young girl in the picture, developing as they did banks of vocabulary and devising a story map for their piece of writing. One exceptional example showed an authentic response to such a stimulus:

> Her mouth was an arch leading to a place full of sorrow and her eyes were a vortex trailing away to a distant place. She was a complete picture of total misery along with her life I thought suddenly.
>
> (Fisher and Williams 2004: 51)

Using props to create narrative

Russell Jones (in Jones and Wyse 2004) reproduces a conversation with a teacher that demonstrates how creativity is achieved in the classroom. The teacher describes how s/he was working with a Year 3 class looking at Native American Indians and read *The Indian in the Cupboard* (by Lynne Reid Banks). Using a papier-mâché figure of an Indian, the teacher asked the class to write about the Indian in the classroom and what would have happened if he had come alive. Mindful of an objective regarding adjectives, the teacher asked the children to think about the adjectives they used. The weakest child in the class, who was working towards Level 1 in literacy, produced an *amazing* story. The teacher said:

> It gave me goosebumps. Some of the class are quite clever children, they came up on Level 3, but for this child not only was the spelling quite good, the structure was there and her use of adjectives was amazing. When I read it out as it should have been read, her face … her smile just got bigger and bigger and bigger!
>
> (cited in Jones and Wyse 2004: 15)

3D virtual worlds

Research by Merchant (2010) found that diverse literacy practices can be enhanced through virtual-world gameplay. In this project, a virtual world was developed with Year 5 and 6 pupils that created a whole community and used 'avatars' (graphical representations of the user/author or the user's alter ego) to interact on screen in 3D scenarios. The aim of the project was to raise achievement in literacy in a small group of project schools. Data showed the work had a significant impact on pupil motivation and performance. Merchant summarises.

> To explore Barnsborough, pupils selected off-the-shelf avatars, entering the metaverse through underground sewers and controlling their avatar with simple keyboard strokes. In the project described here, teachers explained to pupils that Barnsborough had been hurriedly and mysteriously abandoned by its inhabitants. The broad objective for children was to solve this mystery by collecting evidence available in-world in a number of media and textual forms.
>
> (Merchant 2010: 138)

This engagement with 3D worlds involved the pupils in the following literary forms:

- environmental print (e.g. shop signs, graffiti, logos, posters and advertisements);
- tool-tip clues to give additional explanations or commentaries on in-world artefacts that are revealed when the cursor moves over them;
- hyperlinked texts: mouse-clicking on active links reveals a more extended text;
- interactive chat, which was the means of avatar interaction using speech bubbles.

As Merchant says (2010: 147), 'In sum, Barnsborough provided plenty of engagement with a range of old and new literacy practices and provoked a strong sense of motivation in learners.' To be effective, however, such a project requires competent ICT skills in teachers for them to be able to work in such innovative ways.

Common elements in creative approaches

Creative responses by pupils require creative approaches to teaching. Some of the common elements in the examples above include:

- using a range of stimuli for writing;
- ensuring that children inhabit the text and that it becomes a *lived* experience, making any subsequent literacy activities authentic and real;
- using talk and drama as a first step and part of the total learning experience;
- combining a range of genres;
- using ICT to interact in motivational ways;
- linking multimodal texts.

In addition, other triggers for creativity in this chapter have included the use of screen-based text, visual literacy, the moving image and popular culture. All of these excite, engage and draw children into literacy practices.

Key points

- Creativity involves generation, variation and originality of ideas and approaches.
- Multimodal texts combine word and image and often sound to create rich and varied contexts for learning.
- ICT can support social interaction with authentic purpose and audience.
- Popular culture, including computer games, comics, toys and popular music, can act as a springboard into motivational literacy experiences.

Further reading

Branford, H. (1997) *Fire, Bed and Bone*. London: Walker.

Craft, A. (2000) *Creativity across the Primary Curriculum: framing and developing practice*. London: Routledge Falmer.

Cremin, T. (2009) *Teaching English Creatively*. London: Routledge.

Marsh, J. and Millard, E. (2000) *Literacy and Popular Culture: using children's culture in the classroom*. London: Paul Chapman.

Wilson, A. (ed.) (2005) *Creativity in Primary Education*. Exeter: Learning Matters.

Resources for teaching

BBC film website: www.bbc.co.uk/film.

British Film Institute (BFI) downloadable resources: http://filmstore.bfi.org.uk.

BFI, *Starting Stories*: http://filmstore.bfi.org.uk.

BFI, *Starting Stories 2*: http://filmstore.bfi.org.uk.

BFI, *Story Shorts*: http://filmstore.bfi.org.uk.

BFI, *Story Shorts 2*: http://filmstore.bfi.org.uk.

Film education study resources: www.filmeducation.org.

Film trailers: www.apple.com/trailers.

National Curriculum in Action: www.ncaction.org.uk/creativity/index.htm.

Suggested authors of picture books

Janet and Allan Ahlberg (particularly *The Jolly Postman, Each Peach Pear Plum*).

Jez Alborough (*Where's My Teddy?*).

Quentin Blake (particularly *Mrs Armitage on Wheels, Mr Magnolia*).

Anthony Browne (particularly *Changes, Gorilla, The Tunnel, Through the Magic Mirror, Voices in the Park*).

Eileen Browne (*Handa's Surprise*).

John Burningham (*Granpa, Mr Gumpy's Outing, Oi Get off our Train!, The Shopping Basket*).

Mary Hoffman (*Amazing Grace*).

Pat Hutchins (*Rosie's Walk*).

Mick Inkpen (particularly *Blue Balloon*).

Simon James (*Dear Greenpeace, Sally and the Limpet*).

Colin McNaughton (*Boo!, Have You Seen Who's Just Moved in Next Door to Us?, Suddenly*).

Alfred Noyes (*The Highwayman*).

Michael Rosen (particularly *We're Going on a Bear Hunt*).

Jon Scieszka and Lane Smith (*The Stinky Cheese Man and Other Fairly Stupid Tales, The True Story of the Three Little Pigs*).

Maurice Sendak (*Where the Wild Things Are*).

Colin Thompson (*Falling Angels*).

Martin Waddell (*Can't You Sleep, Little Bear?, Farmer Duck, Owl Babies*).

Kit Wright (*Dolphinella, Tigerella*).

4

Understanding language and literacy development

Purpose of this chapter

This chapter aims to:

- provide a broad overview of language development;
- present a range of ways of supporting language development;
- discuss links with language and literacy at home;
- examine ways of developing literacy through play and creativity;
- support early reading development;
- support children's early attempts at writing.

Early language development

The development of language is one of the most remarkable developmental achievements that human beings make. As Hetherington and Parke explain:

> Language is one of the most complex systems of rules a person ever learns, yet children in a wide range of different environments and cultures learn to understand and use their native languages in a relatively short period.
>
> (Hetherington and Parke 1999: 274)

Having a clear understanding of the foundations of language development and how to provide support is crucial to working with young children throughout the primary phase. This chapter aims to provide that underpinning.

Theories of language development

A wealth of research into language development has produced a range of different theories to explain the emergence of communication, language and literacy skills. Essentially, these theories revolve around the role of genetics and environment, although many now agree that it is a combination of the two that determines our development. This section summarises the main theories that have been advanced to explain language development (for more information see the further reading at the end of this chapter).

> ### ACTIVITY: THEORIES OF LANGUAGE DEVELOPMENT: IMPLICATIONS FOR PRACTITIONERS
>
> Read the brief summaries of theories that follow and, together with colleagues if possible, make notes on the role of the practitioner according to each view.

The behaviourist view

Traditional learning theorists invoke the principle of reinforcement to explain language development. According to this view (e.g. Skinner 1957), parents and carers selectively reinforce the sounds a child makes that are most like adult speech and, by showing approval, encourage their child to repeat these sounds. Other learning theories (e.g. Bandura 1977) propose that the child learns primarily through observational learning. According to this theory, the child picks up words by imitation of what s/he hears, and then through reinforcement or generalisation learns to use the words when appropriate.

The nativist view

This theory originated from the work of Noam Chomsky (1957), who proposed that children are born with an innate mental structure that guides their acquisition of language and, in particular, grammar. This he terms a 'language acquisition device' (LAD). The justification for this is that certain universal features are common to all languages (e.g. sentences in all languages contain a verb, subject and object). Children then use a set of innate language hypotheses to derive rules from the language data that they hear. Children acquire complex language quickly, which indicates, this theory proposes, that they could not learn this from fragmented and incomplete environmental input; this skill must be partially innate.

The cognitive view

According to this view, language development is seen as part of general cognitive development. It links to Piaget's (1954) description of mental structures or schemas, which are created by the child's explorations with the environment. This perspective sees the child as a meaning-maker, actively seeking to make sense of the world. This suggests that cognitive development precedes language development and therefore that, for example, children understand the concept of an object before they learn the word for it. From this perspective, children's language development is dependent on their cognitive development.

The social-interactionist view

This view sees the interplay between biological and environmental factors in the acquisition of language. Language is learned in the context of spoken language, but also humans are biologically prepared for learning language. Factors that are important are children's active role – they formulate, test and evaluate hypotheses concerning the rules of language – plus the role of carers in supporting the process. Jerome Bruner (1986) proposed a 'language acquisition support system' (LASS) that contrasts with Chomsky's language acquisition device and emphasises the role of the carer/parents as facilitators of language acquisition. This consists of a series of techniques that adults use to facilitate language – playing non-verbal games, using simplified speech and elaborating or rewording children's utterances.

Development of language in children

Before considering further the impact of such theories on practice, it is important to be aware of the common developmental sequence that children encounter as they become proficient language users. It is vital to bear in mind that this sequence is only a guide; each child is an individual with varying home contexts. Table 4.1 provides a brief summary of the main features.

TABLE 4.1 Stages of language development

Developmental stage	Common features
Preverbal communication	■ From birth: parents' and carers' sounds, movements, smiles and other facial expressions show a type of dialogue – early conversation. ■ 3–12 months: increased ability to use gesture to communicate with and respond to adults. ■ 7–8 months: adults point to draw attention to objects. ■ By 1 year: children are highly skilled at non-verbal communication (e.g. pointing to request something). ■ As they learn language, they combine words and gestures. ■ At 3 years onwards: they reduce their use of gesture and rely more on verbal skills.
Early language comprehension – receptive language	■ Even prenatally, children may develop a preference for their own language. ■ Understanding begins very early. ■ Babies show a preference for human speech rather than other sounds. ■ Two-day-old infants can distinguish their mother's voice. ■ From 1 month old: ability to discriminate speech sounds develops. ■ From about 6 months: children are more able to engage in turn-taking games involving sounds and body movements. ■ 18–24 months: children learn new words at a rapid rate, mapping the concept to the word. ■ 24–36 months: conversation skills develop. ■ From 5 years: understanding develops of non-literal speech.
Babbling and other early sounds – productive language	■ End of first month: vowel-like sounds start. ■ Middle of the first year: babbling (strings of consonant–vowel combinations), common across all languages. ■ End of first year: patterned speech begins – strings of words made up of phonemes from own language that sound like speech but are not. ■ Middle of second half year: cultural differences in prespeech sounds begin to emerge.

Semantic development – acquiring words	■ Vocabulary acquisition proceeds in bursts.
	■ 10–15 months: children usually utter their first words.
	■ About one and a half years: rapid increase in vocabulary (typically about 50 words).
	■ 2 years (average child): vocabulary ranges from 600 to 900 words.
	■ 6 years: vocabulary is about 8000 words.
	■ Learning a word requires linking an appropriate concept with an appropriate sound; this linking is called 'fast mapping'. This is helped by interacting with and reading to children.
	■ Errors illuminate the learning process; for example, 'overextension' (using a single word to cover many different things, such as 'doggie' for cows, horses, etc.) and 'underextension' (using a single word in a highly restricted way, such as 'car' only for the child's family car).
Acquisition of grammar – learning the rules	■ First words are not just naming but expressing ideas.
	■ 1½ and 2 years: two-word sentences – telegraphic speech.
	■ There are stages in learning rules (e.g. use of plurals and past tense).
	■ In third year: children show signs of understanding the rules and use sentences so complex that it is difficult to analyse all the rules they have learned.

Key learning principles in communication

Guidance for practitioners from the DfES (2005a), entitled *Communicating Matters*, refers to these stages of development as strands and presents 'key learning principles' (KLPs) within each strand. These strands are set out below together with the related KLPs.

As you read the strands and the related KLPs, consider how this information could be helpful in working with young children.

1. Knowing and using sounds and signs

This involves having the ability to recognise, comprehend and produce the distinct sounds critical for oral language behaviour, or to recognise, comprehend and produce the individual signs and symbols of alternative modes of communication.

■ KLP: Sounds are heard in the interactive context of language in regular use in social life.

■ KLP: Infants continuously seek and construct patterns of language and communication.

■ KLP: Having common ground for communication, and learning to share attention with other people, gives a context for children's developing language.

2. Knowing and using words

This involves having the ability to recognise, comprehend and produce the particular units of language, in particular words or phrases, that carry independent meanings sufficiently distinct for them to be demarcated from other words or phrases.

■ KLP: Words start to be produced in line with a child's increasing ability to share attention and identify common communicative ground with others in a variety of situations.

- ■ KLP: There is a broad timespan for the production of first words within the normal frame of development; some children might do this at nine months whereas others may not until they are nearly two years old.

- ■ KLP: Word combination starts when children know between fifty and 100 words; it is the number of words they know that is significant rather than their age: adults know on average between 50,000 and 100,000 words.

3. Structuring language

This involves having the ability to recognise, comprehend and produce longer units of language that are organised in systematic ways and that generate more-complex units of communication appropriate for many different purposes.

- ■ KLP: The wider communicative environment in which children find themselves provides the resources with which they learn to construct language; this happens through their increasing experience of social and interactive situations.

4. Making language work

This involves having the ability to recognise, comprehend and produce language appropriate for a range of different social interactions, recognising social conventions and their variations, and combining different modes of communication for full effect.

- ■ KLP: Features of adult–child interaction are culturally determined and conventions for interaction vary, both within and across speech communities. This does not affect the final outcome, in the sense that all children learn to speak and communicate.

Becoming an effective communicator

It is important not only to be aware of the common sequence that children go through in learning language but also to realise that being an effective speaker requires a complicated set of skills. These require the child to:

- ■ engage the attention of listeners;
- ■ be sensitive to listeners' feedback;
- ■ adjust speech to listeners; for example, taking into account age, cultural and social factors (a school child learns to speak differently to a teacher and to another pupil);
- ■ understand it is a two-way process and that there is a need to be both a good speaker and a good listener;
- ■ recognise their own communication skills and be able to evaluate their own messages.

Considering the complexity of the above, it is remarkable that by two years old children are generally very adept. They have learned to adjust speech when talking to other children of different ages; for example, they use more repetitions when talking to baby brothers or sisters than older children or parents. The crucial factor to bear in mind is the interaction they have with others, as children learn from direct instruction and by observing others.

TABLE 4.2 Supporting children's language development

Key factors	Examples
People Play, talk and interaction with other people are the key.	Listen carefully to the child and respond accordingly.
Places School settings – small rooms or the creation of safe areas.	Provide a changing range of play-based areas that encourage talk.
Activities Varied opportunities for talking singing, listening, watching and helping.	Expand and model conversations supported with visual material.
Subjects Ample opportunities for talk about topics that are relevant and meaningful to children.	Read, tell and talk about stories.

ACTIVITY: SUPPORTING LANGUAGE ACTIVITIES

Review the key factors shown in Table 4.2 (people, places, activities and subjects) and the suggested ways to ensure rich linguistic beginnings. Now consider further examples of ways to encourage and support children's language development.

Knowledge and practitioners

Practitioners working with young children should therefore understand, as Whitehead (2004) summarises, that:

- all children are linguists;
- all languages are complex grammatical systems;
- all natural languages are or have been spoken;
- language and thinking are inextricably linked.

Support for children can be provided through symbolic representation of ideas through playing, gesturing, drawing, building, labelling, naming, storytelling and writing. A significant factor in language development is the quality of the relationships that are built up with young children. Whitehead highlights the importance of providing 'genuinely mutual conversations between children and adults, and between children and children' (Whitehead 2004: 106). The Early Years Foundation Stage (EYFS) *Practice Guidance* stresses the importance of this and states:

> To become skilful communicators, babies and children need to be with people who have meaning for them and with whom they have warm and loving relationships, such as their family or carers and, in a group situation, a key person whom they know and trust.

(DfES 2007b: 39)

Supporting children with language difficulties

The Bercow report (DCSF 2008a) reinforced the vital need for developing effective communication skills and examined the services for supporting children and young people with language difficulties. It found that services were patchy across England: what is often described as a 'postcode lottery'. The report recommended better training for professionals working with children, better information for parents, and better identification and support. As a result of this report, several programmes have been developed to provide such support. Every Child a Talker (ECAT) is one example; it is a national project to develop the language and communication of children from birth to five years of age (DCSF 2008b). It focuses on support in targeted settings to provide high-quality early language provision for all children through increased practitioner knowledge in identifying children at risk of language and communication delay and supporting them as early as possible. The programme encourages strong partnerships with families and carers. Full details of the programme and materials can be accessed from: http://webarchive.nationalarchives.gov.uk/20110809091832/http:// teachingandlearningresources.org.uk/early-years/every-child-talker-ecat.

Another programme that supports children in becoming effective communicators was developed by the Institute of Education in Tower Hamlets in London and is entitled *Talking Time* (Dockrell *et al.* 2007). This is an interactive oral language intervention package with a range of resources available to download from the Institute of Education website (www. ioe.ac.uk). It promotes three key skills:

- vocabulary development;
- the ability to make inferences;
- the ability to recount a narrative.

There is, therefore, a range of programmes and resources that support practitioners' understanding of how to support early language development and how to intervene effectively where needed. In schools and other settings concerns should also be referred to a special-needs coordinator, who will seek advice from specialists when required.

Speaking and listening

Language is a tool for thinking as well as being vital for communication. Both are facilitated by interaction with others and through appropriate stimuli. Speaking and listening also underpin children's ability to deal with written language – to read it and to write it.

The EYFS (DfES 2007b) did not use the term 'speaking and listening'; instead it called this 'communication, language and literacy'. In the revised EYFS (DfE 2012a) this is now referred to as 'communication and language' and is seen as one of the prime areas that support learning. Literacy is now separate and included as one of the 'specific areas' alongside 'mathematics', 'understanding the world' and 'expressive arts and design'. Dame Clare Tickell, in her review of the EYFS, explained the rationale for separating communication, language and literacy:

> The development of communication and language skills happens during an optimum window of brain development and is experience expectant (and therefore forms part of the prime), whereas the acquisition of literacy skills is experience dependent since it can occur at any point in childhood or in adulthood.

(DfE 2011b: 99)

Communication and language in the 2012 EYFS are subdivided into three aspects: 'listening and attention', 'understanding' and 'speaking'. In the non-statutory guidance on development, these are categorised under three areas: 'the unique child', 'positive relationships' and 'enabling environments'. Further discussion of this may be found in Chapter 6.

Teaching communication and language

Teaching communication and language in EYFS and later in Key Stages 1 and 2 should build on an understanding of children's early language development. To be effective, teachers should consider the factors set out below.

- Acknowledge and build on the invaluable contribution that home makes to the development of language. Gordon Wells' seminal study found that at school children had fewer interactions with adults than at home and stated: 'for no child was the language experience of the classroom richer than that of the home' (Wells 1986: 87).

- Understand the value of talk and the potential it provides for children's learning. The danger is to value written work as more tangible evidence of learning and to feel that a noisy classroom is evidence that not much work is taking place, and yet the contrary may be the case (as long as the talk is productive and on task!).

- Model the use of talk in a variety of ways, and particularly model the art of being a good 'active' listener. This is clearly signalled by genuinely listening to children and what they have to say and building on their understanding sensitively by asking relevant questions.

- Engage in meaningful dialogue. This notion of encouraging dialogue has become known as 'sustained shared thinking' as a result of the lengthy research undertaken by Sylva *et al.* (2004), known as the EPPE (Effective Pre-school and Primary Education) study. This found that 'excellent' early-years settings encouraged relatively more sustained shared thinking, which consists of episodes in which two or more individuals work together in an intellectual way to solve a problem, clarify a concept, evaluate activities, extend a narrative and so on. Both parties must contribute to the thinking and it must develop and extend.

ACTIVITY: EXPLORING SUSTAINED SHARED THINKING

Read the two extracts from the EPPE study (Sylva *et al.* 2004: 71–3), which illustrate interaction between an adult and children.

- Which example provides evidence of sustained shared thinking?
- Which example illustrates the adult really 'tuning in' to the children's discussion?

Extract 1
Eight children aged 4–5 years and nursery teacher:

Teacher: What area of science did we cover last week?

Joe:	The skeleton.
Teacher:	What is the name of it?
Lucy:	Biology.
Teacher:	This week we are going to be looking at zoology. A zoologist is a person who studies animals. What does a zoologist study?
Joe:	Animals.
Teacher:	A biologist studies?
Ganesh:	Animals.

(Teacher reads from a book about zoology.)

Teacher:	What's the backbone called Ganesh?
Ganesh:	Th- The spine.
Teacher:	Animals with a backbone are called vertebrates. I need you to know that animals with backbones are vertebrates, animals without backbones are called invertebrates.
Teacher:	Harry, an animal without a backbone is called a …?
Harry:	Reptile.
Teacher:	No, a vertebrate [sic]. I've got some things for you to have a look at and then we're going to put them into categories.
Teacher:	Do you think crocodiles have got a backbone?
Ganesh:	A backbone.
Teacher:	What kind of animals are they?
Ganesh:	Vertebrates.

(All the children are invited to look at a poster of vertebrates/invertebrates.)

Teacher:	We are going to look at the different groups these animals fall into. We're going to talk about mammals.
Harry:	It's like a reindeer.
Teacher:	Yes it is, but what's the difference between a reindeer and a starfish?
Harry:	It's like a star.
Ganesh:	The reindeer is a vertebrate.
Teacher:	The female mammal feeds the baby with their own milk. This makes the mammal special. What else feeds with its own milk?
Charlotte:	Cows.
Ganesh:	Tigers.
Teacher:	What are we called? Are we mammals?
Joe:	No.
Teacher:	Why Ganesh?
Ganesh:	No we are. We have a backbone.
Teacher:	Did Mummy feed you? What with?
Joe:	Cows.
Teacher:	No, breast milk.
Ganesh:	And very good it was too.

(Later ...)

Teacher: Something else I forgot to tell you, mammals are warm-blooded. If you cut yourself the blood that comes out is ...?
Harry: Cold.
Teacher: Tomorrow we are going to look at where mammals and arthropods live. What are we going to do tomorrow?
Ganesh: Look at where they live.

Extract 2

The following interaction shows what may be achieved by children of the same age when they are supported and encouraged (DfES 2002b: 45–6):

Tom (boy age 4 yrs 8 months):   How did God make himself?
Teacher: Well in most of the books about God, it says God just is.
Tom: Well how did God make us?
Teacher: I don't know. What do you think?
Tom: I don't know.
Teacher: Well how would *you* make yourself?
Grace (girl age 4 yrs 9 months):   I would make myself happy.
Tom: I think when God made us, we made God.
Grace: He putted [sic] our bones in first and then he putted our blood on the bones and then he putted our skin on.
Tom: No – he opened up our bones and put the blood in us.
Grace: No – if he put it in our bones, the blood wouldn't come out.
Tom: (changing subject) You don't know what's there (pointing to throat). These are microphones to talk. My dad told me.
Grace: You're wrong.
Tom: No! I'm right!
Grace: No *and* your dad's wrong.
Tom: No he's not! He's right ... I want to draw.

(He goes to get paper and pencils.) (Tom returns and begins to draw 'a bone'.)

Grace: That's a funny bone.
Tom: Yes – but it *is* a bone.
Grace: (drawing) He's got long arms to let him make his dinner. Cos my mum's got long arms like me. (pauses and thinks) ... If the blood was inside your bones ...
Tom: (interrupting) I know your blood is out of your bones ...
Grace: (ignoring Tom's comment and pointing to a blood vessel in her finger) Look! So why are you telling me blood's in the bones? ... I know God's got blood.
Tom: No he hasn't.
Grace: Yes he has. Why do you think we have blood and everybody has blood and he doesn't? ... (Showing her picture to Sophie – girl 3:11) Look I done [sic] God.
Sophie (girl age 3 yrs 11 months): That's not God .... It's too little.

Tom: So how did God make eyes and eyelashes?
Teacher: I don't know.
Grace: I know – he does the bone in the eye (pointing to the iris) and then he paints the white.
Teacher: So God paints you does he?
Grace: He painted your eyes.
Tom: No it's not.
Grace: It is.
Tom: How does the paint stay on anyhow?
Grace: (chanting) Easy peasy lemon squeezy.
Tom: I hate 'easy peasy lemon squeezy'.
Teacher: So you don't think Grace's right then?
Grace: I am right and Tom's wrong.
Tom: We're both wrong – well you're wrong and I didn't say anything.

(The following week the teacher brings in a dog's skull and the week after, a skeleton – the discussion about bones and blood continues in detail and in an equally dramatic fashion!)

Supporting children's talk

To support children's learning through talk, a teacher should not take over the conversation but instead guide the children and consider how to:

■   focus on the child and listen to what he or she is saying;

■   summarise what the child has said to check the message has been understood;

■   help the child to focus on significant aspects;

■   show respect for the child's views and support him/her in the next steps;

■   help with sequencing a particular issue, where appropriate;

■   ask genuine questions that respond to what a child has said;

■   treat the child as an equal;

■   make tentative suggestions (e.g. 'Perhaps if …');

■   let the child do most of the talking.

Providing an environment for talk

To develop a climate of meaningful and valued talk, certain prerequisites are necessary. Children need to feel secure and free to make mistakes without being judged. They need to feel their culture or home background is acknowledged and their views are taken seriously. The next step is to ensure that the environment lends itself to talk.

Review the bullet points in the sections below with colleagues and decide which are particularly important.

Classroom areas

■ There should be a rich environment of print – for example, with signs and labels including the home languages of pupils – that encourages children to interact.

■ Role-play opportunities should be provided to encourage talk, in which adults take part.

■ A listening area should be included.

■ Furniture should be arranged to support interaction.

■ Writing areas should permit sharing.

■ A class noticeboard should be provided where children are encouraged to interact using their attempts at mark-making (i.e. when children make representations through drawing or attempts at writing).

■ Reading corners should support interaction with a range of books and print displayed and related to play activities (e.g. a letter from Goldilocks saying she is sorry to the Three Bears).

Opportunities for partner or small-group work

■ Encourage the use of talk partners, having first modelled and discussed how to do this effectively.

■ Ensure children share ideas with their partner before the rest of the class.

■ Provide specific tasks for children to carry out in pairs.

■ Ask children to discover specific aspects about a class topic and then to share with partners/groups and the rest of the class.

Resources to support communication and language skills

■ digital recorders (such as 'talking tins', which record short extracts of speech or sound that can be played back);

■ telephones;

■ dressing-up clothes;

■ puppets;

■ storysacks or storyboards;

■ games that support interaction amongst peers.

In addition, consider:

■ encouraging a range of visitors to the classroom to promote talk about their expertise (e.g. a fire safety officer or farmer);

■ providing opportunities to explore first hand a range of materials and practical equipment as a stimulus for talk.

Activities to promote communication and language

- storytelling or activities that result from shared stories;
- drama techniques such as hot-seating (a device where one person acts in role and others ask questions related to the role; see Chapter 14, on Drama);
- circle time that encourages every child to orally contribute in turn.

Lesson planning

Opportunities for talk need to be carefully planned for. The planning should bear in mind the following:

- Key questions to be asked should be specifically noted in planning.
- Focused group or whole-class work should be included, where appropriate, to provide opportunities for discussion with partners/peers.
- A clear structure should be given to oral tasks, providing success criteria, making clear the time allocated and so on.
- Careful support, as well as monitoring, should be given to pupils by the teacher or teaching assistant.

Useful resources and ideas for planning lessons are provided in *Talk Box: speaking and listening activities for learning at Key Stage 1* by Dawes and Sams (2004). One idea recommended includes the use of an actual box with a range of props, to provide a visual focus, together with resources that relate to a particular lesson, for example items from a story to be read or pictures that depict specific scenes that can promote discussion.

Links with language and literacy at home

For opportunities for talk and the development of literacy to be really effective in the classroom, it is important to build on children's experiences at home. Several detailed long-term ethnographic studies have revealed the richness and intellectual power of young children's language development in secure and familiar domestic settings (Heath 1983; Tizard and Hughes 1984; Campbell 1999; Whitehead 2002).

Meaningful links to a child's home literacy experiences should be encouraged. It is helpful to tune into these experiences and use them as a springboard for further development. This is clearly acknowledged in the both the 2007 and the 2012 editions of the *Early Years Foundation Stage Framework* (DfE 2012a), which advocates partnership working.

It is interesting to note that this has not always been the case; it was not until the late 1960s and early 1970s, following the Plowden Report (CACE 1967), that the case for parental involvement was argued and innovative programmes began to be disseminated and have an effect. Following this, a series of pieces of legislation (the Education Acts of 1980, 1981, 1986 and 1988) all strengthened the rights of parents to be involved in their children's schooling.

Advantages of involving parents

Legislation requires schools to involve parents, and doing so can support children's development in the following ways:

- supporting practitioners in developing a fuller picture of the child;
- helping transition from home to school;
- supporting two-way communication from school to home and vice versa;
- sharing a child's learning with parents;
- providing guidance to parents on how to support children at home;
- extending the curriculum to include contributions from parents and the community.

Many schools have developed effective links, including home/school diaries, to provide an open-door policy to encourage parents to come into school to help and work with their children. Particular projects that involve parents can also help, so that children may be asked to find out with their parents about the history of their name or provide pictures of themselves as a baby (and so on). The Sure Start initiatives, launched by the Labour Government in 1998, focused on enhancing partnership with parents and carers. Within these initiatives, various projects and local initiatives were developed and one of the key areas of focus was to improve children's communication skills. Evaluations of the initiative showed modest impact (Hutchings *et al.* 2007); however, as noted in *The Lancet UK Policy Matters* (2011: 1), 'Although evaluation of Sure Start has been challenging, the balance of evidence suggests that families benefit from the programme.'

A range of research has been cited by the DfES (2003b) in *The Impact of Parental Involvement on Children's Education* to show the value of parental involvement in the development of literacy skills. For example:

- The frequency with which the child plays with letters/numbers at home was linked with attainment in all measures.
- Parents' drawing children's attention to sounds and letters was linked to literacy skills, early number skills and non-verbal attainment.

(DfES 2003b: 1)

Environmental print

Environmental print is the print found in the local environment, such as road signs and street names. It can be an effective bridge between children's experience of literacy at home and their learning in school. Literacy development begins very early as babies are surrounded by print and children begin to understand the symbolic awareness of print. Thus 'CBeebies', 'Toys R Us' or 'McDonald's' are recognised at an early age. At home, children are surrounded by writers (of shopping lists, birthday cards, tax forms, cheques, letters etc.); from observing such practices, children begin to develop rules about writing. The task of the teacher is to help those implicit understandings to become explicit. One of the key vehicles for this is play. This can provide diverse opportunities for literacy; for example, children writing prescriptions in the context of a role-play area set up as a health centre. Classrooms, therefore, should be print-rich and culturally diverse to build on the fertile world of print outside school. This should also include digital literacy linked to socio-dramatic play opportunities; for example, in an 'airport' role-play area the check-in desk could include an age-appropriate database for children to check names, times of flights and so on.

Children can also take part in 'print walks' around the classroom, school or local area, looking for examples of print. Making use of digital photography by the children as well as the teacher can support a range of literacy work in the classroom, encompassing labelling, describing, citing areas of interest or areas for improvement, and actively interrogating the print around the children. Many early-years classrooms provide a print-rich environment with examples of labels and signs clearly displayed: in guided print walks around the classroom, teachers can point out examples of print and what they tell us.

An the awareness of print around them can be a powerful incentive to beginning readers, and one very useful activity is to create environmental scrapbooks consisting of a range of captions and advertisements that children readily recognise. A scrapbook could include wrappers from items such as cereal, crisps, chocolate bars or popular toys. Children love to 'read' the book and parents can be encouraged to make their own. This supports the use of print around children and helps to develop their confidence as print users.

The most significant piece of writing in a child's life is his or her name. How often do you hear young children say, 'Look, Mummy, that is in my name!' as they point to a particular letter on a sign or poster? As many early-years teachers know, 'games with names' are a good way into early writing. Most classrooms have children's possessions labelled with their name and often an accompanying picture. They can then sort their name cards according to those that begin (or end) with the same letter and use them to record who is here, playing in a certain area and so on. When this is accompanied by the child's picture, either current or as a baby, this can generate real interest. It is often illuminating to ask parents to tell the story of the child's name: how it was chosen and where it came from. Names can be a powerful motivator for children, especially when slipped into stories or songs.

Play, drawing and narrative

Children gradually assimilate their everyday experiences into their play. Malaguzzi's (1998) inspirational work with early-years children in the Reggio Emilia area of Italy describes this as the 'hundred languages of children'. These 'languages' may consist of storytelling, singing, dancing, patterning, model-making, drawing or talking. For children, it is through play that meaning is negotiated and symbolism is used.

The importance of early mark-making and drawing to the development of literacy stems from children's attempts to fix their play in time. These attempts to symbolically represent aspects of their play are driven by natural need and by mirroring the examples of literacy they experience at home and in the environment. Thus, a child learns that a shopping list consists of a series of words, each written on a separate line, while a note to someone consists of continuous print (see Figure 4.1).

FIGURE 4.1 Example of emergent writing
Source: Bearne, E. (2002) *Making Progress in Writing*. London: Routledge Falmer, p. 9.

Developing literacy through play and creativity

There is a strong tradition in early-years education regarding play as the key way in which young children learn. Research by Evangelou *et al.* (2009) has shown that play is important socially, emotionally, physically, intellectually and linguistically. This finding is supported by the EYFS, which reinforces its importance for learning:

> The ways in which the child engages with other people and their environment – playing and exploring, active learning, and creating and thinking critically – underpin learning and development across all areas and support the child to remain an effective and motivated learner.
>
> (DfE 2012b: 4)

This is not always well understood by parents, who may feel that school should be 'work' and not 'play'. This is encapsulated by Timothy Mo in *Sour Sweet* (1982). Here a Chinese mother is aghast at her young son's description of school:

> She couldn't believe that Son dropped in an aside that they played with plasticine and flour and water in the classroom. He had been doing that at home for years.

'Bad to tell lies, Son,' she admonished him gently.

(cited in Hall and Robinson 2003: 5)

Later in the story, the mother discovers that her son has no difficulty working with money when helping in the family shop. He tells her that he has played shops at school with plastic meat and pretend money. But she can't believe he could be learning in this way and retorts:

'Clever Boy.' Kiss. 'But bad to tell lies, Son.'

Play is diverse and consists of different forms. Hutt *et al.* (1989) have shown that play consists of 'epistemic play' and 'ludic play'. Epistemic play concerns children exploring and learning by doing. Ludic play includes socio-dramatic play and offers more opportunities for language play, creativity and literacy development. Hall and Robinson (2003) suggest that when planning opportunities for play linked to literacy we should consider:

- a theme that naturally has a range of literacy activities;
- a setting that is relevant to the children's lives but also can extend their knowledge;
- where possible, a visit to a real-life example;
- a setting that can have more than one possible area; for example, a zoo park with an animal-care centre and a customer-care centre;
- a setting that has a range of literate character roles;
- a setting that includes diverse examples of print for different purposes;
- opportunities to allow the children to design and build a setting;
- opportunities for adults to join the children and play in the setting from time to time.

An example cited by Hall and Robinson (2003) involved a focused visit to a local garage to examine what happened there, with a focus on types of environmental print:

- whole-class discussion of the visit including the kinds of jobs they had seen and the roles that would be needed in the classroom, plus the necessary props;
- a thank-you letter to the garage owner following the visit;
- an application to the council for planning permission to build a garage (the children wrote to the Town Planning Department, and in response were asked to fill in a form; the teacher read the form and wrote the children's responses);
- drawing up plans for building a garage, including labels;
- lists of things needed to set up a garage;
- a response to a letter of complaint about plans to build a garage;
- planning the opening with a notice, advertisement, programme of events and name badges;
- job advertisements and applications;
- playing in the garage that encouraged writing: notices, clipboards, lists, instructions (e.g. how to change a wheel), estimates for repairs etc.

Summing up the impact of the project, Hall and Robinson stated that:

During the entire course of the case study the children demonstrated massive engagement in, and enjoyment of, the experience … the children engaged in the writing with considerable intensity and purpose.

(Hall and Robinson 2003: 124)

The project promoted considerable engagement with parents, who helped in many ways including making child-sized overalls, coming to the opening and listening to the children's recounts, all of which involved many literacy experiences.

Developing a love of reading in the early years

In order for children to develop as readers, they need to have experienced the delight that books can bring. This needs to begin early, and initiatives such as Books for Babies have helped to promote it. These first experiences can be multisensory, with books that contain tactile surfaces and other sensory delights. Books such as *The Very Hungry Caterpillar* by Eric Carle and *Dear Zoo* by Rod Campbell contain visual features that extend the playful possibilities. These first experiences are shared with an adult, and for children represent a time of warmth, security and pleasure. Children commonly develop favourite books that must be read again and again. Later, they retell the story from memory, turning the pages as if actually reading the words. Here the young child is switching on to book language, rehearsing for later reading and, importantly, being introduced to the unique voices of many authors.

As experience of literary texts grows, it supports a range of skills, notably expanding children's vocabulary and widening their knowledge and understanding of the world around them. The role of the adult or practitioner is crucial here in mediating the child's understanding, and many authors support the process by encouraging children to interact with their books. One of the skills that can be developed in this way is the ability to predict what will happen next. Prediction is a key skill for readers, as it encourages a constant search for meaning in the text. It is from the early enjoyable experiences of a wealth of children's literature that language-comprehension skills are formed. It is also by playing with words and language, another commonly enjoyable occupation with young children, that the basic building blocks of mapping the sounds and symbols of language are developed. This is explored in detail in Chapter 8.

Emergent writing

Reading and writing are closely interlinked, and these links are supported by speaking and listening. It is by supporting these links that children best learn to become literate. The term 'emergent literacy' refers to the phase when a child is in the process of becoming literate, between approximately six months and school entry. Marie Clay (1979) introduced this term when she described the knowledge and awareness that young children have about print before starting school. Clay emphasises the interrelationship between speaking, listening, reading and writing.

Children begin the process of mark-making early, representing their thoughts about experiences and cultural images. This starts with the way in which young children attach special importance to a toy or blanket. From then on, marks using a range of media are common, from smearing food on a high-chair tray to daubing with paint or crayons. Drawings and writing are produced together and many researchers (Ferreiro and Teberosky 1982; Kress 1997; Hall and Robinson 2003) emphasise the significance of these early drawings that precede and accompany writing.

Understanding early writing is supported by three principles (Goodman 1984):

- *Functional principle*: writing has a purpose for the writer (e.g. putting up a notice).
- *Linguistic principle*: writing is a system that is organised into letters and words.
- *Relational principle*: there is a connection between the spoken and written word.

Emergent writing develops children's creativity and encourages them to experiment. It is this experimentation that helps children not only to understand the difference between drawing and writing (as explored in depth by Ferreiro and Teberosky 1982) but also to crack the writing code and begin to understand the correspondence between letters and sounds. It is not, however, a matter of leaving children alone to learn to write. They need support from teachers, who can respond, monitor and help development as children learn about the writing system and the alphabetic code.

Supporting early writing

A key factor in success is to place writing in a meaningful context and to provide a real purpose in order to make the crucial links with literacy at home. Providing a supportive environment that encourages early writing involves various elements:

- Modelling writing for children in a range of forms; for example, writing letters, notes or filling forms, in addition to scribing for children in shared writing.
- Providing a range of writing materials for children to investigate. For example, a variety of sorts of paper of various colours and sizes, which can be stuck to the floor or table with large pens provided. Other items that can be motivating are diaries, postcards, envelopes, stamps and computers; a range of sorts of print may be displayed, with opportunities to complete forms and such.
- Creating a workshop area; for example, for making small books with a range of supporting materials, such as glue, staples, lists of words, name cards and so on.
- Displaying examples of writing in a range of languages and scripts.
- Producing published examples of the children's work using computers, printers and digital cameras.
- Ensuring a real purpose and audience for writing.
- Having opportunities to practise writing in various ways.
- Providing natural ways into writing alongside play (such as prescription pads in the health centre, telephone message pads and shopping lists in the home corner, and so on).
- Accepting children's tentative attempts at writing.
- Supporting children's fine motor skills in the development of handwriting through a range of exercises.
- Above all, it is important that children see themselves as writers and are not dissuaded from their first attempts.

Talking before writing

One of the keys to encouraging children to write is to provide the time and opportunity to talk about the subject first, with either a partner or an adult. The advantages of this include the following:

- Oral storytelling gives experience of story forms and helps narrative writing.
- Talk partners help shape writing.
- Even very young writers can express their ideas after talk, role play and guided storytelling.
- Talk guides how the text should sound – its style and voice.
- Talk helps children to sequence and structure their writing.
- Talk helps children to check whether their writing makes sense.

Pie Corbett's work on *Talk for Writing* (DCSF 2008c) both supports the oral rehearsal before writing and encourages the collaborative nature of this process.

Narrative writing

Children's exposure to storytelling from infancy establishes a body of knowledge that can be used to develop a writer's voice. It is important for children to become aware that fiction has a recognisable pattern with a chronological structure focused around a complication or problem. This does not have to follow a simple structure or formula (e.g. a beginning, middle and end). Stories can cover a wide range of structures; for example, linear stories (e.g. Jill Murphy's *On the Way Home* or Colin McNaughton's *Suddenly*), circular stories (e.g. Pat Hutchins' *Rosie's Walk* or Eric Carle's *The Bad-Tempered Ladybird*) or journey stories (e.g. John Burningham's *The Shopping Basket* or Michael Rosen's *We're Going on a Bear Hunt*).

It can be useful in making progress in narrative to borrow the models of known stories as starting points. Through this, writers learn to use a prop for a while that then can lead to creating their own writing. Using prompts and aids such as storyboards and story maps can help oral retelling and also assist in planning a story.

Early writing development

The following factors are crucial in developing proficient writers:

- a rich oral experience of telling and retelling texts in preparation for writing;
- frequent rehearsal of sentences orally;
- varied stimulating writing contexts and experiences, often within play settings;
- adults (not just teachers) modelling writing for a range of purposes;
- systematic teaching of phonics;
- direct teaching of handwriting with daily practice;
- regular shared writing to teach the skills of text composition directly;
- displays of a variety of writing, including word lists and work in progress.

The process of writing is a complex one for young children, and can be supported as a child develops increased ability with transcriptional skills (i.e. spelling and handwriting). However, these skills should be taught in real writing contexts in order to enable the child to transfer the acquired knowledge. The process of shared writing with the teacher is an effective teaching strategy.

Scaffolding (supporting) the process

Supporting young children as writers can be done powerfully by modelling the process. Geekie *et al.* (1999) describe 'blackboard stories' and chronicle the development of two girls aged five in a Kindergarten/Reception classroom who within the first year of school became competent readers and writers. Aided by the teacher's modelling of these 'blackboard stories', which consisted of a considerable amount of oral rehearsal of each child's narrative prior to individual writing, each child had a clear 'story' to tell and was able to go about the process of writing it, using at first a combination of drawing and writing but gradually developing correct spelling. One example of a strategy that can be helpful involves children observing sentences modelled by the teacher, sharing ideas with a partner and then, having orally rehearsed their sentence, saying it to their cupped hands. Metaphorically holding this sentence in their hands, children go to tables in the classroom and then individually write their sentences. This symbolic action provides a real aid to the authoring process. Geekie *et al.* (1999) describe the process thus:

1   Make a clear statement about what is going to be written.

2   Identify each word in succession.

3   Either recall words from memory, find them in the print environment of the classroom, or segment them into phonemes and make sound–symbol matches.

4   Reread the developing text in order to remember what has already been written and what remains to be written.

(Geekie *et al.* 1999: 40)

At the heart of the ability to support children's emerging literacy is the need to respond *contingently* to children. This is described by David Wood as follows:

Contingent teaching … involves pacing the amount of help children are given on the basis of their moment-to-moment understanding. If they do not understand an instruction given at one level, then more help is forthcoming. When they do understand, the teacher steps back and gives the child more room for initiative. In this way the child is never left alone when he is in difficulty nor is he 'held back' by teaching that is too directive and intrusive.

(Wood 1988: 81)

In summary, communication, language and literacy development are enhanced by the following factors:

■   practitioners who understand the development process;

■   frequent opportunities for meaningful talk and interaction;

- clear links to experiences at home and in the community;
- provision of a secure environment with sensitive adults who really listen and respond appropriately to children;
- a print-rich environment;
- learning through play;
- first-hand experiences;
- frequent engagement with the wealth of children's literature;
- playing with sounds, words and rhymes;
- modelling by adults of different forms of literacy;
- celebration of home cultures and languages.

Key points

- Early language acquisition is a remarkable achievement and there is a range of theories to explain the developmental process.
- The support and interaction of adults and peers are crucial to this development, and particularly to encouraging sustained shared thinking.
- Providing an environment to promote talk needs careful consideration.
- It is important to acknowledge children's rich language experiences at home and create meaningful links with language and literacy.
- Play is seen as the key way in which young children learn, and providing opportunities for play in the classroom is important.
- Children need opportunities to explore the wealth of children's literature and thus develop early reading skills.
- Early mark-making and writing should be encouraged through a range of resources and opportunities, including modelling by adults.

Further reading

Browne, A. (2009) *Developing Language and Literacy 3–8, 3rd edn*. London: Sage.

Buckley, B. (2003) *Children's Communication Skills: from birth to five years*. London: Routledge.

Dawes, L. and Sams, C. (2004) *Talk Box: speaking and listening activities for learning at Key Stage 1*. London: David Fulton.

Whitehead, M. (2010) *Language and Literacy in the Early Years 0–7, 4th edn*. London: Sage.

5

Knowledge about language

Grammar and punctuation

Purpose of this chapter

This chapter aims to:

- discuss reasons for learning about language;
- examine problems associated with teaching and learning about language;
- present classroom activities to develop children's knowledge about language;
- describe the role of punctuation and how to teach it;
- provide classroom activities to develop children's ability to punctuate accurately;
- look at issues related both to our own development of subject knowledge about language and at ways in which children's knowledge about language can be improved through enjoyable and meaningful activities.

Reasons for learning about language

'We never learned no grammar when we was at school.' What might you think if you heard this said by someone about to embark upon an English course? You might agree with the gist of it and think, 'No, neither did I', or you might hear only the grammatical errors. You might form an opinion about the speaker. In the preface to *Pygmalion*, George Bernard Shaw (1916) wrote: 'It is impossible for an Englishman to open his mouth without making some other Englishman hate or despise him', and examples of deviations from Standard English such as the above might lead us to draw conclusions about social status and even intelligence.

Some 'mistakes' occur when people use regional dialects rather than Standard English. A common error for trainee teachers in many regions is: 'Who is sat nicely?' Then there is the confusion over when to say 'John and *I*' as opposed to 'John and *me*'. However, we do all have quite a sophisticated understanding of English grammar, even if we happily deviate from Standard English several times a day.

Even young children have an understanding of grammar before they begin to read or write. Listen to them talking and note the mistakes they make. For example, 'we wented' or 'we goed' instead of 'we went'; 'we runned' instead of 'we ran'. In using such constructions, children demonstrate that they are aware of the past tense endings of regular verbs but make the mistake of applying these to irregular verbs. They do similar things with plurals, assuming that all plurals end with s, as most do. Therefore, we hear of 'mouses' and 'mans', instead of 'mice' and 'men', because children know about houses and cans and blouses and fans.

Learning about language and acquiring the terminology necessary to discuss it is rather like taking a course on car mechanics. We may be good drivers but have no knowledge of what makes a car work; however, when the car breaks down a rudimentary knowledge of what happens under the bonnet can be useful, and we may save ourselves from being charged for unnecessary work by an unscrupulous garage. If we tell people who regularly ask whether children are 'sat nicely' that they should ask whether they are 'sitting nicely', it is helpful if we can explain why and perhaps provide other examples to reinforce the point (would they ask 'Who is ran nicely?').

ACTIVITY: ANALYSING GRAMMATICAL ERRORS

Which grammatical errors annoy you and why? Make a list and write corrected versions. Can you explain the reasons for the errors?

One of the problems that teachers face when teaching children about language is that many teachers (including us) were given very little explicit instruction during their own schooldays and may lack confidence in their own abilities. There is also a feeling among some teachers and trainee teachers that they managed to achieve good results at school and even university without having had much training in grammar, so why could it be important for others? David Crystal suggests six reasons why we should learn about language:

- 'Because it's there.' We are curious about the world and wish to understand it and grammar is 'no different from any other domain of knowledge in this respect'.
- Because language 'is involved with almost everything we do as human beings' and 'grammar is the fundamental organising principle of language'.
- Because we already have an extraordinary grammatical ability and it may be helpful to describe the rules that govern grammar.
- Because we need to be aware of what went wrong when we have made grammatical errors in speech or writing.
- Because 'Learning about grammar provides a basis for learning other languages.'
- Because after studying grammar we should be 'more alert to the strength, flexibility and variety of our language, and thus be in a better position to use it and to evaluate others' use of it'. Crystal sounds a cautionary note here: 'Even after a course on car mechanics, we can still drive carelessly.'

(Crystal 2004b: 12–13)

Problems associated with teaching and learning about language

Modern foreign languages (MFLs) are increasingly a feature of the primary curriculum in England. Many secondary-school teachers of modern languages assert that before they can begin to teach children a new language they have to spend time teaching them about their own language. The National Curriculum for English and the Literacy Framework should help children to become more aware of their own language and how it works, but this will depend upon teachers having the subject knowledge to teach about it effectively. As Wilson unequivocally states:

> I feel absolutely certain that only by building on their own language knowledge can teachers hope to foster the skills and the enthusiasm for language, and confidence in engaging with it, that children need.
>
> (Wilson 2005: 6)

Why does English present problems?

English is a rich language that has developed over hundreds of years and is an amalgamation of languages from other parts of the world, particularly Europe. This has led to a variety of spellings and some sound symbol correspondences that can be baffling for English-speakers, let alone for foreigners. For example, the 'k' sound in 'kit' is made in different ways in different words, such as cat, sock, queen and school. Add to this the number of homophones (words that sound the same but have different spellings and meanings) in English and it is no wonder that many people struggle with spelling (see Chapter 12). However, homophones provide us with great scope for humour: puns and misunderstandings are central to many jokes. For example:

> Two peanuts walk into a bar, and one was a salted.
> I walked into a seafood disco last week … and pulled a mussel.
> Two fish swim into a concrete wall. One turns to the other and says, 'Dam!'

While some of these subtle (or not so subtle) differences in the meanings of words can make us laugh, they can also lead to exasperation when we try to learn more about our language. The language is littered not only with homophones but also with homonyms, which are words that have the same sound and perhaps the same spellings as others but different meanings. For example, let us look at the word 'fast':

- fast is a noun when one takes part in *a fast*;
- fast is a verb when one decides *to fast*;
- fast is an adjective, as in *a fast driver*;
- fast is an adverb, as in *to drive fast*.

This inevitably leads to problems when we try to teach children about parts of speech. The presence in English of *word class mobility* means that words may be different parts of speech according to the context in which they are used. And it is not only children who find this a difficult concept to grasp: teachers and trainee teachers sometimes have to address their own misconceptions before they can attempt to teach children about parts of speech. Those who may have been taught about nouns and adjectives by being given lists of each were done a disservice by teachers who failed to discuss parts of speech in the context of texts. Thus, we can look at a list of words that can be adjectives and consider how each may be a different part of speech according to how it is used in a sentence. Try this with the list below:

■ green
■ fat
■ light
■ club.

As adjectives, these words could be part of phrases such as:

■ a green dress
■ a fat cow
■ a light meal
■ a club sandwich.

However, they could also be nouns, as in:

■ They played on the village green.
■ He wanted to lose some body fat.
■ She switched on the light.
■ They met at the tennis club.

And three could be verbs, as in:

■ The leaves began to green in the spring.
■ She decided to light a fire.
■ They had to club together to pay the bill.

ACTIVITY: USING WORDS AS DIFFERENT PARTS OF SPEECH

Look at the following words and experiment with using them as different parts of speech:

■ mirror	■ mate	■ boot
■ drink	■ run	■ chair
■ table	■ foot	■ face
■ farm		

You may feel that understanding parts of speech is rather more challenging than you first thought! However, if you have a basic understanding of parts of speech and are aware of word class mobility, you will be well equipped to use the terms with children in the context of whole texts. What will confuse both children and teachers is teaching parts of speech in isolation by using lists on the board and asking children to decide which words are nouns, which are verbs and so on. Apart from being misleading for learners, it just takes one child to give an answer that the teacher does not expect but that is correct for confusion to reign for everyone.

Classroom activities to develop children's knowledge about language

Nonsense sentences

Children should learn grammatical terms in the context of texts and of the language they use in speech and writing. For example, try asking children to read nonsense sentences and then work in pairs or small groups to produce their own. This activity not only forces children to consider and discuss the roles played by different words in sentences but also enables them to be creative and to engage in an enjoyable task. Sentences can be simple and short for younger children but can become increasingly complex for older and/or more able pupils.

Begin by writing a simple nonsense sentence and showing it to the whole class or group. For example:

The blue carrot ate the red dustbin.

Ask the children to look at the sentence carefully and discuss it and then to suggest another sentence that is equally nonsensical and that follows exactly the same pattern. Children who do not know the names of parts of speech will probably talk about the words in terms of their function and so may say things like: 'It needs *the* at the beginning then a word that describes something and then a thing ....' For the time being, this is fine and children *should* be encouraged to think carefully about the functions of words in sentences. However, if when you discuss sentences that you compose with the children's help you explain that words that describe things are called adjectives, this will gradually enable children to develop a vocabulary for their discussions.

Having introduced simple nonsense sentences, you might go on to introduce adverbs and then subordinate clauses so that children could be asked to replicate structures such as:

The pink elephant, who was riding a bike, carefully drank the purple pond.

When they have mastered a few different sentence structures, children could go on to make their nonsense sentences more interesting by making them alliterative ('The boring banana bashfully bought a beautiful brick.') or putting them together into a rhyme. They could be introduced to nonsense verse by writers such as Spike Milligan (e.g. 'On the Ning Nang Nong') and Lewis Carroll (e.g. 'Jabberwocky') and might go on to write their own versions of the poems. Again, in exploring the poems children will need to understand the functions of different words if they are to replicate the style.

ACTIVITY: USING NONSENSE SENTENCES

Why use nonsense sentences rather than 'sensible' sentences? (See the end of this chapter for an explanation.)

Replacing adjectives and other words

Another activity that focuses attention on the functions of parts of speech involves replacing adjectives in a text. Many teachers tell children to vary the adjectives they use and to avoid more mundane ones such as 'nice'. Try presenting children with a text similar to the following as a shared reading activity:

> The weather was nice when we went to Hornsea. We had a really nice time on the beach and we ate some very nice sandwiches. Mum helped us to build a really nice sandcastle and we put some nice flags in it which we bought at a nice little shop next to the beach. Dad played with us while Mum and Gran went for a nice cup of tea and we had a really nice time with him.

Invite children's comments about the text: it is almost certain that they will mention the frequent use of 'nice'. Ask them to consider what the purpose of the word 'nice' is in the text, and encourage them to discuss alternatives. Edit the text with the children's help, and then produce a 'Nice Chart' with the word nice in the middle and a range of alternatives around it. This can lead to a discussion on context, with children being asked to think about the different situations in which an adjective like 'nice' might be used. For example, in the text above it is used to describe weather, food, various objects and a passage of time. The Nice Chart might, therefore, include a collection of adjectives to describe food, weather, clothing, places and so on.

Another activity to promote consideration of varied vocabulary focuses on alternatives to 'said' in dialogue. A shared reading passage could be a starting point:

> 'Leave me alone,' said Chloe.
> 'No!' said Tom. I won't leave you alone until you tell me where you've hidden my book.'
> 'And I won't tell you where it is until you give me my pen back,' said Chloe.
> 'Oh please can I have my book back?' said Tom.
> 'You know what you have to do first,' said Chloe.
> 'Oh all right,' said Tom. 'Here it is.'
> 'Thank you,' said Chloe. 'Your book is under the table.'

Children should be asked to consider how the text might be improved. On this occasion, the punctuation can be studied and can act as a guide to the kinds of verbs that might be used instead of 'said'. There is, of course, no reason why 'said' cannot be perfectly acceptable in many situations, but its repeated use can make dialogue dull and does not always enable the reader to gauge how characters' words are spoken. As an extension activity, children could introduce some adverbs to give a further indication as to how words were spoken. For example, 'shouted angrily', 'whispered secretively', 'muttered crossly'. They could also be asked to look at examples of dialogue from story books in the classroom and could make a collection of alternatives to 'said' as well as a collection of adverbs used with such verbs.

Activities can begin with reading whole texts and moving on to study aspects of the text, which teachers can choose in line with the learning objectives they wish the children to meet. A natural progression is then to move on to shared, guided and independent writing that allows children to reinforce their understanding by using what they have learned and making it a focus of their writing. For the 'nice' adjective work, children could write descriptions of days out or walks around the school grounds, using a range of adjectives to embellish their writing. For work on dialogue, children could be given imaginary scenarios in which a conversation takes place: for example, a parent speaking to a child who has arrived home late. They could hold the conversations in role and go on to work in pairs to write dialogue for the conversations. Having done this, they could read the dialogue to others before inviting their audience to guess which verbs they used to show how the words should be spoken. After showing the words they actually used, they could consider editing their work to make use of any suggestions that they feel might enhance it. By paying close attention to the meanings of the verbs in this way, children will be much more likely to remember them. An excellent lesson was taught by two undergraduate trainee teachers in Bristol in which discussion about varying verbs and adverbs in dialogue was followed by children watching excerpts from a pantomime. They were then asked to suggest how the dialogue could be written using verbs and adverbs to convey the way the lines were delivered. They also engaged in a shared writing activity on stage directions, which provide guidance to actors on how to deliver their lines. The children went on to write and then perform their own scripts with expression and enthusiasm.

A problem-solving/discovery approach to developing knowledge about language

We need to teach children grammatical rules, but we should also encourage them to discover rules for themselves by looking at different texts and discussing them. The children's conclusions can then be tested by presenting them to the teacher and to classmates. For example, here is a mini saga, a story condensed into exactly fifty words.

> Three bears, Mummy, Daddy and Baby, awoke. Breakfast was too hot, so they took a walk. Goldilocks, little girl, sneaked into their house, ate their porridge, sat on their chairs and broke Baby Bear's. She slept on the small bear's bed, but ran away in terror when the family returned.
>
> (Waugh with McGuinn 1996: 118)

By presenting children with the story in this format, we can encourage discussions not only about the key elements of the story but also about ways in which we can express them concisely through careful use of language. When asked to write their own mini sagas, children should be encouraged to consider different sentence structures and the use of punctuation both to separate and to draw text together.

Children can also look at ways in which words that are unnecessary to the meaning of a sentence might be eliminated. For example:

'I have not got any money,' said Tim.

could be rewritten as

'I have no money,' said Tim.

Children could go on to look at other examples of sentences that include the word 'got' to see how often it is really necessary. Other convoluted phrases could be explored, such as:

I myself personally think that it is not unlikely that rain will fall tomorrow.
I think it is likely to rain tomorrow.

At this present moment in time we have an ongoing period of sunshine.
It is sunny.

Sasha has got a new bicycle and Daniel has got one too.
Sasha and Daniel have new bicycles.

In spite of the fact that it was raining, Ruth had not got her hat on.
Despite the rain, Ruth had no hat.

Skilled users of language can add to sentences to embellish them or remove words to make them more concise and easier to understand.

Use of texts: planned opportunities

While one of the great strengths of the Literacy Strategy (DfEE 1998) was its emphasis on the use of texts as starting points for teaching and learning, it also led to many children thinking that poems and extracts from stories and non-fiction texts are merely vehicles for learning about grammatical features. Some sample texts can be contrived in order to reinforce grammatical concepts, but on the whole it is better to focus upon less-contrived texts that provide some examples of word- and sentence-level concepts but that are enjoyable and engaging in their own right, as well as on texts that are written to focus on particular grammatical features.

Excerpts should be seen by children as being part of whole texts and they should be introduced as such. Thus, if a Year 3 class is learning about pronouns, you can find examples in almost any piece of continuous prose without relying upon contrived examples. However, you may wish to reinforce children's understanding by also looking at specially written passages in which a particular noun is frequently repeated so that they can discuss possible pronoun alternatives.

Shared writing

Shared writing offers an ideal opportunity to focus children's attention on grammar, and demonstrates how writers can explore ideas and consider alternatives. Because the teacher is doing the writing, the children are free to discuss it and suggest how it might be structured. In addition, the quality of the writing should be high, given the scope for drafting, editing and revising. Children should, therefore, look closely at what is written and question whether it is accurate. Teachers can encourage this by making occasional deliberate mistakes that children will enjoy spotting, and then justifying their alternative suggestions. Children will also experience and analyse structures that they might not use in their own writing.

A typical activity to develop children's appreciation of complex sentence structures could involve reading a text and then focusing on one sentence, for example:

There was a horrible moment when every breath was held as the ball sped towards the staffroom window; then there was a shattering, crashing sound as the glass exploded into a thousand pieces.

Unlike the work on nonsense sentences, the objective here is not to replicate the sentence structure exactly but to replicate the sentence type. Children might read and reread the sentence to identify that there are two parts: the first describes a moment of tension and the second a dramatic event. As a shared writing activity, they could write similar sentences with tension followed by action. This could form part of a sequence of lessons on story openings and might lead to independent work in which complete stories could be written.

An understanding of language is, then, more than simply having a knowledge of parts of speech, important though that is. It involves looking at language usage and appreciating various possible ways of using language, and leads to an ability to experiment with language and to write in more interesting ways.

What can teachers do to make children more aware of language?

There are some key things we can do to foster children's awareness of language:

- look at a wide range of examples of written and spoken language;
- make collections of words and texts;
- discuss different registers (see Waugh 2000a: 125);
- use terminology when exploring language (e.g. 'tense': see Waugh 2000a: 118);
- provide opportunities for children to write in different styles;
- discuss language and vocabulary in other lessons besides English; for example, physical education, movement, geography, mathematics;
- encourage children to look at examples of incorrect or misleading English and to analyse what is wrong with them (see Waugh 2000b: 119–20);
- encourage children to rewrite texts in different ways (see Waugh 2000b: 128);
- discuss the value of understanding the way language works.

ACTIVITY: REWRITING INCORRECT SENTENCES

Consider your own knowledge about language. All the sentences below are incorrect. Can you work out why and then rewrite them correctly? (See the end of the chapter for answers and explanations.)

Living in Durham has it's advantages.

Give a child lots of books and they will learn to read.

'Whose the comedian who's catch phrase is "Turned out nice again"?' asked George.

A packet of cigarettes are now very expensive.

John knew he could of done better in the test.

The role of punctuation and how to teach it

In this section we will look at the teaching and learning of punctuation. For some children, punctuating their writing is an obstacle when they are just beginning to write down groups of words. Those who experience difficulty with the concept of punctuation might take some comfort from its history.

Until around 1700, only limited amounts of punctuation were used and what was used was designed to help people to read passages aloud. The marks showed suitable places to pause, breathe or change the tone of voice. Gradually, punctuation marks began to be used 'to mark grammatical structure – such as clauses and sentences – and to guide the reader's interpretation of a text' (Graddol *et al.* 1996: 63). It was not until the eighteenth century that punctuation began to look as it does today. However, legal documents have continued to be unpunctuated, probably because they were not intended to be read aloud so early compositors did not bother to punctuate them (see Crystal 1987: 387).

When discussing the use of punctuation with children, talk about why it is necessary. We require punctuation when we write so that we can compensate for the lack of intonation that is possible in speech. However, punctuation can be a matter of style and some people make greater use of commas, hyphens and exclamation marks than others in order to achieve a certain effect upon the reader.

Punctuation marks enable us to define the status of the sentences we write. Through their use we can indicate whether a sentence is a question, a statement or direct speech, and whether a speaker is exclaiming. Punctuation also enables us to separate units of language such as phrases, clauses and sentences.

What is punctuation?

The word 'punctuation' derives from the Latin *pungere*, 'to prick' (think of 'puncture'); this gives *punctus* – 'pierced' – as the participle. Bunting (1997: 44) maintains that there are two main aspects of punctuation: 'rules which must be used and conventions which are more open to interpretation'. She provides the following examples of rules in English:

- capital letters at the beginning of sentences;
- full stops to end sentences;
- question marks at the end of sentences which are questions;
- apostrophes to mark elision (don't) and possession (John's) (*its* is the possessive exception).

(Bunting 1997: 44)

Punctuation is also used in a stylistic way to emphasise certain words, phrases and clauses and to make subtle, or sometimes not so subtle, changes to meaning. Thus, the same words may be given different meanings through varying the punctuation marks. An inability to understand that the placement of punctuation marks can have a significant effect can lead to confusion for a writer's audience and may result in ambiguity. For example, inserting a comma in 'Shoot Waugh!' alters the meaning of the phrase to 'Shoot, Waugh!' (Waugh changes from the person being shot to the person doing the shooting). Linking the teaching of punctuation to meaning will enable children to regard it as important, whereas an approach that deals with the subject separately from children's own writing might not convey the necessity for careful punctuation.

Punctuation and the curriculum

At Key Stage 1, children are taught to punctuate writing with consistent use of capital letters, full stops and question marks and to begin to use commas. At Key Stage 2 they should be using exclamation marks, inverted commas and apostrophes to mark possession and omission.

In order to achieve level 4 in the writing element of National Curriculum English, a piece of work must fulfil the following requirements:

> Full stops, capital letters and question marks are used correctly, and pupils are beginning to use punctuation within the sentence.
>
> (DfEE and QCA 1999: 7, in 'Attainment Targets' section)

The National Literacy Strategy was rather more demanding, requiring Year 1 children to understand full stops, question marks and speech marks and to understand commas and exclamation marks by Year 2. In Year 4 they met colons, semi-colons and possessive apostrophes.

Some teachers will feel uncomfortable about their own knowledge of punctuation, while others will have strong views on the ways in which children should acquire skills in this aspect of language. The next section shows some of the ways in which punctuation might be taught and learned.

Classroom activities to develop children's ability to punctuate accurately

Punctuation may be taught in stages, with teachers taking the opportunities presented in children's reading to explain commas, colons and so on. Some class or group lessons may be used to discuss, for example, the use of capital letters and, while it is important to relate what is learned to children's writing, it may be helpful to provide some illustrative exercises in order to reinforce concepts.

Proofreading

Encouraging children to proofread their work can help with punctuation, especially when they work with response partners. Communicating with someone else through writing can provide the stimulus many children require to develop punctuation skills. Voice-recording work may help some children to realise where it is necessary to indicate pauses, in much the same way as early printers devised schemes for doing the same. Children may devise their own marks initially before having conventional methods explained to them. Such proofreading may be easier for children to manage if they are given a checklist for checking their work, for example:

- Have you put a capital letter at the beginning of each sentence?
- Does each sentence end with a full stop?
- Have you used speech marks to show when someone was speaking?
- Have you used commas to separate items in lists?

(For another example of a checklist, see Chapter 11, 'Developing writing'.)

By providing a checklist, we can enable children to focus on specific aspects of their writing rather than expecting them to spot mistakes in a more general way. Often, children who are simply asked to check their work go away and return a few minutes later having either done very little or added punctuation in a random way.

The sentence

The most basic concept in punctuation is the sentence. Kress (1982) suggests that a key element of learning to write is learning to write in sentences, but cautions that the sentence is not the basic unit in which young children speak. Appropriate use of the comma, colon, semi-colon and paragraph can be taught only when children have an understanding of the nature of a sentence. In the early stages of writing, children place full stops in many places. Sometimes full stops appear at the end of each line of writing because children have encountered books in which sentences are short and contained within single lines.

One activity that develops the concept of the sentence is to provide children with incomplete sentences and to ask them to use their imaginations to finish them. This could lead to a discussion of the nature of a sentence. They may be asked to join beginnings and endings of sentences, choosing from a list. This could lead to some interesting combinations and some discussion of what is possible and impossible, as well as what makes sense and what does not. For example:

The big, brown dog	flies over the hill.
The little sparrow	played football.
The children	begged for a bone.

It can be seen that there are possible combinations here that might be nonsensical – such as 'The big, brown dog flies over the hill' – but that are grammatically accurate. However, one combination is not possible because the subject and verb would not agree ('The children flies over the hill'). Discussion about grammatical accuracy can, therefore, be linked to discussion about punctuation in such exercises.

Commas

Much of children's early writing is made up of lists. The list may be a feature of preparation for writing for experienced writers too. Commas may be introduced when children begin to turn their lists into prose. They might be asked to write descriptions of members of the class using a series of adjectives separated by commas.

At a later stage, the children could examine the use of commas in their reading books and could try to work out why they were used in particular places. Teachers could help them to classify the different uses. For example, commas can be used:

- to separate words in a list;
- to separate the name of a person being addressed in direct speech from the rest of the sentence;
- to separate an adverbial from the rest of a sentence;   ✳ *Hopefully*
- to separate clauses in a sentence.

A story about a comma that saved a human life (see Waugh with McGuinn 1996: 133) may be used to show how the insertion of a comma into text can change meaning dramatically.

Question marks

Asking children to look at a list of sentences and identify which require full stops and which need question marks may help to reinforce the use of punctuation. Providing the children with answers and asking them to write their own questions is a more creative way of developing their conception of the question and its punctuation. For example, children could be asked to think of questions that might produce answers such as:

- 'Half past nine';
- 'Yes, but only on Saturdays';
- 'Florida'.

Exclamation marks

Exclamation marks may be introduced through an oral activity in which children pass a word around and try to say it in different ways, such as loudly, angrily, softly or humorously. They then discuss which are exclamations and are shown that these can be denoted in writing by using an exclamation mark to help readers to understand how they were or should be spoken. The children might go on to write short drama scripts in which there are frequent exclamations. Tabloid newspaper headlines are a rich source of exclamation marks and children could make collections of these for a classroom display.

Speech marks

Many children are confused about the placement of inverted commas when writing dialogue and may gain a greater understanding if they are introduced to them through speech bubbles in comics. They could be given copies of comic strip stories with the speech bubbles blanked out and then be asked to add dialogue. Subsequently, they could write the story using speech marks and adding text to show the identity of speakers.

Walking and reading

Children might be presented with a short passage that is unpunctuated and be asked to read it through. They could go on to walk as they read, pausing briefly where the text seems to include a pause and the need for a comma, and for longer when a full stop might be required. They could begin working individually and go on to discuss with partners where punctuation may be needed.

Apostrophes for abbreviation

Where apostrophes are used to abbreviate words, it is important that children understand that the apostrophes show where letters have been missed out. They might be shown examples and be asked to say what the longer versions would be. At this stage, words such as 'won't' and 'shan't' ('will not' and 'shall not') should be avoided, with the focus being on more regular abbreviations such as 'didn't', 'shouldn't' and 'isn't'.

Children could go on to look at examples of words abbreviated using apostrophes in newspapers and in shops. Football league tables often show teams' names in shortened form and may promote discussion and investigation into the complete spellings. For example, children may find:

N'castle, So'ton, B'ham City, Middlesboro' and Tott'm.

Collections can be displayed together with reference sources, so that children can try to find extended versions. They could also look at road signs with place names abbreviated and could be invited to create their own abbreviations for different places. A development activity could explore some of those abbreviations that tend not to have apostrophes such as 'Utd' and 'Tn'.

Apostrophes for possession

Children often see examples of apostrophes being misused, so a good introduction to using possessive apostrophes can involve children being given examples of sentences that include apostrophes, or they could look for apostrophes in their reading books. They could discuss the reasons for the presence of the apostrophes, both together and with the teacher, before being given some examples of sentences that require apostrophes to be added. They might go on to attempt short pieces of writing that include possessive apostrophes.

Bunting (1997: 54) maintains that 'It may help children to understand that the apostrophe *s* to mark possession represents the *es* form of Old English'. For examples, see Chaucer's *Canterbury Tales*, which were written in the fourteenth century and include *The Nonnes Preestes Tale* (*The Nun's Priest's Tale*) and *The Cokes Tale* (*The Cook's Tale*).

ACTIVITY: USING APOSTROPHES

Look for examples of apostrophes in the environment.

- Make a list of those that are used correctly and those that are not.
- Can you explain why particular errors are made?

Making use of children's reading

The influence of reading in the environment is evident in the misuse of apostrophes, which seem to appear in children's writing before they are taught about them. It is useful to discuss punctuation marks by showing examples in reading books in order to demonstrate correct usage. Group reading sessions can reinforce concepts in punctuation. For example, give children a copy of the same book and ask them to read in turn, changing reader after each sentence or paragraph. They may be assigned different characters in a story and be asked to read dialogue without using words such as *said John* or *asked Jill*. This develops an understanding of the purpose of speech marks and their placement.

Using incorrectly punctuated text

One method of teaching punctuation that is frequently employed is to use unpunctuated or incorrectly punctuated passages that pupils are asked to punctuate. This method draws attention to ambiguities that can arise when punctuation is absent or inappropriate and, if used sparingly and as a follow-up to marking of writing, can be very effective. Children may be presented with pieces of writing and asked to punctuate them in different ways in order to alter their meaning. For example:

the boy sat down on the television there was a herd of elephants in his bedroom his father was tidying up

This could be punctuated in various ways:

The boy sat down on the television. There was a herd of elephants in his bedroom. His father was tidying up.

The boy sat down. On the television there was a herd of elephants. In his bedroom, his father was tidying up.

Similarly, a simple sign could have its meaning changed through variations in punctuation:

PRIVATE. NO SWIMMING ALLOWED.

PRIVATE? NO! SWIMMING ALLOWED.

(Waugh 1998: 17)

Another example invites the reader to show how the same words, punctuated differently, may be used to portray a person as generous or as mean:

At Christmas, Hayley was going to buy lots of things for herself. She was going to buy nothing for everyone else. It was going to be a wonderful time.

At Christmas, Hayley was going to buy lots of things. For herself, she was going to buy nothing. For everyone else, it was going to be a wonderful time.

(Waugh with McGuinn 1996: 69)

Identifying necessary punctuation

Another activity involves the use of a passage presented on an interactive whiteboard, flipchart or overhead transparency with the punctuation covered. Children listen to the passage or read it aloud, and then reread it and try to decide what the hidden punctuation marks are (see Barnes 1997: 18).

Approaches to teaching punctuation

Punctuation may be developed through a variety of approaches, including:

- discussion of punctuation in children's reading;
- discussion of punctuation in children's writing;
- the use of response partners in the drafting process;
- the use of group reading sessions;
- the use of class or group teaching reinforced by exercises.

The first four approaches have formed the bulk of many children's experience of learning about punctuation since the mid-1970s. The use of exercises seemed to fall out of favour with many teachers during the 1960s and 1970s, but there appears to have been a revival of interest from the 1990s, perhaps because of the demands of the National Curriculum and the Primary National Strategy. Exercises need not be dull. Indeed, they may involve children in producing imaginative writing. They enable us to reinforce what has been learned and provide an opportunity to check whether children have grasped concepts. However, they cannot, in themselves, teach children very much. They should be regarded as an adjunct to teaching rather than as a method of teaching, and should not be used in isolation.

Punctuation has been neglected in many works on children's writing and may have been inadequately taught and learned by some teachers. A combination of approaches, with an emphasis on the vital role that punctuation plays in helping us to derive meaning from text, should enable us to raise its status and improve its usage.

ACTIVITY: RESPONDING TO CHILDREN'S PROBLEMS WITH PUNCTUATION

Study each of the following and decide upon your response:

- A Year 1 child puts a full stop at the end of every line, regardless of whether one is needed or not.
- Many of your class of Year 2 pupils seem to have little idea about the use of commas.
- A Year 3 child puts apostrophes before every terminal *s* in her work.
- A Year 4 child uses no punctuation whatsoever, but writes at length.
- Many of your Year 5 pupils do not understand the concept of the paragraph.
- A Year 6 child uses speech marks but he places them around whole sentences, including within them 'he said', 'she said', etc.

This chapter has looked at the importance of developing knowledge about language, both for pupils and teachers. While it has been shown that the English language's complexities can prove challenging for both pupils and teachers, it should also be clear that there are many interesting and engaging ways in which language can be studied and explored as we develop our understanding. We do not need to be graduate linguists to be able to teach children about their language, but a good working knowledge will help us to explain their errors and challenge them to develop their skills.

Key points

- If we learn about language, we are better able to understand our errors and avoid them.

- An understanding of language can help us to develop and improve our writing.

- There are many interesting classroom activities that can develop children's knowledge about language and their punctuation skills.

- Punctuation needs to be understood if we are to use it effectively to convey meaning when we write.

Further reading

Bryson, B. (1990) *Mother Tongue: the English language*. Harmondsworth: Penguin.

Crystal, D. (2004a) *Making Sense of Grammar*, London: Longman.

Mallett, M. (2003) *Primary English Encyclopaedia*. London: David.

Medwell, J. and Wray, D. with Moore, G. and Griffiths, V. (2001) *Primary English: knowledge and understanding*. Exeter: Learning Matters.

Wilson, A. (2005) *Language Knowledge for Primary Teachers*. London: David Fulton.

Resources for teaching

Waugh, D. (1996) *Curriculum Bank Writing at Key Stage 1*. Leamington Spa: Scholastic.

Waugh, D. (2000) *Further Curriculum Bank Writing at Key Stage 1*. Leamington Spa: Scholastic.

Waugh, D. (2000) *Further Curriculum Bank Writing at Key Stage 2*. Leamington Spa: Scholastic.

Waugh, D. with McGuinn, N. (1996) *Curriculum Bank Writing at Key Stage 2*. Leamington Spa: Scholastic.

Explanation for the activity on using nonsense sentences

The use of nonsense sentences makes the activity creative and enjoyable and motivates children to want to produce sentences that will entertain their classmates. It also provides a good link to a genre of writing that can be explored by the class.

Explanations for the activity on rewriting incorrect sentences

Incorrect: Living in Durham has it's advantages.
Correct: Living in Durham has its advantages.

Explanation: 'Its' has an apostrophe only when short for 'it is'. Only pronouns ending in 'one' ('someone', 'anyone' etc.) have apostrophes when possessive.

Incorrect: Give a child lots of books and they will learn to read.
Correct: Give a child lots of books and he or she will learn to read.

or

    Correct: Give children lots of books and they will learn to read.

Explanation: 'A child' is singular so the pronoun should not be 'they'. However, because we do not have a suitable gender-neutral pronoun in English, it has become quite common for people to speak of one person as 'they'.

    Incorrect: 'Whose the comedian who's catch phrase is "Turned out nice again"?' asked George.
    Correct: 'Who's the comedian whose catch phrase is "Turned out nice again"?' asked George.

Explanation: 'Who's' is short for 'who is' – try replacing 'whose' and 'who's' in the sentence with 'who is' and you will see why the sentence is incorrect.

    Incorrect: A packet of cigarettes are now very expensive.
    Correct: A packet of cigarettes is now very expensive.

or

    Correct: Cigarettes are now very expensive.

Explanation: Even though 'cigarettes' is a plural, it is the packet that is the subject of the sentence and this is singular, so the verb must be singular too.

    Incorrect: John knew he could of done better in the test.
    Correct: John knew he could have done better in the test.

Explanation: 'Could of' is a common mistake is made because people hear 'could've' (short for 'could have') and assume 'of' should be used. 'Have' is a verb and 'of' is a preposition, and a verb is clearly needed.

6

Talking to learn

Purpose of this chapter

This chapter aims to:

- clarify the link between talk and learning;
- summarise how cooperative learning can be a powerful vehicle for promoting talk and effective learning;
- analyse the use of teachers' questioning to promote talk;
- discuss the use of talk to support children's development of reading and writing skills;
- examine the different forms of speaking and listening and how these can be planned and managed effectively in the classroom;
- show how to involve children in self-assessment of their speaking and listening skills.

The importance of talk for learning

A wealth of research has shown that talk is a key ingredient in the learning process (Barnes and Todd 1977; Slavin 1983; Corson 1988; Johnson *et al.* 1988; Wells *et al.* 1990; Mercer 2000). One powerful example of the social and collaborative nature of learning is demonstrated by a transcript of a mother and child completing a jigsaw puzzle together (Geekie *et al.* 1999). The way in which the mother scaffolds the unfamiliar process by modelling, thinking aloud and talking to the child, followed by the child using learned strategies to complete the puzzle alone, provides a vivid illustration of supporting the learning process. Geekie *et al.* (1999: 116) describe learning as 'collaborative puzzle solving' and set out seven principles that are involved:

- Learning is often a mutual accomplishment.
- Children learn through guided participation.
- Children profit from the support of more competent people.

■ Effective instruction is contingent instruction – the involvement of adults does not imply simply direct instruction or control of learning.

■ It is the quality of the interaction that is important, ensuring that the child is involved in planning activities and decision-making.

■ Language is the means through which self-regulation of learning behaviour develops.

■ Learning depends on the negotiation of meaning with others.

Adults can, therefore, support children's understanding by performing a number of functions. These include focusing the child's attention on what is relevant, simplifying and interpreting information, holding information in working memory for the child, reminding the child of what is known and what the goal is, alerting the child to success or failure, and shifting the child to an alternative procedure.

ACTIVITY: USING TALK TO SUPPORT LEARNING

Examine the transcript below of paired counting with an older child (Kay, 14 years) and a younger one (Antonia, 3 years), cited in Mercer (1995:11). Discuss the following questions with a colleague:

■ How does talk support the learning?
■ How does the older child support the younger child's learning?
■ What would be the next step for the older child in order to support the learning process?

Antonia:	I do one first. No you do one first.
Kay:	OK. One.
Antonia:	Two.
Kay:	Three.
Kay:	(and so on up to …)
Antonia:	Fifteen.
Kay:	Seventeen.
Antonia:	Sixteen! Yours is sixteen.
Kay:	Sixteen.
Antonia:	Seventeen.
Kay:	Eighteen.
Antonia:	Nineteen.
Kay:	Tenteen.
Antonia:	No! (laughs) Twenty.
Kay:	Twenty.
	Twenty-one. Keep going.

The activity illustrates the use of language as a tool, or a social mode for thinking. As Mercer (1995: 19) states: 'Knowledge is neither accumulated nor discovered by learners: it is shaped by people's communicative actions'.

The role of talk in learning was examined in depth by the Russian psychologist Lev Vygotsky (1986), who looked at the link between language and thinking. He saw our use of language as serving two purposes: first as a 'cultural tool' for sharing and developing our knowledge to support our social life and second as a 'psychological tool' to help organise our individual thoughts. He also felt that these two aspects are integrated to help us become active members of communities. Vygotsky developed the concept of the 'zone of proximal development' (ZPD), which is:

> the distance between the actual development level as determined by independent problem solving and the level of potential development as determined through problem solving under adult guidance or in collaboration with more capable peers.
>
> (Vygotsky 1978: 86)

As a consequence of supporting the learner in this way, Vygotsky (1986: 188) showed that 'what the child can do in cooperation today, he can do alone tomorrow'. The concept of the ZPD has been widely used (and differently interpreted) and one teacher has commented that if ZPD had not been invented by Vygotsky teachers would have needed to invent it! In other words, teachers (and fellow pupils) support learning by guiding the child's next step in his or her understanding.

Bruner (1985) built on this concept and suggested that the learner passes through mental developmental phases that are supported by structured learning experiences. In addition, Bruner asserted that speech is a primary mechanism for thought, and therefore it is vitally important for children to have the opportunity to talk through their ideas. Bruner's term for the support that adults provide in the learning process is 'scaffolding', whereby an adult varies the level of support, gradually withdrawing it as the child gains in competency.

Central to the work of Vygotsky and Bruner are the following strategies, as described by Corden (2000: 10):

- *Modelling*: showing children examples of work by experts.
- *Demonstrating*: illustrating the procedures experts go through in producing work.
- *Supporting* children as they learn and practise procedures.

Mercer (2000), in discussing the ZPD, states that he is more interested in understanding the quality of teaching and learning as an 'intermental' or 'interthinking' process:

> For a teacher to teach and a learner to learn, they must use talk and joint activity to create a shared communicative space, an 'intermental development zone' (IDZ) on the contextual foundations of their common knowledge and aims. This is facilitated by dialogue: 'If the dialogue fails to keep minds mutually attuned, the IDZ collapses and the scaffolded learning grinds to a halt.'
>
> (Mercer 2000: 141)

Like the original ZPD, the IDZ focuses on the guidance of a more experienced peer or adult for a learner, but it relates more to the contributions that both make in a reciprocal process. It is a process of 'interthinking'. Mercer (1995: 104) also presents three ways of talking and thinking:

- *Disputational talk*: this is characterised by disagreement, short exchanges that consist of assertions or challenges, and decisions being reached by individuals, not collaboratively.
- *Cumulative talk*: here pupils work together, often in pairs, to construct 'common knowledge' by accumulation.

- *Exploratory talk*: here pupils work collaboratively and engage critically but constructively with each other's ideas. Challenges are justified and alternatives offered, and progress is made towards a joint agreement. In exploratory talk, 'knowledge is made more publicly accountable and reasoning is more visible in the talk' (Mercer 1995: 104).

Dawes (2002: 128), describing a project that built on the work of Mercer and the idea of interthinking, says interthinking is 'the situation that exists when two or more people achieve real communication with each other, when mental resources are pooled through the medium of talk'.

This project, *Raising Achievement through Thinking with Language Skills* (Dawes 2002: 129), involved classes of Year 5 pupils. It consisted of the following:

- developing ground rules for talk;
- devising a series of ten one-hour talking lessons;
- using exploratory talk (from Mercer);
- employing ICT with specially written software to support exploratory talk;
- using talk across the curriculum.

The results of the project showed that children who had received talk training did better in non-verbal reasoning tests, and the conclusion was that 'Talk-focused children had learnt how to engage more effectively with one another's ideas' (Dawes 2002: 131).

ACTIVITY: UNDERSTANDING THE ZONE OF PROXIMAL DEVELOPMENT (ZPD)

Spend some time ensuring you understand the link between talk and learning based on the concept of ZPD.

- Explain this to a colleague to support your understanding.
- Discuss the impact that this has on teaching.

The status of talk has been considerably raised by extensive research (e.g. Mercer 1995, 2000; Alexander 2000, 2004) that has shown that 'Reading, writing and number may be the acknowledged curriculum "basics", but talk is arguably the true foundation of learning' (Alexander 2004: 5). Following Alexander's (2000) comparative research of primary education across five countries, he developed the concept of 'dialogic teaching' to support the use of talk. This teaching approach aims to harness the power of talk to stimulate and extend pupils' thinking and understanding. Dialogic teaching has been used and researched in a range of schools in London and Yorkshire, demonstrating that it can have real impact on interactions in the classroom. However, it requires considerable time and effort to be effective as it is 'in effect a transformation of the culture of talk and the attendant assumptions about the relationship of teacher and taught' (Alexander 2005). Dialogic teaching consists of the following five elements:

- It is *collective*: children work together on tasks, as a group or class.
- It is *reciprocal*: teachers and children listen to each other and comment/share ideas.
- It is *supportive*: children are supported to discuss their views freely.

- It is *cumulative*: teachers and children build on each other's ideas to create coherent lines of thinking.
- It is *purposeful*: teachers plan and steer classroom talk with specific purposes.

Alexander and others have continued to develop the case for talk as a powerful vehicle for learning in the Cambridge Primary Review (Alexander 2009). Alexander argues strongly for this to be included in the primary curriculum:

> At the heart of the new curriculum is the revised and much strengthened domain of language, oracy and literacy, which also includes ICT and a foreign language. Oracy is considerably more rigorous than what is currently defined as 'speaking and listening' and enhances both literacy and the curriculum as a whole.
>
> (Alexander 2010: 3)

The promotion of 'oracy', a term coined by the National Oracy project in the late 1980s (Norman 1992), refers to a much wider concept than 'speaking and listening'. Howe (1993) sees it as encompassing four interlinked dimensions:

- learning (the power that talk has in enhancing learning);
- the ability to use the resources of language (i.e. vocabulary, non-verbal communication, tone, expression etc.);
- the reciprocal nature of talk (its social nature);
- reflexivity (the ability to reflect on learning through talk).

Work on oracy has led to a number of different initiatives, including Philosophy for Children, the Social and Emotional Aspects of Learning (SEAL) and the work of Creative Partnerships. However, teachers frequently find incorporating talk effectively in the classroom difficult, and Ofsted noted in a review in 2005 a limited range and variable quality of speaking and listening in classrooms studied. One effective method of incorporating talk for learning is through the use of cooperative learning, as set out below.

Cooperative learning

Cooperative learning requires pupils to work together in pairs and small groups to support each other to improve their learning. It is not just 'group work' and requires certain factors to be present for it to be genuinely 'cooperative'. Group work is certainly not new; indeed, putting children together to work in groups is a common occurrence in England. But putting children together and then assuming they will interact and support each other's learning is another matter altogether. However, when implemented properly, cooperative learning presents an ideal method of supporting not only children's learning but also the effective use of talk. The first step is to ensure that pupils are supported with the necessary interpersonal and small-group skills to cooperate. The second step is to structure the tasks to maximise the potential to cooperate. This process needs to be developed in a staged and structured way and teachers require ongoing support. For comprehensive details of how to implement this staged process see Jolliffe (2007).

Certain key ingredients need to be in place for the learning to be cooperative. Johnson and Johnson's (1999) extensive work in this field set out five basic elements that are needed for cooperative learning to be effective:

- *Positive interdependence*: students must feel that they need each other in order to complete the group's task; they 'sink or swim' together.
- *Individual accountability*: cooperative learning groups are successful only when every member has learned the material or has helped with and understood the assignment.
- *Group processing*: this involves giving students time and procedures to analyse how well their groups are functioning, and how well they are using the necessary skills. The processing helps all group members achieve while maintaining effective working relationships among members.
- *Small-group skills*: students do not necessarily come to school with the social skills they need to collaborate effectively with others; teachers need to teach the appropriate communication, decision-making and conflict-management skills to students, and provide the motivation to use these skills, in order for groups to function effectively.
- *Face-to-face interaction*: the interaction patterns and verbal exchanges that take place among students in carefully structured cooperative learning groups benefit their learning.

ACTIVITY: CREATE A GRAPHIC REPRESENTATION

Work with colleagues to devise words and symbols to represent each of these five key elements of cooperative learning, to act as an *aide-mémoire*.

- positive interdependence;
- individual accountability;
- group processing;
- small-group skills;
- face-to-face interaction.

While considerable effort is required to develop cooperative learning, extensive research (Sharan 1990; Slavin 1995; Johnson *et al.* 2001) has shown that it is worthwhile. Three main categories of advantages have been clearly documented, including *improved achievement*, *greater interpersonal skills* and *enhanced self-esteem*.

Teaching cooperative learning skills

Teachers can establish the correct ethos of a 'cooperative learning classroom' by:

- creating a safe environment where risks can be taken without fear of ridicule;
- celebrating diversity and valuing everyone;
- establishing conflict-resolution strategies.

To create this ethos, give students opportunities to build relationships, encourage them to support each other in learning, give them self-responsibility for aspects of the classroom and, above all, ensure that learning experiences are enjoyable.

By creating a safe and supportive learning environment, the teacher will have built the *will* to work together. However, this is not sufficient; the skills of group work must also be taught. Teamwork skills can be divided into task skills and working-relationship skills and need to be explicitly taught in stages, as follows:

- establish the need for the skill;
- define the skill;
- guide the practice;
- generalise the application of the skill.

Specific teamwork skills that are necessary include:

- active listening;
- being aware of the volume of voices;
- helping and encouraging each other;
- ensuring that everyone participates;
- completing tasks;
- resolving conflicts.

A range of structures, principally derived from Spencer Kagan (1994), to facilitate paired and/or group work can be applied to various activities across the curriculum. Some of these are: 'think-pair-share', 'rally table', 'line up', 'three-step interview', 'two stay and two stray' and 'jigsaw groups'. For further guidance on these structures and others, see Kagan (1994) and Jolliffe (2007).

The National Curriculum and National Initiatives

The importance of talk for learning was not fully recognised until the 1960s, when the Schools Council Project (Halliday *et al.* 1964) and the work of Wilkinson (1965) and Barnes *et al.* (1969) promoted an interest in spoken language and literacy in primary schools. The Bullock Report (DES 1975) was devoted entirely to language and welcomed the growth in importance in oral language. It argued that schools should prioritise the speech needs of their pupils. The Oracy Project in the late 1980s, as previously mentioned, further built on this. This project particularly revealed how teachers and children alike undervalued the role of talk for learning at the time. As Mercer (1995) states, 'one of its main achievements was to raise teachers' awareness of the potential value of talk, and so improve the status of classroom talk amongst both teachers and pupils' (Mercer 1995: 92). This research was instrumental in speaking and listening becoming a separate component in the English 5–11 National Curriculum in 1989, and acknowledged the importance of these skills for children's development.

Requirements of the National Curriculum

'Speaking and listening' in the National Curriculum is divided into the following areas:

- knowledge, skills and understanding;
- speaking;
- listening;
- group discussion and interaction;
- drama;
- Standard English;
- language variation.

Two major reviews of the curriculum – the Rose Review (DCSF 2009a) and the Cambridge Review (Alexander 2009) – have both highlighted the central importance of talk. At the time of writing, a further government review is underway that will result in new curricula for English, mathematics, science and PE from 2013 (and other subjects in 2014) to allow for a 'radically different approach' (DfE 2012c). As part of this process, a report issued in 2012 (DfE 2012d) provides an international comparison of different curricula, and, while no clear indication is provided on the position of speaking and listening in the proposed National Curriculum, a comparison of other countries where these are not seen as a separate domain, but rather integrated within reading and writing, is provided. How this will impact on the new curriculum is, at the time of writing, yet to be seen.

The National Literacy Strategy

The importance of talk for learning took a step backwards in 1998 as speaking and listening was largely omitted from the wealth of teaching objectives of the National Literacy Strategy. The result of this, as Smith et al.'s research showed, was that:

> In the whole class section of literacy and numeracy lessons, teachers spent the majority of their time either explaining or using highly structured question and answer sequences. Far from encouraging and extending pupil contributions to promote high levels of interaction and cognitive engagement, most of the questions asked were of a low cognitive level designed to funnel pupils' response towards a required answer.
>
> (Smith et al. 2004: 408)

In 2003, the Qualifications and Curriculum Authority (QCA) produced a document titled *Planning for Speaking and Listening in Key Stages 1 and 2* (QCA and DfES 2003) to support speaking and listening and, in response to widespread criticism of the National Literacy Strategy, a revision of this QCA document was made in order to integrate speaking and listening and the National Literacy Strategy Framework for teaching, entitled *Speaking, Listening, Learning: Working with children in Key Stages 1 and 2* (DfES 2003c). The guidance set out four teaching objectives for speaking and listening each term from Year 1 to Year 6, covering speaking, listening, group discussion and interaction, and drama. These objectives were designed to be linked to other curriculum areas as appropriate. Examples of activities were provided for different year groups. The guidance also emphasised the importance of:

- modelling appropriate speaking and listening;
- encouraging sensitive interaction;
- setting goals with clear success criteria;
- providing opportunities for pupils to practise and reflect on language used.

Speaking and listening was also given more emphasis in the *Excellence and Enjoyment* professional development materials (DfES 2004b); a range of useful materials were provided, including some promoting collaborative and personalised learning. The Rose Review of the teaching of early reading also emphasised the key importance of speaking and listening:

> The indications are that far more attention needs to be given, right from the start, to promoting speaking and listening skills to make sure that children build a good stock of words, learn to listen attentively and speak clearly and confidently. Speaking and listening, together with reading and writing, are prime communication skills that are central to children's intellectual, social and emotional development.
>
> (DfES 2006a: 3)

Speaking and listening, or its broader term, 'oracy', has over the last twenty or more years been subject to a number of initiatives with varying emphases. This inconsistent approach has led to a danger of a lack of expertise by teachers in terms of incorporating it effectively and to a lack of understanding of its true potential.

Strategies to promote effective talk in the classroom

Teachers' questioning to promote talk

One clear way to promote effective talk to is to review the use of teachers' questioning. Research (Galton *et al.* 1999) shows that teachers usually ask closed questions, such as the 'guess what I am thinking' type, where the teacher has a clear idea of the answer and the children have to guess it, rather than open questions that genuinely seek to explore children's understanding and views. Wood (1986) argues that teachers often constrain classroom discussion through inappropriate questions.

The *Excellence and Enjoyment* materials (DfES 2004b) also focused on teachers' questioning, aiming to help them 'to ask fewer but better and more demanding questions – and to use alternatives to questions to stimulate … thinking' (DfES 2004b: 64). While there is a place for the quick, closed, fact-finding questions of the quiz type, it is important to consider whether the questions used provide a cognitive challenge for children. There should be a balance between closed, quick-fix questions and open questions that demand more complex and higher-order thinking.

ACTIVITY

Consider the strategies for effective questioning below and discuss with a colleague which you have used and which you might explore further.

1   *Use a 'no-hands' rule.* This tactic directs questions at particular pupils (rather than a general question with all pupils putting their hands up) and has the potential to differentiate the question according to the ability of the pupil, or to extend it into a real, meaningful dialogue as promoted by Alexander (2004) through dialogic talk. If you are using 'conscripts' rather than volunteers, it is important to have a back-up strategy, allowing pupils to 'pass' or 'ask a friend'. This can also be linked to the cooperative learning strategy of 'numbered heads'; in this method, a number is assigned to each pupil in a group, and then at random a number is called for a pupil to answer, first allowing time for the team to ensure everyone can respond.

2   *Build in wait time.* If a teacher waits at least three seconds for the pupil to think and before answering, there are substantial benefits leading to a greater number of responses, more confidence and 'risk-taking', and this encourages pupils to ask questions in return.

3   *Carefully plan one or two open-ended questions in a lesson that will genuinely extend pupils' thinking.* Teachers might consider placing a minimum requirement on the answer (e.g. pupils should answer in more than ten words).

4   *Allow time for collaboration before answering.* Allowing pairs of pupils to discuss a question for a short time before answering encourages everyone to be engaged, rather than the few who respond. This is often called 'think-pair-share'.

5   *Use probing questions.* When a pupil responds to a question, use a range of questions to get the pupil to clarify and extend the response (e.g. 'Can you tell me more about …?' 'What do you think the next step would be?').

Developing thinking skills through dialogue

There are many ways of promoting thinking skills recommended in the guidance, some of which incorporate partner or cooperative group work, as well as activities to encourage children's questioning. Using a taxonomy or scheme of classification of thinking to support higher-order thinking can be helpful when deciding how to challenge children. Bloom's (1956) taxonomy shows a progression in thinking (see Figure 6.1). Using this hierarchy of thinking skills can help teachers to plan more-effective questions with appropriate cognitive challenge.

Talk and literacy skills

The centrality of talk to reading

Speaking and listening are important not only for learning and developing effective communication skills but also for developing reading and writing skills. Palinscar and Brown (1984) have shown the value of dialogue in supporting children's comprehension skills when reading. The method they suggest involves the reciprocal teaching of comprehension strategies, which were designed to provide a simple introduction to group discussion. The basic procedure is that a teacher and a group of pupils take turns leading a discussion on the content of a section of text they are jointly attempting to understand. Four strategies are practised: 'questioning', 'clarifying', 'summarising' and 'predicting'. Throughout, the teacher provides guidance and feedback to the group. This process can be modified so that the essential features can be used in whole-class discussion, and success has also been achieved with training peer tutors. A further development could be the use of cue cards within groups to replace the role of the teacher.

Dialogue has been shown to be powerful by Rosenblatt (1989), who demonstrated that teacher–pupil and peer–peer dialogue and interaction form an important part of the reading and writing process:

> Group interchange about the texts of established authors can also be a powerful means of stimulating growth in reading ability and critical acumen. When students share their responses and learn how their evocations from transactions with the same text differ, they can return to the text to discover their own habits of selection and synthesis and can become more critical of their own processes as readers. Interchange about the problems of interpretation and a collaborative movement toward self-critical interpretation of the text can lead to the development of critical concepts and criteria of validity of interpretation. Such metalinguistic awareness is valuable to students as both readers and writers.
>
> (Rosenblatt 1989: 173; see also Corden 2004: 139)

One example of this was demonstrated in a video (DfES 2004b) of guided reading in Year 5 using *The Firework-Maker's Daughter* by Philip Pullman (1995). This exemplified the power of discussion, both in pairs and as a group, really exploring and empathising with a character in a book.

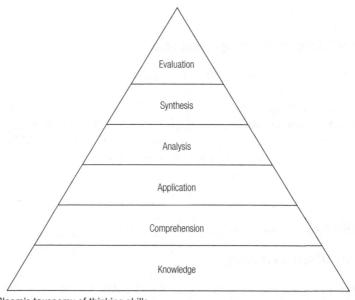

FIGURE 6.1 Bloom's taxonomy of thinking skills
Source: adapted from Bloom, B.S. (1956) *Taxonomy of Educational Objectives: the classification of educational goals. Handbook 1: cognitive domain.* New York: Longmans, Green.

Talk and writing

The advantages of talking before writing were discussed in relation to the early years in Chapter 4, in addition to the work of Pie Corbett and *Talk for Writing* (DCSF 2008c). These advantages persist throughout Key Stages 1 and 2. Giving children the chance to talk about the subject with a partner, in groups or with the teacher, can substantially improve the children's motivation and the quality of what they write.

The effective use of shared writing can support this process, particularly using 'teacher scribing', where the teacher takes contributions from the children and helps mould them into effective writing; or using 'supported composition', where the children work, usually in pairs, to write short sections, building on what the teacher has modelled. Guided writing also provides valuable opportunities to use talk to support the writing process, with a clear focus on a particular aspect of the writing and the chance to engage in meaningful dialogue with small groups of pupils.

The concept of writing workshops is derived from the work of the *National Writing Project* (1989a, 1989b), which showed the value of children getting responses from their peers. From that, the use of response partners became widespread. Where children already have an established 'talk partner' this is easily put in place. Children often need prompts to aid their responses to partners. Using a range of prompts can be very beneficial in supporting children's comments and questions on one another's work. This process needs to be clearly established, ensuring that children are positive about one another's work and can make some helpful suggestions. Modelling the process for children would be beneficial. Examples of prompts for pupils might include:

- 'The best bit was …'
- 'I liked how you …'
- 'I would like to know more about …'
- 'What do you mean by …?'
- 'Do you think you could add …?'
- 'Could this part be cut/moved …?'

Using models from literature can be a powerful springboard into writing, but this needs to be supported by real interactive learning through talk. Corden (2000) provides some vivid examples. In a Key Stage 2 class, children were working on responding imaginatively to characters in stories. The teacher had read extracts from *Matilda* (1989) to show how Roald Dahl used direct action and dialogue description to develop characters. After examining the words that Dahl used, the children developed lists of words to describe characters. For example:

Character:	Miss Trunchbull
Book:	*Matilda*
Author:	Roald Dahl
awesome	loathsome
barbaric	mammoth
bossy	mean
blobby	mountainous
cruel	muscular

ferocious	macho
fierce	spiteful
formidable	strict
gigantic	terrible
grumpy	terrifying
grotesque	ugly
hideous	vicious

(Corden 2000: 59)

This practice eventually led to the children developing a character portfolio with a range of lists of words to describe characters to support their own writing. Such a wealth of material had evolved from the effective use of talk. The research of Bereiter and Scardamalia (1987) demonstrated that successful writers 'think aloud', needing to elaborate and revise as they write. Primary-age children need to see this modelled by teachers. The process of 'metacognition' – that is, understanding and examining the thinking process – can be demonstrated by teachers verbalising their thoughts. For example, during shared writing, the teacher might think aloud: 'Let me see, how shall I start this paragraph? Yes, perhaps some dialogue …. One word would be good to emphasise the suspense …' and so on. See Chapter 12 for further guidance on how to support children's writing.

Boys' under-achievement

Many boys underachieve in writing. In Chapter 3, we gave examples from the Raising Boys' Achievements in Writing project (UKLA and PNS 2004) of how the use of visual stimuli, drama or speaking and listening can engage boys in writing. One might sum this up by saying, 'Let Jack climb the beanstalk before he writes about it.' In other words, action and talk are critical to motivating many boys to write.

Distinctive features of speaking and listening

Understanding the features of speaking and listening that distinguish it from other modes of language can support planning for it effectively in the classroom. It is worthwhile to consider these differences (DfES 2003c):

- It is collaborative: meaning is mainly constructed collaboratively, and spoken language is fluid and open ended.
- Spoken language is more varied in terms of purpose, context and levels of formality.
- Social relationships are mostly enacted through talk.

The key factors to consider for effective talk are topic (the subject matter), audience (who is being spoken to affects the level of formality) and purpose (the underlying reason for the talk). All these will inform the format of the talk.

Progression in speaking and listening

Progression in speaking and listening relates to the following features:

- the ability to contribute;
- the ability to sustain speaking and listening with appropriate language;
- the use of Standard English when appropriate;
- the ability to adapt to different contexts with confidence;
- the ability to understand and verbalise one's own progress.

Guidance provided by the Primary National Strategy (DfES 2003c: 24–7) examined the features of progression for Years 1–6 for all four areas (speaking, listening, group interaction and drama); this guidance can be used for assessment purposes. In addition, the 'assessment focuses' introduced as part of the Assessing Pupils' Progress (APP) materials provided detailed categories and progression to enable accurate assessment. Further discussion of the assessment of speaking and listening can be found in Chapter 16.

Planning for speaking and listening

Opportunities for speaking and listening need to be carefully planned. Clear objectives from the Early Years Foundation Stage to Key Stage 2 and links into Year 7 were provided by the DfES (2003c), which built on the earlier work from the QCA (1999) to ensure a range of activities to support children's progression in speaking, listening, group discussion and drama. These objectives can be accessed at www.teachfind.com/national-strategies/speaking-listening-learning-working-children-key-stages-1-and-2-%E2%80%93-leaflets-and-p. They include exemplars of units of work to show the integration of speaking and listening with reading and writing.

Managing children's talk

The importance of talk for learning has been discussed, but for many teachers the problem is more a matter of how to stop children talking. Table 6.1 lists a range of common issues that you could review and, if possible, discuss with colleagues, adding and amending where appropriate.

The role of the teacher

There are many ways in which the teacher can promote the necessary classroom ethos for developing talk:

- carefully considering the types of questions that promote pupils' engagement and thinking;
- genuinely listening to pupils' ideas;
- displaying warmth and interest in pupils and particularly considering body language (e.g. smiling, eye contact, reassuring gestures);
- showing empathy for pupils' feelings and a caring attitude;

TABLE 6.1 Potential difficulties managing talk in the classroom

Difficulty	Possible solution
High noise level when pupils are working in pairs or groups	■ Work through the issue with pupils and help them to understand the need for talking in appropriate voices (20 cm voices for working with a partner, i.e. voices that cannot be heard more than 20 cm away).
	■ Have a noise meter (a dial in the classroom which shows zones – green: acceptable, orange: getting unacceptable, red: unacceptable).
	■ Appoint a 'noise monitor' or monitors.
Some pupils dominating in small groups	■ Have a specific target of everyone participating in lessons.
	■ Reward pairs or groups where this is happening.
	■ Provide tokens for talk, so that every member of a group must use their token before members can speak again.
Encouraging shy pupils to participate	■ Ensure careful pairings.
	■ Give roles to pupils in groups to ensure all participate.
Gaining the attention of the class	■ Have a zero-noise signal, such as a raised hand.
Pupils talking off task	■ Monitor when pupils are working in pairs or groups with reminders about task, time limits, etc.

■ being alert to pupils who are regarded as outcasts and making efforts to help;

■ having a sense of humour: this can be crucial in developing the right atmosphere, but sarcasm should be avoided at all times.

One way to support this is the use of 'circle time' (Mosley 1996); however, it is important to ensure that this is carried out in the way Jenny Mosley set out. Schools often pay lip service to establishing genuine circle time. Guidance on this is also provided by the DfES in *Excellence and Enjoyment: social and emotional aspects of learning* (SEAL) (DfES 2005b).

Opportunities for talk: activities and resources

Separating spoken language into different areas is helpful, as it focuses on specific ways of using talk and helps to ensure that these important areas are provided for in a balanced way. This can be linked with the following text genres: narratives, recounts, explanations, instructions, reports and persuasion. A range of suggested activities for different categories of spoken language are provided below. You may like to discuss with a colleague which activities are suitable for different age groups.

Narratives

- *Story box*: using a story box or bag of objects, children make up a story to fit.
- *Story basket*: the teacher models the use of a story basket containing the associated objects or props to bring the story alive. Pupils work in pairs or groups to use them.
- *Picture stories*: provide a series of pictures for children to make into a story and then tell to others.
- *Story ingredients*: provide a selection of pictures on card for different characters, settings and objects. In pairs, children choose one or two from each category and make up a story together.
- *Group stories*: the teacher reads the beginning of a story and, in groups, pupils decide how it will end.

Recounts (personal experiences)

- *Memories*: pupils recall things such as their earliest memory, some things that made them happy or sad, something exciting or something worrying.
- *Lost*: pupils talk about a time they were lost. (Use the five Ws – where, why, when, what, who – to encourage children to provide details.)
- *Wishes*: talk about three wishes the children would love to have granted. This could be followed by discussion of the most sensible, exciting and so on.
- *Making excuses*: give examples of situations and excuses people give (e.g. when they are late home from school or forget to do something). Provide some funny examples. Children recount an experience and add an excuse for something that happened.

Explanations

- *Explain an object to a Martian*: pupils choose an everyday object from a selection and put in a box or bag so other pupils cannot see it. They then describe it as if the people listening were Martians and had no experience of it or its function. The other pupils have to guess what the object is.
- *The food game*: sort a set of fifteen to twenty different pictures of food into different groups (e.g. foods that should be eaten hot; food that is in liquid form; food that you eat as a desert). In groups, pupils explain the reasons for their choices.
- *Explain how it works*: pupils are provided with a diagram, such as the water cycle, and then take turns to explain it to a partner.

Instructions

- *Giving instructions*: in pairs, one pupil is given a simple outline picture on which he or she draws in features for which his or her partner has to give instructions.
- *Trust me!* Pupils work in pairs – one of the children is blindfolded and the other has to help a partner get to a designated place by using only verbal instructions.
- *Devise a game*: make up rules for a simple game and then teach them to a partner.

Reports

- *The local park*: pupils prepare to give a verbal report on local facilities. They could also plan possible improvements.

- *The museum*: pupils record their own guided museum tour on audio tape, based on a visit made to a museum.

- *Talking tins*: pupils are provided with some interesting tins containing various artefacts. They work with a partner to prepare a short talk on the significance of the objects.

Persuasion

- *Persuading parents*:
  - to have a pet (provide a situation; e.g. a child who lives in a small house with no garden and whose parents work all day; groups discuss the pros and cons and come to a conclusion).
  - to watch a television programme (provide a situation; e.g. it is late, a horror film).
  - to allow the child to stay at a friend's house.
  - to buy a pair of expensive trainers.
- *Survival*: imagine a situation (e.g. a ship wreck and only a limited number of objects can be carried): which five things would you need to survive? Working in groups, pupils have to persuade each other which objects they need. This could be linked to reading *Kensuke's Kingdom* (Michael Morpurgo) or a version of *Robinson Crusoe*.
- *Advertising*: collect a variety of adverts and discuss the products and the wording of the advertisements. Consider what methods are being used to promote the product. Follow up by asking children to develop their own advertisement, reflecting on target audience, style of advert, wording, visuals, use of colour and layout. This could be in the form of a television advert.

Active listening

Closely linked to being a good communicator is the skill of listening, and this also needs to be clearly taught. The following are important aspects:

- Use the term 'active': listening is not passive but rather something you need to be actively involved with.

- Discuss body language and expectations of what should be seen and heard in the classroom if children are listening.

- Explain that listening is a process that has three basic steps: hearing, understanding and judging (forming opinions on what has been said).

Teaching active listening requires clear steps. The following four steps will help the learning process:

1 *Establish the need for active listening*: this can be done through role play in pairs to demonstrate the effects of not listening (e.g. showing lack of eye contact, bored body

language (yawning, etc.), fiddling with other objects). This should be followed by discussion of key aspects of active listening.

2   *Define the skill*: using a 'T chart' (draw a large T on the board or large piece of paper with either side of the T marked 'sounds like' and 'looks like'), work with the class to draw up a list of what the skill sounds like and looks like. This can then form a poster in the classroom for constant reference while the skill is practised and refined.

3   *Provide guided practice*: make opportunities for pupils to practise with corrective feedback. The teacher monitors, observes, intervenes, coaches, reinforces and encourages. Groups reflect on how well they practised the skill and how they could become more effective.

4   *Ensure generalised application of the skill*: once the skill has been established, the teacher provides opportunities for using the skill in a range of contexts.

Storytelling

Through hearing tales and telling stories, children develop awareness of story, character and plot and a range of narrative techniques, as well as expanding their imaginative capacity. The power of storytelling can be harnessed in the classroom only if teachers are prepared to develop their own storytelling skills and thereby model them for children. Demonstrating a range of techniques – such as skeletal summaries, 'seeds of the story', 'story hands' or 'story mountains' – to recall the story shape can be empowering for children. In addition, by listening to a storyteller, children are more clearly able to recall and understand a narrative through experiencing the use of inflection, expression and eye contact. Encouraging children to tell stories gives them the opportunity to be listened to and develops skills such as oral competence, memory, vocabulary and use of different registers. In addition, once the story has been told, the act of writing it is much more manageable and often far richer. As Grainger states:

> The oral tradition of storytelling underpins and complements the growth of language and literacy. Its spellbinding power can liberate children's imaginations, release their creativity and enable them to weave dreams together, as they journey along the road of never-ending stories.
>
> (Grainger 1997: 10)

Developing storytelling skills

For many teachers, and particularly trainees, the thought of telling a story (rather than reading it out) is a daunting prospect. Following are some ways to gain confidence and competence in the art of telling stories:

■   *Begin with a personal tale*: this could be a memorable moment, perhaps triggered or supported by an object or photograph. The author once told the true story to an assembly of children of a parent's retreat at Dunkirk in the Second World War, complete with a memento (a plate that he was given by a French farmer's wife, stored in his knapsack, that still shows marks from the ricochet of bullets). The children were absolutely enthralled. The experience came alive for them.

- *Try traditional tales*: we are all familiar with stories such as *Little Red Riding Hood*. Telling the story can free the teller to use body language and eye contact to really engage the audience.

- *Remember stories*: it is important to realise that no two retellings will ever be alike; that is part of the charm in embellishing and adapting the stories. Remember the story by distilling it into the key elements, perhaps through a series of keywords jotted on a piece of card. Interestingly, once you are engaged in the story, it usually sweeps you away and you seldom refer to any notes. It is in the process of noting the keywords that you inhabit the story, ready to make it your own as you tell it.

- *Develop your use of voice*: change the expression, range, volume and so on and use gesture. Provide pace by pausing for dramatic effect or speed up to highlight action.

Once the skills have been modelled, you can begin to develop them in children. Similar guidance to the above is needed. Start in a small way with something very familiar and build up to longer tales. Children will find it helpful to work with a partner to support each other: telling the tale to a smaller audience is less daunting.

Assessing speaking and listening

Full guidance on methods of assessment for speaking and listening can be found in Chapter 16. Bear in mind the importance of involving pupils in this process. Table 6.2 illustrates a talk diary, which can be a useful means of doing this. Talk diaries are used weekly to record the types and range of speaking and listening activities the children have been involved in. See Grugeon *et al.* (2005) for further examples. Table 6.2 is an example for use in Key Stage 2; a simplified version could be used in Key Stage 1.

TABLE 6.2 Talk diary for Key Stage 2

Name: Start date: End date:				
	Week 1	**Week 2**	**Week 3**	**Week 4**	**Week 5, etc.**
Talk activities this week:				
Given a talk or presentation to a large audience				
Explained ideas or processes				
Told a story				
Presented an argument with evidence				

Listened and contributed in a small group					
Worked with a partner and used good questioning and summarizing					
Other					
How I have done this week:					
I listened well to my partner					
I spoke clearly					
I used some new and interesting words					
I can add detail to what I am saying					
I can speak to a large audience confidently					
I can speak to a group confidently					
I can ask useful questions					
I can summarise what someone has said					
I can talk appropriately for different occasions					
My targets for next week are:					

Source: adapted from Grugeon *et al.* (2005: 206).

Providing rich and varied opportunities for talk in the classroom is the key to effective learning. Carefully planned with systematic teaching of skills, it will enhance not only the ability to communicate effectively but also the ability to read and write effectively.

Key points

- Talk supports learning through interaction, discussion and collaboration.
- Cooperative learning, correctly implemented, provides an effective vehicle for purposeful talk.
- The place of talk in the English curriculum has varied in prominence and, while there are many examples of innovative practice, the national picture in classrooms is varied.
- Teachers' questioning needs careful consideration to promote effective talk.
- Reading skills are supported through discussion and interaction.
- Talk prior to writing promotes greater engagement by pupils and higher quality of work.
- Planning for speaking and listening should reflect the distinctive nature of talk and provide for a range of opportunities.
- Storytelling can provide a powerful impetus for talk.
- Teachers need to establish clear strategies for managing talk.

Further reading

Corden, R. (2000) *Literacy and Learning through Talk: strategies for the primary classroom.* Buckingham: Open University Press.

Goodwin, P. (ed.) (2002) *The Articulate Classroom: talking and learning in the primary classroom.* London: David Fulton.

Grugeon, E., Dawes, L., Smith, C. and Hubbard, L. (2005) *Teaching Speaking and Listening in the Primary School, 3rd edn.* London: David Fulton.

Jolliffe, W. (2007) *Cooperative Learning in the Classroom: putting it into practice.* London: Paul Chapman.

7

Teaching and learning reading

Purpose of this chapter

This chapter aims to:

- examine the background to the focus on literacy standards and methods of teaching reading in England;
- review historical perspectives and key research findings on the teaching of reading;
- explore models of the reading process;
- provide an overview of research and effective practice in teaching phonics;
- look at the teaching of comprehension skills;
- present a balanced reading programme, including shared and guided reading;
- review support for struggling readers.

Literacy standards

Perhaps no aspect of educational policy has been as widely disputed as the teaching of reading. One reason is the status of reading as 'the key to educational achievement' (House of Commons 2005: 3). The Bullock Report, thirty years previously, stated that reading helps to 'shape the personality, refine the sensibility, and sharpen the critical intelligence; that it is a powerful instrument for empathy and a medium through which children can acquire their values' (DES 1975: 124).

However, it is the economic impact of a workforce with good literacy skills that lies at the heart of keen government interest. In a speech to UNESCO, the US Secretary Arne Duncan (2010) stated: 'in a knowledge economy, education is the new currency by which nations maintain economic competitiveness and global prosperity.' Echoing such concerns in the UK, the prime minister and deputy prime minister set out clearly in the foreword to the 2010 white paper titled 'The Importance of Teaching' that falling rankings in international tests are a key driver in improving standards:

For example, England fell in the PIRLS rankings from 3rd out of 35 in 2001 to 15th out of 40 in 2006. In the most recent PISA survey in 2006, England fell from 4th to 14th in science, 7th to 17th in literacy, and 8th to 24th in mathematics.

(DfE 2010: 3)

Research shows that standards in literacy among English primary-school children remained largely stable between 1948 and 1996. National Curriculum tests in 1995 and 1996 highlighted the concern and indicated that only 48 per cent and 57 per cent respectively of eleven-year-olds were reading at the level expected for their age group (i.e. National Curriculum level 4) (Brooks 1998). As Beard (2000) shows, the evidence from inspection, surveys and research all suggests that, in the years prior to the National Literacy Strategy, early reading in English primary schools was largely taught by individualised methods, which consisted principally of the teacher listening to the child read (e.g. Cato et al. 1992). Indeed, Beard (2000: 246) notes that 'direct teaching of literacy skills was surprisingly rare'. Further studies, as set out above, showed that England fell from third out of thirty-five countries in 2001 to fifteenth out of forty countries in 2006. Thus, the concern about literacy continues and has driven a number of government reports and initiatives both in England and internationally.

More recently, the same concern regarding low literacy standards was expressed by Ofsted in its report 'Reading by Six', which notes that

Too many children in England do not read or write well enough by the time they leave primary school. The proportion of 11-year-olds that reach the expected level (Level 4 of the National Curriculum) in English has stalled at around 80% and the national average point score for reading at the end of Key Stage 1 has remained between 15.6 and 15.7 for the last four years.

(Ofsted 2010a: 5)

The political imperative is therefore clear: literacy standards need to rise to enhance the skills of the future workforce; and evidence from international surveys and test results will reinforce the driving up of literacy standards.

Historical perspectives on the teaching of reading

The debate over the effective teaching of literacy has raged long and vehemently. In the 1990s, fierce arguments took place over the virtues of teaching reading through the 'whole language approach' using 'real' books versus the value of teaching the sub-skills such as phonics. The two positions appeared to be totally polarised and have been described as the 'reading wars' (Goodman 1998). Harrison (2004: 28) noted that 'since around the year 2000, peace has broken out in the UK in relation to the "reading wars" and the place of phonics in early reading instruction'. Harrison attributed this to the fact that the teaching of phonics is now in effect mandatory in the UK. Following this comment, however, further debate was stirred by the House of Commons (2005) report on the teaching of reading and the review by Jim Rose (DfES 2006a), and war broke out once more. Yet again, the place of phonics in the teaching of reading has been fiercely debated by academics and become a topic of general interest hyped by media coverage. The coalition government in 2010 set out clearly its commitment to ensuring that phonics forms a central role in the teaching of reading; Schools Minister Nick Gibb stated in a speech in November 2010:

> There is more to reading than phonics – but there is also a weight of evidence that systematic synthetic phonics, taught in the first years of a child's education, gives children key building blocks they need to understand words, underpins children's attainment of a good standard of reading and can inspire a lifetime love of reading.
>
> (DfE 2010)

The focus on the teaching of reading therefore continues with the role of phonics at the heart of it.

Summary of research findings

During the 1990s, a wealth of research was produced on the effective teaching of literacy, most notably Adams' (1990) seminal work indicating the clear need for explicit teaching of phonics within a meaningful context of texts. Other key findings from Bryant (1993) and Goswami (1995) highlighted the need for developing phonological awareness. The work carried out by Clay (1979), through Reading Recovery, emphasised the need to make explicit how print works, how to effectively link reading and writing, and how to ensure swift intervention when children begin to exhibit a lack of effective progress. Holdaway's (1979) work, on using shared texts to enable teachers to recreate the experience of a bedtime story with a child and parent, began to be replicated to effect. Further work by Australian genre theorists (Littlefair 1991) made clear the need not only to introduce a range of genres to children but also to make the features of each explicit, to enable clearer understanding.

More recently, key developments in neuroscience are providing new insights into the impact of reading on the brain. Advances in brain imaging are beginning to reveal the brain areas that are activated as words are read. As Dehaene (2009: 2) states, 'a theory of reading is materializing. It postulates that the brain circuitry inherited from our primate evolution can be co-opted to the task of recognising printed words'. The impact is that new techniques can be developed, in particular to support children with learning difficulties such as dyslexia. While brain-imaging tools cannot yet precisely track reading progress in the brain, advancements do indicate that literacy development affects the anatomy of the brain and that certain parts are demonstrably 'thickened' in literate brains. In addition, as Dehaene (2009: 209) states, there is a 'massive increase in the exchange of information across the two hemispheres – perhaps explaining the remarkable increase in verbal memory span in literates'. What was also uncovered in this work and in particular through studying those who were illiterate is that, while initially learning whole words may appear to achieve faster results than reading by mapping letters and sounds, this tendency is short lived. A particularly fascinating experiment was carried out by McCandliss (cited in Yoncheva et al. 2006) that provided a new invented alphabet and involved two groups, one that learned to read whole words and the other that learned the letters to construct words. While the whole-word group outperformed the other group on the first day, thereafter the group that had learned the code and were able to apply it to decode words performed significantly better. Thus, as Dehaene summarises,

The punch line is quite simple: we know that conversion of letters into sounds is the key stage in reading acquisition. All teaching efforts should be initially focused on a single goal, the grasp of the alphabetic principle whereby each letter or grapheme represents a phoneme.

(Dehaene 2009: 228)

Nevertheless, how phonics is taught is an ongoing subject of debate. Wyse and Goswami (2008) provide an analysis of discrete teaching approaches to phonics and contextualised methods where phonics instruction is contextualised with sentence-level and/or text-level work such as reading of connected text. They conclude that:

The main conclusion to be drawn from this analysis of phonics instruction studies is that a range of ways of teaching systematic phonics is effective. Considering contextualised systematic phonics instruction versus discrete systematic phonics instruction, there is a need for more research to compare the effectiveness of the two approaches.

(Wyse and Goswami 2008: 704)

Theoretical perspectives on reading

The wide range of research on reading over the last four decades has led to very different theoretical positions or perspectives. Kathy Hall's book *Listening to Stephen Read* (2003) presents the example of eight-year-old Stephen, who is underachieving in reading, and then views ways of helping him from different perspectives. Hall discusses the benefits of using multiple perspectives for providing a range of support, rather than searching for a single 'right' method of teaching reading. The four major perspectives are summarised below.

ACTIVITY: DIFFERENT THEORETICAL PERSPECTIVES ON READING

Read each of the four different perspectives on reading and then answer the following questions, working with colleagues where possible:

- According to the psycho-linguistic perspective, what would the teacher provide frequent opportunities for?
- According to the cognitive–psychological perspective, what specific skills would a teacher ensure are taught?
- According to the socio-cultural perspective, why are links to home and the community so important?
- According to the socio-political perspective, why is it important to carefully select texts for children?

The psycho-linguistic perspective

Following the views of Noam Chomsky (1965) and his study of language development, which suggested that humans are innately disposed to acquire language of their environment, psychologists began to question whether this also applied to written language. The work of Smith (1971) and Goodman (1973) used children's miscues to derive information about the reading process. Goodman's (1967) analysis led him to describe reading as a 'psycho-linguistic guessing game' and suggested that readers use three types of cue simultaneously to make sense of text: graphophonic, syntactic and semantic.

Frank Smith (1971) also argued that reading was not something that could be taught but rather that one learns to read by reading. Teachers do not 'teach' reading but support children during the process. He placed more importance on the non-visual sources (context and prior knowledge) than the actual words. He claimed that readers do not use the alphabetic principle of decoding. The role of the teacher was to create a climate in which children would be motivated to learn and to provide an environment that is rich in natural language. This view can be described as a 'top-down' model whereby the use of text supports the learning rather than the sub-skills such as decoding. Dividing texts into smaller parts for this perspective can jeopardize the meaning. This led to the 'whole-language approach' to teaching reading using 'Breakthrough to Literacy' materials (Mackay et al. 1970), which supported children creating their own texts to read based on their own experiences. In summary, according to the psycho-linguistic perspective, reading is not:

> a linear process of letter-by-letter deciphering, sounding out, word recognition and finally text comprehension. It is not a linear process, they insisted, but a meaning-building (constructivist), problem-solving one.
>
> (Hall 2003: 42–3)

The cognitive–psychological perspective

This perspective sees reading as a staged developmental process. It views the alphabetical nature of written language as the key and also a major hurdle for beginning readers. Various stage models have been presented (Chall 1983; Frith 1985; Ehri 1987) but they all share one important aspect, which is the importance of decoding words. This work suggests that sight word-reading is not a flashcard method but rather a process of reading words by accessing them in the memory. It does not rely on the visual features of the word but relies on connections that link the words to their sounds and meanings, which are stored in the reader's lexicon.

This theory has three main phases. First, the *prealphabet* (or *logographic*) *phase* is where children use the shape or look of the word, storing visual cues in their memory to remember the word, such as the shape of two round eyes in the work 'look'. Second, the *partial alphabetic phase* is where learners have gained some alphabetic knowledge and begin to know the relevant letter–sound (grapheme–phoneme) correspondences. Phonemic awareness is necessary before this can progress and at first children focus on the most important letters. Third, the *full alphabetic* (or *orthographic*) *phase* is reached when readers fully understand the grapheme–phoneme correspondences. At this stage children are also beginning to store in their memories knowledge of common spelling patterns. In summary, the cognitive–psychological perspective sees reading as occurring in stages and as highly dependent on alphabetic knowledge.

The socio-cultural perspective

The emphasis here shifts from the individual to the social and cultural contexts in which literacy occurs. This perspective stresses the symbolic nature of language and thought. Meaning occurs through social interaction (Vygotsky 1978; Bruner 1996). For this perspective, learning to read is concerned with how reading is done in a particular context. The classroom, or school or home or community, is in this view a community of practice. Literacy becomes a multidisciplinary field that can be studied through ethnographic of literacies in their context. It follows that understanding the context and literacy practices in the home is crucial to supporting children's reading. For children it involves learning how to be like a reader in the context of the school. The research of Shirley Brice Heath (1983), who studied the differing literacy practices of various racial groups, showed the real impact on the ways in which the children learned language. There can be a detrimental effect on low-achieving readers who come from lower socio-economic groups, who may be offered a diet of reading that bears little resemblance to their own culture. One way to avoid this is to place more emphasis on meaning that is derived from print than the decoding process. In summary, the socio-cultural perspective asks teachers to take note of the understanding of literacy gained in the home and community to inform the activities in the classrooms.

The socio-political perspective

This view starts from the premise that no knowledge is neutral but is rather based on a group's perspective. The work of Comber (1999) and Marsh and Millard (2000) presents examples of this stance and shows the danger of demotivating pupils through not reflecting children's 'cultural capital' (Bourdieu 1977) in the classroom. This view (also called critical literacy) holds that learning to read includes being able to determine underlying assumptions and biases in texts. It requires the reader to take a critical stance towards images that are portrayed (e.g. about gender, race, ability, etc.). This stance is about making explicit the relationship between the language and the world. It is about learning how attitudes and beliefs about the world are presented by language. This view helps the reader not merely to spot stereotypes but also to understand how texts work to achieve certain effects. Hall (2003: 178) points out that 'Learning to read in this perspective is as much about learning identities and values as it is about learning skills and codes.'

In summary, the socio-political perspective is about understanding the role of literacy skills in empowering pupils to fully participate in society. It sees literacy as bound up with ethnicity, gender, social class, disability and so on, viewing its purpose as social justice.

Reading processes

Historically, the two main approaches to teaching reading have been widely known as 'bottom-up' and 'top-down'. *Bottom-up* approaches view the reading process as building up from letters, spelling patterns and words to sentences and paragraphs. *Top-down* approaches stress the prime importance of the meaning of language for comprehension and for word recognition. More-recent research-based models of early reading and fluent reading suggest that reading is neither top-down nor bottom-up in nature. Instead, sources of contextual, comprehension, visual and phonological information are simultaneously interactive, issuing and accommodating to and from each other (Adams and Bruck 1993). Related research is reported by Rumelhart and McClelland (1986) and Seidenberg and McClelland (1989). A US government report (Snow *et al.* 1998) analysed a large number of research articles and cited five areas of development associated with becoming a proficient reader: decoding, fluency, background knowledge, comprehension monitoring and motivation. Thus, reading is viewed as a combination of bottom-up and top-down.

Models of the reading process

In the past twenty years, a number of such models have been proposed to aid understanding of the reading process. Models of reading that have received particular discussion include the Interactive Compensatory Model, the Word Recognition Model, the Dual-Coding Model, the Searchlights Model and the Simple View of Reading Model.

The Interactive Compensatory Model (Stanovich 2000) suggests that poor readers use contextual information to compensate for weak word-recognition skills. The model has two major components: (1) contextual facilitation of word perception and (2) facilitation of comprehension. Thus, the reader compensates for limitations in automatic processing of the text by slowing down and making use of existing knowledge.

The Word Recognition Model of Seidenberg and McClelland (1989) provides an explanation for word-recognition processing in fluent reading. It is based on connectionist theories of how the mind organises information and learns from text. As we encounter words with similar meaning over many occasions, we develop automaticity in recognising words based on prior experience.

Another model of reading is the Dual-Coding Model (Sadoski 2008). This model draws on several key concepts from other reading models, including the Interactive Compensatory Model, Simple View of Reading Model and Verbal Efficiency Model (Perfetti 1999). In the Dual-Coding Model, both visual and verbal processes of reading work together to improve reading comprehension abilities.

The Searchlights Model contained in the National Literacy Strategy *Framework for Teaching* (DfEE 1998) became widely known and promoted by the National Literacy Strategy prior to the Rose Review of the teaching of reading, after which the Simple View of Reading replaced it. In the Searchlights Model, a number of reading strategies or 'searchlights' help to shed light on the text. These strategies consist of phonics and spelling, grammatical knowledge, word recognition and graphic knowledge and knowledge of context. The model proposed that successful readers use as many of these strategies as possible. However, it was not clear how these elements fitted together. In addition, word recognition seemed to be unconnected to phonics and spelling. Critics of this model noted:

> The 'searchlights' model proposed in the framework has not been effective enough in terms of illustrating where the intensity of the 'searchlights' should fall at the different stages of learning to read.
>
> (Ofsted 2002b: para 58)

An alternative model, known as the Simple View of Reading (Gough and Tunmer 1986), identifies two components: decoding and comprehension. *Decoding* means the ability to recognise words out of context and to apply phonic rules to this recognition. *Comprehension* means not reading comprehension but *linguistic comprehension*, which is defined by Gough and Tunmer (1986) as the process by which words, sentences and discourse are interpreted.

These authors also state that the two interrelated processes are both necessary for reading. This view has been developed since it was first proposed in 1986 and is represented in the Rose Review (DfES 2006a: 77) as shown in Figure 7.1.

The advantages of the Simple View of Reading are that:

- it shows children may not display equal performance in each area;
- it enables clear identification of any strengths or weaknesses and supports appropriate teaching;
- it demonstrates the importance of both word recognition and comprehension;
- it shows the importance of teachers understanding the cognitive processes involved.

Critics of the Simple View of Reading object principally to the over-simplification of what is a complex area. Harrison (2010) states it has been become synonymous with the 'first, fast and only' model of phonics and also that there is a danger of missing elements such as fluency, vocabulary, cognitive flexibility and morphology: skills that are all necessary in becoming an effective reader. However, Hoover and Gough went on to refine the model and acknowledge that

> The simple view does not deny the complexity of reading, but asserts that such complexities are restricted to either of the two components. ... While the simple view provides an adequate account of reading, the task remains to define the components underlying decoding and linguistic comprehension.

> (Hoover and Gough 1990: 151)

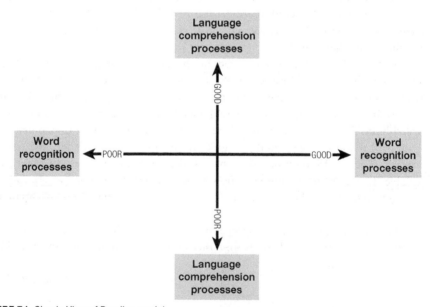

FIGURE 7.1 Simple View of Reading model
Source: DfES (2006a) *Independent Review of the Teaching of Early Reading (Final Report by Jim Rose).* Ref: 0201/2006DOC-EN. Nottingham: DfES, p. 77.

Further exploration of these elements by Hoover and Gough highlights that language comprehension itself includes two domains of knowledge. The first is linguistic knowledge, or knowledge of the formal structures of a language. The second is background knowledge of the context. Hoover and Gough explain that, within these two large domains, linguistic knowledge can be further broken down into:

- *phonology*, which involves knowledge of the sound structure of the language and the elements that convey differences in meaning;

- *semantics*, which deals with the meaningful components of language, at the level of morphemes (smallest units of meaning in a word, e.g. 'pre' in the word 'preschool') or higher levels, which combine such units into words and words into sentences;

- *syntax*, which includes the rules of language that indicate how different classes of words (nouns, verbs, adjectives etc.) should be combined to form sentences.

Background knowledge of the subject or context is also essential for language comprehension.

Hoover and Gough (1990) also demonstrate that word recognition, or decoding, also consists of different elements. These consist of a two broad domains: cipher knowledge and lexical knowledge. Cipher knowledge concerns the systematic relationship between the letters and the sounds. Lexical knowledge consists of knowledge about words and in particular where the relationship between the units of spoken and written words do not follow a systematic pattern. As Hoover and Gough state (2000: 15): 'In English, both systematic and unsystematic (or idiosyncratic) relationships exist, and the successful reader must master both.' This relates to the irregularity of English, in which words such as 'stomach' do not entirely follow the patterns contained within cipher knowledge. Decoding is therefore the ability to recognise systematic relationships between letters and sounds and to have knowledge of the exceptions in a language. Both cipher and lexical knowledge depend on two elements, as follows:

- *letter knowledge*, or the ability to recognise and manipulate the letters of the alphabet;

- *phoneme awareness*, which is the ability to manipulate the units of the spoken word.

Productive use of the two elements above requires an understanding of the alphabetic principle: that there is a systematic relationship between the units of spoken and written words. Underpinning the ability to read effectively is one final element, which involves understanding concepts of print – that is, that print carries meaning and that text in English runs from left to right and from the top to the bottom of the page. A representation of this framework, which explains the underpinning elements of the Simple View of Reading, is shown in Figure 7.2.

As Kirby and Savage (2008: 80) state, while the Simple View of Reading 'serves a useful function as a broad framework', it is important to understand what it is not and that 'continued efforts are required to articulate a complete theory of the cognitive processes involved in reading.' In summary, the Simple View of Reading is useful in providing that broad agenda of what to teach, but it does not fully account for the complex nature of the reading process. The conceptual framework shown in Figure 7.3 helps to expand on this.

In order to become readers as well as listeners, children need to develop processes that lead into their store of word meanings and their store of word sounds from language they *see*. The stores and processes that children need to set up to accomplish this are shown in the unshaded parts of Figure 7.3. The dotted lines leading to 'pronounce word aloud' indicate that reading aloud is optional, since probably most reading is silent.

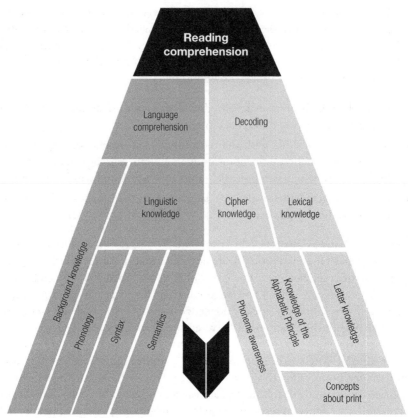

FIGURE 7.2 The reading acquisition framework
Source: Wren, S. (2001) *The Cognitive Foundations of Learning to Read: a framework*. Austin, TX: Southwest Educational Development Laboratory (www.sedl.org/cgi-bin/pdfexit.cgi?url=http://www.sedl.org/reading/framework/framework.pdf).

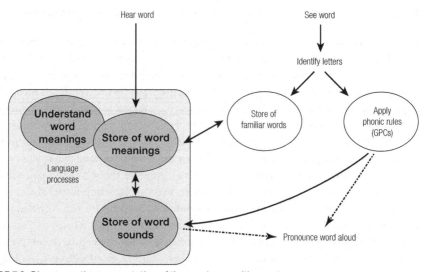

FIGURE 7.3 Diagrammatic representation of the word recognition system
Source: DfES (2006a) *Independent Review of the Teaching of Early Reading (Final Report by Jim Rose)*. Ref: 0201/2006DOC-EN. Nottingham: DfES, p. 86.

ACTIVITY: MODELS OF READING IN PRACTICE

Consider the models discussed and review the following questions:

- What key aspects need to be clearly planned for in teaching reading?
- Which of the models best supports diagnostic assessment of children's reading ability?
- How does linguistic comprehension support reading?

Research into teaching phonics

The teaching of phonics continues to be the subject of considerable debate. The debate centres not only on the effectiveness of phonics as a teaching method but also on the type of phonics teaching used. Much of the recent focus on phonics has stemmed from a research study carried out in Clackmannanshire, Scotland. Rhona Johnston and Joyce Watson (2005) looked at 300 children in the first year of the Scottish primary-school system. They compared three different teaching methods: synthetic phonics, analytic phonics and an analytic phonics method that included systematic phonemic awareness teaching. At the end of the programme, those children who had been taught by synthetic phonics were found to be seven months ahead of the other two groups in reading.

- *Synthetic phonics* refers to an approach to the teaching of reading in which the phonemes (sounds) associated with particular graphemes (letters) are pronounced in isolation and blended together (synthesised). Synthetic phonics for writing reverses the sequence: children are taught to say the word they wish to write, segment it into its phonemes and say them in turn and write a grapheme for each phoneme in turn to produce the written word.
- *Analytic phonics* refers to an approach to the teaching of reading in which the phonemes associated with particular graphemes are not pronounced in isolation. Children identify (analyse) the common phoneme in a set of words in which each word contains the phoneme under study. Analytic phonics for writing similarly relies on inferential learning.

The Clackmannanshire report was widely influential and led to the review undertaken by Sir Jim Rose into the teaching of reading. The final report for the Secretary of State for Education and Skills produced in March 2006 (DfES 2006a) drew on research findings; consultation with practitioners, teachers, trainers and resource and policy makers; and visits to schools and training events. The review made recommendations of best practice in the teaching of early reading and phonics:

- High-quality, systematic phonic work as defined by the review should be taught. The knowledge, skills and understanding that constitute high-quality work should be taught as the prime approach in learning to decode (to read) and encode (to write/spell) print.
- Phonic work should be set within a broad and rich language curriculum that takes full account of developing the four interdependent strands of language – speaking, listening, reading and writing – and enlarging children's stock of words.

- For most children, high-quality, systematic phonic work should start by the age of five, taking full account of professional judgements of children's developing abilities and the need to embed this work within a broad and rich curriculum. This should be preceded by prereading activities that pave the way for such work to start.

- Phonic work for young children should be multisensory in order to capture their interest, sustain motivation and reinforce learning in imaginative and exciting ways.

The recommendations of the Rose Review have since been widely adopted, first by the Labour government and then strengthened under the coalition government since 2010. Measures to monitor the adoption have included a specific focus by Ofsted for the inspection of schools and teacher-training providers, and in the Teacher Standards in 2012 a specific statement that to gain qualified teacher status trainees should 'if teaching early reading, demonstrate a clear understanding of systematic synthetic phonics' (DfE 2011e: para 3).

It is not just in the UK that the focus on teaching reading and the use of phonics has received government focus. In the USA, the National Reading Panel (NRP) report by the National Institute of Child Health and Human Development (NICHD 2000: 2–89) provided a meta-analysis of research into the teaching of reading and concluded that 'systematic phonics instruction proved to be universally effective it should be implemented as part of literacy programs to teach beginning reading, as well as to prevent and remediate reading difficulties.'

The NRP findings from a meta-analysis of evidence-based research indicated that for beginning reading direct, systematic instruction in phonics makes significantly greater contributions to children's development in reading, writing, spelling and comprehension than alternative approaches involving unsystematic or no phonics instruction. The NRP also emphasised that 'systematic phonics instruction should be integrated with other reading instruction to create a balanced reading program' (NICHD 2000: 2–136) and that it should not dominate the teaching of reading.

In Australia, a review of research into the teaching of reading came to a similar conclusion:

> The incontrovertible finding from the extensive body of local and international evidence-based reading research is that for children during the early years of schooling, they must first master the alphabetic code via systematic, explicit, and intensive instruction in: phonemic awareness, phonics, reading fluency, vocabulary, and reading comprehension strategies. Because these are foundational and essential skills for the development of competence in reading, writing and spelling, they must be taught early, explicitly, and taught well.
>
> (Australian Government 2005: 25)

However, even although there have been substantial studies that have reviewed the research literature, the debate still continues, and critics of a focus on systematic phonics argue that there is 'no reliable empirical evidence that synthetic phonics offers the vast majority of beginners the best route to becoming skilled readers' (Wyse and Goswami 2008: 691).

One aspect related to teaching phonics that has received considerable focus concerns phonological development and its role in promoting success in learning to read. It is first important to understand the difference between phonological awareness and phonemic awareness. *Phonological awareness* is the understanding of different ways that oral language can be divided into smaller components and manipulated. *Phonemic awareness* relates to the ability to perceive and manipulate individual phonemes in spoken words. The importance of phonological-awareness training has dominated the research literature in the field and the NRP (NICHD 2000) identified over 2000 studies in the area. Harrison (2004: 41) reiterated the general view of its importance: 'Unless you have phonemic awareness ... it is impossible to gain much from instruction in phonics.' However, language-development studies demonstrate that awareness of phonemes is present at birth and that, by about six months, children begin to extract words from the stream of speech they hear. Babies' early babbling also demonstrates this, with babies around the world saying consonant/vowel sounds (e.g. ba–da). By three years of age, children are generally capable of demonstrating what they know, and one study (Chaney 1992) found that 93 per cent of three-year-olds could listen to a sequence of phonemes and blend them into a word. Of particular interest in this study is that children of the same age had enormous difficulty with what has been regarded as the more simple tasks – rhyming and alliteration. McGuinness (2004) and others have questioned whether, if young children are able to discriminate and manipulate phonemes at the age of three, all children need a specific programme to teach this in readiness for learning grapheme–phoneme correspondences. Such training, however, has been shown to be critical for those children at risk of literacy failure, and Hatcher *et al.*'s (2004) research shows that phonological awareness training in conjunction with a phonics teaching programme is beneficial. Nevertheless, a widely held assumption that specific teaching of awareness of sounds in the environment progressing to voice sounds, as a precursor to teaching grapheme–phoneme correspondences, has led in some cases to a delay in teaching phonics. As the research has shown, phonological awareness is developed alongside effective teaching of phonemes and their corresponding graphemes and most effectively within a broad and rich language curriculum.

Teaching phonics

As a result of the Rose Report (DfES 2006a), the provision of phonics in the Primary National Strategy was revised. Since then, an increased demand for effective phonics teaching has been shown by the specific requirement for it to be inspected by Ofsted, both within initial teacher training and within schools. To monitor the impact, a national screening test at the age of six has been introduced that will report on children's progress. The Rose Report set out the definition of high-quality phonic work and this has since been supplemented by guidance for initial teacher training provided by the Training Development Agency (TDA) in 2011 and revised criteria for high-quality phonic work published by the DfE (DfE 2011e), which sets out that this work should:

- present high-quality systematic, synthetic phonic work as the prime approach to decoding print (i.e. a phonics 'first and fast' approach);

- enable children to start learning phonic knowledge and skills using a systematic, synthetic programme by the age of five, with the expectation that they will be fluent readers and have secured word-recognition skills by the end of Key Stage 1;

- be designed for the teaching of discrete, daily sessions progressing from simple to more-complex phonic knowledge and skills and covering the major grapheme–phoneme correspondences;

- enable children's progress to be assessed;

- use a multisensory approach so that children learn variously from simultaneous visual, auditory and kinaesthetic activities that are designed to secure essential phonic knowledge and skills;

- demonstrate that phonemes should be blended, in order, from left to right, 'all through the word' for reading;

- demonstrate how words can be segmented into their constituent phonemes for spelling and that this is the reverse of blending phonemes to read words;

- ensure children apply phonic knowledge and skills as their first approach to reading and spelling even if a word is not completely phonically regular;

- ensure that children are taught high-frequency words that do not conform completely to grapheme–phoneme correspondence rules;

- provide fidelity to the teaching framework for the duration of the programme, to ensure that these irregular words are fully learned;

- ensure that, as pupils move through the early stages of acquiring phonics, they are invited to practise by reading texts that are entirely decodable for them so that they experience success and learn to rely on phonemic strategies.

To further support the guidance, a range of explanatory notes was provided to ensure that there is no ambiguity regarding the expectations. In particular, note 1 states:

> Phonic work is best understood as a body of knowledge and skills about how the alphabet works, rather than one of a range of optional 'methods' or 'strategies' for teaching children how to read. For example, phonic programmes should not encourage children to guess words from non-phonic clues such as pictures before applying phonic knowledge and skills. High quality systematic, synthetic phonic work will make sure that children learn:
>
> - grapheme–phoneme (letter–sound) correspondences (the alphabetic principle) in a clearly defined, incremental sequence;
> - to apply the highly important skill of blending (synthesising) phonemes, in order, all through a word to read it;
> - to apply the skills of segmenting words into their constituent phonemes to spell; and that
> - blending and segmenting are reversible processes.
>
> (DfE 2011e: 14–15)

The alphabetic code

In order to teach phonics effectively, teachers need to fully understand the English alphabetic code. Unless they have previously undertaken training in linguistics, for many teachers (particularly trainees), this is a new body of knowledge that needs to be explicitly understood. Seymour *et al.* (2003) set out a comparison of word-recognition skills in fourteen European countries; they found that children learning to read in English in their first year of instruction performed far worse than children from any other country. Children from most of the other countries could read over 90 per cent of words accurately, whereas those reading in English could read only 34 per cent of words. Seymour *et al.* (2003) highlighted two key reasons for this: one is the complex alphabetic code and the second is the syllabic structure of English. Both of these require systematic teaching in order to support effective literacy skills.

The complex alphabetic code

If the English language had a consistent and transparent code, every sound would have just one letter assigned to it and it would be very simple to decode. Unfortunately, as we only have twenty-six letters to represent forty-four or more sounds, written English has an advanced code where sounds are frequently represented by more than one letter and letters often represent more than one sound. The alphabetic code is underpinned by the following concepts:

1   Sounds/phonemes are represented by letters/graphemes.

2   A phoneme can be represented by one or more letters; for example, the phoneme /igh/ can be written as 'i-e' (in line), 'igh' (in sight), 'ie' (in tie) or 'i' (in tiger). A one-letter grapheme is called a 'graph', a two-letter grapheme a 'digraph' and a three-letter grapheme a 'trigraph; four-letter graphemes (as in 'weigh' = /w/eigh/) are called 'quadgraphs', though these are unusual.

3   The same phoneme can be represented (spelled) more than one way, as in /or/ spelled as 'or' in fork, or 'aw' as in 'claw' or 'oor' as in 'door'.

4   The same grapheme (spelling) may represent more than one phoneme, as demonstrated by the letter 's', which may make the sound /s/ in 'sip' or /z/ in 'laser'.

To summarise the differences between the basic and advanced codes, the basic code consists of learning one spelling choice for each of the forty or more sounds. The advanced code involves mastering the multiple spellings for each phoneme. For more guidance on teaching the alphabetic code, including the advanced code, see Jolliffe *et al.* (2012), particularly chapter 5.

The syllabic structure of English

Many other languages consist of single consonants followed by vowels. In English, as Ziegler and Goswami (2005) have investigated, there are many examples of two or more consonants together before vowels, as in 'strap'. These consonant clusters can occur at the beginning or end of syllables and create added difficulties for beginning readers and for adults learning the phonetic structure of English, specifically in order to teach phonics.

Progression in teaching phonics

One aspect that has changed significantly in the last few years is the expectation for teaching phonics quickly and commencing early, so that by the end of Year 1 children should have mastered all forty-four phonemes and their most common grapheme representations. The pace of the teaching of phonics was revised following the Rose Report (DfES 2006a). The following six phases were recommended:

Phase 1: developing phonological awareness. *Duration*: Early Years Foundation Stage: communication, language and literacy.

■   Support children's developing language structures and vocabulary.

■   Help children to distinguish between sounds through the use of rhyme, rhythm and alliteration.

Phase 2: beginning of systematic phonic teaching. *Duration*: up to six weeks.

■   Introduce a small number of common consonants and vowels.

■   Blend them together in reading simple consonant-vowel-consonant (CVC) words and segment them to support spelling.

Phase 3: teaches one grapheme for each of the forty-four phonemes in order to read and spell simple regular words. *Duration*: up to twelve weeks.

■   Link sounds to letters (letter names and sounds).

■   Recognise letter shapes and say a sound for each.

■   Hear and say sounds in the order in which they occur in the word.

■   Read simple words by blending the phonemes.

■   Recognise common digraphs.

■   Read some high-frequency words.

Phase 4: read and spell words containing adjacent consonants. *Duration*: four to six weeks.

■   Blend and segment adjacent consonants in words.

■   Apply this skill when reading unfamiliar texts and in spelling words.

Phase 5: learn alternative ways of pronouncing the graphemes and spelling the phonemes already taught. *Duration*: throughout Year 1.

■   Learn alternative ways of pronouncing the graphemes and spelling the phonemes corresponding to long-vowel phonemes.

■   Identify the parts of two- and three-syllable words and be able to read and spell phonically decodable two- and three-syllable words.

■   Recognise an increasing number of high-frequency words automatically.

Phase 6: develop skill and automaticity in reading and spelling. *Duration*: begin in and continue throughout Year 2.

■   Apply phonic skills and knowledge to recognise and spell an increasing number of complex words.

■   Read an increasing number of high- and medium-frequency words independently and automatically.

One of the key aspects of teaching phonics effectively is to ensure that segmenting and blending phonemes are taught explicitly and that plenty of practice is provided. Segmentation means hearing the individual phonemes within a word; for instance the word 'crash' comprises four phonemes – /c/r/a/sh/. In order to spell, a child must segment a word into its component phonemes and choose a letter or letter combination (e.g. 'sh') to represent each phoneme. Blending means saying phonemes together to pronounce a word. In order to read an unfamiliar word phonemically, a child must attribute a phoneme to each letter or letter combination in the word and then merge the phonemes together to pronounce the word (e.g. /f/a/t/ = fat).

ACTIVITY: CHECKING ON TERMINOLOGY

Review the glossary below and work with a colleague to ensure that you understand the terms. For example, you might consider:

■ What is the difference between a phoneme and a grapheme?
■ Give examples of words that contain split digraphs.
■ Define the difference between blending and segmenting.

Glossary

Alliteration   A sequence of words that each begin with the same sound.

Blend   A combination of letters where individual letters retain their sounds.

Blending   Drawing individual sounds together to pronounce a word (e.g. /c/l/a/p/ blended together reads 'clap').

Digraph   Two letters that combine to make a new sound.

Grapheme   A letter or combinations of letters that represents a phoneme.

Initial consonant blend   A consonant or consonants that retain their original sounds but are blended together, as in 'slip'.

Long vowel sounds   The long vowel sounds, as in 'feel' or 'cold'.

Mnemonic   A device for remembering something, such as 'big elephants can always use small exits' to remember the spelling of 'because'.

Phoneme   The smallest single identifiable sound in a word that can change its meaning (e.g. the letters 'ch' represent one sound).

Rhyme   Words that have similar-sounding endings but do not necessarily share the same spelling.

Segmenting   Splitting up a word into its individual phonemes in order to spell it (i.e. the word 'pat' has three phonemes: /p/a/t/).

Split digraph   Two letters that make one sound that are split by a consonant letter (e.g. a-e as in 'cake').

Syllable   A unit of pronunciation with one vowel sound.

Trigraph   Three letters that combine to make a new sound.

Approaches to teaching phonics

There are many of programmes available for teaching phonics. What is important is that the programme adopted by a school should be adhered to 'with fidelity' (DfES 2006a: paragraph 55) – that is, applied consistently – and used regularly. The concept of fidelity concerns consistently working through a defined progression, or framework, in order to teach the entire alphabetic code, not necessarily fidelity to one published programme. The key aspects of effective programmes, identified in the Rose Report (DfES 2006a), are:

■ being systematic;

■ including teaching of blending phonemes and segmenting words into phonemes;

■ providing regular assessment;

■ being multisensory in approach;

■ being manageable within a broad and rich early-years curriculum.

One programme that is clearly multisensory and uses actions to represent phonemes is Jolly Phonics (see Lloyd 1998). This programme is systematic and it is recommended that it is taught quickly and early.

The Teaching Handwriting, Reading and Spelling Skills (THRASS) approach (Davies and Ritchie 1998) introduces children to both lower-case and upper-case letters by name and involves teaching of all phonemes using correct terminology, such as graph, digraph, trigraph, grapheme and phoneme. The THRASS charts, which are fundamental to the approach's operation, provide a visual representation of the English sound system. Each of the forty-four boxes on each chart provides a range of alternative spellings for phonemes. For example, 'cat' 'kitten' 'duck' 'school' and 'queen' for the 'k' sound. This approach does not provide a systematic progression for teaching the phonemes, however, nor does it teach children to blend phonemes.

The Success for All (SFA) approach to teaching phonics (Slavin and Madden 2005) provides an element of multisensory work and highlights the use of blending and segmenting phonemes using a puppet who can talk only in phonemes. It also provides help with the most difficult aspect, learning the long-vowel phonemes, with a rap, and clearly links the reading and writing of phonemes. However, it does not include all forty-four phonemes, and teaches only some of the spelling choices for phonemes.

The Read, Write, Inc. programme (Miskin 2011) aims to be a consistent whole-school approach in which children are grouped across the school by reading ability. Schools using the programme receive training and very specific guidance on implementing it. There is an emphasis on oral work and a clear teaching sequence for the forty-four phonemes, together with application of skills through decodable texts.

Letters and Sounds (DfES 2007a) provides clear guidance for daily discrete sessions that are structured in four parts:

■ *revisit* – to ensure regular revisiting of phonemes taught;

■ *teach* – to provide clear teaching of a new phoneme;

■ *practise* – practising the grapheme–phoneme;

■ *apply* – application in reading and writing.

Letters and Sounds comprises six phases for forty-four phonemes. Children are grouped according to the phase that closely matches their level of attainment. Through continuous assessment and differentiation, pupils are able to progress through these phases at a pace suitable for their individual needs.

Those phonics programmes that meet the criteria for high-quality phonics (revised by DfE 2011d) can be provided to schools with matched DfE funding.

One of the key aspects of effective phonics teaching is to ensure ongoing diagnostic assessment that tracks children's progress and provides additional support where required. For those children that require additional support, phonics catch-up programmes are also available. One such programme, Quick Fix for Phonics (Jolliffe 2012), provides a range of diagnostic assessment activities in order to ascertain how and where to intervene. It then provides a comprehensive teaching programme for all forty-four phonemes in multisensory ways, including visual prompts, raps, mnemonics and actions, with specific support for the complex alphabetic code.

Teaching comprehension skills

Guidance on teaching comprehension has been given less emphasis than phonics, particularly in recent years. The Primary National Strategy provided guidance on teaching comprehension skills in response to the Rose Report (DfES 2006a) that stated that 'Reading comprehension is a highly interactive process that takes place between a reader and a text' (DfES 2006c: 28). The key aspect to consider here is the experiences and cultural background of each child. According to the Simple View of Reading model, comprehension is the product of word recognition and listening comprehension. Once the words are recognised, they can be understood as long as they are in the child's oral vocabulary, but vocabulary is also increased through reading. From an educational viewpoint, this means that practitioners and teachers must encourage the development of oral language skills in order to safeguard children's reading comprehension.

The development of comprehension skills begins with listening comprehension skills (simply comprehending what you hear), which requires the skills of vocabulary knowledge, grammatical skills, pragmatic abilities (the ability to understand and use language in appropriate ways and contexts) and metalinguistic awareness (the ability to reflect on the structure of language to understand non-literal, figurative and metaphorical use of language). Reading comprehension is a less natural act than listening comprehension and requires additional strategies. Teaching strategies that support this are identified in the report of the NRP (NICHD 2000: 19), which states that 'Research on comprehension strategies has evolved dramatically over the last 2 decades.'

Vocabulary

At the heart of supporting comprehension skills is the development of vocabulary in children. This is heavily influenced by the child's home background and other out-of-school experiences. Biemiller (2003) has shown that vocabulary growth is largely determined by practices in the home and that there are considerable differences in vocabulary size in seven-year-olds. Research (White *et al.* 1990) also shows that children from disadvantaged backgrounds typically have a smaller vocabulary and that this gap widens (Beals 1997). Biemiller (2003) also found that vocabulary is a strong predictor of reading success; thus, children from disadvantaged backgrounds can be trapped in a vicious circle unless specific action is taken to remedy this. A publication by the DCSF (2008d), *Teaching Effective Vocabulary*, provides a range of methods of supporting vocabulary development in school, including:

- explicit instruction, particularly regarding difficult words out of pupils' daily experiences;
- indirect instruction, through a rich literary environment and experience of reading materials;
- use of multimedia methods as a visual stimulus for increasing vocabulary;
- use of capacity methods to support development of a larger store of known words through defining word meanings; use of a programme of encounters with new words in different ways; active processing of words and their meanings in a range of contexts;
- play with language through games, songs and jokes, alongside rich opportunities for talk, for example using 'talk partners'.

Teachers need to be alert to planning to teach a number of new words each week that are linked to other literacy work; for example, key words from a text being studied. The creation for children of 'meaningful sentences' that model the use of these words, followed by the children creating their own sentences throughout the week, helps to ensure that the words become embedded.

Strategies for enhancing comprehension skills

The NRP (NICHD 2000) reviewed a range of studies that showed evidence that instruction leads to improvements in comprehension and identified the following broad teaching areas:

- comprehension monitoring;
- cooperative learning;
- curriculum integration;
- graphic and semantic organisers (including story maps);
- question answering;
- question generation;
- summarisation.

It is also important to realise that language comprehension and word recognition are closely integrated. For example, see the following two sentences:

> He thought the girl was pretty.
> He thought the girl was petty.

(cited in Nation 2010: 77)

Thus, one letter makes a fundamental difference to the meaning.

Significant factors in effective comprehension

Oakhill *et al.* (2003), in contrast to the NICHD (2000), assert that there has been relatively little research on the development of comprehension. In their review of the factors that may impede effective comprehension, they cite:

1   *Speed and efficiency of decoding skills.* It is clear that laboured decoding of a text will impact on comprehension as the working memory will be focusing on the decoding process and have little space left for understanding what is read. As Smith (1975) points out, this process makes it difficult to hold earlier parts of a sentence in the memory in order to integrate them with what comes later. So, as Oakhill and Nation state (2003: 157), 'by the time they have come to the end of the sentence, they have forgotten how it began!'

2   *Vocabulary development.* As discussed previously, reading comprehension and vocabulary are highly related; however, knowing the words and their meanings in a text does not of itself guarantee comprehension.

3   *Syntactic development.* This continues to develop in children, and in particular they need to learn that written language is not just 'speech written down' – it takes various forms. Syntactic knowledge includes understanding of sentence construction, including how to extract meaning from sentences that might be in active or passive form. Many children find sentences written in a passive form (e.g. the ball was hit by the boy) rather than active form (the boy hit the ball) much more difficult to understand. Syntactic awareness has been shown to influence reading ability as it helps children to detect errors in their reading and self-correct. It also may support word recognition through activities involving predicting the type of word that fits in a sentence.

4   *Identification of main ideas.* The ability to identify the main ideas in a text has been regarded as the 'essence of reading comprehension' (Johnston and Afflerbach 1985). This has been shown to improve with maturity and needs explicit teaching.

5   *Understanding text structure.* This involves understanding a hierarchical structure in a text and the relative importance of different aspects. In addition, it involves the consideration of how ideas in a text are related. This is also related to an understanding of the features of texts of different genres.

6   *Learning to make inferences.* This has been the subject of considerable research, and in 2007 the Department for Children, Schools and Families (DCSF) commissioned the National Federation for Education Research (NFER) to conduct a review of the research evidence into inference skills for reading and how to teach them.

The report written by Anne Kispal (DCSF 2008e) provides an extensive summary of the literature in this area. It begins by helpfully defining making inferences as 'the ability to use two or more pieces of information from a text in order to arrive at a third piece of information that is implicit' (DCSF 2008e: 2). The key findings from this review are as follows:

■   The ability to draw inferences predetermines reading skills and this in turn affects comprehension.

■ Types of inference include:

- *Coherent inferences (or text-connecting inferences)*. These often involve the use of pronouns and require the reader to link these to named people in the text.

- *Elaborative inferences (or gap-filling inferences)*. These provide additional information in a text but the reader has to draw them out. For example: 'Peter sheltered at the bus stop from the heavy downpour. When he got home his mother was cross.' The reader has to work out that by sheltering he was late home and his mother was worried and then appeared cross.

- *Local inferences*. These consist of inferences between sentences and paragraphs and require the reader to fill in the gaps.

- *Global inferences*. These help to provide a coherent picture of the whole text; the reader has to infer overarching ideas about the text.

According to the report, in order to be proficient at making inferences, a pupil needs to:

■ be an active reader who seeks to make sense of a text;

■ learn to monitor understanding and to check on any misunderstandings during reading;

■ have a rich vocabulary;

■ have a competent working memory.

Inference skills are also helped by having a wide background knowledge and understanding the cultural context of the text. Teachers can support pupils to develop inference skills by:

■ teacher modelling and 'thinking aloud' as they read aloud to pupils;

■ asking themselves questions to demonstrate how they check their understanding as they read;

■ making explicit the thinking processes in drawing out inferences from text;

■ asking questions that are open ended and use 'I wonder why …?' or 'How do you know that …' constructions. Aiden Chambers' (1993) work on 'tell me' questions may be useful here.

Teachers can support this process by carefully considering the following stages:

■ before reading (activating prior knowledge, prediction etc.);

■ questions at key points during reading (but allowing pupils some uninterrupted reading time);

■ ways of responding afterwards.

(For more detail on this, see the section below on 'Teaching a comprehensive reading programme'.)

ACTIVITY: SUPPORTING COMPREHENSION SKILLS

Review some of the key strategies for supporting comprehension skills as outlined on pages 123–124 and also read the section on 'Developing Reading Comprehension' contained in the Core Position Papers for Literacy and Mathematics from the Primary National Strategy (DfES 2006b: 28–39). Discuss the following questions with colleagues:

■   What strategies support active reading?
■   Why does reading comprehension depend on oral language skills?
■   What are some of the key ways of extending children's vocabulary?

Teaching a comprehensive reading programme

For many trainees and recently qualified teachers, the teaching of reading is clouded by the many debates about the correct methods. The following provides guidance on how to put into action the key findings from research and advice from the latest government reports. The simplest way of viewing this is to understand that teaching needs to be simultaneously both *text level* (centred on developing an understanding of how texts work and deriving meaning and pleasure from them) and *word level* (providing the necessary sub-skills of decoding using phonics and building a store of words in the memory, linked to their meaning). Teaching should provide for both of these in structured steps, and below you will find some guidance on how to go about this. Table 7.1 provides a summary of a comprehensive reading programme.

Stage 1: Beginning reading

At this stage, children need a rich diet of books that are explored in an interactive way, relating them to their own experiences. Children should be supported in attending to fine details in the text and pictures, leading to imaginative play. Alongside this, children need to develop their word-level skills, ensuring they develop and consolidate their phonological awareness and begin the systematic teaching of grapheme–phoneme correspondences.

Text level

When working with texts, fiction or non-fiction, the following procedure should be adopted.

1   Before reading:

■   Activate background knowledge of the subject – that is, talk about the book *before* opening it: look at what the picture shows, talk about the title and read the blurb and relate it to the children's own experiences.
■   Discuss any significant new words.
■   With fiction, encourage the children to predict the story.

TABLE 7.1 Teaching a comprehensive reading programme

Stage	Text level	Word level
Stage 1 Beginning reading	Provide a rich diet of books explored in an interactive way, related to their own experiences. ■ Before reading: plan for activating prior knowledge and supporting prediction of fiction prior to reading the text. ■ During reading ensure texts are read for enjoyment and with expression. Provide opportunities for dialogic book talk which is a group activity in which adult and children together develop shared understandings of a book through talk. Use prompts such as 'I wonder why...' rather than direct questions. ■ Support children to attend to fine details through the text and pictures, use of props such as story-sacks ■ After reading: provide opportunities for retellings using storyboards, props, puppets or drama techniques such as hot-seating. ■ Provide opportunities for imaginative play with suitable props.	Alongside the text level work, children need to be taught vital skills to support their development as readers. *Learning about print:* this can be primarily achieved by the use of enlarged texts and the use of a pointer demonstrating how print works – from left to right and back to left and from top to bottom of the page. It can also help understanding of individual words and spacing in between words; identifying individual letters and the concept of a sentence and the punctuation used. *Phonological awareness:* ensuring children develop good listening skills and can discriminate a range of sounds from environmental sounds to larger 'units' of sounds e.g. syllables and rhymes and progress to smaller 'units' to distinguish individual phonemes. *Alphabet awareness:* children should be introduced to the alphabet using letter names for example by using alphabet songs and rhymes. Knowledge of letter names should not be confused with learning phonemes. *Vocabulary development:* begin to explicitly develop children's vocabulary through explicit instruction of words out of pupils' experiences and indirect instruction through a rich literary environment.
Stage 2 Learning to decode	Continue to provide a rich diet of texts exploring texts together. Provide opportunities to apply their developing decoding skills to read independently ■ Before reading: plan for activating prior knowledge and supporting prediction of fiction prior to reading the text. ■ In shared reading continue as for beginning reading, but specifically model blending phonemes to make words. ■ Provide opportunities for practice of blending phonemes to read words using decodable texts. ■ Support the child to continually monitor reading for meaning by stopping them to check they understand what they have read and it makes sense. ■ After reading: review what they have read. Discuss questions and predictions raised before reading. Provide follow-up activities, including writing.	The emphasis is on systematic teaching of phonics at this stage with practice at blending the phonemes for reading and segmenting the words for spelling. ■ Provide systematic instruction in sound/symbol correspondences (decoding) ensuring that the complete alphabetic code is taught. ■ Provide opportunities for children to hear, say, read and write the phonemes taught with plenty of practice and over-learning. ■ Ensure that regular diagnostic assessment is undertaken to track children's progress and intervene with additional support where required. Continue with explicit teaching of vocabulary.

Stage	Text level	Word level

Stage 3 Silent reading	During this time the child moves from the reliance on decoding to develop an increasing number of words recognised automatically. The emphasis shifts to improving comprehension.
	
	In shared reading:
	■ Model activating background knowledge.
	■ Integrate new vocabulary by modeling new words in a sentence.
	■ Support developing cognitive and metacognitive strategies:
	  – using prediction before and during reading
	  – using 'think-alouds' and visualisation
	  – making inferences
	  – understanding the structure of different text types.
	
	In individual reading encourage children to apply the above strategies.
	■ During reading: silent reading begins. Encourage wider reading of unknown texts. Develop greater fluency and appropriate expression when reading aloud. Provide support with pronunciation and word-stress.
	■ Provide opportunities for guided reading
	■ After reading: support children's questioning of the text by using higher and lower-order levels of thinking, using Bloom's Taxonomy. Encourage a personal response. Provide opportunities for drama activities such as hot-seating to support empathy.
	■ Provide opportunities for writing texts related to text type read, in pairs or cooperative groups.
		Ensure that phonemic knowledge is secure and applied in spelling through systematic teaching of spelling.
		
		Continue with explicit teaching of vocabulary.

Stage 4 Independent reading	At this stage the child should be encouraged to read widely and develop personal preferences. In shared, guided and independent reading the emphasis will be on developing children's understanding at three levels: 1 *Literal* understanding of text. 2 *Inferential or deductive* understanding by reading between the lines and encouraging paired and group discussion. 3 *Evaluative* understanding of the text by comparing with other similar texts and specific strengths.	Ensure that phonemic knowledge is secure and applied in spelling through systematic teaching of spelling. Continue with explicit teaching of vocabulary.

Give a purpose for listening by asking key questions; for example, 'What do you think might happen to …?' For non-fiction, have a question to explore for which the answer is in the book.

2   During reading (at this stage of reading it will be through shared reading):

- Consider expression when reading with children: pitch, intonation, stress and patterns of language all help comprehension.

- Ensure the book (if fiction) is read through without a break, either on the first or a later reading, for enjoyment.

- When reading fiction, if possible use props, such as objects from the story, to bring the text alive.

- Stop frequently when examining the text. For fiction, ask summative questions about the story. For non-fiction, closely examine sections to answer specific questions.

- Finish by referring to original questions and predictions.

3   After reading:

- Provide opportunities for a brief review of the main characters and events, or (if the text is non-fiction) what the children found out from the book. This is ideally done through paired talk.

- Follow up later in the same day or on a following day with a more detailed retelling. A variety of techniques can be used, such as paired work; small groups using props such as sequencing cards, storyboards or puppets; or drama techniques such as hot-seating (see page 254) or freeze-framing. (Freeze-framing is a drama strategy involving children choosing a key moment and creating a still picture to illustrate it. For example, children could freeze the moment in *Goldilocks and the Three Bears* when the three bears find Goldilocks asleep in one of their beds and act out their body language and facial expressions.)

- Develop comprehension further with opportunities for imaginative play and props associated with the text provided.

Word level

Alongside the text-level work, children need to be taught vital skills to support their development as readers.

- *Learning about print*: this can primarily be achieved by the use of enlarged texts (big books), in print or on screen, and the use of a pointer. So, as the adult reads and points, children learn the direction of print and identify individual words, the spacing between them and individual letters; they also learn about the concept of a sentence and about the punctuation used. This is supported by the children being encouraged to write in a range of contexts alongside play activities.

- *Phonological awareness*: the first step in ensuring that children develop phonological awareness is to explicitly teach how to be a good listener and to provide additional support to those children who need it. Children then discriminate larger 'units' of sound and then work towards smaller 'units' to distinguish individual phonemes.

■ *Alphabet awareness*: here children should be introduced to the alphabet using letter names (not sounds), for example by using alphabet songs and rhymes. They should also gradually be able to distinguish upper- and lower-case letters and not, as was felt at one time, be exposed only to lower-case letters. The prolific examples of upper-case letters in the environment (e.g. B&Q, BBC, etc.) illustrate that restricting children only to lower-case letters is not necessary. They can then begin to identify initial letter sounds.

■ *Vocabulary development*: begin to develop children's vocabulary through explicit instruction (particularly of difficult words out of pupils' daily experiences and a programme of encounters with new words in different ways); indirect instruction (through a rich literary environment and experience of reading materials); and multimedia methods as a visual stimulus for increasing vocabulary and playing with language through games.

Stage 2: Learning to decode

Text level

1   Before reading:

■ Continue as for stage 1 (beginning reading).

2   During reading:

■ In shared reading, continue as for beginning reading but specifically model blending phonemes to make words.

■ At this stage, independent reading begins. Support the child to use the strategies modelled in shared reading and from developing word-level skills. In particular, the child should be encouraged to apply his or her phonic knowledge by blending phonemes to read words.

■ Support the child with developing vocabulary and understanding new words.

■ Encourage finger pointing to reinforce one-to-one correspondence of written to spoken word.

■ Support children to continually monitor reading for meaning by stopping them to check they understand what they have read and that it makes sense.

■ Provide opportunities for practice using decodable texts.

3   After reading:

■ Review and summarise what they have read.

■ Discuss questions and predictions raised before reading.

■ Provide follow-up activities; for example, writing letters to Goldilocks.

Word level

The emphasis at this stage is on systematic teaching of phonics, with practice at blending the phonemes for reading and segmenting the words for spelling.

■ Provide instruction in sound/symbol correspondences (decoding).

■ Provide opportunities for children to hear, say, read and write the phonemes taught, with plenty of practice and over-learning.

- Ensure that regular diagnostic assessment is undertaken to identify early any child who is not making progress.
- Continue with explicit teaching of vocabulary.

Stage 3: Silent reading

Text level

During this time, the child moves from the reliance on decoding towards recognising an increasing number of words automatically, through a store of word meanings and familiar words. The emphasis shifts to improving comprehension.

1   Before reading during shared reading sessions (also encourage children to apply these strategies in individual reading):
- Model activation of background knowledge.
- Integrate new vocabulary by modelling new words in a sentence.
- Support developing cognitive and metacognitive strategies:
  - using prediction before and during reading;
  - using 'think-alouds' and visualisation;
  - making inferences;
  - understanding the structure of different text types.

2   During reading:
- Silent reading starts for first time.
- Encourage wider reading of unknown texts.
- Develop greater fluency and appropriate expression when reading aloud.
- There is no need for finger pointing.
- Pronunciation and word-stress problems are the main areas of difficulty.
- Provide opportunities for guided reading.

3   After reading:
- Support children's questioning of the text by using higher- and lower-order levels of thinking, using Bloom's (1956) taxonomy (see Chapter 6, pages 93 and 94).
- Encourage a personal response to the text through reading journals.
- Provide opportunities for drama activities such as hot-seating to support empathy.
- Provide opportunities for pupils to construct text related to text type read, in pairs or cooperative groups.

Word level

- Ensure that phonemic knowledge is secure and applied in spelling through systematic teaching of spelling.
- Continue with explicit teaching of vocabulary.

Stage 4: Independent reading

Text level

At this stage, children should be encouraged to read widely and develop personal preferences. In shared, guided and independent reading, the emphasis will be on developing children's understanding at three levels (see Figure 7.4):

1   *Literal* understanding of text.

2   *Inferential or deductive* understanding by reading between the lines and encouraging paired and group discussion.

3   *Evaluative* understanding of the text by comparing it with other similar texts and specific strengths of the text.

Word level

- Ensure that phonemic knowledge is secure and applied in spelling through systematic teaching of spelling.
- Continue with explicit teaching of vocabulary.

Three kinds of questions

Where is the answer found?

Type 1

Right there.

The answer is in the text.

It's 'right there' for you to read.

(literal)

Type 2

Think and search.

Search for clues in the text and think about your answer.

(inferential)

Type 3

On my own.

The answer won't be told by words in the text.

You must find the answer in your head.

Think: 'I have to answer this question on my own. The story won't be much help.'

(evaluative)

FIGURE 7.4 Different levels of reading

ACTIVITY: THE STAGES OF A COMPREHENSIVE READING PROGRAMME

Study the four main stages of a comprehensive reading programme carefully, as outlined on pages 127–133. Then, if possible with colleagues, discuss different age groups to which each stage might apply.

Effective shared and guided reading

The research evidence, like the national reports on Standard Attainment Tests (SATs) performance, indicates that greater use of shared and guided reading and writing is likely to help teachers to teach literacy in a more systematic and sustained way. National surveys suggest that these teaching approaches were not being effectively used (Cato *et al.* 1992; Ireson *et al.* 1995; Wragg *et al.* 1998) and that explicit links between text- and word-level teaching have not being strategically made.

Shared reading

Shared reading, in which teacher and pupils simultaneously read a large-format text aloud, has been especially promoted for younger pupils through the work of Don Holdaway (1979, 1982). Older children can interact with the text with the teacher's support in a number of ways. In shared and guided reading sessions, teachers have the opportunity to

- explicitly teach strategies for enhancing critical understanding and informed reflection;
- model how to use such strategies;
- support children as they practise the use of these strategies;
- encourage children to become enthusiastic, autonomous and thoughtful readers.

Guided reading

In guided reading, the teacher supports a small group of children who are at the same reading level. The children each have an individual copy of the text, which the teacher introduces to the group. The teacher presents a key aspect or question for the children to find out about during reading. The children then read their own copies at their own pace with the teacher carefully monitoring pupils as they read. After the reading, the group discusses the question originally posed by the teacher to support their understanding. This has several advantages over hearing children read on an entirely individual basis:

- It substantially increases the time that children actually spend reading.
- It creates a supportive context for children to read in.
- It supports the explicit teaching of key strategies or aspects.
- It can encourage independent reading.

Helping children with reading problems

As teachers, we need to look for ways to assess children's reading abilities and provide remedial help that will enable children to overcome their problems. The key factor is to diagnose the precise areas of difficulty. One of the most effective ways of doing this is through a 'miscue analysis' of a child's reading (see Chapter 16 for more guidance on this). There are several methods of support for children with reading problems, as outlined below.

Reading recovery

The 'reading recovery' procedure devised by Marie Clay (1993) from New Zealand has been widely used and has been shown to be successful for early intervention with pupils who are having difficulties with reading. This programme requires highly intensive one-to-one daily instruction for a period of twenty minutes until such a time as a child shows proficiency in the key areas of

■ directional movement of print;

■ one-to-one matching of spoken to written word;

■ self-monitoring of own errors;

■ cross-checking of reading strategies;

■ use of multiple cue sources (e.g. visual, meaning, phonic, grammatical);

■ self-correction of errors and self-correction of mistakes.

The actual reading-recovery session typically takes the form of

■ rereading two or more familiar books;

■ rereading yesterday's new book and conducting a running record (miscue analysis);

■ practising letter identification using plastic letters and a magnetic board, and/or word-making and word-breaking;

■ writing a story (including hearing and recording sounds in words);

■ rearranging a cut-up story;

■ introducing a new book;

■ attempting the new book.

This programme, although highly effective, is costly, and teachers are intensively trained to carry it out.

A range of intervention programmes has also been developed for pupils who are falling behind their peers by the National Strategies; for example, Early Literacy Support for pupils in Year 1, Additional Literacy Support for pupils in Year 4 and Further Literacy Support for pupils in Year 5. The key aspect in any intervention is that it should be based on an accurate diagnostic assessment of children's reading ability and any specific issues identified. Progress then needs to be carefully tracked through ongoing assessment.

Key points

- The political imperative for driving up standards in literacy has been discussed.

- A range of research findings have been presented showing the importance of phonics within a meaningful encounter with texts. The importance of early intervention for children who are not making adequate progress with reading has been shown.

- Multiple perspectives have emerged on the teaching of reading: the psycho-linguistic, which emphasises the whole-language approach; the cognitive–psychological perspective, which stresses the staged developmental process and the need for alphabetic knowledge; the socio-cultural perspective, which focuses on literacy practices in the home and community; and the socio-political perspective, which emphasises the need for critical literacy for the purposes of equality.

- Models of the reading process have been reviewed, including the Simple View of Reading Model, which is favoured by the Rose Report and the DfE, which emphasises the need for phonics fast and first alongside developing comprehension skills.

- Methods of developing comprehension and inference skills have been reviewed, including the importance of developing children's vocabulary.

- A suggested teaching programme has been provided that is clearly staged and provides for the teaching of decoding alongside language comprehension.

Further reading

Adams, M.J. (1990) *Beginning to Read: thinking and learning about print*. Cambridge, MA: MIT Press.

DCSF (Department for Children Schools and Education) (2008e) *Effective Teaching of Inference Skills for Reading: literature review* [Ref: DCSF-RR031]. Nottingham: DCSF.

DfES (Department for Education and Skills) (2006a) *Independent Review of the Teaching of Early Reading (Final Report by Jim Rose)*. Ref: 0201/2006DOC-EN. Nottingham: DfES.

Hall, K. (2003) *Listening to Stephen Read: multiple perspectives on literacy*. Buckingham: Open University Press.

McGuinness, D. (2004) *Early Reading Instruction: what science really tells us about how to teach reading*. Cambridge, MA: MIT Press.

Fiction and poetry

Purpose of this chapter

This chapter aims to:

- look at the role of fiction and poetry in the primary classroom;
- discuss the link between children's literature and learning about literacy;
- emphasise the importance of reading to children;
- analyse the art of reading to children;
- offer suggestions for stories and poems to read to children;
- present ways in which stories and poems can be studied and enjoyed.

Children's literature and learning about literacy

We will begin by looking at an extract from one of the best-known children's stories, C.S. Lewis's *The Lion, the Witch and the Wardrobe* (1950), which describes the scene as winter turns to spring and the Witch loses her power over Narnia:

> And however the dwarf whipped the poor reindeer the sledge went slower and slower. There also seemed to be a curious noise all round them, but the noise of their driving and jolting and the dwarf's shouting at the reindeer prevented Edmund from hearing what it was, until suddenly the sledge stuck so fast that it wouldn't go on at all. When that happened there was a moment's silence. And in that silence Edmund could at last listen to the other noise properly. A strange, sweet, rustling, chattering noise – and yet not so strange, for he'd heard it before – if only he could remember where! Then all at once he did remember. It was the noise of running water. All round them though out of sight, there were streams chattering, murmuring, bubbling, splashing and even (in the distance) roaring. And his heart gave a great leap (though he hardly knew why) when he realized that the frost was over. And much nearer there was a drip-drip-drip from the branches of all the trees. And then, as he looked at one tree he saw a great load

of snow slide off it and for the first time since he had entered Narnia he saw the dark green of a fir tree. But he hadn't time to listen or watch any longer, for the Witch said: 'Don't sit staring, fool! Get out and help.'

(Lewis 1950: 108)

ACTIVITY: QUESTION

What is the most likely situation in which children will have encountered this extract at school? Will it have been through listening to the story of *The Lion, the Witch and the Wardrobe* being read to them as a serial, or will they have seen the extract in isolation as part of a literacy lesson?

All too often, teachers take excerpts from children's literature and, rather than putting them in context by reading the whole book, use them to teach children about adjectives, punctuation or speech marks. There is a danger that we are creating a nation of children who can read but for whom reading is seen as something to be done in literacy lessons that involves analysing texts rather than enjoying them. In the extract above they might, for example, be expected to look at the use of adjectives to describe the thaw. The extract has even been used by a rather over-zealous teacher to demonstrate to children that they should not begin sentences with conjunctions! The children were given the task of rewriting the text without any sentences beginning with 'and' or 'but'. Quite apart from the dubious nature of the teacher's assertion that sentences should not begin with conjunctions, it seems almost sacrilegious to interfere with this text from one of the best-loved children's novels ever written.

But is it ever justifiable to use extracts from children's novels as texts to discuss and analyse in a literacy lesson? The answer is, of course, 'yes', but this should be a qualified 'yes'. Children should see such excerpts in context and should ideally explore them as part of an ongoing serialisation of the story, with the teacher reading to them regularly for pleasure. Alternatively, they might be told about the events that lead up to the excerpt and then have the opportunity to read on independently. The excerpt might also be used to whet children's appetites for reading the whole book, in the way that cinemas and television channels show excerpts from films in order to encourage us to watch them.

The importance of reading to children

For some children, it is only in literacy lessons that they ever hear any part of a story being read to them. For some teachers, reading to the class has come to be seen as a luxury to be sacrificed as the pressure to teach a full curriculum and personal, social and health education (PSHE) has grown. So why should teachers read to children? Is this merely an entertainment that has no place in the modern primary school, or does it have both an intrinsic worth and a value to work across the curriculum? Goodwin sums up its importance succinctly:

At all stages of reading development, sharing the experience of a story enables children to understand more deeply and to tackle more complex ideas than they could alone.

(Goodwin 2005: 49)

It is vital that children hear stories being read by skilled readers if they are to know how a book should 'sound'. The teacher provides a model for expressive reading and indirectly demonstrates to the children how to bring text to life. It could be argued that this is the function of shared reading within literacy lessons, but such reading is necessarily short and focused on only part of a story, whereas the sustained reading of chapters can engage children's interest much more effectively. For those teachers who feel the need to justify to others, or even to themselves, reading to their classes on a regular basis, the following points might be considered:

- Children's listening skills can be developed through prolonged exposure to engaging stories.
- Vocabulary can be improved when teachers discuss the words and phrases that authors use.
- Scenarios from stories can provide starting points for discussions about moral issues and can help children to consider how they would act in various situations. This can lead into valuable work in PSHE.
- Children's written and oral work will improve if they have more ideas about phrasing and style derived from hearing good-quality literature.
- Children often lack imaginative ideas for their own writing. By exploring a range of stories, they can be helped to develop their own ideas.
- By reading to children, teachers demonstrate that they value reading and show that it is important.
- An interest in fantasy can be encouraged and may lead to children exploring this genre.
- Listening to stories can help make children aware of their own and others' cultural heritage.
- Class reading of a story presents children with a valuable shared experience. The whole class comes together with a common purpose and a pleasant atmosphere can be created.

The art of reading to children

Of course, none of the above may be achieved if the teacher does not read to the children in a way that engages their interest. Besides being fluent readers, there are other attributes that teachers need if they are to read books to their classes successfully.

Voice, expression, intonation and accents

While it is not necessary to be able to assume accents with the skill of Jon Culshaw, it certainly helps children to follow a story if they can tell which person is speaking from the way in which characters' words are said. Radio plays almost invariably have characters with a range of accents to help listeners tell them apart. Teachers who are not confident about using different accents can still use softer and louder or deeper and higher voices for characters. Using a variety of voices also helps the reader, who may be able to miss out 'he said', 'Jane asked' (and so on) in dialogue, since the voice changes will make it clear who is speaking and whether questions are being asked. More importantly, we need to put expression into our voices when reading aloud so that the listener becomes engaged and senses the enthusiasm of the reader. To develop reading-aloud skills, you might try recording yourself and then listening to the recording to discover whether you are expressive and whether you find listening to yourself engaging.

ACTIVITY: READING ALOUD

Choose a favourite story and record yourself reading a passage of dialogue. Play the recording a few days later and ask yourself:

- Can I tell from simply listening which person is speaking?
- Can I forget that it is me reading and enjoy hearing the passage?

Class management when reading to children

Class-management problems might arise when teachers read to children if the children are not interested in the story or if the teacher does not make use of the skills described above. There are some simple strategies that can be used to limit opportunities for disruption and to give children incentives to behave well and listen carefully (see Chapter 2, on classroom management). A key strategy is to involve the children as much as possible. This might be done by providing additional copies of the book for some children to follow the text and to contribute to the telling of the story by reading the words spoken by different characters. Not only does this engage them with the text and help them to understand the punctuation of dialogue but it also provides the teacher with some of the different voices discussed in the previous section.

Other strategies could include:

- Providing cards with the names of characters for some children to hold while the story is being read. This helps listeners to distinguish between characters and provides a useful resource for word-level work, which might follow.
- Creating a story sack with artefacts related to the story, which can be introduced at appropriate moments. For example, for *The Three Little Pigs* there might be some straw, a brick, some wood and a cooking pot.
- Hot-seating: tell the children beforehand who will be asked to assume the role of which characters in the story to answer questions about their actions after the reading session.
- Reading logs: ask the children to make brief notes on what has happened and to compare these with others. The notes can be used to bring absent children up to date on the events in the story when they return.

Reading beforehand

Before reading a story to children, we need to read it first to become familiar with the text, to check whether any material might prove sensitive for some children and to decide on ideal places for stopping that will leave children in suspense and eager to hear the next part of the story. Just as television producers ensure that their audiences are left wanting more at the end of an episode of a soap opera or drama, so teachers can leave children in suspense as they anticipate what might happen next. Indeed, children may use their reading logs to write their predictions based upon inference from what they have already heard. This can lead to interesting discussions in which children draw upon their knowledge of genres to talk about typical themes, scenarios and endings. Such engagement with texts is far more likely to help children meet literacy objectives for fiction than being shown an extract and having a teacher explain its features.

Choosing stories and poems to read to children

One of the most useful resources a teacher can easily maintain is a children's literature portfolio in which copies of poems and interesting extracts from books may be kept, along with brief synopses of books read and children's reactions to them. The notes can be accompanied by ideas for classroom activities that might be developed as a result of reading. These can stretch across the curriculum. Ideally, portfolios should be shared with colleagues to help create a broad knowledge base and a wider appreciation of possibilities.

ACTIVITY: LISTING YOUR FAVOURITE STORIES

Before reading the next section, which identifies ten children's stories we especially like, make a list of ten of your favourite children's stories.

■ Think about why you like them.
■ How might you introduce them to the children you teach?

Some teachers' knowledge of children's literature may be limited and restricted to stories and poems they read or heard as a child. However, there is an abundance of children's literature that engages and entertains not only children but also adults. By increasing our own knowledge of children's literature, we are better able to guide children's choices and make them aware of what is available. It will also be possible to discuss different types of story, from fantasy to comedy, classic to modern, and adventure to thought-provoking. While it would be wrong to be prescriptive about what children should read, it may be helpful to look at a few well-known children's stories that are well written and stimulating and that represent a range of styles, and to look at how these stories might be enjoyed by children and used to stimulate a range of study across the curriculum. The following stories are presented in an order that might equate with their appeal to different age groups, although it is often difficult to ascribe books to age groups since some continue to be enjoyed by adults while younger children sometimes struggle through very challenging texts (e.g. the *Harry Potter* books) because they are so fond of the stories.

Ten favourite children's stories

For each story, a brief synopsis of the plot is presented, followed by notes on possible classroom activities that could be linked to it. Of course, it is perfectly acceptable, indeed desirable, simply to read the story to children without following it up in any way other than through discussion.

Not Now, Bernard (David McKee)

This book, which the publishers recommend for reading together for children aged three years and over, has brief but repetitive text and attractive illustrations. Its recurrent theme is Bernard's parents shunning his approaches and saying 'Not now, Bernard.' The accompanying pictures, especially of Bernard's father, are often comical and stimulate discussion among children. Even when Bernard is 'eaten' by a monster, which replaces him in his house, his parents continue to ignore him.

Possible activities

■ Discussions could be held about adults and their relationship with children. Do the children ever feel that they are ignored? Do they understand why this might be?

■ The story can be read to children and then with them joining in, especially with the refrain 'Not now, Bernard.'

■ Children could discuss whether or not Bernard is actually eaten by the monster. Could it be that the author uses this device to show that adults sometimes don't even notice children?

The Bear under the Stairs (Helen Cooper)

This beautifully illustrated story is well written and uses language that, while occasionally it may challenge young children, is always engaging and readily understood within the context of the story. William imagines there is a bear living under the stairs in his house and worries about this. He decides to feed the bear and puts food under the stairs, quickly slamming the door before the bear can get him.

Possible activities

■ The story focuses on a child's fear and this might provoke children to talk about their own fears of shadows, ghosts and so on. These could be discussed and children might be reassured to know that such fears are common and almost always unfounded.

■ The story has several rhymes for 'stair' and 'stairs', including 'bear', 'there', 'lair' and 'everywhere', each of which has a different spelling of the same phoneme. This could promote discussion about spelling and about rhyme, and might lead to shared writing of a poem about the bear, followed by independent and guided writing.

■ Each time William slams the door under the stairs, he does so with a 'wham, bang, thump'. The concept of onomatopoeia could be discussed and other examples listed (splash, crash, squelch, crunch, slap, hiss, clang), perhaps as a prelude to writing.

■ The book includes a cross-section picture of William's house at night. Children could look at this and at dolls' houses and might go on to draw their own houses' cross-sections.

The Worst Witch (Jill Murphy)

The author was only nineteen when she wrote and illustrated this humorous and entertaining story, the first in a series. It tells of Mildred Hubble's exploits at Miss Cackle's Academy for Witches.

Possible activities

- Witches appear in many children's stories, usually as forces of evil, such as in *The Lion, the Witch and the Wardrobe*. Children could compare and contrast witches in different stories, making character studies and deciding on the attributes that authors give to witches, both physical and social, in order to convey their characters to the reader.

- Children who enjoy this series will almost certainly enjoy the *Harry Potter* series. Some will have read these or seen the films, so discussions could be held about the similarities and differences between the books.

Clever Polly and the Stupid Wolf (Catherine Storr)

Polly consistently outwits a rather dim but articulate wolf who wants to eat her. The series of books is engaging and promotes discussion. Once children have understood the basic premise of the stories, they can read chapters as stories in their own right as it is not necessary to read the books from beginning to end. 'Monday's Child' is based upon the familiar rhyme about the day of one's birth and is especially recommended.

Possible activities

- Children could learn the well-known rhyme and the names and spellings of the days of the week, perhaps going on to look at the origins of the names and their equivalents in other languages.

- Children could retell the story in poetry form, after an initial shared writing activity and a word-level session on rhyme.

- The story could be retold in strip cartoon format, with speech bubbles.

- The story could be re-enacted as a play, with children planning this and then performing it for their classmates.

- New words could be put to a well-known song to tell the story. Again, this might begin as a shared writing activity.

- Objects could be used as musical instruments to provide sound effects for a 'radio' version of the story.

(For a literacy lesson plan for the two versions of the poem, see Waugh *et al.* 1999.)

Bill's New Frock (Anne Fine)

A boy wakes up one morning to discover that he is a girl. The author does not attempt to explain the gender change but uses it to explore the ways in which boys and girls are treated. Bill finds that his teachers and friends behave differently towards him and he begins to have sympathy with the girls, whose play areas are restricted by the boys' domination of the playground. The story is both amusing and poignant.

Possible activities

- Discussions might be held about the ways in which boys and girls feel they are treated differently in school, perhaps in preparation for a debate on the subject.

- Children could imagine themselves in a similar situation to Bill and write a story.

- Groups could devise pieces of drama, either derived directly from the story or depicting experiences that they have had.

Danny the Champion of the World (Roald Dahl)

This children's novel is based upon a short story for adults that Dahl wrote in 1960. The children's version replaces two friends as central characters with a father and son, who respond to persecution by an unpleasant local landowner by poaching his pheasants. Although the tension and excitement of the poaching expeditions have readers on the edges of their seats, it is the loving relationship between father and son that captivates and inspires discussion.

After waking in the middle of the night and discovering his father has not returned from a poaching expedition and fearing that he may be in danger, Danny drives an old car along country lanes to rescue him. Dahl's description of the night drive is beautifully constructed, with skilful use of punctuation, short clauses and sentences, to give the reader an impression of rapidly changing events and rapidly building tension, culminating in Danny coming face to face with a police car.

Possible activities

- The punctuation of the passage could be discussed to illustrate the value of using commas and full stops carefully to indicate speed.
- Children could go on to write their own paragraphs describing exciting events, at first as a shared writing activity with discussion and then as guided or independent work.
- In PSHE, discussions could be held about whether Danny was right to take the car and drive it when this was clearly against the law. Children might be reminded of the dangers of driving when unqualified and too young to pass a test, but there could also be discussions about famous instances of law-breaking that are now celebrated, such as Rosa Parks' refusal to give up her bus seat to a white man in Alabama, USA, in 1955.

The Midnight Fox (Betsy Byars)

A boy stays on a farm for the summer holidays and sees an unusual fox. He writes to his friend regularly and the two speculate on various topics. The daydream about discovering a new colour (Byars 1981: 48–50) is beautifully written and could lead to some interesting work from children.

Possible activities

- Children could imagine that they have discovered a new colour and tell of the discovery in a news item similar to that in the book.
- Children could try to make and name new colours in a painting lesson.
- Songs and poems about colours could be learned and sung or recited.
- Children could try to describe colours to partners.
- The activity could be linked to reading the poem 'Mimi's Fingers', which appears later in this chapter and in which a blind girl asks about colour.
- Atlases could be consulted to locate the part of the USA where the story is set.

Harry Potter and the Philosopher's Stone (J.K. Rowling)

Orphaned Harry goes to Hogwarts, a school for sorcery, which is reached via Platform 9¾ at King's Cross Station. As in all the *Harry Potter* stories, Harry and his friends have to overcome dark forces to triumph. Each of the stories concerns the solving of some riddle or quest, and there are many nods to Rowling's classical education and interest, which may lead the reader into the worlds of Greek and classical myth.

Possible activities

Comparisons could be made between Hogwarts and boarding schools in other stories, for example *The Worst Witch*.

- Children might listen to and read children's versions of Greek myths and discuss similarities and differences between their style and that of the *Harry Potter* stories.
- Children could write their own versions of key events.
- The rules for Quidditch could be written out and compared with rules for sports children have played.
- Children could write their own stories about Harry Potter, using existing characters but also, perhaps, inventing new ones.

Kensuke's Kingdom (Michael Morpurgo)

This beautifully constructed story tells of a boy marooned on a desert island who discovers there is another occupant: a former Japanese soldier (Kensuke) who does not know that the war is over. At first their relationship is strained, but gradually they come to know and like each other and to work together for survival. Kensuke teaches the boy to paint, and they become so close that Kensuke begins to fear his friend's rescue.

Possible activities

- The story is told in the first person. This could lead to discussions about possible bias in the way events are related. Does the author portray himself in a constantly good light or is he honest enough to describe his errors?
- The opening line instantly captures the imagination of the reader ('I disappeared on the night before my twelfth birthday, July 28 1988'). Other stories' opening lines could be studied and this could lead to shared writing of opening lines and eventually to independent work. A collection of opening lines could be displayed alongside copies of books.
- The book provides maps of the island and a map of the world showing Michael's voyage. Children could find out more about the places visited and could use Google Earth to look more closely.

Goodnight Mister Tom (Michelle Magorian)

Will is evacuated from London to stay with Tom Oakley, an old man who is initially reluctant to take him but who proves to be an excellent carer. As the story unfolds, it emerges that Will was abused by his mother and that this has had an effect upon him. The story describes life in wartime England with superb attention to detail, and the relationships between Tom and Will, and Will and his friend Zach, are portrayed beautifully and, at times, movingly.

Possible activities

- There are obvious areas for discussion about relationships and about Will's experiences at home, though these may need to be handled delicately.

- Children could find out more about evacuation and children's lives during wartime. They might also look at other novels that feature evacuees, including *Carrie's War* by Nina Bawden (1974) and C.S. Lewis's *The Lion, the Witch and the Wardrobe*.

ACTIVITY: DEVISING ACTIVITIES FOR A FAVOURITE BOOK

Now that you have read about the ten books above, consider how, using one of the favourite children's books you chose for the previous activity, you could devise worthwhile activities that would engage children's interest and enhance their enjoyment of the story.

Enid Blyton

Anyone with a knowledge and love of children's literature would easily be able to suggest ten quite different books to represent genres that would be equally captivating for young and old readers alike. Our selection is not intended to represent a top ten. Indeed, as soon as prescriptive lists appear, as they did in prequels to the National Curriculum in 1990, lovers of literature become indignant about omissions. However, one author whose absence from such lists has provoked little outcry, but who was the best-selling children's writer of the twentieth century and whose books continue to sell in huge numbers, is Enid Blyton.

There is a strange and now predictable response from trainee teachers when they are asked what they read as children, if Blyton was their favourite. With chin moving towards chest they often, almost shamefully, mumble something like: 'Enid Blyton, but I think that's frowned upon now, isn't it?' In some quarters, Blyton's books are regarded as unchallenging and not especially well written, but they continue to sell in huge numbers and have been, for many children, the first books that they read eagerly from cover to cover. Indeed, in a *Guardian* interview (Duerden 2012), Michael Morpurgo happily admitted that his own children love Blyton's books because, regardless of the faults of cardboard characterisation and pedestrian style, there is a cliffhanger on virtually every page. Blyton's books are page-turners in which the stories rattle along at a pace, leaving the reader eager to know what happens next. The problems that some critics have with Blyton's work revolve around issues such as sexism, racism, class distinction and use of language. It is not difficult to find examples of the first three in some of her stories, although it should be remembered that she was born in 1897 and wrote in a different era, when most people were less conscious of political correctness. Recent editions of some of Blyton's books have been 'sanitised': the names of the golliwogs are now Wiggie, Waggie and Wollie rather than Golly, Woggie and Nigger; 'I say' has been replaced with 'Hey' and 'queer' with 'odd'; Dame Slap has become Dame Snap, and now scolds naughty children rather than smacking them; and Fanny and Dick have been changed to Frannie and Rick.

An excerpt from *The Three Golliwogs* may make uncomfortable reading, perhaps moving some of those who speak of changes to the books as 'political correctness gone mad' to think again:

> Once the three bold golliwogs, Golly, Woggie, and Nigger, decided to go for a walk to Bumble-Bee Common. Golly wasn't quite ready so Woggie and Nigger said they would start off without him, and Golly would catch them up as soon as he could. So off went Woggie and Nigger, arm-in-arm, singing merrily their favourite song – which, as you may guess, was *Ten Little Nigger Boys*.
>
> (Blyton 1968: 51)

Of course, anyone who wishes to be critical of Blyton can easily focus upon extracts that appear to condemn her whole output, but it should be remembered that these are not typical of all of her work. It should also be borne in mind that Blyton is far from the only author from the past to have written in a way that now seems offensive and anachronistic: try looking at Hugh Lofting's *Dr Dolittle* (1920), in which the Sleeping Beauty will not marry the black prince until he becomes white.

ACTIVITY: CHOOSING SUITABLE BOOKS FOR CHILDREN

In considering our choices of books to present to children, it may be helpful to focus upon the following questions:

- Is it acceptable to leave some books off classroom shelves because teachers are offended by their content? If so, which would be omitted?
- Should literature be modified to bring it in line with current thinking? If so, what would you change?
- Are children capable of seeing authors' work as products of the times in which they wrote?
- How do we know what children might enjoy?

Helping children to choose books

If children have a limited knowledge of literature and have explored few different genres, they will, when faced with choices, be rather like people faced with a menu in a foreign restaurant. Will they choose something exotic and take a risk, or will they stick to what they know? It is the teacher's job to ensure that their knowledge of the literature menu is broad enough for them to be able to make informed choices and not to be afraid of the unknown or unfamiliar. We should, therefore, ensure that we introduce them to a wide range of texts, including both modern and classic stories.

It is very tempting to choose only those stories that will make children laugh – after all, as teachers we all want to see our pupils happy. However, children also enjoy stories with moral dilemmas, adventure stories, and stories that make them afraid for the characters.

Stories set in the distant past, especially when the period described is one that children are studying, will not only engage their interest but also add to their knowledge and give them an insight into how people actually lived. For the Romans, try *The Eagle of the Ninth* by Rosemary Sutcliff or Caroline Lawrence's series of Roman Mysteries; for the Vikings, Terry Jones's excellent *Erik the Viking* will both inform and entertain. Topics on the Victorians can be brought to life through reading stories by Joan Aiken, whose books are often set in a period similar to the Victorian era but in which there is a different monarch. *The Elephant War* by Gillian Avery, which is based upon a real event from 1882 when Jumbo the Elephant was to be taken from Regent's Park Zoo to work for Barnum's Circus in America, both paints a picture of Victorian life and promotes debate and discussion. Michael Morpurgo's *Private Peaceful* and *Warhorse* are set during the First World War and build tension while drawing the reader into an unfamiliar period. Both have now been made into films, which should ensure the books' continued popularity.

For the Second World War, there are several excellent books written by people who were alive at the time; for example, the previously mentioned *Carrie's War* by Nina Bawden and *Goodnight Mister Tom* by Michelle Magorian.

Stories from different cultures and countries will expand children's understanding of how other people live and how they solve problems; for example, *Handa's Surprise* by Eileen Browne, *We're Going on a Lion Hunt* by David Axtell and *Dragon Mountain* by Tim Vyner.

Books that extend thinking and challenge ideas are plentiful; many by Anne Fine fall into this category, including *The Tulip Touch*, in which a popular girl befriends an unpopular one. Stories by Jacqueline Wilson and Judy Blume are equally thought-provoking and can be linked to PSHE discussions.

We hope that these suggestions will encourage you to explore children's fiction more widely, both for your own enjoyment and for that of your pupils, many of whom might be unlikely to experience a wide range of literature without guidance from an experienced reader.

Poetry

'Hands up if you like poetry!': a question aimed not at a class of children but at a group of trainee teachers, and one that traditionally produces a disappointingly small number of raised hands. For many, poetry at school was limited in range and at secondary school was studied, analysed and learned to enable students to pass exams. There's even a word for fear or hatred of poetry: 'metrophobia'! This legacy of negative attitudes to poetry is perpetuated by some teachers, who see poetry either as something to be avoided or as a genre that they must explore with their pupils in order to meet literacy objectives, but not one that they will dwell upon for any longer than is absolutely necessary.

ACTIVITY: THINKING ABOUT POETRY

- Can you recite any poems by heart?
- Did you enjoy poetry at school?
- Do you ever read poetry now?
- Do you ever write poetry?

If our responses to the above questions are largely negative, how can we encourage children to enjoy poetry and discover its significance as a literary genre and as a vehicle for developing a love and understanding of language? A good starting point is to ensure that teachers are aware of a range of poems of different types and have heard these read aloud and understand their features. Just as a portfolio of children's literature is a valuable career-long resource, so a burgeoning anthology of poetry will prove invaluable, both as a resource for literacy lessons and for sharing with children purely for pleasure. These might be drawn from some of the popular anthologies that are available cheaply, including the excellent *The Works* series (Cookson 2000; Moses and Corbett 2002). The poems in the Cookson anthology are divided into genres to cover the types described in the old Literacy Strategy, while Moses and Corbett (2002) have sections for each subject in the primary curriculum. While this may seem rather functional, the anthologies can of course be enjoyed in their own right without teachers feeling that they are merely vehicles for learning about language.

Having built a collection of varied and interesting poems, teachers need to reflect upon the value of sharing these with children. The value will be considerably enhanced if teachers learn to read the poems well, with expression and intonation and without falling into some of the traps that inexperienced readers succumb to, such as pausing at the end of each line of a narrative poem after the rhyme, rather than reading on to sustain momentum and help listeners understand what is being read to them. BBC Radio 4's excellent *Poetry Please* programme, usually broadcast on Sunday afternoons, features high-quality readings of well-loved poems and provides a good model for anyone wishing to read poetry to others. Read well, poetry will engage children and encourage them to want to talk about what they have heard. Read poorly, poetry will arouse the negative feelings described above.

Exploring poetry with children

In this section we will look at examples of poems and ways in which they might lead to discussion, literacy work and cross-curricular study, as well as giving pleasure to readers. The poems have been chosen partly because they are short enough to be looked at as a whole on a screen, and so might be studied within a single lesson, but mainly because of the quality of the language used, their imagery and the way in which the poets capture the imagination of the reader.

'Mimi's Fingers' (Mary O'Neill)

'Mimi's Fingers' begins by informing the reader that the narrator is blind, and then proceeds to describe how she manages to understand her environment through other senses, particularly touch (see Sweeney 1999). The description is simple yet clear and the poem ends with a twist that is thought-provoking. Only colour cannot be understood through touch, and Mimi does not have a clear idea of the concept of colour.

> I know a snowflake as a melting star,
> The sticky-thick of honey and of tar.
> Colour alone my fingers cannot do.
> Could you, could you, tell me about blue?

Having listened to the poem and read it with the teacher, children could be asked to consider how they would describe colour to a blind person. The importance of clear descriptions can be emphasised, as can the need to be aware that someone who had never been able to see would not understand descriptions that relied upon any prior knowledge of what things looked like. Study of the poem can be linked to reading Betsy Byars' *The Midnight Fox* (1981), with Tom's discovery of a new colour being discussed as well. An obvious cross-curricular follow-up is in art, where colour-mixing could lead to descriptions of the colours created and a study of a paint chart might prompt children to invent names for their colours that could be used in their own poems and prose about colour.

'November' (Thomas Hood)

'November' has a regular pattern, with each line beginning with 'No' and telling the reader about things that cannot be seen or enjoyed. The final line is simply 'November', so that the reader discovers only at the end what the poem is about. This poem is best introduced with the title and final line concealed, as children always enjoy the twist at the end and this promotes discussion. 'November' was written in 1844 so some of the vocabulary may be unfamiliar to children and may require some explanation, although children should be encouraged to use the context of unfamiliar words to attempt to understand their meanings. Reading the poem could ultimately lead to discussions on the use of apostrophes for omission, a device used by poets to ensure their words scan and fit in with the rhythm of the poem. Children might look at *t'other* and *'em* and could discuss what the full versions might be and go on to examine wasn't, couldn't, shan't, won't and so on. The poem also offers scope for writing in a similar style, perhaps on the subject of November or using a different prefix or word opening such as 'De' for December (delightful, delicious, deep snow, depart), or even 'Uni' for United.

> No sun – no moon! No morn – no noon –
> No dawn – no dusk – no proper time of day.
> No sky – no earthly view –
> No distance looking blue –
> No road – no street – no 't'other side the way' –
> No end to any Row –
> No indications where the Crescents go –
> No top to any steeple –
> No recognitions of familiar people –
> No courtesies for showing 'em –
> No knowing 'em –
> No travelling at all – no locomotion,
> No inkling of the way – no notion –
> 'No go' – by land or ocean –
> No mail – no post –
> No news from any foreign coast –
> No Park – no Ring – no afternoon gentility –
> No company – no nobility –
> No warmth, no cheerfulness, no healthful ease
> No comfortable feel in any member –
> No shade, no shine, no butterflies, no bees,
> No fruits, no flowers, no leaves, no birds –
> November!

'Jabberwocky' (Lewis Carroll)

Lewis Carroll's 'Jabberwocky' offers great scope for creativity and language study, since it is replete with invented words that can be interpreted by readers. It may perhaps be interesting to point out that chortle, galumph and burble, all accepted words in the modern lexicon, were first coined here! Classes have written their own versions, both with accepted English words replacing Carroll's inventions and with invented words. In deciding which words to use, children have discussed the functions of the words, identifying parts of speech in order to determine appropriate substitutions. The poem also lends itself extremely well to performance, with children's interpretation of the text being linked to actions. In one example, 130 Year 6 children performed 'Jabberwocky' under the guidance of an English teacher during a day's pre-visit to their secondary school.

> 'Twas brillig, and the slithy toves
> Did gyre and gimble in the wabe;
> All mimsy were the borogoves,
> And the mome raths outgrabe.
>
> 'Beware the Jabberwock, my son!
> The jaws that bite, the claws that catch!
> Beware the Jubjub bird, and shun
> The Frumious Bandersnatch!'
>
> He took his vorpal sword in hand:
> Long time the manxome foe he sought –
> So he rested by the Tumtum tree,
> And stood a while in thought.
>
> And as in uffish thought he stood,
> The Jabberwock, with eyes of flame,
> Came whiffling through the tulgey wood,
> And burbled as it came!
>
> One, two! One, two! And through and through
> The vorpal blade went snicker-snack!
> He left it dead, and with its head
> He went galumphing back.
>
> 'And hast thou slain the Jabberwock?
> Come to my arms, my beamish boy!
> O frabjous day! Callooh! Callay!'
> He chortled in his joy.
>
> 'Twas brillig, and the slithy toves
> Did gyre and gimble in the wabe;
> All mimsy were the borogoves,
> And the mome raths outgrabe.

The invented words should promote discussion about pronunciation and thus consideration of phonemes and graphemes. Words might be related to more familiar ones as children debate how to say them and what they might mean, with dictionaries referred to as they justify their ideas. For example:

- Should 'gyre' be pronounced with a soft g as in 'gyrate' or a hard g as in 'gate'?
- Is 'raths' pronounced as 'baths' with a short a as in most northern English accents or a long a as in parts of southern England?
- Does 'tulgey' have a hard or soft g?

Most of the invented words seem to be phonically regular and accessible to young readers, ensuring that children should be able to make a good attempt at reading the poem even before they have begun to decide what it might be about.

'The Eagle' (Alfred Lord Tennyson)

This short poem begins with an alliterative first line and a first verse that enables us to picture the bird in his isolation, surrounded by sky ('the azure world') in lonely lands. His talons are referred to as hands, perhaps helping us to get a greater sense of how it might feel to be an eagle clinging to a mountain side. In the second stanza, the bird's lofty position is emphasised and the waves are personified as wrinkled and beneath the eagle's mountain walls. The final dramatic line reminds us of the eagle's power and speed as it falls like a thunderbolt towards its prey.

> He clasps the crag with crooked hands;
> Close to the sun in lonely lands,
> Ringed with the azure world, he stands.
> The wrinkled sea beneath him crawls;
> He watches from his mountain walls,
> And like a thunderbolt he falls.

The poem has a pattern that could be replicated, first by the teacher through shared writing and then by children. Each line in each of the two stanzas rhymes. Collections of rhyming words appropriate for eagles or other creatures could be made, and alliteration and similes discussed. See Chapter 11 for other examples of short poems with regular structures.

More activities using poetry

Of course, a study of poetry does not have to be restricted to classic poems. Children might explore the following:

- rhymes that are used to remember things (mnemonics), such as 'Thirty days hath September' to remember the number of days in each month, and 'Never Eat Shredded Wheat' to remember the points of the compass;
- nursery rhymes, which can be explored by young children and learned by heart, as well as by older children, who might explore the hidden meanings behind some of them, for example, 'Ring a Ring o' Roses' and the plague;

- the lyrics of songs, including hymns, which can sometimes be difficult for children to understand;

- jingles used in advertising: children could go on to write their own to advertise school and local events;

- rhymes in greetings cards: many tend to be trite and children could be asked to try to improve upon existing ones;

- short comic verse such as that of Spike Milligan;

- longer comic verse, for example Roald Dahl's *Revolting Rhymes* (1982) and poems by Pam Ayres, Allan Ahlberg, Michael Rosen, Roger McGough and Kit Wright;

- ballads and narrative poems;

- structured poems with a clear syllabic pattern such as limericks, haiku, cinquains and triolets;

- free verse without rhyme;

- 'nonsense' poems;

- poems written by children;

- extracts from descriptive 'adult' poetry, such as 'Ode to Autumn' by John Keats, the witches' brew in *Macbeth* by Shakespeare or 'Daffodils' by William Wordsworth;

- poems from different cultures.

Children should be encouraged to perform and even record poems to develop their oral and presentational skills. They might do this individually or in pairs, but may also work in groups to devise performances, perhaps including choral speaking.

Finally, one reason for reading poetry to children and discussing it with them is to help them to write their own. This can be done initially through shared reading, followed by shared writing, with the teacher modelling poetry writing. Discussion can take place about making the poem scan and about rhymes. Teachers can show how they explore possibilities for rhymes, perhaps by taking a key word that they wish to use and then making a list of possible rhymes. The resulting word banks will not only help children with their own rhymes but also support their phonic understanding, and can provide opportunities for them to explore words, using dictionaries to check whether the words they create actually exist and if so what they mean.

ACTIVITY: WRITING STRUCTURED POEMS

Looking at the examples of structured poems below, try to work out their pattern and then replicate it by writing a poem of your own in each style. Not only will this help you to remember the features of the poems but it will also help you to see some of the challenges children face when asked to write poetry. See the end of the chapter to check whether you have correctly identified the poems' structures.

Haiku

Watching the moon rise,
Seeing the western sun fade,
My worries lie down.

Beautiful feline,
Stalk your unsuspecting prey.
So quiet, deadly.

(see Waugh with McGuinn 1996)

Triolets

David Dean read lots of books
His friends all gave him funny looks
He couldn't put them down
David Dean read lots of books
He brought them home in a fleet of trucks
From the library in town.
David Dean read lots of books
His friends all gave him funny looks

Louise McCarthy sits in front of me
She's the kind of girl I'd like to be
She has long hair
Louise McCarthy sits in front of me
I'd really like to ask her home for tea.
I wouldn't dare.
Louise McCarthy sits in front of me
She's the kind of girl I'd like to be.

Cinquains

Never
Keep your shoes on
When you get into bed
Because you will make the clean sheets
Dirty

I love
To hear the sound
Of happy young children
Dashing around the school playground
Yelling.

(see Waugh 2000b)

In this chapter we have looked at the importance of fiction and poetry in the classroom and at the importance of reading both stories and poems to children, as well as at some of the skills that teachers will require to be able to do this successfully. We have also examined a range of stories and poems and have considered some of the ways in which curriculum-related work might be linked to sharing them with children. In addition, we have looked at some issues related to choosing literature to share with children.

Key points

- Stories and poems are an important part of the primary curriculum and should be shared with children regularly.

- Reading aloud to children is a skill that requires development and it is important that teachers hone their skills if they are to engage their pupils' interest.

- Stories and poems can be starting points for activities both in literacy lessons and in other areas of the curriculum, but these activities should be meaningful and should enhance rather than detract from children's enjoyment of the texts.

- Teachers should build up a knowledge of children's literature and should think carefully about the choices of texts they make for sharing with their classes.

Further reading

Carter, D. (2000) *Teaching Fiction in the Primary School*. London: David Fulton.

Gamble, N. and Yates, S. (2002) *Exploring Children's Literature*. London: Paul Chapman.

Goodwin, P. (2005) 'Creative young readers', in A. Wilson (ed.) *Creativity in Primary Education*. Exeter: Learning Matters, 44–57.

Children's books

Aiken, J. (1962) *The Wolves of Willoughby Chase*. London: Jonathan Cape.

Aiken, J. (1964) *Black Hearts in Battersea*. London: Jonathan Cape.

Aiken, J. (1968) *The Whispering Mountain*. London: Jonathan Cape.

Avery, G. (1960) *The Elephant War*. London: Collins.

Axtell, D. (2000) *We're Going on a Lion Hunt*. London: Macmillan.

Bawden, N. (1974) *Carrie's War*. London: Puffin.

Blume, J. (1988) *Just as Long as We're Together*. London: Pan Macmillan.

Blume, J. (2003 [1972]) *Tales of a Fourth Grade Nothing*. London: Macmillan.

Blume, J. (2006 [1974]) *Blubber*. London: Macmillan.

Blyton, E. (1968) *The Three Golliwogs*. London: Dean & Son.

Browne, E. (1995) *Handa's Surprise*. London: Walker.

Byars, B. (1981) *The Midnight Fox*. London: Puffin.

Carroll, L. (1972 [1871]) 'Jabberwocky', in *Through the Looking-Glass and What Alice Found There*. London: Macmillan.

Cookson, P. (ed.) (2000) *The Works*. London: Pan Macmillan.

Cooper, H. (1993) *The Bear Under the Stairs*. London: Corgi.

Dahl, R. (1977) *Danny the Champion of the World*. London: Puffin.

Dahl, R. (1982) *Revolting Rhymes*. London: Puffin.

Fine, A. (1992) *Bill's New Frock*. London: Longman.

Fine, A. (1997) *The Tulip Touch*. London: Puffin.

Jones, T. (1989) *Erik the Viking*. London: Robson.

Lawrence, C. (2001) *The Thieves of Ostia*. London: Orion.

Lewis, C.S. (1950) *The Lion, the Witch and the Wardrobe*. Harmondsworth: Penguin.

Lofting, H. (1968 [1920]) *Doctor Dolittle Stories*. London: Cape.

Magorian, M. (1998) *Goodnight Mister Tom*. Harmondsworth: Penguin.

McKee, D. (1980) *Not Now, Bernard*. London: Red Fox.

Morpurgo, M. (1999) *Kensuke's Kingdom*. London: Egmont.

Moses, B. and Corbett, P. (2002) *Works 2: Poems for Every Subject and Occasion.* London: Pan Macmillan.

Murphy, J. (1974) *The Worst Witch.* London: Young Puffin.

Rowling, J.K. (1997) *Harry Potter and the Philosopher's Stone.* London: Bloomsbury.

Storr, C. (1967) *Clever Polly and the Stupid Wolf.* London: Puffin.

Sutcliff, R. (2004 [1954]) *The Eagle of the Ninth.* Oxford: Oxford University Press.

Vyner, T. (1996) *Dragon Mountain.* London: Collins.

Wilson, J. (1993) *The Suitcase Kid.* London: Corgi Yearling.

Wilson, J. (2004) *Midnight.* London: Corgi Yearling.

Wilson, J. (2006) *Clean Break.* London: Corgi Yearling.

Structured poetry: answers

Haiku (Japanese and created by Matso Basho)

- Three lines.
- Each line has a fixed number of syllables.

Watching the moon rise	(five syllables)
Seeing the western sun fade	(seven syllables)
My worries lie down.	(five syllables)

Beautiful feline,	(five syllables)
Stalk your unsuspecting prey.	(seven syllables)
So quiet, deadly.	(five syllables)

Triolets ('triplet'): a French verse form

- Eight lines with two rhymes (rhyme scheme shown below).
- Five of the eight lines are repeated or refrain lines.
- First line repeats at the fourth and seventh lines.
- Second line repeats at the eighth line.

Louise McCarthy sits in front of me	(A)
She's the kind of girl I'd like to be	(A – rhymes with first line)
She has long hair	(B)
Louise McCarthy sits in front of me	(A – identical to first line)
I'd really like to ask her home for tea.	(A – rhymes with first line)
I wouldn't dare.	(B – rhymes with third line)
Louise McCarthy sits in front of me	(A – identical to first line)
She's the kind of girl I'd like to be.	(A – Identical to second line)

Cinquain (a form first produced by Adelaide Crapsey)

- Five lines.
- Each line has a fixed number of syllables.

Baby	(two syllables)
Happy, smiling!	(four syllables)
Babbling, eating, crawling	(six syllables)
His very first birthday party	(eight syllables)
Perfect	(two syllables)

Pudding
Hot and steaming
Juicy, crunchy, tasty
It all disappeared in a trice
More please!

9

Reading and writing for information

Purpose of this chapter

This chapter aims to:

- explore reading and writing of non-fiction;
- give examples of using everyday texts;
- describe various genres of texts;
- provide strategies for effective interaction with texts;
- suggest activities in the classroom for each year group.

This chapter provides possible activities in the classroom and explains how programmes of study can be devised to incorporate a range of genres and diverse activities that will develop children's skills and engage their interest.

Non-fiction literature

Many of children's early experiences of reading focus on fiction, with stories and poems, including nursery rhymes and songs, figuring strongly. However, as they learn about the world around them, children become increasingly curious about plants, animals, transport and natural phenomena. They also find that the literature in their environments is predominantly non-fiction. For example, they will see notices, signs, advertisements, letters and timetables. We are surrounded by text when we walk down the street or turn on the television or computer, and even when we look around our homes. Children need to make sense of all of this text; they need to understand how it can be useful and know what it tells us. As they develop as readers, they then need a broad diet of texts that reflect the real world as well as fantasy. Boys, in particular, often prefer non-fiction texts (e.g. see Canada Council on Learning 2009). Look, for example, at the popularity of Top Trumps cards and at the way children extract information from them.

Unlike most of the fiction texts that children have access to, many of the non-fiction sources they find all around them are not specifically written for children. As Brien maintains,

> When working with non-fiction in literacy or across the curriculum, the barrier between the text written specifically for children's learning and the abundance of real-life sources has broken down almost entirely. Children access the same material as the rest of the population and learn from it in new ways.
>
> (Brien 2012: 141)

Even quite young children often have access to the internet, which provides them with the potential to find out almost anything they want to know. However, it also provides a wealth of unedited material that reflects the opinions of the authors and that has not been scrutinised by editors in the way that printed material often is. Given this mass of available 'information', it is vital that children understand that what they read may not necessarily be true and that they need to explore information about topics from a number of sources. Thus, the National Curriculum for English at Key Stage 1 stated that children should 'understand that texts about the same topic may contain different information or present similar information in different ways' (DfEE and QCA 1999: 46).

Even at this early stage, children should also 'use the organisational features of non-fiction texts, including captions, illustrations, contents, index and chapters, to find information' (DfEE 1999: 46). There are, inevitably, implications for the Key Stage 1 classroom, which might have reference areas equipped with dictionaries, thesauruses, encyclopaedias, directories and databases. Children can begin to appreciate the value of such materials if they become part of a 'literate' home corner. This might include writing materials (including electronic), a telephone directory, catalogues and timetables.

Children are expected to develop quite sophisticated study skills, not only to enable them to meet the requirements of the curriculum but also to enable them to find and make use of information from a range of sources, which has grown considerably as information technology and paper publications have expanded and become increasingly accessible.

Focusing on the Victorians

To illustrate ways in which texts may be used with children to develop their understanding of the features of different genres and their ability to extract information and produce their own texts, let us look at a series of possible lessons for a Year 2 class. (Similar lessons can be found in Waugh 2005: 174–91.)

The starting point for the lessons, which are linked to work in history on the Victorians, could be some pictures of children in a Victorian classroom. By introducing the topic with pictures, the teacher can make it accessible to children whose reading skills might prevent them from being engaged from the outset. This technique also enables children to draw upon prior knowledge and to bring their own ideas to discussions. They can look at the pictures and comment upon similarities and differences between the Victorian classroom and their own, while posing questions about things that they do not recognise or understand. Initially, the discussions might be held in pairs, with partners sharing ideas in preparation for whole-class discussions.

Having encouraged children to look closely at the pictures, the teacher can ask for their ideas and write these on the board in note form; for example, 'high windows, rows of desks, big stick'. The teacher can go on to model writing by asking the children to suggest how the notes might be turned into sentences. This initial activity can be used both to stimulate interest in a topic and to set the agenda for future study, including independent research by children using books, the internet and other resources, both at school and at home. Indeed, the teacher might at this stage introduce a 'Know, Want, Learned' grid, as shown in Table 9.1 (Wray 2004: 41).

In the left-hand column of the grid, the teacher should write a list of things the children already claim to know about the Victorians while in the central column the teacher should write a list of questions children would like answered during their study of the topic. The list can be added to in future lessons, and can be prominently displayed so that children are encouraged to find possible answers to the questions in the central column.

In the next lesson, children can be introduced to simple text that provides information about aspects of school life in Victorian times. Before reading the text to the children, the teacher should ask them to scan it and discuss what information it might contain, justifying their ideas by talking about titles and subtitles and any key words they notice. After reading the text to the children and then with them, the content should be discussed before focusing on unfamiliar vocabulary and spellings. As discussed elsewhere in this book, it is important that children see texts as meaningful and worth studying in their own right, and not simply as vehicles for learning about spelling, grammar and punctuation. However, this should not prevent teachers from looking for opportunities to explore word- and sentence-level aspects within the context of whole texts.

Independent, paired or group work, which might follow the shared whole-class work, could involve children in finding out more about Victorian school life, writing their own versions of parts of the text or making up questions for each other that could be answered by reading the text carefully.

TABLE 9.1 The 'know, want, learned' grid

What do I know about this topic?	What do I want to know about this topic?	What have I learned about this topic?

A further lesson might focus upon fact, fiction and opinion, with children looking as a class at some statements prepared by the teacher. For example:

- Some Victorian teachers hit children with canes when they were naughty.
- Children wrote on slates in Victorian schools.
- Victorian schools were better than modern schools.
- Victorian schools had computers.

After reading the sentences to and then with the children, the teacher could ask them which of the sentences they think are true and which are untrue. The sentence 'Victorian schools were better than modern schools' should be looked at carefully and children should be asked whether they agree with it, based upon what they have found out so far. They can be asked to justify their opinions. The teacher can then go on to write further sentences with the children's help, with children supplying ideas for ones that are fact, fiction and opinion.

Further lessons might focus on other aspects of Victorian children's lives, such as games, toys, clothes and work. Once again, children's interest might be aroused through the use of pictures, simple texts, websites and artefacts.

The method of working described above enables children to make links between subjects and allows teachers to use texts associated with foundation subjects within English lessons. This cross–curricular approach chimes well with the Primary National Strategy's emphasis on making links between curriculum subjects and areas of learning (DfES 2006c: 13).

ACTIVITY: PLANNING FOR NON-FICTION

Look at Cremin's (2009) suggestions for ways in which teachers can scaffold children's reading of non-fiction texts and consider how these might inform your planning for non-fiction. Cremin suggests we can do this by:

- helping children to see a genuine purpose for engaging with the text;
- helping them to activate any prior knowledge they have on or around the text;
- preparing them for the kind of vocabulary they might meet;
- giving them experience in hearing and using formal registers;
- modelling active reading of the text and the strategies they use;
- supporting children in understanding the text;
- ensuring that any response to the text involves the reader in remodelling the information.

(Cremin 2009: 132)

Using everyday texts

Although books of lesson plans and texts for use in literacy lessons are available, it is important that the texts used in the classroom are, wherever possible, real texts of the type children might meet in everyday life. Teachers should make collections of suitable texts; these might include timetables, advertisements, television programme listings, information leaflets, programmes for plays or sports events, tickets, letters, forms, lists and notices. Such texts make good starting points for discussions about textual style, vocabulary and presentation.

Another excellent resource is newspapers. Although a variety should be available, teachers may wish to consider the contents carefully before making some of the national tabloids available in the classroom. Local papers tend to have the advantage that they are generally well written and their style tends to be accessible for able readers at Key Stage 2, with fewer examples of esoteric phrasing and hyperbole than many national papers. In addition, their contents are related to the children's local area. Within newspapers there are examples of a range of non-fiction genres, including the following (see below for more detailed explanations):

■   discussion (articles that examine different sides of arguments);

■   persuasion (editorials and advertisements);

■   instructions (recipes);

■   explanation (articles that give information about, say, another country);

■   recount (accounts of an event).

A display of the anatomy of a newspaper with extracts enlarged for easy reading can form a useful interactive resource that groups of children may work on independently or as part of guided work. A natural progression from reading newspapers is for children to produce their own. There are several computer programs that can enable them to produce text with a professional appearance and these can not only be printed for distribution but also be sent to readers as email attachments. This is a particularly good idea where a class has a partner school, perhaps in another country.

Genres of texts

The range of texts that children should work with as part of the Revised Framework for Literacy (DfES 2006b) is wide and reflects the kinds of texts that adults meet in everyday life. Six main non-fiction text types are set out below (based upon descriptions in the National Strategies (DfES 2008) *Support for Writing*).

Recount texts

Purpose: to retell events for information or entertainment. Text structure:

■   orientation – scene setting, opening;

■   events – recount the events as they occurred;

■   reorientation – a closing statement.

Language features:

■   written in the past tense;

■   in chronological order.

Example: a biography of William Wilberforce.

Instruction or procedural texts

Purpose: to instruct on how something should be done through a series of graded steps. Text structure:

■   goal – a statement of what is to be achieved;

■   materials/equipment needed;

- sequenced steps to achieve the goal;
- often a diagram or illustration.

Language features:

- written in the imperative (e.g. 'mix the ingredients');
- in chronological order;
- impersonal rather than named individuals.

Example: a recipe for a cake.

Report texts

Purpose: to describe the way things are. Text structure:

- an opening, general classification;
- more-technical information;
- a description of the phenomenon.

Language features:

- present tense;
- non-chronological;
- focus on generic participants (e.g. sparrows in general).

Example: a report on Victorian schooling.

Explanation texts

Purpose: to explain the processes involved in natural or social phenomena or to explain how something works. Text structure:

- a general statement to introduce the topic;
- a series of logical steps explaining how or why something occurs;
- these steps continue until the final state is produced and the explanation is complete.

Language features:

- simple present tense;
- uses time connectives (e.g. 'then', 'next');
- uses causal connectives (e.g. 'because', 'so').

Example: an explanation of the rain cycle.

Persuasion texts

Purpose: to argue the case for a point of view. Text structure:

- thesis – an opening statement (e.g. 'vegetables are good for you');
- arguments – often in the form of elaboration;
- reiteration – summary and restatement of opening position.

Language features:

- simple present tense;
- focus mainly on generic participants;
- mainly logical rather than time connectives (e.g. 'this shows', 'however', 'because').

Example: an essay on why we should recycle waste.

Discussion texts

Purpose: to present arguments and information from differing viewpoints. Text structure:

- statement of the issue – a preview of the main argument;
- arguments for and supporting evidence;
- arguments against and supporting evidence;
- recommendation – summary and conclusion.

Language features:

- simple present tense;
- generic participants;
- logical connectives (e.g. 'therefore', 'however').

Example: a discussion of the arguments for and against building a new bypass.

ACTIVITY: USING DIFFERENT TEXT TYPES

If they are to develop an understanding of these text types, children will need to explore them through shared reading and writing, and will also require strategies for reading them and extracting information. Look at the different text types described above and try to think of examples of writing that you have used or seen used in the classroom for each one.

Reading and interacting with texts

Finding information and making notes

With computers available in virtually every primary classroom, children do not necessarily need to make notes by hand when reading texts. They might, for example, use highlighting or cut and paste to select key words or phrases. However, they will still need strategies for selecting relevant information. Teacher modelling can help them to see how skilled readers skim texts for key words or key information, for example by looking down a timetable to find a particular train or bus, looking at television listings for a programme or using an alphabetical list such as an index to find a word. If the teacher models these strategies and talks about them, drawing the children into discussions about techniques, this will demonstrate to the children ways in which they may work independently.

Another approach is to preview a text, gaining an overview by looking at pictures, charts, maps, headings and subheadings. This alerts the children to prior knowledge and provides a 'big picture' that enables them to put details into context.

Note-making can be seen as part of the drafting process, which is now well developed in many schools. Although children should be encouraged to be accurate, they should also realise that notes do not have to be written in 'best writing', as their purpose is to inform future writing and they are not an end in themselves.

Children should be encouraged to discuss their notes with others as well as cooperating in research. For example, a group of children might be given the task of finding out about early flying machines. They could first determine what they already know and identify questions that they would like to answer. They could then discuss where the relevant information might be found and divide up the task of reading about the subject. A wall display showing different parts of books and their functions (title page, contents page, index, etc.) would be a useful reference point. Information can be presented to the rest of the class in a variety of forms, including:

- telling or taping;
- radio or television presentations;
- newspaper articles;
- posters and brochures;
- plays;
- charts and diagrams;
- booklets and books;
- instructions and/or question sheets for others;
- letters.

Library skills

Many schools organise libraries along Dewey lines so that children see a progression from primary-school library use to the use of public libraries and those in secondary schools. Whichever method is used to organise books, children need to be shown how it works and there should be discussion about the probable location of books on different subjects. Children will need to learn how to use the alphabet to help in their research and should be shown as soon as possible how to find subjects by using their second, third or even fourth letters.

Gaining access to non-fiction texts

Inevitably, some children will experience problems when working with non-fiction texts, particularly if their previous reading experiences have revolved mainly around narrative texts. Key questions can be asked about the text and strategies devised that will help children to gain access to texts. Four questions about texts that children find difficult are suggested in a core position paper (DfES 2006c: 39):

- Is it too dense?
- Are there too many unknown or difficult words?
- Is the author's style accessible?
- Is the genre familiar?

We have used these questions to offer suggestions for strategies to support children.

Is it too dense?

A lot of information may be presented in a short piece of text and it can be difficult for readers to extract key points or even to know what to look for. Supportive strategies could include:

- discussing the subject with the children before they look at the text;
- asking them to think of questions they would like to answer by reading it;
- discussing what they already know about the topic;
- talking about the way in which the text is set out, including the use of maps, charts and pictures;
- encouraging children to survey the text before attempting to read it in detail, to see what it might be about and to look for some of the items discussed previously.

Are there too many unknown or difficult words?

Information texts often contain unfamiliar vocabulary, which can frustrate children as they attempt to read and extract information. Before reading, teachers might

- produce a word bank, discuss it with the children and display it;
- ask more able children to partner others to turn the word bank into a glossary;
- encourage the children to read on beyond any difficult words and then use the context to try to work out what the words might mean.

Is the author's style accessible?

Often non-fiction books may appear attractive and well presented but a closer look reveals that the authors may know more about their subjects than they do about presenting information in an accessible way. If we use information texts that are not written specifically for children, the problem inevitably increases. Before reading such texts:

- read the text aloud to the children;
- work with the children in shared writing to produce non-fiction text and to discuss phrasing and style;
- spend time talking about layout;

- use shared reading to show how headings and subheadings can be used to guide readers to what they want to find out;
- discuss key words that often feature in non-fiction but that may be unfamiliar, such as 'however' and 'therefore'.

Is the genre familiar?

It is not only authors' styles that may challenge children but also the nature of the genre they are reading. Many non-fiction texts are written in the present tense, yet stories are written in the past. Often styles change within a text, with information being presented in prose and then in charts or in lists, or sections being presented in a different genre, such as instructional (this is a feature of this chapter, with bullet points beginning with imperative verbs).

Supporting children when using non-fiction texts

Strategies could include the following:

- Ensure that they often read a variety of genres in shared reading.
- Display a range of genres in the classroom.
- Use a highlighter and an overhead projector or whiteboard to show children how key points can be identified and used as signposts for re-presenting information.
- Make use of graphic organisers to present information extracted from texts and work with children to show them examples. For example, they might use a Venn diagram with two overlapping circles to present information about two contrasting environments, with the area of overlap representing similarities. A web chart or spider chart can be used to identify key points about a topic, with further information placed around each point. This also helps children to plan for writing about a topic and enables them to divide up the task between them.

Readers need to understand, above all, that non-fiction texts are usually read in a quite different way from narratives, which are read from beginning to end. Often, we skim non-fiction texts for information or use reference devices such as contents pages or an index to find what we want to know. We often refer to the same book many times over a long period without ever reading it from cover to cover. If children are to develop the ability to use non-fiction texts effectively, they will need to have lots of opportunity to see a range of genres and discuss their features, as well as to develop the ability to use their knowledge of alphabetical order and reference devices to locate information quickly.

Literacy lessons should be opportunities to talk about the features of non-fiction texts and the ways in which they differ from fiction and poetry texts. The following sections explore some activities that could be used in the classroom with different year groups, either as part of literacy hours or as part of cross-curricular work focused upon non-fiction texts.

Early Years Foundation Stage: activities in the classroom

At this stage, children will be curious about the world around them and may be unfamiliar with written texts. Some will have looked at books and may already be able to read, but for some school will be virtually the only place in which they have the opportunity to share texts. The Primary National Strategy (DfES 2006c: 23) states that most will learn 'how information can be found in non-fiction texts to answer questions about where, who, why and how'. Activities might focus on notices and signs around the classroom, with attention being drawn to those that will help them to find things or to know whose drawer is whose. They might be asked, in turn, to go and find notices, copies of which are held up by the teacher. This might be followed by a 'hunt for print' walk (see Jolliffe *et al.* 2005), in which they first read notices in the classroom and then go and look for some of them around the school with the help of the teacher or a classroom assistant. The activity can then lead to children attempting to write their own notices.

Lists are a key element of early reading and writing and might focus initially on children's names and then on items in the classroom. When non-fiction texts, particularly in big-book format, are shared, children might help the teacher to make a list of things they have learned or key points from the text. They may go on to write their own lists, using simple texts to find names of animals, types of transport and so on.

Year 1: activities in the classroom

In Year 1, children should begin to 'distinguish fiction and non-fiction texts and the different purposes for reading them' (DfES 2006c: 25), and should be familiar with the anatomy of a book. By using big books, teachers can draw attention to features such as blurbs, contents pages, indexes, titles, subtitles, authors and illustrators. Children can look at such features to help them to decide what a book might be about and whether it might contain the information they are looking for. The words 'fiction' and 'non-fiction' can be used and children can be shown examples of each to promote discussion about genres. There are many excellent non-fiction books available that possess all the features one would expect in textbooks written for adults.

Children can be shown different books on the same topic and this can lead to discussion about the level of detail provided, the different ways in which information is presented and the relative quality of the books. Children should be shown examples of charts, diagrams and illustrations as they learn about different ways of presenting information. Labelling activities may be differentiated so that all children are challenged, and children can go on to produce their own charts and diagrams. This work can be linked to other subjects, with geography work involving labelling maps and creating simple diagrams with lists of the features of contrasting environments. In history, children might sequence events using arrows, numbering or other devices. In converting lists and diagrams of sequential events into prose, children can be introduced to words such as 'first', 'then', 'next' and 'finally', which will also be useful to them in story-writing. For all of these activities, the provision of word banks will not only support the children but also offer opportunities for word-level study and the development of increased phonic knowledge.

Year 2: activities in the classroom

Although they may have used them in Year 1, children should be introduced, in greater depth, to ordered texts such as dictionaries, encyclopaedias, indexes, registers and glossaries as part of literacy work in Year 2. An understanding of alphabetical order will be vital and children can also be shown how to use the second and third (and so on) letters of words to place them in lists. Most children in Year 2 learn to 'explain organisational features of texts, including alphabetical order, layout, diagrams, captions, hyperlinks and bullet points' (DfES 2006c: 27).

Many of the concepts met in Year 1 should be revisited, with concepts such as fiction and non-fiction reinforced through discussion about different types of texts. Displays of a variety of texts will provide stimuli for discussion and for independent and group work.

Year 2 children should be working towards being able to make simple notes about the information they have discovered, perhaps noting in brackets the page of a book or the source where they found it.

Instructions and directions feature strongly in Year 2, so work on recipes and map work in which journeys are plotted between places can be useful. Instructions and directions should be part of shared writing, with children talking about the use of imperative (or 'bossy') verbs as well as 'left', 'right' and words that denote a sequence of events such as 'first', 'next', 'then' and 'finally'.

A class book on an historical or geographical topic might be produced, both as shared and independent writing, with children learning how to use captions, headings and subheadings. This might be produced electronically, using an interactive whiteboard or a word-processing or desktop publishing package. This can be linked to the children's work in ICT, with teachers modelling techniques such as importing pictures and diagrams and changing fonts and layout so that material is presented in an interesting way that will attract readers' attention.

Year 3: activities in the classroom

In Year 3, many children begin to read with some fluency and to enjoy finding books to read independently. They need to be made aware of the huge range of literature available to them and, perhaps, to be guided towards texts that they will find accessible but not frustrating so that they gain satisfaction from their reading. An exploration of their hobbies and interests could be a good starting point for putting together a display of books that can be discussed and be available for children to borrow. These might be divided into fiction and non-fiction or children could be given the task of sorting them into these two categories, drawing upon their growing understanding of different genres.

The concept of alphabetical order will need to be revisited and reinforced as children begin to make greater use of reference books. The classroom should have a plentiful supply of reference texts such as dictionaries, thesauruses, encyclopaedias, atlases and directories. It is important that the reference materials children encounter at this stage are attractive and stimulating. A greater understanding of reference texts will be gained if children also have the experience of creating their own as a shared writing activity. A glossary of key terms for a topic could be a starting point, with children looking at examples of glossaries and dictionary definitions in shared reading before producing their own. More-able children might look at a range of definitions of the same word or term in a variety of sources before agreeing upon their own version.

Reading aloud by the teacher should not be restricted to fiction but should include poetry and non-fiction. Extracts from different non-fiction texts can be read to children to whet their appetites for independent reading as well as to foster discussion of the differences between fiction and non-fiction. The extracts could also be displayed alongside complete copies of books so that children can try to identify which book which extract was taken from, using scanning to look at subject matter, style and presentation.

The texts that are discussed, even in the literacy hour, might include maps, diagrams, charts and lists. In looking at the place names on a map, children will need to work out how they might be pronounced, drawing upon their growing phonic knowledge. While most British towns and cities have names that are sufficiently phonically regular that children should be able to find a place after listening to an initial phoneme or cluster of phonemes, others with irregular pronunciations, such as Alnwick (pronounced 'Anik'), Belvoir ('Beaver'), Hawick ('Hoik') and Woolfardisworthy ('Woolsery'), can be used to provoke discussion. After all, many common children's names seem to defy common phonic knowledge (e.g. Chloe, Siobhan, Stephen, Thomas etc.), so encounters with other examples should not surprise them.

To emphasise the concepts of fact and fiction, children can be given statements and asked to find out whether they are true or false. The Primary National Strategy states that most Year 3 children should be able to 'identify and make notes of the main points of sections of text' and 'explain process or present information, ensuring that items are clearly sequenced, relevant details are included and accounts are ended effectively' (DfES 2006c: 28). Following are some examples of activities that provide opportunities for children to extract and present information.

Rainbowing

After working on a topic, each member of each group is allocated a number, letter or colour and then meets with all the others with the same number, letter or colour to share ideas and compare what each group discovered from their texts. Children are provided with a real audience for their speaking and will be able to listen and respond to a range of people. They will also be able to share ideas, insights and opinions.

Jigsawing

The class is organised into groups with each member of each group being given an aspect of the topic on which to become an expert. The experts from each group meet to share ideas and then report back to their groups. Many of the benefits that are derived from rainbowing may be found here, but children will also have the opportunity to show their own 'expertise' and to explore, develop and explain ideas. Simple computer databases can be devised so that children can develop skills in recording and research. One that records children's heights, weights and so forth and that may be amended throughout the year can provide a good starting point.

Character quiz

Children might write statements about an historical character, based upon research from the internet, and then display or read the statements and ask the rest of the class to try to identify the characters.

Fact or fiction?

Reference books and the internet might be used to produce statements that may or may not be true. Others have to conduct their own research to check the veracity of the statements.

Initially, teachers may wish to provide some statements and ask the whole class or group to check their veracity. This could be a useful guided reading activity, focused on locating information, for a group of children.

Dictionaries and thesauruses

Dictionaries should be appropriate for pupils but there should always be a large and more comprehensive version available for looking up words that do not feature in children's dictionaries. If they are to be able to use reference books successfully and without frustration, it is important that children understand alphabetical order as early as possible.

Literacy-hour activities on non-fiction should focus on making notes, recording information, identifying key words, locating information from different sources and presenting it using devices such as flow charts. Make use of information technology to enable children to 'publish' their work.

Year 4: activities in the classroom

Most children in Year 4 will, according to the Primary National Strategy, 'learn to use knowledge of different organisational features of texts to find information effectively' and will be able to 'Summarise and shape material and ideas from different sources to write convincing and informative non-narrative texts' (DfES 2006c: 30). Children's interests and hobbies can provide useful starting points for developing their reference skills if books for the classroom are chosen carefully. Such texts should include features such as contents pages, indexes, glossaries, maps, charts, illustrations and diagrams.

Children should be able to 'offer reasons and evidence for their views, considering alternative opinions' (DfES 2006c: 30). They may, for example, be asked to work with others to identify key points from an historical story and then dramatise the story and perform it for the rest of the class. The different versions could be compared with those of other groups and children could be asked to explain their interpretations.

Following are some examples of activities suitable for Year 4 children.

Persuasive writing

In order to see the power of writing as a tool for persuasion, children might look at a range of advertisements, noting the kinds of words used, the presentation (including varied font sizes), illustrations and the use of adjectives and adverbs. A real writing activity could follow, with children preparing advertisements for school events such as sports fixtures, class assemblies, plays, fetes or fairs. Children should be encouraged to plan and discuss their advertisements, working in small groups to determine font sizes, vocabulary choices, illustrations and so on. The computer might be used to enable them to import pictures and make use of colour and varied fonts.

Wray (1995: 76–7) provides an example of the way in which the same event can be interpreted differently by different authors, and such examples might be used to show children how their use of language can be important in the way they provide messages to their readers. Children could compare reports on the same event from different newspapers before producing their own reports, either written or presented as television or radio news items. A class newspaper could then be produced using a desktop publishing package.

Historical artefacts may be used as an alternative to texts and as a stimulus to using texts to find out information about the artefacts. Children might make notes about the item's appearance, smell and feel, before turning their notes into a presentation, perhaps using Powerpoint. This can lead to discussions about descriptions, presentation and interpretation, with other children being asked to research the artefacts to find out more about them.

In Year 4, children will 'organise text into paragraphs to distinguish between different information, events or processes' (DfES 2006c: 31), and so will need to explore and discuss ways in which texts are organised. Follow-up activities might include writing sections of a textbook as part of a group, with the authors of each section then having a real incentive to read other people's work in order to avoid repetition and ensure comprehensive coverage of issues.

Educational visits

Educational visits, which may range from short walks in the school's locality to residential trips, offer a rich source of material to stimulate both reading and writing. Children might prepare for a journey by looking at atlases, road maps and websites such as Multimap to find out possible routes, and they could go on to use Google or a similar search engine to find out about some of the places they will pass through as well as those they will visit. They may produce an itinerary for the journey and perhaps create a sheet of 'Things to look out for' for classmates. Reports about the visit need not necessarily be set out in prose form and could involve lists, diagrams or charts. For example, if they visit a factory or an industrial museum, they could record the production processes using flow charts, while a visit to a supermarket could be recorded on a floor plan with brief descriptions of places of particular interest. For all visits, the provision of information in advance will help alert children to what they might see as well as to aspects that may be of particular interest.

Year 5: activities in the classroom

In Year 5, most children learn to 'make notes on and use evidence from across a text to explain events or ideas' and to 'compare different types of narrative and information texts and identify how they are structured' (DfES 2006c: 32). The range of material that children have the opportunity to read should be wide, and they should be introduced to texts that are not necessarily written for children, such as newspapers and reference books. They may also make use of the internet to seek out information or may be given access to CD-ROMs that feature databases and encyclopaedias.

Following are some examples of activities suitable for Year 5 children.

Historical events

In order to gain a strong insight into the sequence of events that led to a particular conclusion, children might make use of their reading and research to re-enact historical events to perform for classmates. Their interpretations can then be discussed and this may lead to revisions and additions. In working in this way, children tend to retain a knowledge of events and this is helpful if they go on to write about them. It also opens up their interpretations to a wider audience and encourages the sharing of ideas and knowledge.

A range of texts

In order to help children acquire the ability to compare texts and to understand the different ways in which they are structured, teachers need to provide a range of materials including reference books, catalogues, timetables, newspapers, magazines, programmes for sports or drama events, brochures, pamphlets and printouts of computer texts, as well as access to CD-ROMs and the internet. Besides comparing and contrasting different text types, children might also look at different versions of the same text types, perhaps examining timetables to determine which are the most user-friendly or comparing pamphlets from tourist information offices to decide which present places most appealingly. The logical progression from such activities is for children to produce their own texts, often using computers to produce attractive and professional-looking work.

Gift shopping

Catalogue shops, which can be found in most towns and cities, usually provide customers with free catalogues, which can be a rich source of material for literacy development. Activities might begin with work on alphabetical order, with children using the index to find different items, and dictionaries to find alternative names for items that do not appear to be listed. For example, they might discover that 'spoons' would be found under 'cutlery' and 'plates' under 'crockery'.

A further activity could be linked to mathematics, with children being given an (imaginary) amount of money to spend on gifts and being challenged to spend as much of it as possible without exceeding their budget. In attempting this, they would need to use reference skills, read descriptions of items, make choices and record them, as well as doing a lot of addition and subtraction.

Information skills

Central to children's development of research skills is a sound understanding of alphabetical order. Without this, searching for information becomes a tedious or random activity. Besides singing the alphabet to help them memorise it, children should be given lots of opportunities to study alphabetical texts. These could include pages from dictionaries, which can be enlarged using a projector. In looking at a single page, children will see that words that begin with the same letter are arranged according to their second, third and fourth letters (and so on). Children can also be shown other features of dictionaries; for example:

- the first and last word on each page is usually printed at the top of the page to enable easy reference;
- phonetic spellings are given to aid pronunciation;
- plurals and adaptations into different parts of speech are provided;
- alternative definitions are given.

They might go on to look at examples of different dictionaries, ranging from simple picture dictionaries to adult dictionaries and dictionaries related to particular topics. Comparisons between presentations could be made, and they could look up the same word in each dictionary to see how it is defined at different levels.

The class could go on to make its own dictionary, drawing upon definitions from a range of published works. This could be a wall dictionary, with each word presented on a separate piece of paper and arranged in alphabetical order. As words are added, children will need to place them correctly and this will reinforce their understanding of alphabetical order. A light-hearted stimulus for this could be showing children an excerpt from *Blackadder the Third* in which Baldrick accidentally burns Samuel Johnson's dictionary and he, Blackadder and the Prince Regent set about making a replacement. A further activity could revolve around definitions (perhaps not Baldrick's 'big wobbly thing with fish in it' for sea!), with children taking turns to give the definition of a word and its initial letter or letters and asking others to use dictionaries to find the mystery words; for example, 'It begins with E-L and means "first born", what is it?'

Reorganising text

A piece of information text can be divided into paragraphs or sentences and cut up for children to work in pairs or small groups to organise it logically. They will need to discuss the concepts of introduction and conclusion and use semantic skills to determine an appropriate order. In addition, they will need to look for words that provide clues about the order, such as 'finally', 'secondly' and 'however'.

Diagrams and charts

Examples of diagrams and charts from newspapers and magazines can be displayed to stimulate discussion about various forms of presentation, and so that children have models for producing their own diagrams and charts.

Encouraging close reading

Children can be given pieces of text to read as the teacher reads the same text but with errors and amendments. As they listen to the teacher reading the text, they should mark the places where the teacher's version differs from theirs. This encourages both careful listening and close reading. A possible activity is to include several antonyms (e.g. 'irregular' instead of 'regular', 'possible' instead of 'impossible', 'mistrust' instead of 'trust'). This can lead to discussion about the ways in which prefixes can be used to modify words and to change their meanings – for Year 5, the Primary National Strategy states that most children learn 'less common prefixes and suffixes such as im-, ir, and -cian' (DfES 2006b).

Cloze work

Cloze work involves removing words from text and replacing them with lines, and asking children to read the text and use semantic and syntactic clues to decide the most appropriate words to fill the gaps. Words might be removed at regular intervals, such as every tenth word, or particular parts of speech such as nouns, verbs or adjectives might be removed. The best cloze exercises do not have only one possible solution for each missing word, as these provoke discussion and debate and allow children to interpret and justify choices.

Posing questions

Rather than being asked questions by the teacher when they have read a piece of information text, children might write their own questions for the teacher and others to answer. They should be encouraged to think of both closed and open questions, with some requiring simple factual answers and others demanding inference and interpretation.

Year 6: activities in the classroom

Children should, at this stage, be able to 'appraise a text quickly, deciding on its value, quality or usefulness' (DfES 2006c: 34) and be able to skim and scan to seek out key points or particular details. Activities should be challenging, purposeful and related, wherever possible, to the world outside school. Year 6 children are likely to 'participate in whole-class debate' (DfES 2006c: 34) too, and this section includes a focus on different types of texts including those that might promote discussion and debate while encouraging children to 'recognise rhetorical devices used to argue, persuade, mislead and sway the reader' (DfES 2006c: 34).

Following are some examples of activities suitable for Year 6 children.

Environmental issues

This activity might be linked to work on 'The town' described in Chapter 11 (on developing writing). A map of the locality or of an imaginary area could be the initial text, with children being told about certain scenarios that have been chosen by you to fit in with issues of importance to the children. Perhaps a new bypass might be proposed and children have to discuss the best route or indeed whether the bypass is desirable at all. Alternatively, you could tell them exactly where the bypass is to be built and let them begin their discussions from that point. They might research bypasses and debates about their construction on the internet to find out typical arguments for and against. The work could be linked to other work in science on the protection of wildlife, as well as to geographical work on land features.

A debate or discussion could involve children taking on different roles, with some being planners and builders who have an interest in ensuring the bypass is built; some being local councillors in favour of the bypass or opposed to it; some being local residents; and someone, perhaps the teacher, acting as chairperson of an inquiry into whether the bypass is needed and where it should go.

In preparation for the debate, children should be encouraged to research carefully and be able to justify their views. It may be a good idea to 'plant' some key questions or issues by asking some children to focus on these. For example, someone may be a shop owner who is concerned that the bypass will take away trade from her shop because there will be fewer passing cars, while someone else may be a parent concerned about road safety who feels the bypass will make the town's roads safer for his children. Ideally, the debate will be based upon a real local issue, but in any case it may provide an opportunity to invite in a local councillor so that children can ask questions and find out more about how such issues are decided.

The debate might take place over several days and children could prepare campaign literature, write letters to a class newspaper and even record a phone-in to their own 'radio station', which could be played as part of an assembly.

Reference area

A Year 6 class reference area will include encyclopaedias, atlases, spelling dictionaries and timetables for local transport services and for school. Other information sources might be changed regularly to take into account the particular topic that the class is studying or to reflect children's interests. Timetables of television programmes as provided in Sunday colour supplements of newspapers such as the *Observer* and *The Independent on Sunday* or the television guides provided by the *Telegraph* and *Guardian* on Saturdays could be included, and children could use these as a starting point for writing their own synopses of programmes and films they have watched. They might use sources such as *Halliwell's Film Guide* to find out more about programmes. Since many newspaper television reviewers make extensive use of film guides when describing films, this could lead to discussion about précis and paraphrasing. Children may also discover similarities between comments about films in different newspapers, since many of these are provided by the Press Agency and are sold to newspapers.

Sports fixture lists and league tables for football teams including (if one exists) the school team can arouse a great deal of interest, as can soccer reference books such as *The Rothmans Book of Football* or the much cheaper *Playfair Football Annual*. Similar reference sources for other sports, including cricket, rugby, athletics, tennis and American Football, can be found, often in discount bookshops. *The Virgin Book of British Hit Singles*, which details all records that have appeared in the top-seventy-five best-sellers list since the inception of the charts, offers lots of scope for developing reference skills, and children may be interested to find how many of their current favourites were first recorded when their teachers were children! Ideally, a computer will be available as an additional source of information and a tool for recording findings.

If children are given 'ownership' of the reference area, with opportunities to add their own texts, write texts and display them, as well as to make extensive use of the area, this will add status to the use of reference sources and will make using them a natural part of school life. Visits to local libraries can show children how reference sources can be organised and displayed and may introduce them to types of texts they have not previously encountered.

Précis

If children are to produce class newspapers that offer limited space for reports, they will need to develop the art of writing concisely. A task that can help them to develop this ability might use, as a starting point, a story, newspaper article or a section from a text book. Set the children a target of, say, 100 words and ask them to rewrite the passage using exactly that number. Encourage them to think carefully about unnecessary words and about choosing phrasing that is economical with words without destroying the message. They might also discover that they are a few words short and so have the opportunity to add more description or make use of some words that are often superfluous such as 'got', or 'in spite of' instead of 'despite' (see Chapter 5, 'Knowledge about language', for more examples).

Desert Island Discs

This popular BBC Radio 4 programme has been running since 1942 and involves celebrities being interviewed about their lives and choosing eight pieces of music, a luxury and a book they would take with them if they were to be marooned on a desert island. Children can draw upon their research skills and knowledge of music and literature to write about their own choices, with some being recorded or performed for the class. They would need to explain the reasons for their choices and perhaps how particular pieces of music remind them of events from their lives. This could be linked to the following activity on 'Memories'.

Memories

Year 6 is usually the children's final year before transferring to secondary school. They might be asked to write about their school careers so far, including their happiest day, school trips, plays, assemblies, sports matches and people who have left an impression on them. Examples of autobiographies and memoirs could be read or shown to children and they might listen to an edition of *Desert Island Discs* or watch *This is Your Life*. The final versions of the children's memories could be produced as books, including photographs, and might be printed as treasured souvenirs of the children's primary education and early childhood. An end-of-year presentation to the rest of the school and to parents could allow them to share these memories and may enable them to end their primary-school education on a high note by demonstrating many of the skills and abilities they have acquired.

The wider curriculum

The Primary National Strategy makes demands upon teachers and pupils that will require close scrutiny of the whole curriculum, as well as that for English. There is a natural link with subjects such as history and geography, given the emphasis on non-fiction texts throughout the strategy.

Texts from across the curriculum can be used to provide the range of literature that is demanded by the National Literacy Strategy and teachers can use these to model approaches to non-fiction. Children's understanding of devices such as captions, labels, headings, subheadings, indexes, contents pages, charts and diagrams should no longer be left to chance, but should be developed explicitly through direct teaching and through children's own writing.

ACTIVITY: DEVELOPING CHILDREN'S USE OF NON-FICTION TEXTS

Consider your responses to each of the following questions:

- What do you consider to be essential features of a Key Stage 1 classroom in which children are able to develop their understanding of non-fiction texts?
- What do you consider to be essential features of a Key Stage 2 classroom in which children are able to develop their understanding of non-fiction texts?
- How can computers be used effectively to promote reading for information?
- Which factors will teachers need to take into account when planning for children to use computers to find information?

Key points

- Children need to encounter a range of different types of non-fiction texts and develop strategies for extracting information from them.
- There are many simple classroom activities that can help children to engage with texts in stimulating and interesting ways.
- Classrooms should be well stocked with all kinds of reference materials and children should be guided in the use of these materials.

Further reading

Canada Council on Learning (2009) *Why Boys Don't Like to Read: gender differences in reading achievement* (www.ccl-cca.ca/pdfs/LessonsInLearning/02_18_09-E.pdf).
Cremin, T. (2009) *Teaching English Creatively.* London: Routledge.
Wray, D. (2006) *Teaching Literacy across the Primary Curriculum.* Exeter: Learning Matters (chapters 4 and 5).

Resources for teaching

Head, C. and Waugh, D. (2007) *50 Shared Non-fiction Texts for Year 1.* Leamington Spa: Scholastic.
Jolliffe, W., Head, C. and Waugh, D. (2004) *50 Shared Texts for Year 1.* Leamington Spa: Scholastic.
Jolliffe, W., Waugh, D. and Taylor, K. (2005) *All New 100 Literacy Hours, Year R.* Leamington Spa: Scholastic.

10

Learning and teaching in a multilingual classroom

Claire Head

Purpose of this chapter

This chapter aims to:

- differentiate terminology and discuss the problems of pupils for whom English is an additional language;
- show the important role that language plays in children's lives at home and at school;
- describe how teachers can create a multilingual literacy environment and use this as the springboard for learning and teaching;
- provide a range of teaching strategies that can be employed to support learning across the curriculum.

This chapter will discuss how teachers can support pupils who are in the process of learning English as an additional language (EAL). Language is intrinsically linked to a person's sense of home, culture and self-esteem and it should be valued and respected. Pupils who are new to English will encounter some difficulties in school settings but teachers can adopt a range of effective strategies that will help to positively engage all pupils in active learning.

> Language makes accessible culture, culture includes the bilingual pupils' experience, and experience shapes knowledge … if teaching strategies encourage, value and support the use of bilingual pupils' home language, the children are more likely to share their language and culture freely without feeling that they are the centre of attention.
>
> (Blackledge 1994: 58; see also Devereux and Miller 2003: 74)

By taking a broad and flexible approach to 'literacy' in the classroom, teachers can extend and enhance children's understanding of the role language plays at home, at school and in the wider world. This chapter explores how teachers can ensure that bilingual learners have access to the whole curriculum by building on their existing linguistic skills and by using a range of practical strategies that will help children to improve their knowledge about language in meaningful contexts.

Approximately one million pupils, more than 10 per cent of the UK school population, speak English as an additional language (School Census, January 2011). Over 300 languages are spoken in UK schools by pupils who are in various stages of adding English to their language repertoire. Inevitably, most teachers will work alongside some of these children at some point in their career. Remembering that language is acquired by interaction is the first step teachers must make in preparing to meet pupils' specific individual needs.

Terminology

This section explains several terms.

Bilingual

Pupils who are bilingual can function in two languages. This ability positively enhances cognitive development and bilingual speakers are able to switch back and forth between two languages (some more competently than others). Some teachers feel that the term 'bilingual' can be misleading as it does not indicate the help that children who are learning a new language alongside their first language will inevitably need. Gregory (1997: 8) suggests a more appropriate term for these children is 'emergent bilinguals'.

Multilingual

This term describes people who are able to converse in and control three or more languages (there is controversy regarding how proficiently 'multilingual' people should be able to do this).

English as a second language

This is not an accurate term because for many children English is the third or fourth language they are becoming familiar with. Some children speak one language at home, a different language with their grandparents and another language to teachers at school.

English as an additional language

This term is used to describe children who are in the process of learning English on entry to school. It implies that children are learning English in addition to their existing linguistic skills. This is the terminology used most frequently in Literacy Strategy publications, although some educators feel that 'EAL learners' implies that these children have a weakness to surmount. They argue that 'bilingual' learners is a much more positive term for children who are developing new language skills by building on existing strengths (Brent Language Service 2002).

Mother tongue

This term describes the language most commonly used in a child's home. It is also referred to as a child's 'home language' or 'first language'.

Supporting minority-language pupils

The difficulties children encounter when learning a new language, especially when that language is the main language of instruction in the classroom, must not be underestimated or ignored by teachers, but that does not mean that these pupils have learning difficulties. Assessment in the child's home language should access prior learning and check whether the child has any special educational needs. Pupils often understand and know much more than they are able to express in a new language. Teachers should view a child's multilingual or bilingual talents as an asset in the classroom: it is often the monolingual teacher who faces the challenge!

Jim Cummins' (1996) theoretical framework for minority student intervention and empowerment suggests that minority-language pupils are 'empowered' or 'disabled' by four characteristics of schools:

- *The extent to which a child's home language and culture is incorporated into the school curriculum*: do children feel their home culture is valued or rejected? Schools may celebrate different festivals and consequently demonstrate knowledge about these beliefs and respect for them. Faith assemblies may be lead by religious leaders from the local community who work in partnership with the school. Successful schools create a curriculum that values and reflects pupils' identities and cultures.

- *Community participation*: how are children's parents and extended families encouraged to participate in their child's education (e.g. family literacy programmes, book fairs, library visits, help with translating)?

- *Encouraging children to become active seekers of knowledge*: use of interactive teaching strategies such as reciprocal teaching with bilingual support teachers.

- *Assessment and diagnosis*: with a view to evaluating how the curriculum can best serve the child, rather than focusing on how the child can fit in with the system. It is important to consider work from across the whole curriculum when assessing language competence. In order to raise standards of achievement levels for minority ethnic groups, it is essential for schools to use assessment data to proactively target specific groups and individuals.

Ofsted (1999) evidence indicates that the following ethnic groups consistently underachieve compared to their white British counterparts: Bangladeshi, Pakistani, Gypsy/Roma children and Travellers of Irish Heritage pupils, and African Caribbean boys. Strong leadership from head teachers to raise awareness about equal opportunities is crucial (TTA 2000).

Schools need to develop policies and whole-school approaches that cultivate these empowering characteristics in order to nurture the development of all their pupils and to celebrate linguistic and cultural diversity.

Bilingualism as an aid to children's learning

The Welsh Language Board (1999) advertises the benefits of bilingualism in education in their pamphlet for parents entitled *Two Languages: twice the choice* (cited in Kenner 2000: 15). They argue that some of the positive skills bilingual learners develop include:

- more-creative and flexible thinking;
- increased curricular achievement;
- ease in learning a third language;
- twice the enjoyment of reading and writing;
- access to two cultures and worlds of experience;
- enhanced economic and employment benefits.

Researchers such as Charmian Kenner (2000) and Jim Cummins (1996) argue that children's self-esteem can be positively developed if their home language, which is part of their cultural identity, is valued and welcomed in the classroom. This means allowing children to actively engage with their home language and English as part of everyday teaching and learning in school. Activating children's prior knowledge about language is the first step in creating a learning environment that fosters a positive curiosity in all pupils about language and how it can be used to enrich our lives.

Studies that compare approaches to the education of bilingual children highlight the importance of allowing children to learn a new language alongside their home language, integrating the two. Thomas and Collier (1997, cited in Edwards 1998) investigated the impact that different intervention programmes had on a large number of children who started primary school with little or no English. The aim of the study was to compare children who attended two-way bilingual programmes, where they studied both English and their home language in equal proportions, with children who were withdrawn from some lessons to devote more time to focusing exclusively on the sounds and structures of English in special classes for learners of a second language. Research findings indicated that there was little difference in the academic performance of children in these two groups by the end of Key Stage 1; however, results in the next four years showed that the children in the two-way language programme consistently performed better than the 'withdrawal' group and attained a higher level compared to the level achieved by average monolingual English speakers. This evidence supports an approach to teaching and learning that advocates drawing upon what children already know about language to help them in their acquisition of another language.

Theories surrounding the process of second-language acquisition highlight the following common principles that teachers need to build on in their classrooms (modified from Gravelle 2000: 4):

- Second-language acquisition is based on and impelled by a desire to communicate.
- Second-language learners must be treated as communicators from the start.
- The emphasis should be on meaning rather than form.
- Language learning takes place with and through other learning.
- Language learning requires models of natural speech in a range of normal settings.
- Language learning is extended and developed through exposure to a range of environments and language models.
- Language learning is a creative process that involves making errors and formulating rules.
- Language learning is a risk-taking process so a supportive environment is important.
- Language learning is not a linear process.

- Experience of listening is part of language learning.
- Bilingual learners already have at least one other language to build on.

Pupils for whom English is an additional language have particular language and learning needs that must be taken into account if the literacy development of these pupils is to be effectively supported. How can teachers ensure that their planning is effective for all pupils – including those children who have differing and continually changing needs? The best starting place is to find out as much as possible about each child's home language and culture.

Finding out about home literacy

Teachers need to acknowledge and value each child's home language as this is essentially tied up with who that child is and who he/she has the potential to become. The suggestions summarised below are based on research conducted in a South London nursery class by Charmian Kenner (2000).

- If possible, enlist the help of bilingual teachers or assistants and home–school liaison officers who have knowledge about the local community.
- Display multilingual 'welcome' posters around the school to signal to parents your appreciation and recognition of the different languages that are part of the community. This can act as the starting point for further communication with parents or carers.
- Communicate your interest in children's literacy at home by asking parents about bilingual literacy activities, such as videos, television stations, tapes, books and magazines. Ask parents whether children can bring some of these into school so you can talk about them with their child and the rest of the class (e.g. a Gujarati newspaper, a Chinese calendar, an Arabic alphabet chart). Inclusion of these materials as part of the classroom environment may encourage parents and children to enter into a dialogue with you about family literacy at home. This will be a useful springboard from which you can continue discussions during parent–teacher conferences.
- Listen to the children in your class as they interact with the home literacy resources in different areas of the classroom. Children may explain to their friends how their family uses specific items.
- Take time to build up your relationships with parents and children – you are not checking up on the sorts of books children read at home or whether children practise their handwriting. You are demonstrating a genuine interest in what children already know about language so that you can celebrate and build on this experience, with the help of parents, in school.

Language surveys

One of the ways that teachers can find out about the linguistic diversity in their class and demonstrate that they are interested in their pupils' culture and language skills is by conducting a language survey. Ideally this should be a whole-school survey so that teachers can collate information that will help them to meet the needs of all pupils, for example by structuring learning groups, informing planning, devising assessment tasks, recruiting bilingual support staff or organising family literacy activities and parents' meetings.

The following questions were devised by a group of Year 4 pupils from Larkrise First School, Oxford:

- Which languages do you speak?
- Do you know quite a lot of that language?
- Which country does that language come from?
- Which language do you speak at home?
- Which language do you speak the most?

(Edwards 1998: 12)

Teachers can use a simple set of questions like this to interview each child in their class at the start of the academic year. Questions should be adapted to suit different age groups and may need translating into the child's home language.

Children who are new to English

Some of the children who are new to English may also be new to the UK. Children who are refugees or asylum seekers could also be suffering from the trauma of having to leave their familiar home and belongings and may also have been separated from members of their family. A new school is a bewildering environment for these children and their emotional needs must be taken into account as class teachers help them to settle in to a new life. Some of these children may encounter 'culture shock' (Cohen-Emerique 1999; see also Baldock 2010) as they try to navigate their way through personal interactions in unfamiliar circumstances, surrounded by new customs and different social perspectives. It is important that teachers and fellow classmates attempt to develop 'intercultural competence' by remembering that 'If the other person is different, I am different for the other person' (Baldock 2010: 45). Teachers can help these children to feel welcome and more confident in school by

- teaching them the names of key adults who can help them at school;
- taking them on a tour of the school and showing them how to get to the toilet, dinner hall and main entrance;
- spending some time in the classroom with pupils showing them where materials and books are kept;
- naming objects around the room (this could be done one playtime as it is less daunting for the child if he/she can spend a little time with the teacher without interruptions from other children in the class);
- helping the child to learn numbers, body parts, colours, clothes, shapes, days of the week and appropriate answers to simple questions (key words and 'survival' language);
- showing how to form the letters in his or her name.

It helps to involve other children in this process: you could develop a buddy system so that the child's peers can help by acting as mentors as well as friends. It is also important to establish a good relationship with the child's parents or carers so that you can reassure them about progress and begin to build links between home and school.

Links between home and school

Teachers and schools can create a positive, multicultural atmosphere that nurtures and values language and cultural diversity by

- translating literature that goes home for parents to read into their children's home languages (e.g. school booklets, letters, reading records);
- offering regular parents' meetings to keep parents informed and update them on new school initiatives (e.g. reading at home, preparation for assessment tasks);
- letting parents know that bilingual staff will be on hand to translate the information and to discuss issues with parents;
- learning how to greet parents in their home language;
- encouraging parents to explain concepts and themes to children in their home language.

Parents and carers and members of the local community can be encouraged to become part of school life by helping with many aspects of the curriculum. The following ideas can be put into practice with any age group:

- *translating*: labels, class books, making dual textbooks, instructions for games, children's stories, number lines for display;
- *storytelling*: telling stories to children, tape recording versions of stories in different languages, helping children to write stories in their home language;
- *cooking*: preparing food with children and talking about the ingredients and the process in their home language, naming fruit and vegetables in English and in the child's home language, finding out about food from different countries, visiting a greengrocer's and naming the foods on display (talk about the environmental print);
- *songs and rhymes*: teaching these to children in different languages and helping children to learn about different cultural traditions.

Creating a multilingual literacy environment

The learning environment that teachers create for children needs to stimulate and feed their interest in learning about literacy. The print that teachers surround their pupils with should reflect their own enthusiasm about language and how it can be used. It should also send a clear message to everyone about the value of reading and writing – in all its guises. When setting up your language-friendly classroom, try to do the following:

- Ensure reading areas contain dual-language texts.
- Include recorded stories, rhymes and songs in children's home languages in the listening corner.
- Display meaningful labels that the children have helped to make.

- Encourage children to use and take notice of a messages board: messages need to be relevant and real so that children recognise the vital importance of communicating in this way.

- Display writing in English and in children's home languages: this could include writing volunteered by family members.

- Encourage children to bring home literacy materials into school and display these carefully in the classroom.

- Support and encourage children's experiments with multilingual writing in the mark-making and role-play areas. Encourage Key Stage 2 children to write in their home language and talk about the composition and transcription of the piece with their peers.

- Seize opportunities to compare differences and similarities between languages, for example when reading a dual language text: this helps children to understand how writing works.

- Invite parents and carers into the classroom to look at how home literacy materials have been used and to show parents their children's writing.

- Display alphabets and scripts in the children's home languages.

Teaching strategies that foster successful learning

It should be remembered that there is no evidence that language is acquired just by listening; language is acquired by interaction with other language users in meaningful social contexts.

(Morris and Collins 2002: 4)

Teachers need to be reflective and to recognise that their own teaching styles can be varied and matched to the learning styles of the pupils in their care. When choosing resources, teachers must be sensitive to the cultural value systems that will affect children (e.g. 'The Three Little Pigs' would not be appropriate as a shared reading text for Muslim pupils as pigs are regarded as unclean by Muslims). Establishing a positive relationship between teachers and their pupils is the vital component of any successful learning environment. It is through this dynamic rapport that teachers can raise their pupils' self-esteem, which goes hand in hand with their ability to achieve. The teaching strategies outlined below are aimed at EAL learners but teachers will recognise that the 'good practice' described will enhance the quality of learning and teaching for all children.

- Teach children how to record their ideas and information in a range of ways (e.g. charts, drawings, diagrams).

- Try to include visual resources to explain new concepts and activities, such as story maps, mind webs and picture prompts (referred to as 'key visuals' by Brent Language Service 2002).

- Make good use of the pictures in big books by drawing children's attention to the image that matches the text and by asking children questions related to their own experience to establish meaningful contexts.

- Choose books that have predictable, repetitive texts with large pictures to model reading strategies to EAL learners. It is also helpful to use story props or sequencing pictures to help children retell familiar texts.

- If possible, plan shared delivery of whole-class activities through partnership teaching, in which a bilingual teacher and a monolingual teacher work together to introduce new concepts and activities (this sort of double act needs a little rehearsal to work effectively).

- Ensure you give the children opportunities (and time) for active listening.

- Provide scaffolded writing tasks: writing frames with visual prompts if possible (large versions of these need to be modelled before the children use them independently).

- Focus on, praise and reinforce children's growing ability to use language to communicate rather than being overly concerned with sentence construction, vocabulary choices and pronunciation until children grow in confidence.

- Encourage children to consult a bilingual dictionary, a thesaurus, glossaries and key-word lists.

- Allow plenty of time for repetition, revision and revisiting as children spiral through the curriculum and assimilate and accommodate new knowledge and skills.

- Ensure you allow children to engage in different learning styles and incorporate practical and manipulative tasks into lessons so that children do not become too tired through the constant challenge of working in words alone.

- Identify key vocabulary and the language challenges for the children involved in each lesson at the planning stage.

- Be aware of the complications caused by the use of figurative and idiomatic language and develop a range of strategies to tackle this with the children (e.g. 'rich scripting', 'shared imaging' and 'word-weaving' are excellent strategies devised by McWilliam 1998). (See explanations later in this section.)

- Plan activities that encourage peer interaction and collaborative learning (use cooperative learning techniques and activities that demand real communication, such as jigsaw exercises and barrier games).

- Place a special emphasis on speaking and listening and ensure this has been built into your planning for every activity.

- Look for opportunities to make cross-curricular links.

- Build in time for pre-tutoring and post-tutoring around the literacy hour: time for a teacher or bilingual support teacher to introduce a new text to give children a 'way in' to the lesson before shared reading begins, and, at the end of a lesson, time could be built in to talk to a bilingual child or a group about key points, to allow time to revisit and reflect, and to remedy misconceptions.

Language diversity across the curriculum

Topic work related to a particular theme can be the starting point for children (and their teachers) to learn about different languages and cultures. The following themes can act as the springboard for this type of valuable cross-curricular work:

- food;
- ourselves;
- celebrations;
- light;
- homes;
- weddings;
- communication;
- the history of writing;
- newspapers from around the world.

ACTIVITY: WORKING ON CROSS-CURRICULAR THEMES

- Work in pairs to brainstorm ideas about a cross-curricular theme.
- Identify activities that link to different curriculum areas and suggest an inspirational starting point to stimulate pupils' interest.

Words and their meanings

The use of metaphors, clichés and idiomatic phrases enriches language and is embedded in the shared culture of the language users. Mastering and understanding this sort of subtlety contributes to the emotional and social aspects of communication as well as aiding children's understanding. Teachers often attempt to simplify their explanations and instructions when talking to EAL learners, but avoiding figurative language is almost impossible as it is enmeshed into every aspect of written and verbal communication (McWilliam 1998). Instead, teachers need to embrace the opportunities to engage children in the exploration of language and how it is used in order to extend pupils' vocabulary and to arrive at shared meanings. Fitzpatrick (1996) argues that accepting that figurative language is part of everyday life in the multilingual classroom means that teachers need to remember the following advice:

- [Figurative language] is what we take for granted.
- It is often the key to understanding.
- It is often the trigger for misunderstanding.
- We cannot avoid figurative language so we have to 'manage' the meaning.
- Anticipate multi-meanings of words which are key words in the topic or in the way you intend to talk about the topic.
- Use analogies or extended metaphors which relate to children's experience.
- When multi-meaning words occur, explore them in a wide variety of senses but particularly those which make semantic connections with the focal new meaning.
- Use the children's understandings of possible meanings as the baseline wherever you can.
- Create a classroom 'consciously curious' about the meanings of words.

(Fitzpatrick 1996, cited in McWilliam 1998: 86)

Norah McWilliam (1998), in her practical and inspirational book *What's in a Word?*, suggests three strategies that teachers can use to encourage children to become 'consciously curious' about words and their multiple meanings: rich scripting, shared imaging and word-weaving.

Rich scripting

Rich scripting is a technique that allows teachers to check pupils' comprehension of key words and phrases associated with a new topic or activity. It is more than simply defining key words and technical vocabulary, because rich scripting encourages children to seek the meanings of these words in a variety of contexts. Investigating how words can change their meaning depending on how they are used allows children to draw on their own cultural knowledge as they interpret new words.

Take the topic 'water' as an example. Meaning-seeking strategies could include use of thesauruses or dictionaries, paired consultation in home languages, use of an overhead projector to share findings, examples of multiple meanings and idiomatic phrases, and so on.

Samples of evidence children could collate for 'water' include:

> liquid, body of water, water course, seas, rivers, channel, stream, beck, pool, pond, lake, mere, tarn, loch, creek, fiord, strait, spring, spa, my eyes are watering, water the garden, you can take a horse to water …, wet, saturated, soaked, sodden, drenched, like a drowned rat.

(More examples of this process, a 'rich scripting' proforma and a very useful checklist can be found in Chapter 3 of *What's in a Word?*)

ACTIVITY: RICH SCRIPTING

Try rich scripting a suitable word from your cross-curricular theme, for example 'home'.

Shared imaging

Shared imaging is about establishing a common framework in the classroom and recognising that, because we all have different life experiences, and perhaps different cultural experiences, we may imagine different images or meanings when we hear the same words. We need to help children to match meanings and images to the words we share and as teachers we need to remember that this process is one of negotiation. McWilliam (1998) cites the example of a secondary-school pupil who says he does not understand subtraction but knows how to do 'take-aways'. When talking to a Year 2 class of children (whose families came from India and Pakistan), one of us made the mistake of assuming that our 'images' of woodland creatures (squirrels, foxes, badgers) would be the same as the children's. This was clearly not the case, as the question 'What sort of animal do you think might live in a forest?' was met by answers such as monkeys, snakes and tigers. Our images may be fuelled by memories of trips to English woods to collect conkers and stories of *The*

Animals of Farthing Wood and *Winnie-the-Pooh*. Many of the children in this class had visited very different forest areas and had heard stories steeped in a different cultural tradition. Similarly, teachers should not be surprised by children's literal responses to idiomatic expressions that are culturally acquired (e.g. 'pull your socks up!'). The process of shared imaging actively promotes collaborative meaning-seeking and creates a positive atmosphere in which children feel they can share their ideas and have fun with words.

Word-weaving

Word-weaving is a strategy associated with rich scripting that helps children to 'extend their semantic investigation across their home languages' (McWilliam 1998: 173). The class are given a target word and they have to work together to investigate it (using dictionaries, thesauruses and glossaries, putting the word into different sentences, looking for synonyms and metaphors etc.). The aim of this activity is to collect information about the target word and to present it on strips of paper that are woven together in a 'loom' on display in the classroom. Children can be encouraged to ask adults at home to help them by translating the target word and by identifying words and phrases with the same meaning as the target word. Once the loom is complete, it can be used as the starting point for other activities (shared imaging discussions or as a resource for shared writing).

Key points

■ Learners of EAL may spiral through the curriculum as they encounter language in meaningful contexts.

■ Assessment plays a vital role in helping teachers to identify and respond to individual needs.

■ Learning a new language involves taking risks, making mistakes and being creative. Teachers need to ensure that they promote this sort of climate in a supportive school environment.

■ The opportunity to work and learn alongside people from different cultures and with different languages reminds us that there are lots of different ways of living life and communicating with each other. One of the important lessons we learn (at school and at home) is that we can benefit from sharing our experiences and cooperating with others.

Further reading

Baldock, P. (2010) *Understanding Cultural Diversity in the Early Years*. London: Sage.

Cohen-Emerique (1999) *Le choc culturel*, 'Revue Antipodes', 145, 11–2.

Conteh, J. (2003) *Succeeding in Diversity: culture, language and learning in primary classrooms*. Stoke-on-Trent: Trentham Books.

Kenner, C. (2004) *Becoming Biliterate: young children learning different writing systems*. Stoke-on-Trent: Trentham Books.

Siraj-Blatchford, I. (1994) *The Early Years: laying the foundations for racial equality*. Stoke-on-Trent: Trentham Books.

Resources for teaching

National Association for Language Development in the Curriculum (NALDIC), an organisation working for pupils with English as an additional language, offers support material and teaching resources. See www.naldic.org.uk. Recent research and statistics can be found at www.naldic.org.uk/eal-advocacy/eal-news-summary/150112.

Mantra Lingua offers resources for primary classrooms such as posters and dual-language texts. See www.mantralingua.com.

Support and guidance is available from the former Department for Children Schools and Families (DCSF). See *New Arrivals Excellence Programme: CPD modules*. Ref: DCSF 00041–2008DWO-EN.   www.education.gov.uk/publications/standard/publicationdetail/page1/DCSF-00041-2008. This guide is aimed at induction procedures for new arrivals and includes a self-evaluation tool.

11 Developing children's writing

Purpose of this chapter

This chapter aims to:

- describe how to develop early writing;
- examine the role of the teacher in modelling and discussing writing;
- discuss ways of developing children's ability to work independently;
- explore the importance of both transcription and composition in writing;
- consider the importance of handwriting;
- look at the importance of talk for writing;
- describe how to create a writing classroom;
- suggest practical activities for the classroom.

The development of early writing

In this chapter we will look at the development of writing from early stages to the more sophisticated writing that many children in Key Stage 2 are capable of producing. Many factors associated with developing early writing continue to be important in later years as children develop their writing skills. We will consider the changing nature of written communication and think about how this might affect the ways in which we teach children about writing.

Writing begins with speech and reading, and the following are crucial in developing early writing:

- a rich oral experience of telling and retelling texts in preparation for writing;
- frequent rehearsal of sentences orally.

Many children arrive at school having heard stories and poems being read or told to them. They have a good understanding of the concept of a story with a beginning, middle and an end. Others, however, are less fortunate and have not benefited from a key stage in their development as both readers and writers. Children who have experienced a rich diet of literature in their early years are more likely to understand the purpose of writing and to know that we write to convey meaning, share ideas, communicate and entertain. It is vital that the oral experience continues (or is initiated) in early-years school education, with teachers devoting considerable time to reading to and with their pupils and discussing what they have read with the children.

Writing and the Primary National Strategy

The National Literacy Strategy and subsequently the Primary National Strategy responded to difficulties found to be common to many primary schools; specifically, that the teaching of reading was far more systematic and better structured than the teaching of writing. Although the National Curriculum English Order sets out a model of the writing process (children should learn to plan, draft, revise, edit, present and evaluate their writing), it is easy to misinterpret this by treating it as a simple linear process that can result in a sequence whereby:

The teacher prepares and stimulates ideas of writing with the class.

The children write independently.

The teacher responds, discusses, marks, etc.

This sequence indicates that the teaching of writing can be reduced to teaching by correction (i.e. teaching after the event instead of teaching at the point of writing). *Teaching at the point of writing* focuses on demonstrating and exploring the decisions that writers make in the process of composition. The writing process therefore becomes not linear at all but rather iterative. Drafting, revising and sometimes the presentation of the text are all aspects of a common process involving constant rereading and improvement. This shows why shared writing was given such a prominent place in the literacy hour and why it continues to be a valuable pedagogical strategy.

The role of the teacher in modelling and discussing writing

Shared writing

Shared writing is a powerful teaching strategy and is much more than merely scribing for pupils. It enables teachers to model how a skilled writer works at the point of writing, demonstrating the compositional process. It shows how links are made between reading and writing and how to use similar techniques to achieve particular effects. It 'scaffolds' some of the transcriptional aspects of writing, as well as the style and construction of sentences, and can demonstrate particular aspects, such as how to plan, draft and edit text. Scaffolding, in writing, involves building up a framework that children can use to write around, perhaps using headings, titles for paragraphs, or key phrases such as 'Firstly …', 'After that …', 'Next' and 'In the end …'.

There are three broad teaching techniques that can be used during shared writing sessions: teacher demonstration, teacher scribing and supported composition.

Teacher demonstration

The teacher demonstrates how to write a text, how to use a particular feature or how to compose a text type, maintaining a clear focus on the objective(s). The teacher thinks the process aloud, rehearsing the sentence orally before writing it, and shows how changes are often made to the construction or word choice. At least two sentences are demonstrated in this way, and the teacher does not at this point take contributions from the children.

Teacher scribing

Here, pupils make contributions building upon the teacher's initial demonstration. The teacher focuses the pupils' suggestions and challenges them in order to refine their understanding and compositional skills.

Supported composition

The focus here is on children's composition. Children might use dry-wipe boards or notebooks to write in pairs, or individually, a limited amount of text, sharply focused upon a specific objective. This is a quick activity and once sentences are complete they are held up for the teacher to make an immediate assessment. The aim is to practise until most of the class have mastered the objective to the point where they can apply it.

Guided writing

Guided writing sessions should be scheduled to take place with different groups in a class. The principles of shared writing also apply to guided writing, the main difference being that guided writing is an additional supported step towards independent writing. Guided writing should be planned with three major purposes in mind:

- to support children in planning and drafting their work based on the model provided in a shared writing session;
- to revise and edit work in progress through a group discussion;
- to provide differentiated support for particular groups.

Independent writing

Because of the constraints of time, guided writing cannot always be used as a stepping stone into independent writing. However, most children should be able to manage the transition from shared writing into independent writing as long as the shared writing provides the necessary support. Shared writing can be used to scaffold independent writing sessions by providing, for example:

- a worked plan or writing frame for children to write to;
- writing for children to complete;
- an outline for children to expand;
- a clear narrative ending or punch line, with known steps towards it, to be retold to create particular effects (e.g. tension).

Developing children's ability to work independently

The techniques described above support children's writing during the writing process and not merely before or after the event. A typical sequence that leads from hearing a story to participating in writing one might be as follows.

The Tiger Who Came to Tea

The teacher tells the children she is going to read them a story about, say, a tiger who comes to someone's house and asks for something to eat and drink (*The Tiger Who Came to Tea* by Judith Kerr, 1968). Before showing the book cover, questions can be asked to draw out children's prior knowledge and to engage their interest:

- What do you know about tigers?
- Has anyone ever seen a tiger in a zoo?
- Where do tigers usually live?
- What do they eat?

By being shown pictures and talking about tigers, children can begin to acquire an interest in the unusual theme of the story. Next, the children can be shown the cover of the book and asked what they think might happen in the story. Is the girl frightened of the tiger? Does the tiger look fierce?

Having set the scene for the story, the teacher can now read it to the children, perhaps involving some children, either simply by giving them labels to hold or wear with the names of different characters or, where there are strong readers, asking them to read some of the lines spoken by their characters.

While reading the story, there will be opportunities to pause to discuss what has happened and to predict what might happen on the next page. Children could be asked to discuss these things in pairs, before sharing their ideas with the class.

At the end of the story, after discussions and comments, a shared writing activity could involve children imagining that a tiger came to their house and asked for tea. In pairs, they could think of opening lines before sharing them for the teacher to choose one to write on the board. As she writes, the teacher will talk about what she is doing, think aloud about spelling and modelling clear handwriting. When the sentence has been written, it can be read and reread with the children, and their suggestions for modification invited and included. In modelling writing in this way, teachers demonstrate how writers work and show how the spoken word can be recorded in writing.

As children develop as writers, they can be given dry-wipe whiteboards on which to write their ideas during shared writing sessions, before sharing them with the class. Not only does this foster participation and cooperation but it also enables the teacher to monitor and assess children's knowledge and understanding of writing.

ACTIVITY: PLANNING A CHILDREN'S WRITING ACTIVITY

How would you plan a lesson for Year 4 that would lead to children being able to write a story with a beginning, middle and end? Think about

- examples of texts you would share with them;
- modelling and demonstration;
- supported composition and scaffolding;
- guided writing activities;
- independent writing.

Stimulating children's writing

Good teachers of writing constantly seek new and interesting contexts and experiences for their pupils to stimulate their writing, as well as modelling writing in different genres. For example, for an Early Years Foundation Stage or Year 1 class, the writing might centre around an incident in the play area or could focus on stories about a soft toy's adventures. A particularly successful activity involves the introduction of a teddy bear that the children discover in their classroom one morning with a name tag around its neck (a phonically regular name such as Ben or Sam might be used). On subsequent days there are postcards from the bear, which can be read to the children and replies written. Occasionally, the bear may reappear with souvenirs from his travels, including books, postcards, maps and pamphlets, all of which can be shared with the children. These may be authentic or created by the teacher to make them easy to read.

Eventually, the shared writing activities may lead to guided writing, with children attempting to produce their own postcards to send to the bear. At this stage, many children's writing will be 'emergent' and may not obviously resemble normal graphics. There is considerable value in such writing, both because the children feel able to communicate through writing and because it enables the teacher to see what the children know about writing and what they need to learn to take them to the next stage. Thus, there may be evidence of phoneme–grapheme correspondence in some parts of the words written but not in others, or the child may show evidence of understanding that writing begins at the top left-hand corner of the page and moves to the right and down the page. Pencil grip can be observed and letter formation noted. Sometimes these might be corrected during writing, but more often teachers will leave this for a more opportune moment, perhaps in a class lesson, rather than stopping the flow of the child's writing at the point of composition.

Creating a literate environment

Allied to children's development of writing through shared and guided sessions will be a systematic teaching of phonics, a discussion of new words, and regular teaching of handwriting with daily practice and modelling by the teacher. In addition, teachers will create a literate environment for their pupils, with displays of children's writing and of writing for children. Where there is a play area, writing can become part of it, with different themes offering different opportunities. For example:

- A café could have children acting as waiters and writing down orders for their 'customers'.
- Shopping lists could be made for visits to the class shop.
- Tickets could be made for a station ticket office, as well as timetables, place names and notices. Children could write and record station announcements ('apologies for the late arrival of the 11.30 train'). (See Chapter 1, on pedagogy, for further ideas.)

As children's confidence in writing develops, the principles upon which early writing development are founded will continue to be important. The stimuli for writing will still involve oral rehearsal, shared reading and shared writing. Teachers' modelling of sentences may be at an increasingly sophisticated level, but it will still be important for children to see and engage with different idioms and styles of writing, as well as with varied sentence structures. The tools for writing will continue to include sound phonic knowledge, confidence in spelling or attempting to spell the words they need, and a comfortable, legible style of handwriting. Increasingly, children will make use of word processing as well as handwriting, and drafting, editing and revising will grow in importance as children move towards producing polished pieces of writing that can be shared with classmates and with other classes and with teachers, parents and other audiences.

Handwriting

At a time when adults increasingly use keyboards rather than pens and pencils, and children, too, make extensive use of electronic communication, it may seem odd that schools should be expected to focus upon developing children's handwriting. However, there are many sound reasons for doing so. Medwell and Wray (2007) point out that the National Curriculum for England and Wales focused on handwriting being fluent, joined and legible but did not mention speed – an important attribute when we wish to get our ideas down quickly without forgetting them. Medwell and Wray maintain that:

> Handwriting, and in particular the automaticity of letter production, appears to facilitate higher order composing processes by freeing up working memory to deal with the complex tasks of planning, organizing, revising and regulating the production of text. Research suggests that automatic letter writing is the single best predictor of length and quality of written composition in the primary years.
>
> (Medwell and Wray 2007: 11–12)

They go on to assert that more boys than girls find handwriting difficult and that this is likely to affect their compositional abilities. Intervention to teach handwriting to children who have problems can, they maintain, improve not only their handwriting but also their composition.

There is, then, a need for *automaticity* so that composition can be helped by fluent handwriting and children can focus on what they write without being preoccupied with the mechanics of writing. Teachers need to find a balance between transcription and composition so that children are able to set out their ideas in such a way that they and others can share them. Later in this chapter, we will see an example in the section 'How not to teach writing' where this was not achieved.

So what should children be able to do in handwriting? Brien (2012: 109) maintains that they need to understand that:

- clockwise and anti-clockwise movements – making the right movement is essential in handwriting;

- many of our letters start with an anti-clockwise curve: a, c, d, e, f, g, o, q, s;

- another important group start with a downstroke: b, h, i, j, k, l, m, n, p, r, t, u, y (in most styles);

- the other lower-case letters are the ones which start with a slanting downstroke: v, w, x;

- z doesn't fit into any of these groups, and both e and s are slight anomalies.

According to Brien, if children start a letter at the right point and know the first movement, they are unlikely to go far wrong.

Of course, there are many different handwriting programmes and schools adopt a range of styles, but Brien's suggestions are a solid generic staring point. It is worth considering, too, what teachers need to be able to do if they are to successfully model handwriting. A key starting point is to follow school style when writing on the board in shared writing and on children's work (Graham and Kelly 2003). This may involve making changes to the way you form some letters and learning different ways of joining letters. It is also important ensure hold your pen correctly. This excites more discussion than most topics when introduced in lectures and workshops in teacher-training courses. Many people whose handwriting is legible and neat find it difficult to accept that their pen grip is 'incorrect'. A simple way to get used to the most widely accepted way of holding a pen is to take it between thumb and index finger about one to two centimetres from the tip and dangle it before flipping it over so that it rests on the hand and middle finger.

What about left-handers?

Most people write with their right hands and in the past many left-handers were forced to do so as well. Fortunately, schools are rather more enlightened these days and accept that left-handers can benefit from acquiring some simple techniques. Browne (1993: 81) suggests that we consider the following:

- *Light*: ideally, a left-hander needs the light to come over her right shoulder so that she is not writing in the shadow of her own hand.

- *Paper*: a left-hander needs to have the paper on the left side of the centre of the body. The paper needs to be tilted to the right so that the writer can see what she is writing.

- *Pencil hold*: encourage a left-handed writer to hold the pencil or the pen a little further from the point than a right-hander so that the writing is not obscured. It may be helpful to introduce children to a pencil grip to find the right place for their fingers.

- *Position*: make sure that a left-hander is not sitting too close to the right of a right-hander when writing. This will avoid their arms colliding.

- *Speed*: allow for slower writing until competence increases.
- *Teaching*: demonstrate to left-handers with your left hand whenever possible.

Finally in this section, it is worth noting that there are claims that successful handwriting has a link with successful spelling, especially where a cursive style (joined) is adopted, as strings of letters such as '-tion' and '-ing' can be seen as whole units and these can be practised in handwriting lessons (Graham and Kelly 2003).

Creating a writing classroom

Chapter 2, on classroom management, includes guidance on managing writing sessions and you could read that section in conjunction with the section that follows. There are some key principles that need to be considered when planning not only for individual lessons or phases of lessons but also for the class throughout the year. A key element is to create an environment in which writing is celebrated and in which children feel confident and comfortable and able to write without distraction. The latter is probably the greatest challenge.

Although we want to encourage children to think of themselves as real writers and authors, the typical model for independent writing in school is hardly the way in which published authors write. Many great works of children's literature would probably not have been created had authors had to sit at tables surrounded by perhaps twenty-nine other authors, maybe vying for the use of resources such as rubbers, dictionaries and thesauruses! Roald Dahl, for example, did most of his writing in a draughty summerhouse in his garden well away from distractions, although J.K. Rowling did write some of the early *Harry Potter* stories sitting in a café with her daughter sleeping in a pram next to her.

In the classroom, there will be times when children will need to discuss their ideas for writing and write these cooperatively with a small group or with a writing partner. Even when writing independently and individually, discussion, sharing of ideas and sharing of work will still be important. Periods of quiet work followed by discussion enable children to concentrate for manageable sessions while still allowing them a break from composition and an opportunity to talk about their work. By building these into planning, teachers make class management easier for themselves: setting lengthy periods of silent working is not only unrealistic for most classes but also creates a discipline problem that would hardly exist if children knew they would be given the chance to talk at regular intervals. Consider, too, what the rest of the class will be doing if all groups are not writing at the same time. If a writing group is placed adjacent to a group holding a lively discussion or planning a piece of drama, the likely distraction will inevitably lead to a reduction in concentration and quality, as well as to frustration for writers.

Regular intervention by the teacher to highlight good work and good working practices also creates a positive atmosphere in which success is celebrated and children's attention is drawn to what they should be doing and what they might strive to achieve, rather than to what they are doing wrong. These interventions also enable teachers to monitor progress and to draw attention at suitable times to misconceptions, common spelling errors, and interesting use of vocabulary and phrasing. However, while errors should be noted, it is vital that children are not afraid of making mistakes. The following section may be read as a cautionary tale for anyone planning a writing lesson.

How not to teach writing

Making children fearful before they put pen to paper seldom leads to good, creative, imaginative writing. This method was capably illustrated by a student whose lesson was witnessed many years ago.

On the chalkboard was a list of dos and don'ts:

- Draw a neat margin.
- Put the date at the top left-hand side of your page.
- Do not cross out.
- Do not use a rubber.
- Use capital letters at the beginnings of sentences and full stops at the ends.
- Do not misspell any of these words: because, their, there, once ….

The student went through the list with the class of eight- and nine-year-olds in a stern and rather hostile manner, before telling them that they were to write a story about life in a Victorian factory.

Within five minutes of starting work, two children were crying because they had incurred the student's wrath by putting the date on the wrong side of the page, and several others, having surmounted that hurdle, had gone on to sit chattering or chewing pencils as they tried to think about what they might write. An atmosphere of trepidation pervaded the classroom, and children, afraid of making mistakes, left their seats clutching blue spelling dictionaries to ask for words that they almost invariably knew how to spell. The lesson gradually fell apart and little was achieved.

The student, during the post-lesson discussion, blamed the children and stated that they were a dreadful class, full of lazy boys and chatty girls. He would prefer to teach older children, he said, who could do more and needed less help. In fact, the problem had been the student's attitude to the task and the animosity that he conveyed to the pupils. There had been little discussion about what life in a Victorian factory might be like, and he had not read any stories or poems to them to provide ideas. Instead of showing the children that he was interested in what they would write – the composition – he gave the impression that it was only the transcriptional aspects of the writing with which he was concerned. Children were asked to write but were not given guidance on which genre of writing was appropriate: should they write a narrative or a piece of non-fiction? If they were to write non-fiction, should they write an explanation, a discussion or a persuasive piece? In this lesson there was limited guidance and no modelling, and the wrong atmosphere was created, and the task was depicted as a chore rather than as a pleasant activity.

ACTIVITY: TRANSCRIPTION AND COMPOSITION

- Try holding your pen with the hand that you do not usually write with.
- Now try writing a sentence that describes the most interesting thing you have seen in the last week.
- Now try doing the same with the hand that you normally write with.

■ Did you produce more interesting writing with your writing or non-writing hand?

■ Your composition was probably better when you used your preferred hand, because your focus was on composition rather than transcription. What does this tell us about the challenges young children face when a strong emphasis is placed upon transcription and they are also expected to produce good composition?

Course tutors had tried to convey to students in lectures the importance of making writing an enjoyable act. They had told the students that children's spelling was more likely to improve if they were encouraged to attempt words that were new to their written vocabulary, safe in the knowledge that their teacher would help them to spell the words correctly rather than penalise them for making mistakes. They had talked to students about the importance of children being encouraged to experiment with language. This is not to suggest that spelling and accurate writing are unimportant: far from it. Accuracy is vital if readers are to be able to enjoy what they read, but there are times when real writers concentrate on ideas rather than presentation, leaving editing and revising until later. Michael Morpurgo admits that when he writes he gets his ideas down quickly and worries about spelling and grammar later when the time comes to turn the ideas into books that others will enjoy reading. If one of our most successful and experienced authors works in this way, perhaps we should reflect upon the demands we make of children when they are asked to write.

We will see, in the examples later in this chapter, how the writing process can be developed to foster increasing concentration on accuracy as a piece of writing develops.

ACTIVITY: CONSIDERING HOW PUPILS PERCEIVE WRITING

Before moving on to other aspects of writing, it is worthwhile considering a classroom in which you work or have worked to assess how writing might be perceived by pupils. How would you answer the following questions?

■ Are quiet writing areas available?

■ Are vocabulary lists and word banks available and easy to use?

■ Does the teacher have time to help children?

■ Do the children ever see the teacher writing?

■ Is children's writing displayed and regularly shared with the class and others outside the class?

■ How often do the children write for people other than the teacher?

■ Do children always know why they are being asked to write?

■ Do children have opportunities to work with others as well as individually?

■ Do children often use the word processor?

■ What do the children think the teacher is looking for when responding to their work?

Responding to children's writing

As we have seen, teachers' responses to children's work can have a profound effect upon their pupils' attitudes to writing. Teachers' responses will, of course, be largely focused upon the learning outcomes determined for the lesson, but this does not mean that in a lesson in which the focus is use of speech marks teachers should only check children's work for accurate punctuation of dialogue, ignoring content. As a general rule, it is best to comment upon content before presentation. If children feel that the only reason they are writing is to demonstrate proficiency in transcription, writing ceases to be regarded as a purposeful activity and a means of communication. Central to ensuring that writing is valued in its own right is ensuring that children have an 'audience' for their writing, and that this audience is not always only their teacher. As Lambirth (2005: 58) has argued, 'Real writing – writing for real audiences – is a struggle, but the labour becomes worthwhile when the author knows that his/her work will be read, respected and valued as a genuine and authentic attempt at meaning-making.' Knowing whom one is writing for should help dictate style, use of vocabulary and idiom, as well as content, so that Year 6 children writing for Year 2 pupils will write differently from when they write their own versions of, say, a Joan Aiken story.

Marking a child's work should, ideally, take place with the child present. However, this is not always possible and inevitably teachers find themselves taking home piles of exercise books. Inevitably, too, this can lead to inattentive marking and a focus purely on secretarial aspects of work. How much easier is it to skim through a story, pick out and underline three spelling errors and write 'a good try' at the foot of the page than to read the story properly, comment upon events and structure, and then draw attention to errors and misconceptions, concluding with a meaningful comment that shows the child that the teacher has really read his or her work.

A strategy that many teachers use to encourage accuracy is to ask children to check their work before handing it in for marking. This often results in children returning to their seats, adding a full stop or two and then returning. If checking or proofreading is to be done effectively, children need to know what they are looking for. A solution is to provide a checklist for children to look at when rereading their work (see Chapter 5, on knowledge about language, for another example). This might include some items as standard, but others will be focused upon the particular learning objectives for the activity. For example, if a piece of story-writing were to follow work on dialogue, the checklist might be as follows:

PLEASE CHECK THE FOLLOWING BEFORE SHOWING YOUR WRITING

1   Does each sentence begin with a capital letter?
2   Does each sentence end with a full stop, question mark or exclamation mark?
3   Is every word legible?
4   Does each person's speech begin on a new line?
5   Have you opened and closed speech marks?
6   Have you varied the verbs you have used to show how people spoke (e.g. 'whispered', 'called', 'muttered')?

The first three items might be common to all checklists, but the others would vary according to learning objectives, with the total not exceeding six items.

The response to children's writing should not be restricted to the teacher. Where a healthy atmosphere of constructive criticism is developed, children can listen to and read each other's writing and offer suggestions and comment on secretarial errors. This might be done in class or group sessions, or through writing partners with whom children regularly discuss and share writing.

Providing a varied diet

The Literacy Framework in England provided a wide range of writing tasks with interesting and varied starting points offered in the example materials. With such a wealth of ideas and activities also available through published resources and websites, no teacher need be short of stimulating ideas for children's writing. We are now, thankfully, past the stage where children equated quantity with success in writing, and one beneficial side-effect of the limited time available for independent writing within the literacy hour was an increased emphasis upon shorter, structured writing, such as reports, opening paragraphs, definitions and various types of poetry including haiku, cinquains, limericks and triolets. Of course, teachers did not always expect completed, polished pieces of work within a twenty-minute period but rather used the literacy hour as a starting point for extended and more adventurous writing.

The starting point for many writing activities should be whole-class shared writing in which the teacher models writing for the children, drawing upon their ideas and showing them how these can be presented. This can be followed by an exploration of the features of different text types, for example considering style, phrasing, presentation and vocabulary. Children can then work independently of the teacher and individually, in pairs or in groups to produce short pieces of writing during literacy lessons. Subsequently, these short pieces may be starting points for extended writing.

What is essential is that the teacher shares a range of genres with the class and models each one that the children are expected to attempt to reproduce, discussing all the time the features of the genre and inviting the children to put forward their ideas for replication through shared writing.

Supporting children's spelling

We have seen in Chapter 2, on classroom management, some strategies for overcoming what for some teachers is a constant problem: children's repeated requests for help with spelling. In Chapter 12, on spelling, we will see that spelling needs to be taught and learned through a range of activities, some of which involve investigation and trial and error, while earlier in this chapter we saw how an overemphasis upon correct spelling at what should be a drafting stage can stifle creativity and inhibit young writers. During writing sessions, teachers need to achieve a balance between supporting those children whose progress would be seriously hampered without help with spelling and encouraging children to behave as real writers and to use the strategies real writers use when faced with a problem with spelling. If children are to succeed and teachers are to be able to guide and support them, teachers need to do more than spend writing lessons writing spellings into little blue books.

Before writing begins, teachers and children can work together to produce word banks to provide, displayed for all to see, lists of words that they anticipate might be needed. Once these have been made, teachers should read them with pupils, perhaps arranging them on cards in alphabetical order for easy reference. As children are writing and need to spell other unfamiliar words, they should first attempt to spell them independently, drawing upon their phonic knowledge and perhaps using a reference chart such as THRASS (Davies and Ritchie 1998) or the Read Write Inc. 'Simple Speed Sounds' chart of consonants and vowels, which develops into a 'Complex Speed Sounds' chart and shows a range of spelling alternatives for spelling choices. Good attempts at independent spelling should be praised before discussions with individuals, groups and perhaps the whole class take place, to determine how a word should be spelled. At this point, reference to an etymological dictionary could help the teacher to explain an unusual spelling or a particular prefix, suffix or root word. For example, a child wishing to spell 'petrified' could discover that this means literally 'turned to stone', while he may find that 'decimated' means 'reduced by a tenth'. There are obvious follow-up teaching points that could then be made, for example talking with children about other words that begin with 'dec-' that relate to the number ten, including decagon, decimal, decade and December (once the tenth month).

The provision of dictionaries at different levels, as well as thesauruses, will help children to find the spellings they need, as well as introducing them to new words that they might use.

Children's perceptions of writing

The National Writing Project's fascinating booklet *Children's Perceptions of Writing* (1990) records children's comments about writing, which include some thought-provoking, as well as amusing, views. Typical attitudes found in the book can be summed up by the following:

> Writing is for you to be able to know more words and to do neater writing. Writing shows your teacher how you are progressing.
>
> The thing you need mostly for writing is that you should concentrate. You should not start talking. Then you will not be a good writer.
>
> People who have got pensions write because it will give them something to do before they die.

We would like to think that writing in schools has evolved since 1990, but experience suggests that this is not always the case. It is likely that anyone reading this chapter has seen, experienced or even given writing tasks as punishments. Writing out lines ('I must learn not to give writing tasks as punishments') or one-page 'essays' ('Why it is a bad idea to give writing tasks as punishments') and other writing tasks were traditional punishments in many schools, and sadly continue to be in some. We need to consider how children's perceptions of writing will be affected if they see that teachers often use it as a punishment. Of course, writing is not the only aspect of the curriculum that is used in this way. We have seen games lessons abandoned when teachers were unhappy with children's behaviour and children given arithmetic to do instead, and we have frequently seen art, design technology or PE curtailed and replaced by silent reading when pupil conduct fell below teachers' expected standards. Strangely, we have never seen maths abandoned in favour of PE, or silent reading replaced by games or art in similar circumstances.

What do we convey to children when we use some subjects as punishments? We tell them that these activities are unpleasant or at least less pleasant than other aspects of the curriculum. A tutor was once summoned to a school to talk to an irate headteacher who felt that student teachers had undermined the school's policy of developing positive attitudes to writing by keeping several children in at lunchtime to write lines. He was quite right! If children are to succeed in writing, they need to perceive an intrinsic value in what they are asked to do. They need to see writing as:

- a means of communication and something that can be enjoyed both by the writer and the reader;
- having a purpose and an audience;
- an activity that teachers value and celebrate through reading examples aloud to the class, sharing with other teachers and displaying so that others can see.

Teachers can elevate the status of writing considerably by showing that they too are writers. This can be done in various ways. For example:

- Before asking children to write in a particular genre (e.g. haiku, limerick, report, story opening), teachers might attempt the activity themselves at home. Not only will this help teachers to understand the challenges their class might face but it will also provide an example that the children can see and perhaps model their own writing upon.
- As children begin work on a piece of writing, the teacher might do the same, using the opportunity to demonstrate discreetly how writers behave and the working conditions that they need in order to be able to concentrate. ('Is anyone else finding it difficult to work when some people are chatting?')
- Shared writing may usefully be very teacher-centred occasionally, with teachers composing a short piece of writing while narrating the thought processes that they are using, and showing that they edit and revise as they write and after reflection.

It is not only the teacher who can model writing. Classroom assistants, other adult helpers and professional writers might also demonstrate their writing skills and discuss the writing process with pupils. In addition, older children might have younger pupils as writing partners, producing shared pieces and drawing upon the ideas of both while the older children act as scribes.

Practical activities for the classroom

Children in the same class should be given regular opportunities to write cooperatively, sharing and discussing ideas and developing both content and presentation. This is a practice that adults make use of too, with jointly produced reports, co-written songs (Lennon and McCartney, George and Ira Gershwin, Gilbert and Sullivan) and co-written novels (Nicci French, who writes thrillers for adults, is actually a husband-and-wife team).

A drafting activity

We need, as teachers, to consider whether writing can be good only if it is neat. While legibility, like accurate spelling and good use of grammar, is important when we write for others, we also need to consider writing as having stages. When children are preparing a piece of writing, they may need to begin by making rough notes, just as real writers do. At this stage, they will chiefly be writing for themselves and presentation will be low on their list of priorities. 'The Fog' (see Figure 11.1) was a drafting activity that illustrates this process.

This piece of writing was undertaken by a Year 5–6 class and the stimulus was a few minutes spent on a foggy school field at the beginning of the day. The children were asked to look, smell, touch and listen and to make notes about what their senses told

FIGURE 11.1 Example of drafting by a Year 6 child

them. In the classroom, they were asked to 'splatter' their ideas onto drafting paper, using short phrases and clauses, and to keep writing for two minutes as they put their ideas down on paper before they were forgotten. They were told that, at this stage, neatness and accuracy were not as important as their ideas and that they need not worry about making mistakes or about untidy handwriting.

The next stage was to take the ideas and sort them into an order in which they might be used in a finished piece of writing. Ideas could be discarded or added to, but again presentation was a low priority. In the example, it can be seen that the student (Claire) circled and numbered items and then wrote them in a list on a second piece of paper.

The third stage was to develop the ideas into sentences, and the draft shows that Claire behaved as a real writer by crossing out ideas she did not wish to use and reordering others. The final draft is neat and accurate, and followed discussion with the teacher and some marking. The description conveys an image of a foggy morning that would probably not have been achieved had Claire been asked to write neatly and accurately as soon as she returned to the classroom from the foggy field. If we look at the Primary National Strategy core learning in literacy for Year 6 (DfES 2006b: 34–5), we can see that Claire has addressed several aspects, including the following:

- Use a range of appropriate strategies to edit, proofread and correct spelling.
- Understand how writers use different structures to create coherence and impact.
- Integrate words, images and sounds imaginatively for different purposes.
- Use varied structures to shape and organise text coherently.
- Use different styles of handwriting for different purposes.

Cooperative writing using pictures

In this section and the next, two writing activities will be explored in order to demonstrate how some of the principles discussed earlier can be applied. The activities have been chosen because they could be attempted at different levels and with different year groups, with the degree of teacher support and the scope of the activities varying according to children's abilities. The first activity is described in greater detail than the second, which is followed by a challenge for the reader to consider in the light of his/her experience in the classroom and what has been read in this chapter: to devise appropriate activities for a chosen year group.

Group writing using pictures

This first activity is based upon a collection of stimulating pictures. For a general lesson, these can be taken from magazines and colour supplements. Simply cut out a selection of pictures (adverts are particularly good and you can leave out references to products if you like) and then attach them to pieces of A3 paper. The activity has clear stages, but for younger or less-able children you may need to give a higher level of teacher modelling than for others. The possible stages are set out below, but some could be left out, depending upon children's abilities.

1   Mount two large pictures on the board and explain to the children that you have written a short description of one of them. Ask them to listen carefully as you read your description and to wait until you have finished before deciding which of the two pictures you are describing, supporting their judgement by referring to what you wrote. Display the description so that they can refer to it.

2   Leave the other large picture in the centre of the board (or use an interactive whiteboard with a picture in the centre, if available). Explain that you would like the children to help you to produce a description of the picture so that, if it were displayed along with several others, anyone reading the description would be able to identify the picture. Look at it with the children and ask them to suggest short phrases to describe various features. For example, for a beach scene: clear, blue sky; white, sandy beach; crashing, white waves; bright, orange sun. Write the children's suggestions in the space around the picture and continue to add to these as they have more ideas.

3   Having produced notes as the basis for a more refined piece of writing, ask children to discuss how they might turn some of the phrases into sentences, perhaps combining phrases or adding further adjectives and adverbs.

4   With the children's help, compose a short piece of descriptive writing to describe the picture. This could be prose, perhaps with a word limit of fifty, or a poem with or without rhyme.

5   Provide each pair of children with a picture mounted on A3 paper and ask them to work together to make notes on the paper around the picture with descriptive phrases. These could include feelings generated by the picture as well as descriptions of what can be seen.

6   After a few minutes, ask each pair to pass their picture and notes on to another pair, but not to discuss what they have written or to draw attention to errors. Ask the new pairs to look at what has already been written and then to add their own ideas.

7   Pass the pictures and notes on once more after a few minutes for further additions from another pair of children.

8   Ask the children to return the pictures to their original owners, and allow some discussion between all of the six authors involved.

9   Explain that the original writers can now draw upon everyone's ideas to help them to produce a short, descriptive piece of writing. Tell them that you will be displaying all of the pictures and all of the pieces of writing, but not next to each other. The writers need to make their descriptions good enough for readers to be able to match them to the appropriate pictures.

This activity can be done as part of work in a range of subjects. For example, for history a selection of pictures related to a period about to be studied can serve to alert children to prior knowledge as well as to raise questions about the period. The pictures used could be prints of famous paintings or paintings by a particular artist (these can be found cheaply in books in discount bookshops) and the activity might be linked to art appreciation.

There are several points in the process at which teacher intervention might take place to make points about various aspects of writing. The extent to which this is done will depend upon the abilities of the children, but there can be opportunities for discussing vocabulary and for talking about spellings and about punctuation and presentation. Modelling of text types could feature and the activity could be linked to a genre that has recently been studied. The pictures activity, then, features shared reading and writing; note-making; cooperative work; and drafting, editing and revising, with many opportunities for word- and sentence-level study as well as writing in different genres, and leads to accurate and careful presentation.

The town

This second activity is, again, potentially cross-curricular and offers opportunities for a wide range of writing in different genres. Again, the activity is suitable for a range of year groups and can be tailored to the learning objectives needed for a particular class. It focuses on a map or plan of a town that can be designed by the teacher or by children, or may be taken from a published source (Waugh 2000b). The map should include shops, key facilities such as police and fire stations, a medical centre, religious buildings for different faiths, schools, recreation areas, housing and industry. The programme, which could extend over several weeks and which might cover a range of learning objectives, could include the following:

1   A shared reading activity at the beginning of the programme looking at the plan and reading labels and, if one is provided, a key. Any new or unfamiliar words can be discussed in terms of their etymology, with prefixes and suffixes and root words studied, as well as phoneme–grapheme correspondence.

2   Instructional shared writing asking children to give directions for travel between different points, using left and right as well as points of the compass. There can be discussion about imperative (sometimes referred to as 'bossy') verbs, and other sources of instructional writing might be examined.

3   Discussion about the use of capital letters for names, with a focus on (for example) when 'street' and 'road' have capitals and when they do not.

4   Letter-writing between characters from the town.

5   Drama and speaking and listening work involving children in role as characters from the town.

6   Fiction writing about events in the town.

7   Persuasive writing about campaigns for improvements to the town or about controversial issues such as building a new road in a conservation area or building a power station or factory.

ACTIVITY: CREATING A PROGRAMME OF WORK

Look again at the suggested activities for work on 'The Town' and make notes on ways in which you could adapt these and add others to create an engaging and worthwhile programme of work for a year group of your choice. In doing so, consider the following:

■   How will you engage and sustain children's interest?

■   Which aspects of the English curriculum will you cover?

- Which different genres of writing and reading will children encounter and how will you model these for them?
- How can you make the activity 'real' by relating it to other aspects of the curriculum and to children's own environments?
- Which different 'audiences' will be available for children's work?
- How will you create a suitable classroom environment for children to work in?

If, when you attempt this activity, you find you have lots of ideas for answering these questions, you are either a skilled teacher of writing or this chapter has been successful in promoting thinking about writing (or both!).

Writing in the twenty-first century

For some adults, writing is an onerous task and one to be undertaken only when absolutely necessary. Yet for others it is a pleasure and an integral part of daily life. People probably write more now than ever before, with texting an almost constant activity for some and with extensive use of email having replaced letter-writing for many. Millions of people, who might not previously have put pen to paper, now communicate electronically. Radio and television programmes often feature emails and texts as instant audience reactions to topics, and these are shared with millions, while many people have their own websites or 'blogs', which are used to express their opinions.

Within the constraints of space for this chapter, the focus has inevitably fallen upon pen-and-paper writing, but as teachers we need to embrace and understand the electronic age in which children are growing up and exploit their interest in communication as we develop their writing skills. Chapter 13, 'Using technology to enhance the learning and teaching of English', will explore some of these methods of writing in greater detail, but it is worthwhile to ponder upon this new age of communication before moving on.

ACTIVITY: EMBRACING ELECTRONIC COMMUNICATION

Crystal (2009: 3) asks whether there has ever been a 'linguistic phenomenon which has aroused such curiosity, fear, confusion, antagonism, fascination, excitement and enthusiasm all at once?'

- How will you take into account children's experiences of electronic communication when devising activities to develop their writing skills?
- Have you found any examples of children using text speak inappropriately when writing at school?

Key points

- It is important to create the right environment for writing, with the nature of the classroom, the attitude of the teacher and the topics chosen for writing being central.

- The role of the teacher in modelling and discussing writing is central to children experiencing a range of texts and genres and understanding how to produce their own.

- Children need to develop the ability to work independently, both for their own benefit and for that of the teacher, who needs to be able to spend time supporting and guiding writers rather than simply giving help with spellings.

- Children need to write for different audiences and purposes and to know that what they write will be read by others.

- The nature of writing outside the classroom is constantly changing as technology advances, and this has implications for how we approach writing in the classroom.

Further reading

Brien, J. (2012) *Teaching Primary English*. London: Sage.

Browne, A. (1993) *Helping Children to Write*. London: Paul Chapman.

Crystal, D. (2009) *Txting: the gr8 db8*. Oxford: Oxford University Press.

DCSF (Department for Children Schools and Education) (2008c) *Talk for Writing*. Nottingham: DCSF.

DfES (Department for Education and Skills) (2006b) *Primary National Strategy: primary framework for literacy and mathematics*. Ref: 02011/2006BOK-EN. London: DfES.

Graham, J. and Kelly, A. (2003) *Writing Under Control*. London: David Fulton.

Tomkins, G.E. (1994) *Teaching Writing: balancing process and product*. Englewood Cliffs, NJ: Macmillan.

12

Spelling

Purpose of this chapter

This chapter aims to:

■ discuss problems in the English spelling system;

■ describe phonic approaches to teaching spelling;

■ examine the place of word lists in teaching and learning spelling;

■ discuss the teaching of spelling rules and spelling principles;

■ develop strategies for teaching and learning spelling;

■ describe ways of finding out what children know about spelling;

■ suggest classroom activities to develop good spelling.

Problems in the English spelling system

> Shakespeare himself did not spell the name the same way twice in any of his six known signatures and even spelled it two ways on one document, his will, which he signed Shakspere in one place and Shakspeare in another. Curiously the one spelling he never seemed to use himself was Shakespeare.
>
> (Bryson 1990: 116)

While poor spellers may take some comfort from the efforts at spelling of England's most revered playwright, in the twenty-first century poor spelling is viewed by many as a sign of lack of intellect or carelessness and can certainly damage people's career prospects. Many employers discard badly spelled application forms.

■ *Support for Spelling* (DCSF 2009a: 2) maintains that a balanced spelling programme includes five main components:

- understanding the principles underpinning word construction (phonemic, morphemic and etymological);
- recognising how (and how far) these principles apply to each word, in order to learn to spell words;
- practising and assessing spelling;
- applying spelling strategies and proofreading;
- building pupils' self-images as spellers.

This chapter will explore the components of a balanced approach to spelling, while drawing attention to some of the problems inherent in our spelling system and the obstacles these may place in the way of children's spelling development.

The lexicon of the English language has developed over hundreds of years from a variety of languages including French, Norse, Germanic languages, Latin and Greek. This means that there are inconsistencies in the pronunciation of letters and clusters of letters, because many words have retained a pronunciation similar to that used in the language from which they are derived. Thus, we have 'ch', which teachers have tended to teach makes the sound 'ch' as in 'chip', also making a 'k' sound in words with Greek origins, such as 'chemistry', 'charisma', 'school' and 'character', as well as in names like 'Chloe', and a 'sh' sound in words with a French origin, such as 'chef', 'charade' and 'chute', as well as in names like 'Charlotte'.

As Williams (1965: 244) argued, when spellings were first compiled in dictionaries, many spellings were altered 'by men ignorant of their origins, confident of false origins'. 'Island', 'scissors', 'scythe', 'could' and 'anchor' replaced 'iland', 'sissors', 'sithe', 'coud' and 'ancor' without affecting pronunciation. However, similar false alterations such as 'fault', 'vault' and 'assault' (which needed no letter 'l's) have perpetuated their errors into both spelling and pronunciation.

Phonic approaches to teaching spelling

Synthetic phonics involves segmenting for spelling and blending for reading, with children listening to the sounds or phonemes within words and attributing graphemes to them when writing.

The inconsistencies in English orthography lead some people to argue that a phonic approach presents problems. However, while when children build a word by segmenting it into its sounds and then representing these with graphemes to spell it they may make mistakes (e.g. 'feat' for 'feet', 'bote' for 'boat' and 'thay' for 'they'), they are making what Brien (2012: 105) describes as 'comprehensible misspellings'. Brien argues that good attempts at spellings that are phonically plausible help teachers to identify aspects of spelling that need to be addressed.

Let us take one simple consonant-vowel-consonant (CVC) word, fox, and explore the spelling possibilities in order to see the problems children face.

The initial sound could be represented by 'f' or 'ph'. 'Ff' is another alternative, although this is not found at the beginnings of words other than names (e.g. 'Ffion'). The vowel sound will probably present few problems, although many words in children's early vocabularies have the 'o' sound represented by 'a' ('was', 'what', 'want'). The final sound is problematical and often leads to interesting spelling choices such as 'foks', 'focs' or 'focks'.

This is because 'x' usually has two phonemes (try sounding 'fox', 'box' and 'fix' and notice how your mouth shape changes), except in a few words such as 'xylophone'.

ACTIVITY: TEACHING SPELLING

Try looking at other simple words and consider how you would teach their spellings to children by anticipating possible misconceptions. For example, you might look at 'who', 'school', 'said' and 'we'.

Table 12.1 provides examples of different ways in which the same letters may be pronounced and illustrates the challenges we face when using a one-letter-makes-one-sound approach to spelling. Although some variations – like 'c' having a 'ch' sound (as in 'chip') in 'ciabatta' – result from recent word imports and are uncommon, many letters are frequently pronounced in different ways in different words.

TABLE 12.1 Problems with the idea that one letter makes one sound

a	apple, woman, snake, car	n	nip, hymn
b	big, thumb	o	on, go, woman
c	cat, city, ciabatta	p	pig, pneumonia
d	dog, dune	q	queen, Iraq
e	end, the, women, café	r	run, bar
f	fit, of	s	salt, sugar, rose
g	go, huge, gnome	t	tiger, debut
h	hit, hotel, oh	u	up, tube
i	ink, fir	v	vase
j	jam, jalfrezi	w	wall, write
k	kick, knot	x	fox, xylophone
l	log, calm	y	you, by, hymn
m	mop, mnemonic	z	zip, azure

A similar chart of spelling choices could be produced for the classroom, perhaps involving children in its construction. Alternatively, THRASS (Davies and Ritchie 1998) produces charts with pictures and words, words, and graphemes to show possible spelling choices for the forty-four sounds in English, while the Read Write Inc. 'Complex Speed Sounds' chart has a similar function.

There is little wonder, then, that when Peters (1970) asked a thousand ten-year-olds to spell 'saucer' fewer than half of them did so correctly, and that those who wrote it incorrectly gave 209 different spellings.

ACTIVITY: WAYS OF SPELLING 'SAUCER'

Think of the word 'saucer'. Spend two minutes trying to see how many different phonically plausible ways you could spell it. This should help you to see how and why children make mistakes.

Despite the many anomalies in English spelling, children still need to learn to spell accurately and they need strategies to help them to do so. Virtually every English word has some phonic regularity, as well as other clues that can help us to learn how to spell it successfully. Look, for example, at some simple words that often present problems because they include sound–symbol correspondences that do not necessarily conform to those many children learn when sounding out the alphabet: 'was', 'of', 'once', 'your', 'would'.

For 'was' there are two problems: the medial 'a' is commonly taught as 'a' sounds in 'bag', and the final 's' as in 'sit'. Here, however, the 'a' has the sound of /o/ in 'hop' and the 's' the sound of /z/ in 'zip'. Not surprisingly, children often write 'wos' or even 'woz' (Kilroy woz 'ere!). Do we simply teach 'was' as a whole word or does it provide an opportunity to look at some other words in which 'a' has an 'o' sound as in 'hop' and 's' a 'z' sound? We looked at 'want' and 'what' earlier and there are other examples (often beginning with 'w' such as 'wander', 'wasp' and 'warrior'), while 's' is frequently pronounced as 'z' in, for example, 'as', 'is', 'has', 'please', 'revise' and 'phrase'. Learning how to spell 'was' can, then, provide an opportunity to extrapolate and to enhance children's phonic awareness.

Similarly, 'of' presents problems if children have learned only that 'f' has a /f/ sound as in 'fog'. Indeed, 'of' is frequently misused in another way, with many adults writing 'could of', 'would of' and 'should of' instead of 'could've', 'would've' and 'should've'. This error probably emanates from the way we speak in abbreviating 'could have' to 'could've', and the fact that people, perhaps subconsciously, relate the ''ve' sounds to similar sound they hear for 'of' in 'bag of chips', 'packet of nuts' etc.

'Once' is possibly the hardest word to explain, given that it begins with a 'w' sound as in 'wing' that is represented by an 'o'. This also occurs in 'one', which is another problematical spelling compounded by the presence of a 'w' in 'two', which must be very confusing for children learning English numbers. 'Once', despite its difficult beginning, has a regular ending, '-nce', which can be found in many words such as 'dance', 'chance', 'mince' and 'prance'.

'Your' and 'would' present problems if children learn only that the vowel digraph 'ou' is sounded as 'ou' as in 'about', but at least they have phonetically regular beginnings and endings.

While the use of phonics is a key method of learning to spell, it has also been argued that children need to know when this strategy is appropriate and when it is unlikely to work. As Mudd maintained:

> 'Sounding out' usually only works effectively if one knows the spelling alternatives to be selected for particular words; for example, the good speller knows that 'once' may not be sounded out to produce the correct spelling, whereas he or she knows that 'went' may be successfully sounded out.

(Mudd 1994: 138)

Goswami and Bryant had similar reservations, maintaining that

> Children's invented spelling is often wrong because they seem to be using a phonological code too literally when they spell. This of course is not really a surprise, because it is impossible to spell English properly just on the basis of letter-sound relationships. No one who relies just on a phonological code will ever spell 'laugh', 'ache', or even 'have' properly.
>
> (Goswami and Bryant 1990: 53)

The role of the teacher is to help children to develop strategies to enable them to learn spellings and be able to apply what they have learned to new words. One method is to teach words in families so that children see that there are common patterns in words. For example, for 'your' they could also learn 'pour' and 'four', while for 'would' they could learn 'should' and 'could'. This might require a development from synthetic phonics into analytic phonics, which involves looking at patterns within words. For example, Support for Spelling (DCSF 2009b: 61–2) has an activity related to groups of words with the letter strings '-igh', '-ough' and '-ear'. The choice of words for this activity is interesting, and includes 'rough', 'though', 'through' 'thorough' and 'thought'. Children can, then, conduct spelling investigations to find out which sounds are most commonly represented by the letter strings and, for example, whether the position of the letter strings in a word affects their pronunciation. This can be followed by careful teaching of principles. Therefore, the much-maligned teaching of word lists needs to be considered.

Teaching word lists

The main reasons that some educators have questioned the value of giving children lists of words to learn include:

- Children are often sent home with words to learn but without any strategies to help them to learn them.
- Sometimes teachers simply write the lists on the board on Monday morning for the children to copy into books, without discussing the words, their meanings or their spellings.
- Sometimes the words are either not relevant to children's needs or not related to each other in such a way that general 'rules' about spellings might be deduced.
- The inevitable spelling tests that follow can compound children's sense of being poor spellers and create a sense of failure for some.
- Some teachers think that they have taught spelling if they give children spellings to learn, and do little else to develop their pupils' spellings abilities.

Of all the arguments against giving children lists of words to learn, the last is probably the most important. Learning to spell involves much more than learning words by rote. In particular, it involves developing the ability to extrapolate and to apply what one learns about spelling some words to other words. In order to do this, we need to see that, however irregular some words may appear, there are usually others that follow the same pattern. We also need to learn about common prefixes and suffixes and understand how these can be used to modify meanings of words. If children are to be given lists of words to learn, it is important that teachers spend time talking with them about spellings and relating what they learn to more general principles about spelling. It should be remembered that if children were given ten words a week to learn throughout their primary school lives they would learn only around 2700, assuming that no word was ever repeated. Bouttell (article in *The Guardian*, 12 August 1986, cited in Crystal 1990) maintained that by the age of twelve an average child has a vocabulary of 12,000 words. The need to extrapolate and to generalise from knowledge acquired is, therefore, crucial.

We should not only discuss the words that appear on the lists but also talk about other words that may be derived from them. We should differentiate the lists according to the spelling abilities and vocabulary needs of the children. However, some words may be common to all lists if they relate to a particular topic that all children are studying. Table 12.2 has some sample lists for a Year 5 class who are studying novels, stories and poems by significant children's writers.

All the lists can be looked at by all of the groups, with links made between words such as 'prefer' and 'preference', 'extract' and 'excerpt', and 'illustrate' and 'illustrator'. There might be discussion about the ways in which prefixes or suffixes can be used to modify words, so that we can take the word 'enjoy' and get 'enjoyable', 'enjoying' and 'enjoyed', or 'sequence' can be turned into 'consequence', 'sequential', 'sequentially' and 'subsequent'. As long as examples are given in sentences, children will begin to appreciate that words are often related to each other and that we can often work out what unfamiliar words mean by looking for the roots within them.

The strategy of teaching related words together is far from original. The word lists in Schonell's *Essentials in Teaching and Testing Spelling* (1957 reprint) were based upon the written material of seven- to twelve-year-olds. Schonell maintained that homophones should be separated to avoid confusion and so *'new'* and *'knew'*, *'him'* and *'hymn'* and *'there'* and *'their'* each appear in different lists. *'There'* would be learned in conjunction with *'where'* and *'here'*, while *'new'* would be linked to *'few'*, *'chew'* and *'dew'*. Schonell (1957: 12) asserted that 'The first essential is that children should be taught words which they use frequently in their written work and that they should not waste time learning words which they seldom use.'

TABLE 12.2 Sample word lists for a Year 5 class

Lowest ability group	Middle ability group	Highest ability group
prefer	preference	characteristic
enjoy	enjoyable	rhyme
setting	character	dialogue
author	illustrate	sequence
verse	Carroll	metaphor
Lewis	Dahl	illustrator
blurb	describe	illustration
cover	description	incident
publish	paragraph	excerpt
publisher	extract	situation

Developing children's fascination with words

If spelling lists are to be used to foster an interest in vocabulary, teachers need to take time to talk about words and their derivations. This will inevitably require some research in etymological dictionaries, but the benefits will be considerable both for pupils and teachers. *Support for Spelling* (DCSF 2009b) includes a range of useful activities as well as guidance for teaching and lists of words and can be an excellent starting point.

Common prefixes could be studied through looking at words familiar to children, who could then be encouraged to apply their knowledge of these and examples of root words to help them to understand new words. Thus, they might look at the prefix 'sub-', which means 'under', 'less', 'lower' or 'inferior', in words such as 'subway' and 'submarine' and then try to work out the meanings of 'subaqua', 'submerge', 'substandard' and 'subtract'. An understanding of morphology is important here. Morphemes are the smallest units of meaning in words, so 'happy' is a single morpheme while 'unhappy' has two morphemes: 'un-' and 'happy' meaning 'not happy'. As spelling develops from being simply a matter of making graphemes and phonemes correspond, an understanding of morphemes and their functions increases in importance.

Children's fascination with words can be fostered through a variety of classroom activities. Despite criticism of the use of weekly word lists for children to memorise for tests, many teachers persist with these, sometimes citing parental pressure as a reason. However, if used imaginatively, these lists can provide a valuable learning tool. Dictionaries can be used to find alternative meanings and, sometimes, alternative spellings. The lists can provide a starting point for children to make collections of, say, synonyms and antonyms both in school and at home with the help of parents.

It is the broadening of knowledge about words that will enable children to develop their spelling abilities rather than simply the memorising of lists. Teachers often complain that children can spell words in a test but seem unable to do so a few days later in their written work. Perhaps if they were to engage children more deeply with the words and take the time to discuss etymology and strategies for learning how to spell those words, their pupils might be better able to work out how to spell them when the test is a distant memory.

Teaching spelling rules and spelling principles

Ask any group of English speakers to tell you a spelling rule and it is almost guaranteed that they will chorus: 'i before e except after c'. We remember this partly because it has a short, memorable rhyme, but the rule has many exceptions including 'seeing', 'their', 'weigh', 'sleigh', 'neighbour' and 'being', words that children meet frequently. The rule is better amended to take into account the exceptions, and many people prefer 'i before e except after c when the word rhymes with me' (think of 'chief', 'thief', 'shield' etc.), which takes into account where common exceptions can be found.

It is interesting is to ask people to name another spelling rule: they usually find this difficult. Gentry (1987: 31) argued that most spelling rules were of little use and maintained that the following rules were the only ones worth learning:

■   the rules for using full stops in abbreviations;
■   the rules for using apostrophes to show possession;

- the rules for capitalising proper names and adjectives (e.g. 'The Pink Panther');
- the rules for adding suffixes (changing 'y' to 'i', dropping the final silent 'e', doubling the final consonant);
- the rule that English words do not end in 'v';
- the rule that 'q' is followed by 'u' in English spelling.

Gentry goes on to argue that we should 'teach only the rules that apply to a large number of words, not those that have lots of exceptions' (Gentry 1987: 31). Significantly, he does not include 'i before e except after c' in his short list.

McGuinness (2004: 44) goes further and cites studies that showed that the only rules that were 100 per cent consistent 'specified which letters formed digraphs (*sh* in *ship*)'. She concludes: 'There are no spelling rules. Forget about rules. Forget about generalizations.'

However, despite the complexity and inconsistency of English spelling, we maintain that there are some general principles that are worth looking at with children. The problem with many rules is that in order to understand them we need quite a sophisticated knowledge of linguistic terminology, and it may be that by the time we have acquired this we will already have internalised the rules through our everyday reading and writing. For example, a principle that children begin to apply is 'double the consonant when adding -ing where verbs contain short vowels': 'hit' becomes 'hitting', 'bat' becomes 'batting', 'hop' becomes 'hopping' and so on. The rule is widely applicable, although there are some exceptions ('benefiting'), but the terminology may challenge the pupils who need to learn the rule. Of course, they should learn about consonants, vowels and verbs, but combining the three terms in one rule may over-face many children.

One solution to the problem of learning the principles of spelling is to adopt an investigative approach whereby children are asked to look at lots of examples and try to work out the principles for themselves. Their ideas can then be discussed by groups or by the class, with teachers addressing misconceptions and rules being written as a shared writing activity. Try this yourself in the following activity.

ACTIVITY: MAKING WORDS ENDING IN 'Y' INTO PLURALS

Look at the following and then write a rule for making words ending in 'y' into plurals:

- baby – babies
- lady – ladies
- monkey – monkeys
- day – days
- hobby – hobbies
- body – bodies
- guy – guys
- boy – boys

(For a possible solution, see the end of the chapter.)

Peters (1975: 115) maintained that 'a generalisation of probabilities for spelling may be developed as we become increasingly familiar with the look of our language in writing.' For example, we might point out similarities between and within words, perhaps beginning with a child's name. Thus, Ian might learn that part of his name features in 'triangle' and 'Martian'. Peters (1975) argued that the essence of teaching children to spell lies in teaching them how to learn letter strings. Mudd (1994: 159) summed up her experience of teaching spelling rules thus: 'I have found that, though these rules are generally of great interest to those who are already good spellers, they need very explicit teaching to be helpful to most novice spellers.' However, she went on to advocate the teaching of generalisations rather than rules, with exceptions being pointed out.

Teaching children how to learn to spell

So far, we have looked at phonics, word lists and spelling rules. We now describe a range of spelling strategies in order to demonstrate that, while we may use phonic knowledge as a key strategy when we first learn to spell, as we develop our understanding of our language we are able to draw upon other tactics too. By the time children reach Year 4 they might be expected to use their knowledge of phonics, morphology and etymology to spell unfamiliar words, as well as to develop personal strategies for learning new words. These personal strategies might be drawn from some of the approaches described in this section.

Look, say, cover, write, check

Peters (1975) argued that visual perception of word form is crucial to learning how to spell. Children should be presented with words used in the course of free writing, supplemented by useful variants, and be shown how to learn them using the following routine: *look* at the word, *say* the word aloud, *cover* the word, *write* the word from memory and *check* that the word has been written correctly. If the word is misspelled, the process should be repeated.

'Look, say, cover, write, check' (or 'look, cover, write, check') is one of the most widely known and commonly used strategies that teachers encourage children to use when learning spellings. In order to determine how useful it can be, and to explore some other useful strategies, it would be helpful to look at some strategies as we attempt to learn how to spell words that often challenge even the best spellers.

ACTIVITY: TESTING YOUR OWN SPELLING

Look at the words below and decide which of them you might usually struggle to spell accurately. Better still, ask a friend to test you on the spellings before you look at them.

supersede	accommodation	liaise	correspondence
embarrass	raspberry	graffiti	separate
Wednesday	Mediterranean	harass	idiosyncrasy
definitely	necessary	weird	focused

Origins of words

If, as is quite likely, since the words in the activity were chosen because many people find them challenging, you made some mistakes, then you are on the way to understanding the problems children face when learning to spell. Even if you got all the spellings correct first time, it is still possible to reflect upon how you did this. Let us look at some of the words and consider which strategies we might deploy when learning them.

'Supersede' is often misspelled as 'supercede' by people who do not understand its etymology. 'Super' means 'above' or 'beyond' and *sedere* means 'to sit' in Latin (think of 'sedate', 'sedan', 'sedentary' and 'sediment'), so 'to supersede' is 'to sit above' or 'replace' someone. In understanding 'supersede', we can apply our knowledge to other words beginning with the prefix 'super-', such as 'supervise' ('to oversee' – think of 'vision', 'visual', 'visor' and 'visit'), 'supernatural' and 'superman'. In using our knowledge of word derivations, we are using a cognitive approach to spelling. We might also use this approach to help us to spell 'definitely', which is often misspelled as 'definately'. However, if we know that the word is derived from 'finite', it is much more likely that we will spell it with an 'i' rather than an 'a'.

Mnemonics and over-articulation

For some words, we may know or devise mnemonics to help us to remember how to spell the tricky parts. For example:

- I should be embarrassed if I put two 'r's in 'harassed'.
- 'Separate' has a rat in it (sep *a rat* e).
- 'Accommodation' has double beds (to remember the double 'c' and double 'm').
- I liaise whenever I can (to help us remember to put an 'i' after the 'a' in 'liaise').
- It is necessary to have one collar and two sleeves (to help us remember that 'necessary' has one 'c' and two 's's).

For some words with silent letters, we may over-articulate by sounding the silent letters in our heads. Just think how you remember to spell 'Wednesday' and you will understand what is meant by this term. We may do the same thing for 'raspberry', 'February', 'gnome' and 'pneumatic'.

Phonic knowledge

The above strategies are useful both when learning the tricky parts of words and in internalising their spellings, but, when we reflect on the other strategies we bring to bear, we can see that phonic knowledge is also vital. However, once we have acquired sufficient phonic understanding to cope with simple words, we need to develop strategies to help us with the more complicated ones. Central to learning such words is an ability to identify the parts of words that we need to pay particular attention to, such as the double letters in 'accommodation'. Our phonic knowledge will help us with the rest. It may, therefore, be a useful strategy when presenting children with spellings to learn to begin by giving them a test, so that they can determine what they already know and what they need to learn. Providing that this is done in a non-threatening way, that marks are not collected or shown to others, and that children understand the purpose of the exercise, this can be a valuable method of helping them to learn and to determine strategies for learning.

A natural development of the strategies described above is for children to investigate words themselves. While the grammar exercise books that were widely used until the 1960s seem dull and boring today, they can be a rich source of lists of similes, synonyms, homonyms, antonyms, collective nouns and so forth, which can induce a fascination for words in some readers. Such lists encourage children to think about vocabulary. They might, as one class did, devise their own collective nouns after reading and giggling over those in *The New First Aid in English* (Mciver n.d.: 19–20). 'A crawl of caravans' was apparently inspired by a long journey from the South of France by one pupil, while others came up with 'a grumble of teachers', 'an irritation of younger brothers and sisters' and 'a defeat of English footballers'. In looking at the examples provided, the children explore spelling and make use of dictionaries both to look up unfamiliar words and to find new ones for their own use.

Handwriting and spelling

Peters (1985) maintained that handwriting can be a vital factor in influencing good spelling and argued that the teaching of groups of letters through joined script reinforces the child's concept of the serial probability (the likely order in which letters appear in words in English) of letters within words. She stated that

> There is no question that children with swift motor control write groups of letters ... in a connected form and this is the basis of knowledge about which letters stick together. This is the crux of spelling ability, for handwriting and spelling go hand in hand.
>
> (Peters 1985: 55)

Charles Cripps (1988, 1998), who based his work on Margaret Peters' research, developed a joined handwriting scheme, *A Hand for Spelling*, in which he emphasised the importance of free-flowing handwriting and argued that 'Spelling is a visual skill. Good spellers look carefully at words and it is through this visual familiarity that they learn the possibility of certain letters occurring together' (Cripps 1988: 1).

Interestingly, two of the major systematic synthetic phonics programmes have differing views on joined handwriting. The Jolly Phonics Parent/Teacher Guide asserts that 'In time a child will need to learn joined up (cursive) writing. It helps the fluency of writing and improves spelling' (p. 5), while Read Write Inc.'s teacher's guide maintains that teaching joined handwriting early means that children's efforts 'go into the physical process of writing rather than what they are writing' (p. 11).

Reading and spelling

The assumption that children's spelling abilities improve as their reading improves is challenged by Carless (1989), who maintained that spelling and reading are quite different skills and pointed out that fluent readers are sometimes very weak at spelling:

> A fluent reader will use semantic, syntactic and graphophonic cues in order to read words. However, he does not need to look consciously at every word, as a swift reader

uses only partial cues to gain meaning, and so is highly unlikely to use all cues available to him at once.

(Carless 1989: 16)

Thus, mistakes in reading, providing they do not alter the sense of a passage, are relatively unimportant, while a spelling mistake reflects the writer's skill in using language. Frith (1980) studied good readers who were poor spellers and found that the majority of their errors were phonetic misspellings caused by a lack of close attention to the text 'in order to assimilate serial probability' (as described by Carless 1989: 17).

Although Carless (1989) conceded that reading must have some influence upon spelling, she argued that spelling cannot be 'caught' through reading and writing activities alone and must, therefore, have a place in the primary-school curriculum.

Finding out what children know about spelling

The activities described in this section are designed to enable teachers to find out what children know about spelling, and in particular to find out about their level of phonic understanding. For example:

- Do they understand that phonemes can be represented by graphemes?
- Are they aware that some phonemes can be represented by many different graphemes and that some graphemes can represent several different phonemes?
- Can they build words using logical groups of graphemes?

Try the following, but be prepared to vary strategies as you discover the ability levels of the children with whom you are working.

Words containing 'ea'

Make a set of cards with words containing the 'ea' digraph (see Waugh *et al.* 1999: 152). Include words such as 'bread', 'idea', 'break' and 'early' as well as several in which 'ea' makes an 'ee' sound such as 'each', 'please', 'treat' and 'bean'.

- Ask the children which sound the letters 'ea' make. Talk about the most common sound made by the digraph, but encourage the children to discover that 'ea' often makes other sounds, especially as in 'bread', 'dead', 'head' and 'dread'. You might also talk about 'read' and 'lead', which can both be pronounced in different ways.
- Cut out the 'ea' words and ask the children to sort them according to the phoneme that 'ea' represents in each.
- Look at a piece of writing that includes 'ea' words and ask the children to find them and pronounce them.
- Ask children to look at a range of texts to investigate 'ea' words and to decide which are the most common sounds for 'ea'. This could be linked to data-collection work in mathematics and to data-presentation work in ICT.

Grapheme cards

Make a set of cards of common graphemes. Include both the most common representations of the forty-four phonemes, including the letters of the alphabet and common vowel and consonant digraphs, and some that occur less frequently, as well as those that have been discussed in recent spelling lessons. The cards can be used over and over again so you may wish to cover them with a clear film to protect them. They can be used in a variety of ways:

- Ask children to spread them out face up and then take turns to take one. You should play too, to model the activity. Explain that they are going to make words using at least three graphemes. Continue to take turns to take graphemes until each child has three. If someone is struggling to make a word, help him or ask others for suggestions. Ask if anyone can take another grapheme and make a word with four phonemes. If children misspell words, look to see whether their mistakes are phonically plausible. Show them how to spell the words correctly.

- Ask children to sort the graphemes into graphs, digraphs and trigraphs, or into vowel digraphs, consonant digraphs and consonant blends.

- Work as a group cooperatively to build as many words as possible or to make the longest word possible. When a word has been made, help the children to learn its spelling.

- Ask the children to match graphemes that represent the same phonemes. For example, 'kn' and 'n'; 'ch', 'k', 'ck' and 'c'; 'ea', 'ee' and 'ie'. Ask them to tell you a word that has each grapheme in it.

- Turn all the graphemes face down and ask children to take turns to turn one over and name a word that includes that grapheme.

- Ask children to take turns to turn graphemes over and place them on the table face up. The object is to use each grapheme to build a word. For example, Sam turns over 'ch' and has to name a word that includes 'ch'; Pam turns over 'ea' and has to put it with 'ch' and suggest a word that includes 'ch' and 'ea'. If she cannot, ask someone else. If no one can name a word, turn the card face down again and ask the next child to choose a different one.

ACTIVITY: USING GRAPHEME CARDS

We first used the grapheme cards with trainee teachers working with groups of children in an inner-city school. They were a huge success and both trainees and children soon found new and more adventurous ways of using them.

Try to devise some ideas of your own. This is best done if you make some cards and try out activities with colleagues.

Classroom activities for developing good spelling

Daw *et al.* (1997) looked at factors associated with high standards in spelling from Reception to Year 4 and found that the following were features of those classrooms and schools where spelling standards were high:

- active use by children in their writing of displays of spelling, the alphabet, key words, letter strings and so on designed to promote learning;

- an interest in language permeating the teaching of pupils, with opportunities to discuss words being taken up constantly across the curriculum;

- clear understanding of approaches taken by other teachers throughout the school and constant use of a few key strategies;

- early and systematic teaching of phonics, extensive use of rhymes in the early years, mastery of letter names as well as sounds and effective early reading;

- an early but systematic move through the first stages of writing, with independence always the goal but structure always sufficient to produce coherent legible text;

- a systematic approach to covering major spelling regularities, including teaching and discussion, learning words and assessing progress through regular testing;

- high-quality teaching with regular brief instruction sessions to the class, group or individuals to maintain an interest in spelling and a fascination with words and their meanings;

- appropriate differentiation within a context of high expectations for all pupils;

- teaching methods and resources deployed to encourage pupils to experiment and become independent as spellers from an early age;

- pupils' writing marked regularly with the indication of some spelling errors as part of the feedback provided to help them to improve;

- parents involved in helping their children learn spellings at home regularly, as well as hearing reading.

Daw *et al.*'s (1997) conclusions resonate with much of what has already been stated in this chapter and elsewhere in this book (see Chapter 7, on teaching and learning reading). In this section, we will explore some practical activities that might be used in the classroom, or at home by parents and children, in order to ensure high standards in spelling and to make spelling interesting and enjoyable. The age group of the children for which each activity might best be suited is deliberately not suggested, since abilities vary greatly within classes and some activities normally designed for younger children might be appropriate for older strugglers while others, usually the preserve of older pupils, may be adapted for use with very able younger pupils.

Developing an interest in letters and words

In the Early Years Foundation Stage and Key Stage 1, children can create collages of letters, make pastry letters, create patterns using groups of letters, trace letters in sand or cut letters out of newspapers to make sentences (like ransom notes!). One teacher encouraged the children to add to her list of what she called 'silly words' (those that were irregular) and to find others that were called 'easy words'. Children can make collections of foreign words seen in shops and on television and can be encouraged to look for deliberate misspellings on household products and businesses ('Kwikfit', 'Weetabix', 'Betabuy' etc.).

Playing games that highlight sounds and letter strings

I-spy, rhyming games, tongue-twisters and work on alliteration all emphasise word relationships. A particularly successful and amusing activity involves children in creating spoonerisms, beginning with names ('Bavid Deckham') and moving on to other items of interest such as football teams ('Roncaster Dovers') and television programmes ('Brig Bother'). They will soon realise that some names are more difficult than others because of the presence of letter and sound combinations that do not feature in English, and that words beginning with vowels are difficult to spoonerise. However, even when the spoonerisms do not work, children will be learning something about the combinations of letters and initial sounds that are possible and impossible in English spelling.

Using 'environmental print'

Many teachers take children on 'literacy walks', encouraging them to look at signs and symbols in the environment. Alternatively, photographs, slides and websites can be used to show the proliferation of 'literature' that exists all around us. Children can follow this up by learning spellings from the environment and discussing strategies for doing so.

Using dictionaries and thesauruses

In successful classrooms, these are readily available and children are shown how to use them. Teachers select dictionaries appropriate for their pupils, and there is always a larger and more comprehensive dictionary available for looking up words that do not feature in the children's dictionaries. Many thesauruses are suitable for use in primary classrooms and children can become so absorbed in them that they go off at tangents looking up several words as their interest grows. It is important that children understand alphabetical order as early as possible if they are to be able to use reference books successfully and without frustration (see Chapter 9, on reading and writing for information).

Helping to develop drafting techniques

For some teachers, drafting involves children writing a piece of work, having it marked and then copying it out. In classrooms where children are encouraged to develop independence in drafting and see the teacher as an audience for their writing rather than merely the marker of their work, writing tends to be more adventurous and better presented. Children need to learn how to check their work. For some, being told to do this leads to confusion, while for others it is an intrinsic part of writing that fosters careful consideration of word structures and reference skills (see Chapter 11, 'Developing writing' for a guide to checking writing).

Using word processors and spellcheckers

The word processor enables the writer to amend and adapt work easily and produces print, in which children often find it easier to spot their spelling mistakes than in handwriting. Spellcheckers can be useful, but children should be encouraged to use them with caution (one does not recognise 'headteacher' and offers the peculiarly apt 'heartache' as an alternative). This extract from a poem by Jerry Zar (1992) might serve as a warning and stimulate an interest in homonyms and homophones:

I have a spelling checker.
It came with my PC.

It plane lee marks four my revue
Miss steaks aye can knot sea.
Eye ran this poem threw it,
Your sure reel glad two no.
Its vary polished inn it's weigh.
My checker tolled me sew.

Reducing stress in writing sessions

For some teachers, a writing session is a stressful occasion in which little time is available for sitting with children to discuss their work. Often, this situation could easily be avoided. For example, the excessive use of personal spelling dictionaries tends to create a dependency culture in which children become over-reliant upon their teachers for help with every word that they do not feel completely confident of spelling correctly. Some teachers encourage this by telling children that they expect accurate work first time with no spelling mistakes. Besides being an unreasonable demand to make of young children, this also negates much of what the writing process is really like for adults as well as for children. Most adults draft important pieces of writing and try out spellings by writing them down to see whether they look right. Alternatively, they continue their writing and then check spellings at the end or when they reach a natural break.

Children in classes where the spelling book rules tend, in our experience, to produce stilted and unimaginative work and actually do not spell as well as those who are encouraged to attempt spellings and then check them. For some children, the spelling dictionary provides an excuse to stop work and join the queue that inevitably follows the teacher around the room. Often, children reach the front of the queue and have forgotten which word they were going to ask for, or have not opened the book at the right page.

If one argues against the use of spelling books in this way, one may be accused of devaluing spelling, but this is far from the case. In one of the National Writing Project's publications, *Responding to and Assessing Writing* (1989a), a teacher describes how she refused to help children with spellings and encouraged them to 'have a go'. After some initial reluctance, the children accepted the approach. The teacher reported:

> What has surprised me most is that this approach has actually led to a marked improvement in the children's spelling. I did not realise just how well they could spell without my aid. I now feel I was holding them back and not giving them the confidence they needed to attempt their own spellings. They had more experience and knowledge than they or I had realised. It is especially significant that this improvement was seen in the majority of children, representing a wide range of abilities.
>
> (National Writing Project 1989a: 15)

It is this independence, allied to a programme of teaching spelling in a systematic way, that, we are confident, serves children best and allows teachers time to spend with children discussing writing and keeping them on task. Simple guidance can be given to children to enable them to sustain the momentum of their writing when they wish to use a word they cannot spell with confidence:

- Underline the word or circle it and check spelling later or write the word in different ways and choose the one that looks right.

- Segment the word into its sounds, write as much as you can and fill in details later (e.g. 'b-tiful').

- Tap out syllables quietly and write the word bit by bit (e.g. 'yes-ter-day').

- Ask someone, look at a chart or word bank or use a dictionary.

Another way in which individual children's spelling might be monitored and developed is through the use of *spelling cards*. In this system, each child has a card that is kept on the teacher's desk or in some easily accessible place. Whenever a child has a word corrected by the teacher or asks for help with a spelling, the word is written on the card by the teacher. The child looks carefully at the word and then returns to his or her place and tries to write the word correctly. He or she then checks that the word is written correctly and, if it is not, repeats the exercise. The cards are regularly given out to the children and they spend time looking closely at the words before being tested on them by classmates. Each child builds up a store of words that he or she uses regularly and that can be referred to whenever necessary using the 'look, say, cover, write, check' method. The words may be copied, by the children, into personal dictionaries for easy reference. This method has the advantage of being an individual approach to spelling and it does not preclude the use of other spelling lists or tests. Children can achieve success at their own levels and testing is less stressful when carried out individually rather than in a whole-class situation.

ACTIVITY: THINKING ABOUT SPELLING

Having read the chapter, look at the questions below and think about your views and discuss them with a colleague.

- How would you conduct a formal spelling lesson?
- Should invented spelling be tolerated?
- When should spelling instruction begin?
- Which spelling rules should be taught?
- What is the purpose of spelling tests?
- How can phonics be taught as a basis for spelling?
- Should teachers correct every mistake in a piece of work that is to be displayed?

The importance of spelling

US President Andrew Jackson, a poor speller, maintained: 'It's a damn poor mind that can think of only one way to spell a word!' While it may be true that it requires intelligence to apply a range of strategies to the problem of accurately spelling words in a language full of irregularities and exceptions, it is, nevertheless, important that children leave school able to spell accurately and knowing strategies for attempting those words that challenge them. Even though many people have access to a word processor with a spellchecker, it is still, as we have seen, quite possible to misspell words, particularly in a language so rich in homonyms and homophones.

This chapter has explored a range of strategies for developing children's spelling. The principal approach to early spelling promoted by the government and Ofsted is the use of phonic knowledge, and this is central to teaching and learning spelling. However, this approach needs to be allied to others as children develop as writers if they *are* to succeed. In many professions, application forms that include spelling errors are routinely discarded. An inability to spell accurately can, then, be both educationally and financially costly.

Key points

- The English spelling system is problematical because of the number of phonic irregularities, but this should not prevent teachers from making extensive use of phonics when teaching spelling.

- There are many strategies that can be used to teach and learn spelling. A key objective for teachers is to arm children with a range of strategies that will enable them to learn spellings independently.

- Teachers need to develop the sensitivity to know when it is important to use errors as teaching tools and when to show tolerance of mistakes that, if highlighted, might deter future attempts at writing.

Further reading

Montgomery, D. (1997) *Spelling: remedial strategies*. London: Cassell.
Topping, K. (2001) *Thinking Reading Writing*. London: Continuum.

For guidance on the principles and practice for Jolly Phonics, see http://jollylearning.co.uk/overview-about-jolly-phonics. For guidance on the principles and practice for Read Write Inc., see http://ruthmiskinliteracy.com and Miskin, R. (2011) *Read Write Inc.: Phonics Handbook. Oxford:* Oxford University Press.

A spelling rule for plurals of words ending in 'y'

If the word ends with a consonant before the 'y', take off the 'y' and add '-ies'. If the word has a vowel before the 'y', add 's'. The key to remembering this is the word 'key', which we all know has the plural 'keys' and not 'kies'.

13

Using technology to enhance the learning and teaching of English

John Bennett and Richard English

Purpose of this chapter

This chapter aims to:

- explore technology enhanced learning in English;
- put forward arguments for using technology in learning and teaching English;
- describe specific ways of using technology in the teaching of English.

> No child can be an effective communicator in a world which has been transformed by the new technologies without acquiring the skills needed to make selective and effective use of ICT.
>
> (Becta 2009: 2)

Information and communications technology (ICT), more broadly considered in this chapter simply as technology, is an essential component of our everyday lives and is used by most of us both at work and in leisure activities. It also features strongly in the world of education, with most primary schools now generously equipped with computers, interactive whiteboards and an increasingly widening range of other technological gadgetry. With all of this now at their fingertips and with the need to prepare young people for a technology-rich world, the continuing challenge for schools and teachers is to ensure that the potential offered by technology is fully realised, so as to enhance teaching and learning not only with regard to the English curriculum but also in all aspects of primary education. The aim of this chapter is to get you started on the road to making the best possible use of technology in your English teaching. The chapter ends with a list of useful online resources.

What do we mean by technology in schools?

ICT is still a commonly used term in education and stands for 'information and communications technology'. Many people interpret ICT in a narrow way, considering it to be simply synonymous with 'computers'. Yes, computers do represent one aspect of ICT, but it is far more wide-ranging than this. This chapter will use the word 'technology', which encompasses ICT but allows a broader interpretation in order to avoid confusion with ICT, which is taught in many schools as a separate curriculum subject. Some aspects of technology have been commonplace in schools for many years, for example CD players, radios, televisions, DVD players, electronic calculators, overhead projectors, telephones, fax machines and photocopiers. More-recent additions include digital cameras, video cameras, Blu-ray players, eBook readers and smart phones. Even our understanding of the word 'computer' now includes variants such as laptops, notebooks, handhelds and tablet computers (such as the iPad and various Android-based devices), as well as an increasing range of peripheral equipment that can be connected to a computer, notably digital projectors and interactive whiteboards. Now add to this the high-speed internet access found in most schools and the increasing availability of wireless networking (WiFi), internet-based programmes and Web 2.0 (online interaction, collaboration and sharing) and we have an environment for children that is rich in technology in the broadest sense.

Many schools are running their own websites and, either individually or in partnership with their local authority, schools also have learning platforms (virtual learning environments, or VLEs) through which children can access software and files both within and outside school. Software, as well as hardware, availability has increased in schools and there is growing use of free open-source and web-based software, which enables schools with limited budgets to provide a good range of programmes for pupil use. Not only that, but open-source and web-based software is often free for home users, meaning that many children can use the same software at home as they do in school.

Although high-quality technological resources are increasingly commonplace in primary schools, not all established teachers are enthusiastic about them or make the best use of the facilities they offer to enhance learning and teaching. Possible reasons include lack of self-confidence in the use of technology, limited awareness of what is possible and limited time to explore the uses of the technology. Other teachers remain unconvinced that some technology has the potential to transform teaching and learning. The next section provides a persuasive argument for utilising technology in all aspects of your work in primary schools, with a particular emphasis on teaching English. At every stage, you can reap the benefits offered by technology, from preparation and planning, to teaching and learning in the classroom, through to assessment, recording and reporting to parents.

ACTIVITY: USING TECHNOLOGY IN THE CLASSROOM

Make a list of reasons why you ought to be using technology in your teaching, with a particular emphasis on the teaching of English. Remember to think of technology in its broadest sense.

- What are the potential benefits to you?
- What are the potential benefits to your pupils?
- Are there any particular individuals or groups of pupils who would benefit?

When you have answered these questions, compare what you have written with the discussion presented in the next section.

Why use technology? How can it enhance teaching and learning?

The first point to make justifying the use of technology relates to the nature of the high-tech world in which we live. Just think of the wealth of electronic gadgetry that we have in our homes and carry around in our pockets, as well as the technology we encounter when we shop for food (whether we go through the supermarket checkout or avoid it by using the do-it-yourself fast lane or shopping online) or when we fill the car with petrol, withdraw money from the bank, pay for a meal out or a round of drinks in the pub, have the electricity meter read, or borrow a book or CD from the library. Personal technology has taken huge leaps forward in recent years, with devices such as smart phones, iPads, MP3 players and eBook readers such as the Kindle becoming a part of everyday life for many people, some of whom may not actually own a desktop or laptop computer. Personal communication takes place virtually, through emails, text messages, tweets, Skype and social networking sites, perhaps more than in the physical world. At work there are very few occupations that do not involve the use of technology in some form. When thinking specifically of English, we need to acknowledge that pupils are growing up in a world where every aspect of language is explored through technology: from simple things such as using a mobile phone to listen to somebody, through multimodal texts ('texts' that are made up of a variety of media, such as web pages with video, sound, graphics and hyperlinks), to whole virtual worlds in which children can explore and interact with others. We need to prepare pupils to be citizens in a technology-rich world, from the earliest stages of their schooling. This alone should be sufficient justification for ensuring that all pupils experience technology in a positive way, not just in English but in all areas of the curriculum. As Becta notes:

> As technology becomes a greater part of everyday life, it is only natural that it becomes a central and essential part of 21st century learning. Learners already engage extensively with technology and they expect it to be used in school.
>
> (Becta 2010: 3)

Successive governments have acknowledged the importance of technology by either including it as a subject in its own right in the curriculum or stressing its importance as a set of cross-curricular skills, usually as ICT. In teaching or using technology in English in primary schools, it is important to consider the content and expectations of the National Curriculum but equally important to bear in mind that technology changes quickly and new ideas, methods and technologies should be incorporated when appropriate, even if the National Curriculum does not mention them.

Computers are fast and powerful and can therefore carry out low-level mechanical chores very efficiently, thus freeing up time for the user to spend on higher-level skills. One example is a teacher employing a spreadsheet to analyse pupils' marks; another is a pupil using a word processor to cut and paste text, to check spellings or to count the number of words in a document. The computer does the donkey work so that the user can concentrate on things such as analysis and interpretation (in the case of the teacher) and creative writing (in the case of the pupil). Computers can also store and retrieve huge quantities of information, both locally (e.g. using hard disks, CDs, DVDs and memory sticks) and also remotely via networks, intranets and the internet (including access through online storage and cloud computing). Consequently, teachers, pupils, parents and carers are able to access rich and varied resources that were simply not available a few years ago, all through the click of a few buttons, using a few taps on a screen or via voice commands.

Technology allows information to be presented more accurately and more attractively than by most traditional means, so that it engages the attention of the user. Why rely on a scruffy, hurriedly written piece of text on the whiteboard when you can produce a more effective visual aid with a computer? Technology is also inclusive, in that the information can be presented in a variety of ways according to the size of the audience and the special needs of particular individuals. Another feature of the information being presented is that it can comprise various media or modes of communication such as text, graphics, sounds, animations and video: hence the expressions 'multimedia' and 'multimodal'. This, together with the often interactive nature of the materials being presented, captures the interest of the user and motivates him or her to want to learn.

Benefits of technology for pupils

It would be easy to get into a discussion of learning theories, behaviourism and constructivism and of Piaget and other psychologists, but instead let us consider one simple fact: children learn what they choose to learn. We cannot force pupils to learn, and this requires us to inspire, to motivate, to open doors and to make children want to learn. Technology can play a key part in achieving this. Many of us have anecdotal evidence of how children are motivated by technology, and there is a body of research literature to support these beliefs (Becta 2003a, European Schoolnet 2006). This evidence suggests that technology can have a positive impact on pupils' levels of concentration, self-confidence, self-esteem, independence and behaviour. There are particular benefits for those who are reluctant learners or have special educational needs. When using technology, the pupil is required to employ different skills from those needed when using pens, pencils, sheets of writing paper, dictionaries and other paper-based materials. These pupils usually adapt to the technological approach more readily than the traditional one and their much-needed success raises their self-esteem (Becta 2003a). In terms of presentation, their story or poem will look just as impressive as those produced by the rest of the class, and can be displayed on the wall or uploaded to the school's learning platform or website along with everyone else's. One specific target group that could benefit from these sorts of technological approaches is boys, who typically are reluctant to engage in the writing process or read fiction.

Technology can provide access to the curriculum for children with a special educational need of a physical nature; for example, those with poor motor control who find it difficult to produce legible work by hand can use a keyboard or other input device. Speech-recognition software means that those with severe physical disabilities can simply speak and see their words appearing on the screen. Visually impaired pupils can increase the font size or zoom factor when viewing text on the screen or have the text on the screen 'read' to them by the computer. Dyslexic pupils can change the font and background colours to improve their ability to read text accurately, make use of programmes that help with organisation and use programme features to help with checking text .

Technology can benefit pupils with special educational needs in other ways. First, computer-based learning materials often break down the skills and content being taught into small, achievable steps, thus allowing the learner to demonstrate measurable progress. Second, there are major advantages in terms of the learning taking place 'in private'. The child can work at his or her own pace without fear of appearing slow or holding back the rest of the class. If a mistake is made, the child does not have to worry about looking foolish in front of everyone else and he or she can simply have another go, usually after being given additional hints or clues by the computer. Systems such as SuccessMaker Enterprise (www.rm.com) provide this kind of environment and support. The computer can never replace good-quality interaction with an effective teacher, but the instant, impartial feedback it offers is something that the teacher is not always able to match.

Research has also shown that, with computer-based activities, pupils are more likely to be creative, to experiment and to take risks, which is precisely what we want them to do, for example when engaging in the creative-writing process (Becta 2003b).

Benefits of technology for teachers

So, technology has got a lot to offer for pupils, but what's in it for you? Well, if your pupils are benefiting in the ways described above, clearly it is going to assist your role as an effective teacher, but there are some additional specific benefits to be aware of. The widespread availability of technology, particularly the internet, means that you now have easy access to a huge bank of ready-made resources. Why reinvent the wheel when someone else has already created that lesson plan, interactive whiteboard resource, activity sheet, PowerPoint presentation, poster, instructional text or set of flashcards that you want to use? There are many excellent websites, often set up by teachers, that provide these kinds of resources, usually free of charge or for a small joining fee (see the 'Useful websites' section at the end of the chapter). In many cases these websites accept submissions from teachers, so if you have created electronic resources yourself you can make them widely available by sharing them on the internet. A good example of this system is provided by the Times Educational Supplement (www.tes.co.uk), where a vast range of free resources is available. It is important to remember that not every resource that is uploaded is going to be appropriate for the actual class of children you are working with and the quality of resources varies hugely, so the use of professional judgement about the suitability of resources is essential. Of course, one of the biggest benefits of electronic resources is that if you find a resource online that doesn't quite meet your needs you can in many cases edit it and so still get the use from it and save yourself some valuable time. Many resources, in a variety of formats, are available and most, including .pdf files, which in the past were hard to edit, can be edited with the right software. If you have not started to make use of the internet in this way, you really do not know what you are missing out on, so why not investigate some of the websites listed at the end of this chapter?

Specific tools, such as interactive whiteboard and presentation software, word processors, graphics and desktop publishing packages, make creating your own attractive, stimulating resources a straightforward and satisfying task. You can create professional-looking printed materials as well as presentations and visual aids to display on a computer screen or project onto the wall, and because these are stored electronically you can edit and add to them for future use. It is also much easier to adapt these resources for different children or groups, offering opportunities for effective differentiation. You can share the resources with colleagues in your own school and more widely, via the internet or other networking. By encouraging this sort of sharing culture, ultimately everyone benefits. Making use of shared folders on the school's computer network or learning platform and uploading to teachers' websites (such as at www.tes.co.uk) is an excellent way of promoting this way of working. The more that staff put in to it, the more they get out of it, both literally and metaphorically.

In summary, then, from the teacher's perspective, technology enables you to

- access or create stimulating resources;
- distribute or display them attractively to individuals, groups and whole classes of pupils;
- capture the interest of your pupils and motivate them to want to learn;
- address the issue of inclusion by providing all pupils with access to the curriculum;
- share your resources with colleagues and teachers in other schools;
- carry out many of your administrative tasks more effectively and efficiently.

There are many things that are done better with technology than without it, and this is demonstrated in the rest of this chapter, which provides you with a range of tips, ideas and advice for using technology in your English teaching.

Using technology to support and enhance the teaching of English

Having read the previous section, you should be aware of the potential for using technology. The range of possibilities is vast and so it is helpful to think in terms of broad categories of use. We could distinguish between those occasions when it is the teacher who is using the technology and those when it is the pupils who are using it. Alternatively, we could think in terms of *where* the technology is being used, and identify activities that take place in the classroom, in the computer suite or at home as part of homework tasks.

The following suggestions are not intended to be a definitive or complete list of the ways in which technology can be used in the teaching of English. A complete book could be written on this theme and still it would not cover all of the possibilities. Instead, the suggested activities and approaches are designed to stimulate your thoughts about how to start using technology in your English teaching, and also provide an opportunity to discuss some key issues related to the use of technology. The suggestions will be presented using the four interdependent areas of English as a basis (speaking, listening, reading and writing).

Speaking and listening

By the time children leave primary school, we expect them to be able to 'talk and listen with confidence in an increasing range of contexts' (DfEE and QCA 1999: 55). For the vast majority of the time, the skills required to do this can be developed without the need for technological resources, and this is just as it should be, as direct interaction with others, through speaking and listening, is the basis of human communication. However, there is the potential for using radio broadcasts, podcasts, CDs and talking books to model the spoken word for children of all ages, encouraging the development of speaking and listening skills. With young children this might mean listening to stories, poems and nursery rhymes, whereas with older children this could be extended to include plays. You could make use of websites, television broadcasts, DVDs and Blu-ray discs, which contain visual as well as audio elements. There is the potential for working with the whole class or with a small group, or for pupils to work independently of the teacher either individually or in pairs. If only some of the pupils are engaged in these activities, it is important to ensure that the audio is not a distraction to the rest of the class. Headphones and earphones are an almost essential resource and you can use a 'splitter' device to allow two or more pairs to be connected to the same source.

You and your pupils could also use audio-recording facilities, which are available through computers and various digital recording devices (e.g. digital voice recorders and many MP3 players and smartphones). Pupils' speaking activities could be recorded, played back and used as the basis of discussion. Pupils could make their own digital recordings of their stories and poems, retell or read ones they have heard or are working on, present radio-style non-fiction reports, act out plays, and explore many other speaking activities, all recorded and stored digitally, so others can listen to them. Although it is often blocked by individual school or local-authority internet access policies, YouTube (www.youtube.com) has many examples of children presenting poems and stories and there are other websites that children's digital recordings can be uploaded to (e.g. http://performapoem.lgfl.org.uk), bearing in mind the issues of confidentiality and online safety that must always be considered (for information on this refer to www.thinkyouknow.co.uk and the Byron Report (DCSF 2008f)).

Another category of technological resources that could be used to enhance these two aspects of your English teaching, particularly with children in the Early Years Foundation Stage and Key Stage 1, is multimedia talking books. These incorporate text, pictures, animations, the spoken word and music in a way that will capture the interest of children. They have been available on CD-ROM or DVD for a number of years, and are now increasingly available on the internet. Try to be creative in the ways that you use these resources by not thinking solely in terms of individual pupils using them at the computer as a way of filling a few spare moments. Yes, these resources were designed primarily to be used by pupils, but you could also use them with the whole class or a focus group to support speaking, listening and responding activities.

Pupils should increasingly engage in the creation of multimedia or multimodal texts as they progress through primary school, using software such as Kar2ouche (www. immersiveeducation.eu). One aspect should be the inclusion of recorded commentary from the children themselves. This can be as simple as adding sound files with the children reading out what the pages say, but more varied ideas should be considered, such as adding hyperlinks to sound files where children give definitions of key words, providing additional spoken material or even including evaluative comments.

Technology can also be used to support group work and discussion. As with others aspects of speaking and listening, much of the work here can and should be done without utilising technology. However, this area does provide an excellent opportunity to make use of any classroom computers that are available. In English, and indeed in many other curriculum areas, there will be occasions when you arrange your pupils into groups and ask them to discuss a particular issue, with one person taking on the role of scribe and another feeding back to the whole class. There are two potential problems with this much-used approach. First, it is difficult for all pupils in the group to read what the scribe is writing because this is being done by hand, and for some members of the group it is upside down. Second, when the written work is submitted, there is the danger of associating the handwritten sheet more with the individual who has produced it than with the group collectively. There is a simple way to overcome both problems: use a computer. The scribe becomes the typist, everyone in the group can see the text clearly on the screen (increase the font size if necessary), and the printed product can be genuinely associated with the group rather than the individual who typed it.

Advances in technology and the fact that the cost of that technology tends to reduce has led to a situation in which it is possible for schools to set up videoconferencing facilities, either through bespoke videoconferencing systems or through the use of software or systems such as Skype (www.skype.com). These facilities open up a whole new world of possibilities for the use of technology, particularly for language work. Through any form of video conferencing, it is possible for children to engage in interviews, discussion and remote observation, interacting with people from across the globe. This may be something as simple as talking with children at a school in another UK location about projects they are mutually working on, but the facility also offers the opportunity to speak to authors, to have a poet read a poem to a class and then be available to talk about it, to interview a politician, to discuss world issues with children from around the world (encouraging development of modern foreign language learning) and many other possibilities. Multimodal online discussions, which can include speech and video, are relatively easy to set up, using tools such as VoiceThread (www.voicethread.com), which children can contribute to both in and out of school, providing content moderated by the teacher. With the growing use of social networking and the ease of contacting people quickly via the internet, setting up such activities is easier than it ever was.

Drama is an area associated strongly with the development of speaking and listening skills, alongside work on reading and writing. Drama requires pupils not only to be involved in role play and the creation of dramatic pieces but also to respond to performances. Television broadcasts, DVDs, Blu-ray discs and multimedia content on the internet can all be used to model good practice (and bad!) in drama and also provide opportunities for discussion and evaluation, linking with children's literature or themes that the pupils are considering.

Another way of utilising technology to enhance drama work is to use a video camcorder or digital video recorder to record pupils' own performances, with a view to evaluating and improving their own work or as finished performances to present to audiences. There are many devices that can now record short video clips digitally and with a quality that is absolutely fine for classroom use, including many digital cameras, smartphones, tablets and devices specifically designed for this sort of classroom use, such as the Digital Blue cameras (www.digitalblue.org.uk).

When engaging in these drama activities, children will clearly be developing their communication skills related to speaking and listening, but, in order to prepare for a performance, they will also be working on storyboarding, writing scripts, generating ideas, considering characters and making choices about the types of language that will be used – all contributing to their progress in English.

Video editing has become a real possibility for children and there are programmes available that make editing digital video relatively easy, particularly for Key Stage 2 children. This opens up whole areas of possibility for the development of visual literacy and in terms of all the language work around the production of films. Linked to the video-editing possibilities is the chance for children to create animations through the use of digital video. Short stop-frame animation films are easily produced using basic skills, a camera and a computer with video-editing facilities.

When children engage in these approaches using different media, they are often very enthusiastic and it could be argued that, because much of their engagement with language comes through multimodal experiences rather than the written word on the page, it is important both to capitalise on those experiences and to teach children how the different forms of visual literacy work. Again, once these works of art have been produced, they can be shared via the VLE or the internet, giving the children a real audience for their work, and this is something else that often increases engagement and the potential for learning.

Reading

Two aspects of the development of reading skills are learning to recognise words and learning about word structure and spelling. These two key sets of skills require pupils to be able to read fluently and spell words accurately, and teachers employ a variety of approaches to achieve this. A frequently used approach is to present a text for pupils to read, often working with the whole class. Typically, the text takes the form of an interactive whiteboard resource, a big book, a poster, a photocopied sheet or the teacher's own handwriting on an interactive whiteboard, flipchart or paper shown via a visualiser (basically a device that transfers an image to a projector and then onto a screen). Interactive whiteboards, visualisers and projectors open up a huge range of possibilities in presenting texts for pupils to read and discuss. A simple way to get started is to type your text into a word processor or presentation software. This software-based approach offers a number of benefits:

- A handwritten text is usually rubbed out when you have finished with it and so the time spent writing it could be considered as time wasted, particularly since you will have to write it all out again the next time you want to use it. With an electronic text, however, once it has been created it can be used again and again. This may sound obvious, but it will save you a lot of time in the long run.

- Not only are electronic texts available to use again but also you can edit them before you use them each time. So, if you want to change some of the words or phrases in the text in order to emphasise a particular point, you can do this very easily and quickly.

- Electronic texts can be shared with colleagues in school and indeed beyond your own school, via the internet. The most arduous aspect of using electronic texts is creating them in the first place, so why not share the workload? If every member of staff in a typical primary school created four or five electronic texts each term, by the end of the year the school would have built up a resource bank of over one hundred texts to which everyone could have access. The easiest way to store them is in a shared folder on the school's computer network.

- You can interact with electronic texts more effectively than with texts presented in a traditional way. Even if you do not have all the coloured pens and highlighters afforded by an interactive whiteboard, you can use the standard features of most word processors. These will allow you to highlight text, change the text colour of particular words or phrases, insert additional or alternative text, separate a block of text into paragraphs and so on. This form of text-mapping or text-marking allows you or the children to highlight key words, features and phrases. The benefit of an interactive whiteboard is that you can do all of these things at the board itself, but even without one you can still interact with the text effectively through the computer keyboard.

An alternative to creating your own texts is to make use of those that have been created by other people and made available on the internet. Some require a live internet connection while others can be downloaded for use later. As with your own electronic texts, make sure you share your internet discoveries with your colleagues so that the school as a whole benefits, not just you. Several websites that provide ready-made texts are listed at the end of this chapter.

All of the above suggestions can work well within phonics sessions and the potential for presenting multimodal texts to the children relates well to the multisensory approach expected for early readers. Technology can be used to help develop phonological awareness, for example through the use of sound and video clips. Graphemes can be modelled using an interactive whiteboard and sounds can be added to files to illustrate the phonemes and blending in action. Segmenting of words into the graphemes representing sounds can easily be replicated using basic software, such as simple graphics software and interactive whiteboard software, which allows the teacher or the pupils to move letters or groups of letters around on the screen. Of course, the pens and highlighters that are part of interactive whiteboard software can be used by pupils and teachers to highlight parts of words, write graphemes into phoneme frames or simply to demonstrate the required letter formation. There are programmes specifically designed to promote the learning of phonemes and graphemes and there are also phonics games available to play via the internet, all of which can be used to support pupils' development of an understanding of phonemes and graphemes and the key skills of blending and segmenting (e.g. Phoneme Pop at www.ictgames.com).

The use of CDs and multimedia talking books has already been mentioned in relation to the development of pupils' speaking and listening skills. These can also be used to support the development of reading. In the case of CDs, it is essential that the publisher has provided a printed version of the audio book so that pupils can follow the text while listening to it. In fact, many of the best-known children's books can now be purchased with an accompanying CD and audio book versions may also be available. Computer-based multimedia talking books typically display the text on the screen while the story or poem is being read by the narrator. A helpful feature of many such talking books is that individual words are highlighted as they are being spoken. The use of these resources is not, on its own, going to teach pupils to read fluently, but they do provide another string to your bow in your attempts to address this key aspect of literacy. When choosing resources of this kind, it is worth checking that the accent used for narration is appropriate. In some cases multimedia resources are produced in the US and the slightly different pronunciation of some words may be problematical.

As with reading, the teaching of spelling requires a multipronged approach, and one aspect of this could be the use of computer-based 'drill and practice' software for both phonics and further spelling practice. Rather like junk food, there is a lot of this about and if consumed in large doses it is not good for you or your pupils. But in small doses, as part of a balanced diet of approaches to the teaching of spelling, there is nothing wrong with it. It does offer many of the benefits to individual learners identified earlier in this chapter, but what we do not want is pupils spending lengthy periods of time at the computer using these resources. Typically, in many of these programmes, a word appears on the screen for a set time, possibly accompanied by a visual cue; the word is read out by the computer; and then the words disappears and the pupil has to type the word he or she has just seen and heard. It is an electronic version of the 'look, say, cover, write, check' type of spelling practice. The word lists are usually fully customisable and there is often a management system that enables the teacher to track the performance of individual pupils (for strategies for learning spellings, see Chapter 12).

While on the theme of spelling, this is an appropriate point to discuss the use of spellcheckers by pupils when they are using a word processor, but before that there are a couple of questions for you to think about.

ACTIVITY: USING A SPELLCHECKER

- To what extent do you use the spellchecker when word processing?
- Do you think that using a spellchecker has had a positive or a negative effect on your ability to spell words accurately? Give reasons for your answer.

Spellcheckers are to literacy what electronic calculators are to numeracy: their use is the subject of much debate. Some teachers will not allow pupils to touch an electronic calculator until they have developed the ability to recall number facts and have sound mental skills. Similarly, there are teachers who believe that using a spellchecker will make pupils lazy and have an adverse effect on their ability to spell accurately. Some would even talk in terms of banning the use of both calculators and spellcheckers in primary schools. However well-intentioned these views might be, these tools are part of our everyday lives and so instead of 'protecting' pupils from them we should be teaching pupils to make the best possible use of them. Yes, calculators should not be used as a prop for simple arithmetic and similarly spellcheckers should not be seen as a substitute for learning to spell. In fact, you have to be quite good at spelling and reading in order to use a spellchecker effectively. Typically, if you have misspelled a word the spellchecker will offer a list of alternatives. Unless your initial attempt is reasonably close to the correct spelling, you are unlikely to be offered sensible alternatives, and, even if you are, you have to be able to make sense of what is on offer. You and your pupils also have to be aware of the limitations of spellcheckers. First, you may correctly spell a word but simply use the wrong one; for example, 'After I had eaten my super I went straight to bed.' A spellchecker will not spot that it should be 'supper' not 'super' (did you spot the mistake?). Second, the spellchecker does not recognise some perfectly acceptable words. Two common examples that you may already have come across are 'headteacher' and 'numeracy'. A further complication is the use of US spellings. Teachers and pupils need to ensure that the spellchecker settings are for UK English, not US English. These issues need to be discussed with pupils, otherwise they will not make efficient use of a valuable tool (see Chapter 12 for a poem that illustrates the limitations of spellcheckers).

What conclusion did you reach when answering the questions posed above? What effect has using a spellchecker had on your spelling? Many people believe that spellcheckers improve your ability to spell accurately. Sometimes words that used to be spelled incorrectly may now present no problems at all, as a result of being constantly reminded of errors by the spellchecker.

Earlier in this chapter, we mentioned the use of electronic texts in the teaching of reading. Electronic texts can also be used to address comprehension of texts and responding to those texts. There is no need to repeat the points made earlier, so instead this section will be used as an opportunity to consider what we mean by 'texts'.

ACTIVITY: CONSIDERING TEXTS

- What do you understand by the term 'texts'?
- List all the things that could be included in the primary curriculum as constituting 'texts'.

Most people consider 'texts' in literacy to refer to the printed word in the form of books, magazines, newspapers and newsletters, and these media are the ones that pupils in primary schools spend the vast majority of their time working with in literacy lessons and the wider curriculum. Of course, in modern conversation, the word 'text' is probably used more now as shorthand for a mobile phone text message! In our gadget-filled, high-tech world, an increasing proportion of the written 'texts' we encounter are not in the traditional form. For example, now we read web pages, email messages, mobile phone text messages, interactive reference CD-ROMs and DVDs, eBooks and tweets. Using a computer-based multimedia encyclopaedia, or more usually an online information service such as Wikipedia (www.wikipedia.com), is a very different experience from using the traditional paper-based equivalent in the school library. Both types of reference source have a part to play in the education of primary-school pupils, but their changing patterns of use in our everyday lives must be reflected in primary learning and teaching, with increasing use of electronic texts in schools keeping pace with the changes in the wider physical and virtual worlds. New 'texts' require new skills and so it is essential that these are integrated into the primary curriculum, otherwise pupils will not be equipped to fully understand and effectively engage with them. When pupils are provided with opportunities to retrieve, select, describe and interpret information from texts, these should include the non-traditional varieties. The same is true when pupils are analysing the content, structure and organisation of texts or commenting on the author's use of language. By incorporating these electronic texts into your English teaching, you will provide a more varied and richer experience for your pupils and one that will better equip them for the world in which they live.

It is important to avoid confusion between using electronic texts to enhance and extend literacy learning and teaching and the notion of digital literacy. Digital literacy is a broader term; as Becta notes, 'The combination of skill in using technology, plus knowledge and understanding, is what we call digital literacy' (Becta 2009: 8). Using electronic texts in literacy is therefore just a part of the bigger picture: the development of the skills, knowledge and understanding required to utilise modern digital technologies – digital literacy for short.

Writing

When we consider developing writing skills utilising technology, the obvious example is pupils using a word processor to create texts. There is huge potential here, but, despite word processors being widely available, many teachers exploit them in only a very limited way; in addition, there are other types of programme that teachers should also be using that can both support and enhance the writing process.

Effective writing comprises planning, drafting, evaluating, redrafting and editing, culminating in the production of the finished text. Often, when it comes to creating texts with a word processor, pupils do all but the final stage away from the computer. The planning, drafting and editing are done by hand on paper and then the teacher sends the pupils off to the computer to type neat copies. This is not the best way to use word processors to enhance the writing process. Genuine word processing requires a variety of skills that allow the writer to create a text almost from scratch while sitting at the computer. With more computers and other devices offering word processing facilities available in schools than ever before, there should be plenty of opportunities to provide pupils with sustained periods of time to create electronic texts, from the planning stage through to final publication or printing, thus enabling pupils to do some genuine word processing. In order to make the best possible use of a word processor, pupils must be taught the necessary skills. Do not assume all pupils will pick up keyboard skills for themselves. In fact, many primary schools now include explicit learning of typing skills from an early age. You will also need to teach most pupils how to cut, copy and paste text, how to change font types and sizes, how to use tab-stops and bullet points, how to use the spellchecker and thesaurus, and how to insert tables and graphics, to name just a few. As arguably the dominant method of producing texts in the modern world, one could easily argue that teaching word processing skills is more important than teaching handwriting skills, but, until such a time when legible handwriting is not a skill that is required, handwriting must still be taught. Of course, it is also possible to argue that, in the future, even typing and the current word processing skills will become redundant, as voice commands and speech-to-text becomes more sophisticated.

When teaching pupils how to use a word processor effectively, ensure that they are using a tool that is suited to their requirements. Typical industry-standard word-processing packages such as Microsoft Word may well be suitable for pupils at upper Key Stage 2, but younger children may need to use something that is more child friendly. There are several widely used packages, for example Clicker (www.cricksoft.com) and Textease Publisher (www.textease.com), and there are also some online and free downloadable programmes that provide many features, such as WriteOnline (www.cricksoft.com), SmartWrite (www. camboard.co.uk), OpenOffice (www.openoffice.org) and Google Documents (www. google.com). Two useful features of some of these programmes are built-in word lists and the ability to speak the text that has been typed.

The word lists are usually organised alphabetically, rather like a dictionary, and/or under topic headings such as 'The Romans', 'People who help us', 'The water cycle', and so on. Completely new word lists can be created by the teacher and it is usually possible to edit the existing lists. By offering this facility to pupils, we give them a greater degree of independence when engaging in the writing process and also reduce the amount of time they spend deliberating over spellings or trying to think of particular words.

How about the digitised speech facility offered by many of these child-friendly word processors? The temptation is to think that it is little more than a gimmick, designed to amuse and interest the pupils, especially when you discover that the first thing that they do is type in all the rude words they know, just so they can hear them being spoken by the computer! This is similar to children looking up rude words when they are given a dictionary to use. We do not prevent pupils using dictionaries, so we should not banish the digitised speech facility on the basis of children's natural curiosity. In fact, it can be of great value if used carefully. First, children will be motivated to write if they know that the computer will read the work back to them. Second, it provides a proofing tool to complement the spellchecker. Earlier, we saw that a spellchecker will not identify a correctly spelled but incorrectly used word, as in the sentence 'After I had eaten my super I went straight to bed.' A child hearing that sentence being read is likely to spot the mistake and therefore be able to correct it before the teacher needs to. Third, if children listen to their writing, rather than just reading it, it will help them to evaluate its content and structure and thus make improvements. Finally, digitised speech helps to reinforce the links between writing, reading, speaking and listening. We are not suggesting that what the pupils hear on the computer should be held up as a good model of how to speak, but it can at least make a contribution to the breaking down of the dividing barriers that sometimes exist between the different aspects of literacy teaching.

Something that teachers do for pupils of all ages is model the writing process, typically now by writing on an interactive whiteboard or dry-wipe whiteboard. One problem is that you have to spend large amounts of time facing the board rather than your pupils, reducing the potential for effective interaction and increasing the potential for misbehaviour. Another problem is that the editing and revision process that takes place as a result of your discussions with pupils creates what could be seen as an untidy text, which is littered with crossings out and insertions. Both of these potential issues can be resolved by using a word processor to model the writing process. You can position yourself so that you can use the computer while facing the class, with the keyboard on your lap if necessary. Additionally, by using a wireless keyboard, you do not have to be close to the computer, you avoid the hazard of trailing cables and you can hand the keyboard over to a pupil to contribute to the writing of the text. 'Yes,' you are probably saying, 'but isn't it important that we model handwriting as well?' Yes indeed, but handwriting is not the main focus here and there will be many other occasions when it is and you will model it on the interactive whiteboard, dry-wipe board or visualiser. 'But isn't it important that pupils see all the crossing out and insertions so that they can appreciate the evolutionary stages through which the text has passed?' If that is something that you feel strongly about, then all you have to do is save the text at frequent intervals, using a different name each time. You can then display the text on the screen at any given stage in its development by simply opening the appropriate file. Of course, you may wish to model the editing process that the children will be using themselves with pencil and paper, in which case a visualiser is a very useful device that can project the image of you actually writing up on to a screen for the pupils to see. In this case, the visualiser can be placed so that it is possible to simply look up from what you are writing to monitor the class.

Earlier in this chapter, the issue of what we mean by 'texts' was discussed, and that same issue has implications here. Assuming that 'texts' means more than simply paper-based materials, you should be comfortable with the proposal that 'writing' should not be restricted to creating traditional texts. In other words, we should be providing pupils with opportunities to explore and author all of the 'texts' that they experience as end users. We would not dream of teaching pupils how to read without also teaching them how to write, because each one assists the development of the other. This is equally true of non-traditional texts. So pupils should not only be digesting and interacting with web pages and multimedia presentations but also be producing such materials themselves. Only by doing this, and having considered issues such as purpose, audience, content and structure, will pupils fully develop an understanding of the power and potential of these modes of communication. Also, because writing these materials requires different skills from those needed to produce a traditional piece of text, you might find that pupils who find writing a challenge or a chore are more likely to be motivated and succeed when given the opportunity to create digital materials.

At the planning stage when writing, technology offers some very useful facilities to support pupils' work. With a basic word processor, obviously children can plan their work and then simply use that plan as the basis for their writing, extending their notes into full sentences and paragraphs, building on their planned structure. The best way to approach this would be to copy and paste the original plan, so that the initial ideas are still available. Software that can assist pupils at the planning stage, such as mind-mapping software, is readily available. Mind-mapping software enables representations of story plans, either in a free-flow form or as flowcharts, so pupils can set up headings and subpoints easily to help them shape their writing. They could even add images and sounds in some of these packages, using the mind map as a sort of electronic 'working wall' or scrapbook, a store of ideas and prompts around the basic story plan. This non-linear organisation of ideas is often particularly useful for children with specific learning difficulties, who benefit from seeing the 'bigger picture' when working. This kind of software and approach in format is particularly suitable when working on non-fiction texts. In fact, some of the most commonly used resources for non-fiction texts, the 'skeletons' created by Sue Palmer (2006), use diagrams that can easily be recreated using mind-mapping and flowchart software.

At a more basic level, writing frames can obviously be created using software and printed for pupil use, editing them to take account of differing pupil needs. Those frames can also be presented in a huge range of digital formats for pupils to work on using computers: mind maps, word-processed tables and structures, newspaper pages, non-fiction text, posters, magazine pages, wikis, web pages, blank playscripts. Giving the formats means that the creative content is the focus, but teaching about structure and format is, of course, very important as well and that teaching should include comparing the value of using the different approaches, physical and digital, to communicate as effectively as possible.

In all of the above, technology offers new or enhanced ways of working and a further possibility is presented by the opportunity to write collaboratively. Through the use of a facility such as PrimaryPad (www.primarypad.com), children and teachers can collaborate in the writing process, viewing the same text as it evolves together.

Imaginative use of technology in English can lead to all sorts of possible writing activities and forms with the children. Get to know the software and technology that is available to you and the children, try things out for yourself and be creative. Think about the different types of traditional and electronic texts and ensure you give the children a variety of experiences with different electronic ways of presenting the various types of text.

ACTIVITY: DIGITAL TEXTS

Think about your own daily experience with digital texts, both reading and creating. Which software or systems do you use? Can those be used with children? How can you ensure that children both access and create a wide range of digital texts? Here are a just a few possible ideas.

The pupils could create:

- web pages or sections for the school's VLE about aspects of the school, topics children are working on or their local area (there are many good examples of these available on the internet; use them as models and inspiration);
- posters using desktop publishing software;
- information leaflets using desktop publishing software (using various folds and sizes);
- instructional multimedia texts (e.g. how to play a game, with photos, audio or video clips);
- interactive photo albums of school visits, with captions, spoken commentary and hyperlinks to further information;
- interactive non-fiction texts with tool tips or hyperlinks to definitions of words;
- shape poems created using word-processing or graphics software;

- branching adventure stories, using hyperlinks that the reader follows to progress through the story in different ways (a great way of exploring character decisions and plotting a story);
- calligrams created using graphics software;
- animated poetry, where either the words move, the poem is 'clicked through' or multimedia is used to enhance the poem;
- class blogs, which can be accessed by parents and carers, to help them support the learning;
- texts using limited numbers of characters or letters, for example Twitter-style versions of stories (very useful as part of the planning process, to really focus on the key points of the story);
- mobile phone 'text' conversations between characters in a story;
- wikis based on the themes being covered;
- Facebook-style home pages for story characters;
- word clouds, using online tools such as Wordle (www.wordle.net, www.tagxedo.com);
- captions, thought and speech bubbles to add to digital images – for example, digital graphic writing using Comic Life (www.comiclife.com), comic creation (www.bitstripsforschools.com), Microsoft Photo Story 3 (www.microsoft.com) or Kar2ouche (www.immersiveeducation.eu);
- online story creation and sharing (www.storybird.com).

The role and future of technology in teaching English

Having read this chapter, it is hoped that you will have at least started to appreciate the role that technology can play in the teaching of English. It can be used by you to support your teaching and by your pupils to enhance their learning across all aspects of the English curriculum. Within the constraints of a single chapter there is a limit to the ideas that can be discussed and the advice that can be offered, but you should be beginning to realise that by embracing technology you can work more efficiently and more effectively, motivate your pupils, and provide a curriculum that better reflects the world in which they will live as adults.

The technology and software available to schools changes very quickly and teachers need to keep as up to date as possible with the new resources, both hardware and software, that become available. Open-source software can often be used in school and at home for no cost, as can applications that run on the internet, meaning that the transfer of work to and from home is easier than ever, although there are equality implications to consider where children do not have internet access. The increasing use of mobile devices, tablet computers of various forms and interactive technology such as electronic 'voting' systems that can be used for response and assessment should all be explored by teachers. The same is true of the myriad possibilities for language work within virtual worlds, in which children can interact with each other and a range of environments, through text reading and input, speaking and listening. These virtual worlds open up endless opportunities for providing children with reasons to read, write and communicate verbally, based on and within virtual experiences. Imagine if you could take your class for a walk around a chocolate factory, through a wardrobe door, into the past or the future, or into a situation where they could interact with characters from a story or 'become' those characters – taking drama and role play into more visually stimulating environments than most classrooms or school halls. There is real potential in such experiences and they link with the experiences many children have of computer games, online gaming and other online communities, but with a clear focus on using the power of the technology and the virtual experiences to stimulate learning.

The best teachers of English will always look for creative, inspiring ways to use technology to enhance the learning experience of the children and the quality of their own teaching. They will keep up to date with advances in technology and create exciting and inspiring opportunities to use current and emerging technologies to engage their pupils in activities that promote both digital and traditional literacy.

Key points

- Technology in this chapter is taken to incorporate what has been known as ICT (information and communications technology).
- Technology that can be used in schools goes beyond computers.
- Technology offers benefits to teachers and pupils in the teaching and learning of English.
- There is much potential for utilising technology across all aspects of English.
- In the teaching of English the term 'texts' must be interpreted as meaning more than simply paper-based materials.
- Electronic texts or multimodal texts, which might incorporate a variety of media, can be utilised to enhance the work on speaking, listening, reading and drama.
- The term 'writing' must be interpreted more broadly so that it provides opportunities for pupils to create electronic materials such as web pages, multimodal texts and interactive multimedia.
- Computer-based activities can contribute to the development of pupils' phonic and spelling skills.
- Sufficient emphasis should be given to the development of word-processing skills so as to reflect its importance in everyday life.
- Teachers need to keep up to date with the advances in technology, including concerning hardware, software and Web 2.0 opportunities, constantly looking for ways to use that technology to enhance learning

Further reading

Barber, D. and Cooper, L. (2012) *Using New Web Tools in the Primary Classroom*. Abingdon: Routledge.

Becta (British Educational Communications and Technology Agency) (2003a) *What the Research Says about ICT and Motivation*. Coventry: Becta (www.becta.org).

Becta (2003b) *What the Research Says about Using ICT in English*. Coventry: Becta (www.becta.org).

Becta (2009) *Becta's contribution to the Rose Review*. Coventry: Becta.

Becta (2010) *The 21st century teacher: English – using technology to enhance English teaching*. Coventry: Becta.

Becta NATE (2009) *Primary English with ICT: a pupil's entitlement to ICT in primary English.* Coventry: Becta.

Bennett, R. (2004) *Using ICT in Primary English Teaching.* Exeter: Learning Matters.

DCSF (Department for Children Schools and Education) (2008f) *Safer Children in a Digital World: the report of the Byron Review.* Nottingham: DCSF.

DfEE (Department for Education and Employment) and QCA (Qualifications and Curriculum Authority) (1999) *English: the national curriculum in England (Key Stages 1–4).* London: DfEE and QCA.

DfES (Department for Education and Skills) (2004e) *The ICT in Schools Survey 2004.* London: DfES.

DfES (2004f) *The Motivational Effect of ICT on Pupils.* Nottingham: DfES.

European Schoolnet (2006) *The ICT Impact Report: a review of studies of ICT impact on schools in Europe* (http://ec.europa.eu/education/pdf/doc254_en.pdf).

Ofsted (2009) *English at the Crossroads.* London: Ofsted.

Palmer, S. (2006) *The Complete Skeleton Book for Non-Fiction Text Types.* Kirkby-in-Ashfield: TTS.

Useful websites: online texts

Big books at the MAPE website: www.mape.org.uk/activities/BigBooks/index.htm.

Children's storybooks online: www.magickeys.com/books.

Giggle poetry: www.gigglepoetry.com.

Google book search: http://books.google.co.uk.

Online literature library: www.literature.org.

Page by page books: www.pagebypagebooks.com.

Poetry Archive: www.poetryarchive.org.

Project Gutenberg: www.gutenberg.org.

Sebastian Swan big books: www.sebastianswan.org.uk.

Stories from the web: www.storiesfromtheweb.org.

14 Drama

Purpose of this chapter

This chapter aims to:

- explore the role of drama in the primary school;
- provide strategies for effective teaching and learning using drama;
- consider ways of developing both children's and teachers' confidence in drama;
- suggest activities for use in the classroom for drama.

> The most significant kind of learning which is attributable to experience in drama is the growth in the pupils' understanding about human behaviour, themselves and the world they live in. This growth of understanding, which will involve changes in customary ways of thinking and feeling, is likely to be the primary aim of drama teaching. A secondary aim will be an increased competence in using the drama form and satisfaction from working within it.
>
> (O'Neill and Lambert 1982: 13)

Drama is not a subject in the primary curriculum: it is only at secondary school that children meet drama as a discrete entity – a subject in which they can gain qualifications. Some educators claim that drama's lack of prominence is the result of governmental emphasis on training rather than creativity and, indeed, Davis and Byron (cited in Fleming, 1994) even maintained that when the National Curriculum was developed some believed the government placed limited emphasis upon drama because drama encourages independent thinking: something they suggest the government did not wish to encourage! However, each incarnation of the National Curriculum in England and Wales has included drama within English, chiefly as part of speaking and listening. *The Literacy Framework* (DfES 2006b) made drama one of its twelve strands and provided details of what children should be able to do in each year group, and more generally:

4. Drama

Use dramatic techniques, including work in role to explore ideas and texts

Create, share and evaluate ideas and understanding through drama

(DfES 2006b: 16)

Interestingly, a 2003 DfES publication stated: 'Drama needs to be explicitly taught in its own right and can also be used as a tool for understanding in subjects across the curriculum' (DfES 2003c: 2). Woolland (2010: 1), too, maintains that 'drama should be seen as a subject in its own right *at the same time* as being a powerful learning medium.'

Just as in any other subject, there are skills that children need to develop in drama. We should strive for high-quality work in this area in the same way that we do in mathematics, science or history. Nevertheless, as O'Neill and Lambert (1982) maintain (see above), there is much more to drama than simply being a competent actor. Our attitude will influence the approach that children take to drama, and this may be affected by a number of factors:

- we may not be aware of the range and scope of drama work and its potential in the primary school;
- we may lack confidence in our own ability in drama or feel self-conscious about aspects of presentation and performance;
- we may be enthusiastic about the idea of drama work in the primary school but lack ideas for lessons or be unsure how work might be developed.

This chapter will address the issue of confidence in drama as well as suggesting a range of activities for different types of drama and exploring ways of planning for drama effectively. It will build upon the discussion of the value of drama described in Chapter 3, 'Creative approaches to teaching literacy'.

What do we mean by drama?

Drama can involve at one extreme performing to an audience and at the other brief activities with children sitting at their tables. In between, there is a range of activities that might take place in workshops with whole classes, groups, pairs or individuals. What is clear is that drama is not simply about performance; therefore, we should not consider that we have covered drama with our classes if we have simply put on a play or done a class assembly.

Fleming (1994) identified the characteristics of a balanced approach to drama. Interestingly, the first two of these relate to recognising and establishing drama as a discrete subject with its own curriculum. Others include:

- acknowledging that particular emphases in drama are appropriate at different ages;
- identifying that there is a place for performance, but acknowledging that this involves different activity from drama workshops;
- recognising that asking children to take part in performances too soon can have a negative effect;
- recognising that drama competences should not be based on superficial aspects of work.

It is clear, then, that drama has many facets. Woolland (2010: 2) describes the 'building blocks' of drama as:

- *role or character*: acting as if you were someone else or as if you were yourself in another situation;
- *narrative*: ordering a sequence of events or images in such a way that their order creates meaning. This is not necessarily the same as storytelling and story plotting, which are examples of the ways in which narrative can be used;
- *language*: verbal and non-verbal (including body language, facial expression, use of space).

While Woolland cautions against over-simplifying drama, he maintains that the building blocks help us to see a continuum from preschool play to theatrical performance. The range of activities in between is neatly summed up by Grainger (2005):

> Drama, like storytelling, draws on a complex web of different sign systems which includes facial expression, body language, intonation, gesture, mime, movement and space. These combine to communicate in sound, image and movement.
>
> (Grainger 2005: 38)

Teachers' confidence in drama

Fleming (2003: 3) maintained that 'many teachers lack confidence and expertise to plan drama-centred literacy', suggesting that a certain level of knowledge or skill is required to teach drama. Taylor (2000: 97) argued that teachers' perceptions of a typical drama classroom – 'disorder, excitable behaviour and boisterous demonstrations' – may inhibit them from engaging with the subject. Drama often gives children an opportunity to express themselves and to take a lead in proceedings. Where teachers feel that they may lose control of their classes (and this can be true of PE, D&T, art and other lessons too), there may be a tendency to play safe and limit movement and noise. However, drama can take several forms, many of which need not even involve children leaving their seats. For those who have reservations, it is worth considering Woolland's 'four big myths' about drama (1993: 13):

- you need to be a good actor;
- you need to be creative and arty and inventive and have lots of wonderful ideas;
- you need time on the timetable put aside for drama;
- to do good drama you need the school hall.

Grugeon *et al.* (2000: 121) assert that 'children generally love drama but their teachers may be shyer to dive in and try it.' They suggest this may be attributed to some of the following:

- perhaps they (teachers) are anxious that they may lose control of the children;
- they have never experienced drama themselves;
- lack of confidence;
- they think it means moving all of the furniture;
- they just do not know what they are missing.

Kempe and Lockwood (2000) suggest that teachers avoid drama because of the demands it makes on time, space and class management and because they are unsure about what learning outcomes might be achieved. Garvis and Pendergast (2011: 1) discuss teachers' self-efficacy and its impact upon their approach: 'If teachers have strong self-efficacy in the teaching of arts education, they are more likely to incorporate arts in the classroom.'

Brien urges teachers to be adventurous and to resist the temptation to play safe:

> Oral language is children's great strength; good teaching always starts with identifying, consolidating and drawing on existing knowledge and capabilities so in order to do justice to any curriculum area the teacher has got to overcome any reluctance to permit the glorious cacophony of children's active learning.
>
> (Brien 2012: 21)

Of course, it is the thought of a 'cacophony' that may deter some teachers from engaging in drama activities with their classes! However, Woolland (1993) adds a further 'myth' about drama always being noisy, pointing out that people have sometimes interrupted his drama lessons because they didn't realise anyone was in the room! As he states: 'Quiet, rapt attention is as much a characteristic of good drama practice as invigorating (and loud) discussion' (1993: 14). Perhaps, then, drama need not hold fears for inexperienced (or experienced) teachers. Look at the activity below and think about your own attitude to and experience of drama.

ACTIVITY: YOUR THOUGHTS ABOUT DRAMA

Consider your own experience of drama both as a pupil and as a teacher.

- What did you like and dislike about drama?
- What would you like to have done more of?
- How would you feel about being in role in a drama activity with your class?

Building children's and teachers' confidence

There are many simple activities that we might not at first consider to be drama that not only engage and interest participants but also help to build their confidence. These can often be used at the beginning of drama lessons, but may also feature as part of other lessons. For the teacher wary of losing control of a class and for children who are self-conscious or otherwise inhibited, these activities make a good starting point. However, we should be careful not to make our drama work simply a series of ice-breakers, and the activities may often be developed into more-challenging drama work.

Some simple activities involve expressing emotions through gesture and then through limited vocabulary. These can be particularly inclusive where children with English as an additional language or those with limited vocabularies or confidence are involved.

Who is the leader?

This simple activity requires children to sit in a circle while one person leaves the room or looks away. The teacher indicates who is the leader and everyone has to assume the same position, expression and activities as that person. Teachers need to model this first to show what might be possible and, perhaps, what is not allowed. The leader might clap, wave, yawn, stand or sit (and so on) and the others need to take care not to give them away by staring too intently when the person who left the room returns and tries to identify the leader. This may seem like little more than a party game, but children learn to use physical expression, subtlety and disguise and to mirror actions. It can be an ideal warm-up to a workshop.

Adverbs

Children can either remain in their seats or move into a circle. Use some adverbs that children have recently met or that you introduce to them, such as 'slowly', 'lethargically', 'attentively', 'nervously', 'anxiously' and 'excitedly'. Ask children to sit in the manner of the adverbs. When they are confident in this, ask them to stand, walk, look and so on. Not only does this activity help them to use gesture and physical expression but it also teaches them vocabulary kinaesthetically and makes clear the function of adverbs.

Verbs and adverbs

Make sets of cards, some with adverbs written on them and some with verbs. Give them out to everyone in the group or class and ask children to sit in a circle and hold them up so that everyone can see. Choose pairs of children, one with an adverb and one with a verb, and ask them to perform actions accordingly ('walk hesitantly', 'wave excitedly' etc.). This can be developed into a more random activity with two piles of cards (one of verbs and one of adverbs) being placed face down and children taking one from each pile without showing the class (in pairs) and then performing the actions for others to guess what the words are. This could lead to work on scripts, noting stage directions and writing scripts that include these.

Rhubarb, rhubarb, rhubarb

This activity works well with children with limited vocabularies and those learning English, but it is also invaluable for shy children and, in fact, everyone who wants to develop expression and gesture. Begin by sitting children in a circle and asking them to use only the word 'rhubarb' to express different emotions – go around the circle with everyone using the same emotion at first. For example, they might say it angrily, sadly, quietly, affectionately or hesitantly. This can be a good development of the adverbs activity and usually leads to lots of laughter as children turn to the person on their left to say the word.

'Rhubarb' is reputedly the word that extras in plays and films say to each other when the director wishes to create the impression of a buzz of conversation. The activity can be developed so that children move around the room and have to meet and converse with (say) three other people whom they do not usually talk with, using only the word rhubarb. Be sure to draw proceedings to a close by saying 'Rhubarb' firmly when you want them to sit down again!

Drama and knowledge about language

By acting out pieces of text, children can gain a better understanding of both meaning and structure. Reading that involves or is followed by dramatic activity helps children to focus more closely on the use of vocabulary and punctuation.

Speech marks

Give some children roles when reading a story and provide them with additional copies of the text. They should read the words spoken by their character, using different expression and intonation based upon context and language clues such as verbs ('whispered', 'shouted', 'muttered', etc.) and verbs and adverbs ('called frantically', 'whispered pleadingly' etc.). Children might go on to use passages of dialogue in a script format by presenting only the spoken words. After performing for the class, children could listen to the dialogue bit by bit and suggest verbs and adverbs that might have appeared in the original text.

Punctuation

Give some children different punctuation marks (full stops, question marks and exclamation marks) and write some simple phrases and sentences such as 'More tea', 'You like worms', 'You think that was good' and 'Dogs are better pets than cats'. Show the sentences to the class and ask the children with punctuation marks to take turns to say the sentences as if their punctuation mark was at the end. So, 'More tea!' would have a different meaning from 'More tea?' or 'More tea'. Encourage other children to suggest how the sentences might be spoken and ask them to use gesture for additional effect. They might go on to create their own sentences for each other to punctuate and say, and could then write some of these down, adding verbs, adverbs and so on (e.g. '"More tea!" grumbled Adam, who was already full.'; '"More tea?" asked Mr. Jones, holding the teapot over David's cup.').

Reading aloud

Encourage expressive reading by asking children to read independently before reading aloud with appropriate expression. They might annotate text to remind themselves where they need to use a particular expression or where they might include sound effects or visual aids to enhance the entertainment value of their story for their audience. They might go on to make recordings that could be listened to by classmates and children from other classes.

Scripts from dialogue

During whole-class work, show children how dialogue from a novel can be written as a playscript. After modelling scripts for them, provide groups with extracts of dialogue from familiar stories so that they can produce their own scripts. They might do this with pens and paper or could cut and paste using a computer.

Drama in shared reading

Ask children to play the roles of characters from the story you are reading. Either give them copies of the book, so that they can read their characters' dialogue while you and the rest of the class read the rest of the text, or provide cards with dialogue that can be displayed and discussed. Encourage children to look at the way in which the author intends the words to be spoken ('... yelled Tom'; '... whispered Chloe nervously' etc.) and ask them to say the words with appropriate expression.

A further development is for children to listen to a story and then re-enact it in small groups. Try telling stories as well as reading them, making use of gesture and actions, and encourage children to tell stories either individually or in groups.

Drama and speaking and listening

Clipson-Boyles (2003: 4) states that drama 'brings language alive by providing meaningful context'. The activities described in this section provide opportunities for participants to put themselves into and reflect upon situations through being in role.

Hot-seating

Hot-seating involves children assuming the roles of characters from stories, historical events or drama, taking on the roles of key characters and answering questions from the rest of the class in role. Grainger (2005: 40) maintains that this is a 'useful probing technique which seeks to develop knowledge of a character's motives, attitudes and behaviour and increases awareness of the complex nature of human behaviour'.

Forum theatre

This involves a performance or part of a performance being shown twice. During the replay, members of the audience ('spect-actors') can ask for the drama to stop so that they can replace one of the characters and show how they could change the situation and produce a different outcome. Different alternatives can be offered by different spect-actors. The other actors stay in character but improvise as they respond to the spect-actors. The teacher manages the communication between the players and the audience

Conscience alley

Sometimes called 'decision alley', 'conscience alley' involves someone in role walking between two rows of other children with those on each side offering different views on the action he or she should take. Perkins (2012) describes how this worked with a Year 3 class that had listened to Anthony Browne's story *The Tunnel*, in which Rose has to decide whether or not to go through the tunnel. When the dilemma was reached, children worked in pairs to discuss what Rose might be thinking. They then formed two rows and the teacher played the part of Rose, walking between the rows as children whispered their comments to her and acted as her conscience.

Perkins (2012) cautions that the 'alley' should be quite wide so that the person walking through does not become intimidated, and that children should whisper their views rather than shout them. This approach could be used in a variety of situations, including history, RE and PSHE lessons, as well as in English. While it does require some space, it does not have to be part of a drama workshop and might be used as a stimulus for discussion or persuasive writing.

Freeze frames

Children might look at examples of famous pictures that show a tableau in which it is clear that different people have different roles and perhaps views. As part of a drama workshop or as part of sharing a story, groups might create their own tableaux to represent scenes from the story. Others can look at the tableaux and discuss them, and characters can be brought to life one by one and asked to express an opinion or say something about what they are doing or to answer questions in role. As Grainger (2005: 40) suggests: 'Freeze frames offer a useful way of capturing and conveying meaning, since groups can convey much more than they would be able to through words alone.'

Drama and cooperative learning

Drama is seldom a solitary activity, even though we may sometimes ask children to do things independently. The DfES (2003c) guidance on speaking and listening states that, to develop their skills in drama, children need to learn to:

- improvise and work in role, creating and sustaining roles both individually and when working with others;
- script and perform plays and stories using language and actions to express and convey situations, characters and emotions;
- respond to their own and others' performances, commenting constructively on dramatic effects, characterisation and overall impact.

All of the above require children to work together and this can be invaluable not only in developing successful drama work but also in promoting socialisation, sharing of ideas and reflection. For some children, working with others in role is easier than working together as themselves. They are able to voice opinions they might otherwise feel inhibited about, and they can be more confident about expressing themselves if they feel that their character is responsible for what is said.

Drama and poetry

There is great scope for using poetry as a stimulus both for small-group and whole-class drama. The poem below, which was written in Victorian times, has some challenging and rather antiquated vocabulary that children can discuss. Ask them to remain seated and to act out each line as you read it. How would they look like a sage (a wise person)? How would they show they had a pigtail? What would they do to show they were 'wondering' and 'sorrowing'? Once children feel confident about the vocabulary, try involving everyone and begin with them standing in a space. If you take part yourself, you will help remove some of the children's inhibitions, but do encourage children to focus on what *they* are doing and ask them to try not to look at others as this tends to distract them and make them feel self-conscious. If they do feel awkward, it is best not to force them into the activity.

'A Tragic Story' (William Makepeace Thackeray)

There lived a sage in days of yore,
And he a handsome pigtail wore:
But wondered much and sorrowed more
Because it hung behind him.
He mused upon this curious case,
And swore he'd change the pigtail's place,
And have it hanging at his face,
Not dangling there behind him.
Says he, 'The mystery I've found –
I'll turn me round' – he turned him round;
But still it hung behind him.
Then round and round, and out and in,
All day the puzzled sage did spin;
In vain – it mattered not a pin –
The pigtail hung behind him.
And right, and left, and round about,
And up and down, and in and out,
He turned; but still the pigtail stout
Hung steadily behind him.
And though his efforts never slack,
And though he twist and twirl, and tack,
Alas! still faithful to his back
The pigtail hangs behind him.

Children might go on to work in groups to develop their performance of the poem, with some, or even all, reading it aloud. They could then perform for the rest of the class.

Once children have been introduced to the idea of performing poems, they can be given poems in groups to work out how they might perform them. 'Jabberwocky' by Lewis Carroll (see Chapter 8) can be ideal for older children, as can 'The Fence', which we first encountered around thirty years ago but which seems untraceable except in a different form written by Christian Morgenstern and translated from German. Both versions are presented below:

'The Picket Fence' (Christian Morgenstern)

One time there was a picket fence
with space to gaze from hence to thence.
An architect who saw this sight
approached it suddenly one night,
removed the spaces from the fence,
and built of them a residence.

The picket fence stood there dumbfounded
with pickets wholly unsurrounded,
a view so loathsome and obscene,
the Senate had to intervene.
The architect, however, flew
to Afri- or Americoo.

The version we have used with success is as follows:

'The Fence' (author unknown)

There was a fence
With spaces, spaces, spaces.
Spaces you could look through,
If you wanted to.
An architect who saw this thing,
Stood there one summer evening,
Took out the spaces with great care,
Took out the spaces with great care,
Took out the spaces with great care,
And built a castle in the air.
The fence was utterly dumbfounded.
Ooooh!
Each post stood there with nothing round it,
A sight most terrible to see.
They charged it with indecency!
The architect then ran away,
Ran away, ran away,
To Africa, to Africa, to Africa
Or, America!

Children work in groups of around six, with at least one reading the poem as others devise ways of portraying the words through actions. As with 'A Tragic Story', children will need to discuss more-challenging vocabulary, such as 'architect' and 'indecency' (you may wish to adapt to avoid this). As groups work on their performances, stop the class occasionally and ask them to show parts of their work in order to give others ideas. Finally, ask each group to perform, and invite constructive criticism and suggestions for adaptations. It is often best to begin by asking the class what they thought was 'really good' about a performance before looking for suggestions for improvements.

Teacher in role

Stockard and Mayberry (1992: 32) suggested that 'students learn most where teachers are actively involved in teaching', and drama provides an ideal opportunity for teachers to engage with children through what Heathcote (1984) termed 'teacher in role', in which the teacher steps in and out of role in the class drama work. Woolland (2010: 44) maintains that teaching in role is 'a strategy, a means to an end; it is not an end in itself. The purpose is to offer a way of intervening which challenges and focuses the work, which moves it on, which creates learning opportunities and deepens the understanding of the participants.'

'Teacher in role' can involve teachers taking on a significant role in class or group drama that guides children through a story, or it can involve minor roles that challenge children's thinking at certain points in a dramatic activity. For example, for a large part, the teacher might play the part of the Big Bad Wolf in *The Three Little Pigs*, visiting houses built by the pigs and making threats and arguing with them. For a minor role, the teacher might visit groups and pose a question or give a warning about impending danger and then step aside to let children discuss. What is important is that the teacher steps out of role occasionally, perhaps using a prearranged signal such as removing a hat or scarf or sitting down. This can be the signal for children to step out of role too and sit in a circle to discuss the drama and what has happened so far. The teacher can ask questions about the children's response to his or her character and might even ask them for advice on how s/he might play the role more effectively.

Goode and Heathcote (1982: 5) suggest that taking part in drama in this way may feel awkward for some teachers, who may see it as 'resulting in a damaging loss of status'. Reluctance to participate might also be caused by teachers feeling 'that once they have embarked on a role they will have to stick with it for the rest of the lesson' (Woolland 2010: 44). However, Heathcote (1984) proposed the idea of teacher in role with the intention that the teacher should come in and out of role whenever he or she feels it necessary. Thus, awkward moments can be avoided if children are aware that the teacher can revert to being their teacher at a given signal.

An important by-product of the teacher being in role is that it raises the status of drama for the children. By showing that s/he is a willing and enthusiastic participant, the teacher conveys to the children that this is a valuable activity.

Drama and writing

Written work may not be a regular outcome of drama activities, but it has a place since drama can be a good stimulus. Grainger (2001: 6) suggest that two kinds of writing can emerge through children being in role:

■ *writing in role*: writing undertaken from inside the lived experience of drama and written during the imaginative action;

■ *writing alongside role*: writing from a distance, written after the lived experience of drama.

The first-hand experiences that drama can offer should help children to develop ideas for their writing, as well as developing their sensitivity to the feelings of characters. The *Talk for Writing* resources encourage the use of drama, maintaining that

> The first-hand experience of a bear hunt or environment walk could be recorded by fastening various objects or pictures onto a story stick. Crucially, such techniques support children in recounting orally a story or experience they have shared, in the correct order. Accompanied by drama and discussion these multisensory approaches can scaffold children's understanding through into their writing. The use of visual prompts, real objects and other props will also allow

children learning EAL to access the story or recount more readily, while the regular re-telling and oral rehearsal will extend their familiarity with the structures of spoken English as well as developing their vocabulary.

(DCSF 2008c: 8)

A whole-class piece of drama could lend itself to written work, if children are able to make notes when 'stepping out' of the drama. For example, a favourite whole-class activity is a development of an activity described in O'Neill and Lambert's (1982) *Drama Structures*. Our version of *Darkwood Manor* begins with children sitting in a circle, ideally on chairs, with a large space in the middle and a gap between two chairs that can act as a wide entrance to Darkwood Manor. This can be done in the school hall, but we have also done it on the school field on a warm summer day! Children will need note pads and pencils, which they can place under their chairs.

With the children seated in a circle, explain that you will be taking part with them in a drama activity. Tell them that you will cease to be their teacher and become a character in the drama when, say, you put on a jacket, and that that will also be a signal to them that they will be in role too. Ask them to stand outside the entrance with their notebooks and pencils, and put on your jacket. Immediately assume the role of an estate agent who wants workers to restore the manor. Ask who is a carpenter, electrician, glazier, bricklayer, plasterer (and so on) and invite those who raise their hands to look carefully at the work that needs to be done and to make some notes so that they can give you a cost estimate. Go through the different trade roles and ensure that everyone has told you a role, and then ask the tradespeople to go into and around the outside of the manor to look at the work that needs to be done. At first some children may be a little unsure, but we usually find that many are quite enthusiastic and there can be tutting and intakes of breath at the state of the building!

As soon as you feel the drama is flagging, stop everyone by taking off your jacket and raising your hand – this prearranged signal is very effective if children know that they need to raise their hands too and come out of role. Ask the children to return to their seats, and invite their views on what has just happened. What do they think about the person who was asking about their trades? Why do they think s/he wants to restore the manor? What kinds of things did they do when asked to look at the work that needs to be done? How did they feel about being in role?

Explain that you will be in role again shortly and ask them to go back to the outside of the manor. For the next stage of the drama, we usually give not-very-subtle hints that the agent wants the manor to be restored cheaply and superficially so that a quick sale can be made. The agent becomes rather a shady character, which can lead to some interesting discussions later when the children have to be very conscious that the person whose character they may be criticising is not actually their teacher!

The drama can develop in different ways and some classes have led it along lines that we had not envisaged. Where things may be heading in a direction you are not comfortable with, it is a good idea to come out of the drama and discuss this with the children. With some classes, we have introduced another character who is said to live in the house (who can also be played by the teacher with a different item of clothing, or by a child or teaching assistant) and have told them to ignore him because he tells lies about the manor being haunted just because he doesn't want to be evicted when the manor is sold. We have also asked the tradespeople to make phone calls to their bosses or families to explain the situation. There is huge scope for introducing a range of drama activities within a whole class-drama such as this one set around Darkwood Manor, and there are also many possibilities for writing, which might include:

- tradespeople writing reports and estimates for their work;
- notes about different characters, which could lead to descriptive writing;
- notes about the story as it unfolds, which could lead to children writing their own stories about Darkwood Manor;
- descriptions of Darkwood Manor accompanied by drawings – we have found that chalk and charcoal pictures on dark paper work especially well.

When using the teaching sequence for writing (see Chapter 11), we often make use of texts as the stimulus for writing. Drama offers an alternative that can be accompanied by text, but it may also provide children with ideas for narrative; help them to remember a sequence of events they will write about; or provoke thought about some of the complexities of characters and situations.

Planning drama workshops

Where time is set aside specifically for drama, it is important to plan in a structured way so that you, as a teacher, feel comfortable about what will happen and children feel secure about what they are being asked to do. The teachfind website (www.teachfind.com/teachers-tv/ks12-drama-teaching-drama-structured-approach) includes video material of professional development for teachers in which a drama lesson is modelled. A structure is suggested for drama lessons that involves the following:

- *Agreement*: Ground rules are set and agreed to by children. These could be related to *communication, cooperation* and *concentration*.
- *Warm-ups*: These might involve team work, physical warm-ups, communication and so on and prepare children for the work ahead.
- *Focus*: A focus for the drama might be provided by pictures, objects, extracts from text, a question, a story, an event or a poem. The focus should ensure that all children have some basic knowledge of the topic.
- *Development*: This might involve children working in groups, perhaps creating still images or tableaux to portray an aspect of the topic.
- *Creation*: Children create a longer piece of drama, perhaps linking a series of images or actions together to tell a story or recount an event.
- *Performance*: In a workshop, performance involves showing you or other people in the class what has been done, rather than performing for another audience. Children might show extracts from their work or, if it is short enough, a complete piece. Where time is limited, you might go around to each group and observe rather than having a series of mini performances for the whole class, or you might ask children to show other groups their work.
- *Evaluation*: This gives you and the children an opportunity to reflect on what has been achieved, what they have learned and how their work could be improved, and to consider what the next steps might be. Importantly, this is also a quieter time when children can calm down after vigorous and exciting activity before their next lesson.

ACTIVITY: PLANNING DRAMA LESSONS

Look at the suggested structure for a drama lesson above and consider how you might use it to plan for one of the following topics:

- Victorian schools;
- retelling *Goldilocks and the Three Bears*;
- the volcanic eruption at Pompeii;
- 'Jabberwocky'.

Consider each aspect of the structured plan and what you and the children would do.

Performance Drama

The Literacy Framework (DfES 2006) includes performance drama at every level, although for Years R to 4 this generally involves responding to performances. By Year 5, however, children are expected to be able to

- perform a scripted scene making use of dramatic conventions and
- use and recognise the impact of theatrical effects in drama

and in Year 6 they should be able to

- devise a performance considering how to adapt it for a specific audience.

If children are to perform successfully for audiences, they will need to develop a range of drama skills, including use of gesture, voice and movement. A key challenge is getting children to be aware of the audience and the need to ensure everyone can hear them and understand what is happening, without making the children self-conscious when they are acting. It is important that they are given opportunities to reflect on their own and other people's performances, and that they have the opportunity to observe scenes in which they are not participating so that they can consider the impact of the ways in which people act. Giving children opportunities to watch performances, both from other children and from professional actors, is essential if they are to realise what is possible and experience the impact that good performance can have upon an audience.

Woolland (1993) argues that the school play involves both presentation and production, but maintains that it should emerge from classroom drama and be based upon good practice that furthers work from the curriculum. School plays may sometimes be put on as a public-relations exercise, because parents want and expect to see their children perform (you only have to attend a nativity play to see this), but Woolland (1993: 145) cautions: 'It is also worth bearing in mind that even if the school play is mainly a PR exercise, we surely want the PR to be about what we actually do.'

Conclusions

Heathcote (1984: 147) maintained that 'research into language and education has demonstrated the importance of experiences for children which provide meaningful contexts in which to use language for a variety of purposes and drama facilitates this need in an ideal way.' Many of the activities described in this chapter offer children opportunities to engage in activities that can be related to other aspects of the curriculum, as well as to situations in which they might find themselves.

While it is clear that drama in primary schools can take many forms, there are some key elements that emerge as important if drama work is to be successful. These are neatly summed up by the DfES (2003c) document on speaking and listening, which maintains that when teaching drama we should remember to:

■   model language that is appropriate to the role, context and theme;

■   challenge children to move beyond the familiar and everyday;

■   build in time to reflect on both the meaning of the drama and how it is enacted;

■   structure activities in a unit of work to build children's skills in drama and work in role and also their understanding of themes and ideas;

■   vary the techniques used so that children develop a repertoire and make progress in performance, working in role and evaluation;

■   establish ground rules for drama sessions so that children have a clear framework within which to create roles, explore movement or develop scenarios.

Key points

■   Work in drama can take many forms and does not always require use of large spaces and timetabled lessons.

■   Drama can be linked to reading, writing, developing knowledge about language, poetry, cooperative learning and study across the curriculum.

■   'Teacher in role' is a useful device that can help to engage children with drama. By providing a model and showing that they enjoy being in role, teachers can raise the status of drama for their classes.

■   There are some key elements that need to be considered when we plan for drama.

Further reading

Bolton, G. (1986) *Selected Writings on Drama in Education*. Harlow: Longman.
Clipson-Boyles, S. (2003) *Drama in Primary English Teaching*. London: David Fulton.
Davis, D. and Byron, K. (1988) 'Drama under fire – the way forward (2)', *2D*, 8(1), 26–27.
Fleming, M. (1994) *Starting Drama Teaching, 1st edn*. London: David Fulton.
O'Neill, C. and Lambert, A. (1982) *Drama Structures*. London: Hutchinson.
Perkins, M. (2012) *Observing Primary Literacy*. London: Sage.
Taylor, P. (2000) *The Drama Classroom*. London: Routledge.
Woolland, B. (2010) *Teaching Primary Drama*. Harlow: Pearson Education.

15

Planning for English

Purpose of this chapter

This chapter will examine:

- the planning process as part of the teaching cycle;
- core principles in planning for aspects of English;
- planning in the Early Years Foundation Stage (EYFS);
- creating links across the curriculum;
- planning units of study;
- planning individual literacy lessons.

Planning for literacy in 2012 presents both opportunities and challenges. The demise of the National Strategies, with their national frameworks and detailed units of work, has left a vacuum for teachers. While this has left some teachers de-skilled and de-professionalised, for others it has provided opportunities to work more creatively. As Alexander points out, this is a shift in emphasis and teachers need to move towards 'repertoires rather than recipes' (2010: 37). As a repertoire, the many resources of the National Strategies, some of which still reside in the National Archives, are a fruitful source of teaching material. A second aspect concerns the two major reviews undertaken in 2010 – the Rose Review of the Curriculum and the Cambridge Review. Both have much to say about the nature of the curriculum, although they vary in many respects. Irrespective of these reviews, the coalition government is again consulting on a revised National Curriculum and indications signify a much more traditional subjects-based curriculum. The DfE (2012c) has indicated that less prescription may result, but whether this will offer real opportunities for teachers to have more say over what they teach is yet to be seen.

The planning process

Planning for English is particularly complex due to the many layers the subject encompasses, once usefully described by the National Literacy Strategy as text level, sentence level and word level. The planning process needs to be seen as part of a continuous teaching cycle in which observation and assessment feed into planning of appropriate learning. Understanding this cycle is the key to effective planning. This process can be summarised in the cycle illustrated in Figure 15.1.

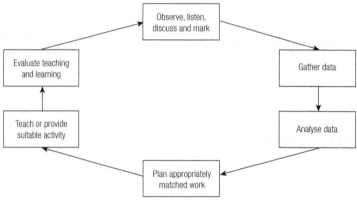

FIGURE 15.1 The planning cycle

Principles of teaching English

Planning needs to be based on a clear understanding of the generic/core business of the teaching of speaking and listening, and reading and writing, and their interrelationship.

ACTIVITY: PLANNING UNITS OF WORK

Review the core aspects below in Table 15.1 and with colleagues discuss the interrelationships between them. In particular, consider:

■ When beginning a unit of work on a specific genre, what type of activities would you start with?
■ To what extent is the core teaching of each aspect discrete?
■ To what extent do the different modes of English overlap?

Following consideration of these aspects, review the section 'A sequence for teaching literacy' below.

A sequence for teaching literacy

Understanding the core teaching principles can help when planning a coherent sequence for teaching in a unit of work. This is underpinned by speaking and listening skills and considerably enhanced when opportunities for talk are specifically planned for. Based on

TABLE 15.1 Core aspects of teaching speaking and listening, reading and writing

Core teaching of speaking and listening	Core teaching in reading	Core teaching in writing
■ Teach and model the necessary skills to speak and listen for a wide range of purposes in different contexts; provide appropriate activities and opportunities to practise. ■ Teach pupils active listening and ways of responding to show understanding and recall. ■ Provide opportunities for interaction in pairs and groups. ■ Support the development of speaking and listening skills for learning and for a wide range of purposes in different contexts. ■ Explore ideas and texts through drama to develop and share ideas in varied and creative ways.	■ Introduce the text (establish a purpose for reading). ■ Teach and practise decoding (e.g. blending phonemes, using decodable texts, etc.). ■ Teach comprehension strategies (e.g. summarising, rereading, having a question or focus to look for). ■ Teach techniques to navigate texts (e.g. skimming, scanning, paragraphs and topic sentences, page layout). ■ Provide opportunities to respond to text (e.g. likes, dislikes). ■ Include specific reading objective(s) (e.g. to identify issues).	■ Teach analysis of texts for structural and language features and how to derive principles of effective writing from these models. ■ Provide introduction to writing (gathering content for writing, deciding on purpose, audience and form of writing). ■ Plan and teach the writing process as appropriate (planning, drafting, revising and editing).

an understanding of core principles for teaching literacy, it is also necessary to understand the sequence of teaching in planning a unit of work. Figure 15.2 shows how this progresses through three phases, where phase 1 creates initial interest through familiarisation with the text type and immersion in the genre, principally by reading examples, and phase 2 analyses the key features and concentrates on capturing ideas/gathering information ready for phase 3, where, through a process of teacher modelling and scaffolding, pupils go on to independent writing in the genre. Although the example in Figure 15.2 shows the conventional route from reading to writing, units may vary from this sequence and the circles can be sketched out accordingly. This sketch can then be used to inform the more detailed unit plan.

The work carried out by Pie Corbett and published by the National Strategies in *Talk for Writing* (DCSF 2008c) provided guidance on how talk underpins each step in teaching literacy and specifically writing, and how it needs to be embedded at every phase of the teaching sequence:

■ before reading;

■ during reading;

■ during all stages of writing;

■ after writing.

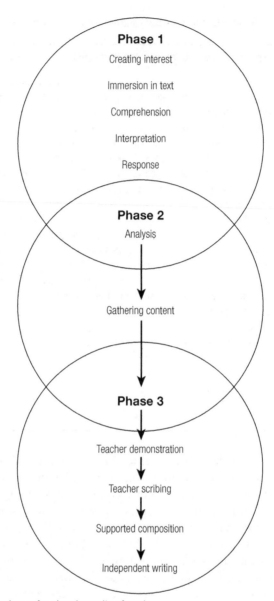

FIGURE 15.2 Planning phases for planning units of work

Progression in skills

It is particularly helpful to have a clear understanding of progression in planning for literacy. The Primary Framework (DfES 2006b) provided a clear progression of skills and expectations by year groups. For a useful summary of progression in skills in reading and writing, see the Lancashire Literacy Team 'Key Skills in Reading' and 'Key Skills in Writing' documents (available from: www.lancsngfl.ac.uk/nationalstrategy/literacy/index. php?category_id=532). These provide guidance on expectations for age-appropriate reading and writing skills for each year group.

Planning for communication and language and literacy in the Early Years Foundation Stage

Planning for learning in the EYFS needs to provide a range of experiences that encompass all areas of learning. These were amended to seven areas under the revised framework from September 2012:

- three prime areas: communication and language; personal, social and emotional development; physical development;
- four other areas: literacy, mathematics, expressive arts and design, understanding the world.

This is set out in more detail in Figure 15.3:

Area of Learning and Development	Aspect
Prime Areas	
Personal, Social and Emotional Development	Making relationships Self-confidence and self-awareness Managing feelings and behaviour
Physical Development	Moving and handling Health and self-care
Communication and Language	Listening and attention Understanding Speaking
Specific Areas	
Literacy	Reading Writing
Mathematics	Numbers Shape, space and measure
Understanding the World	People and communities The world Technology
Expressive Arts and Design	Exploring and using media and materials Being imaginative

FIGURE 15.3 Development matters in the Early Years Foundation Stage

Getting the balance right

Practitioners working in the early years need to use the EYFS framework and accompanying guidance to provide core provision and enhanced provision to match each child's individual learning journey. This means providing a range of resources and experiences in an 'enabling environment' that is designed to encourage children to play, explore, 'have a go' and think together with their peers and teachers. It is important that practitioners recognise opportunities to sustain children's interest and to support children as they make new discoveries. As the *Statutory Framework for the Early Years Foundation*

Stage states, 'Each area of learning and development must be implemented through planned, purposeful play and through a mix of adult-led and child-initiated activity' (DfE 2012a: 1.9).

Long-term plans (often referred to as 'core provision planning') provide an overview of the coverage related to different themes or areas of learning across the year. These should ensure that children will not repeat similar activities in a year; provide guidance on the use of the outdoor and indoor environment; and suggest a range of stimuli that relate to children's previous experiences. Specific visits to places that will support the children's learning can be very beneficial (such as visiting a garden centre, if this is the focus for learning). Also, providing first-hand experiences in the setting can bring learning alive for young children, for example by inviting visitors to talk about specific aspects and to bring a range of resources (e.g. inviting a fire safety officer with a range of resources – even a fire engine!).

A medium-term plan involves providing an outline of activities and resources linked to the relevant development statements and 'early learning goals' from the EYFS Framework and guidance. The EYFS covers progression through areas of learning and development from zero to five years, setting out under 'development statements' the progression of knowledge, skills, understanding and attitudes that children will need to attain the 'early learning goals' by the end of the EYFS. This guidance on what children will typically learn at each age phase is designed to help practitioners to plan experiences and activities under the three themes that underpin all learning and development in the EYFS:

a unique child + positive relationships + enabling environments = learning and development

Following the Tickell Review (DfE 2011b), from September 2012 it is recommended that communication and language should be given greater emphasis than literacy in the early stages of young children's development. This is prompted by research that highlights the time-sensitive link between early brain development and the acquisition of communication and language skills, which 'happen during an optimum window of brain development' (DfE 2011b: Annex 8:98). The revised EYFS guidance emphasises the primary role that communication and language experience plays as the starting point for children's successful language and literacy development.

Planning should be informed by ongoing assessments and should be collaborative with colleagues, parents and other agencies as appropriate. Short-term planning (this includes enhanced provision) is often weekly, with practitioners setting out learning intentions for each activity based on children's interests and needs and related to the next steps in development towards early learning goals. These goals have been substantially reduced under the revised framework in 2012, in order to streamline paperwork for teachers and to ensure their focus in the classroom is on interaction with the children. The EYFS emphasises the importance of planning within an ongoing cycle of observation and assessment; this should be related to common developmental patterns and to planning and resourcing in order to provide effective learning and teaching (see Figure 15.4).

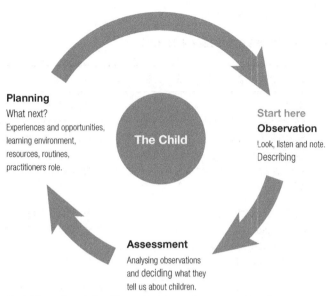

FIGURE 15.4 The Early Years Foundation Stage planning and assessment cycle
Source: DfE (2012b: 3).

Planning at Key Stages 1 and 2

Cross-curricular links

Planning for English should not be seen as discrete: clear links should be made across the curriculum. This can be facilitated by creating curriculum maps, which can provide an overview of all areas across the curriculum that are being taught over a term. These provide helpful ways of linking subjects to provide meaningful learning experiences for pupils. An example is given in Table 15. 2.

Working in a cross-curricular or thematic way has received increasing interest in recent years both in primary schools and more recently in secondary schools, and writers argue for a breakdown in subject boundaries (Alexander 2010; Robinson and Aronica 2009).

The cross-curricular approach teaches a number of subjects while using a theme or topic as a central core. For example, a topic on autumn may include some scientific investigations, various types of writing (English), mathematical surveys, collage (art) and so on. This approach was first advocated by Plowden in 1967 (CACE 1967: 555), who noted that 'children's learning does not fit into categories'. As Kerry (2011: 7) points out, 'throughout a long career in education I have been convinced not only that this assertion is correct but that it applies equally to effective learning in any context.'

The creative curriculum or thematic approach has stimulated many schools to develop engaging projects. Ofsted's (2010b) survey of creative approaches that raise standards noted that well-organised cross-curricular links allowed scope for independent enquiry. The report also found that 'Cross-curricular projects contributed to developing a broad range of skills needed for later success, including the ability to work both independently and collaboratively' (Ofsted 2010b: 11).

TABLE 15.2 Example of a curriculum map

Rearranged curriculum map: Year 4 Term 1

Week	1	2	3	4	5	6	7	8	9	10	11	12	13	14

Geography / History

History
What was it like for children during the Second World War?
Link narrative reading/writing with making storybooks (D and T) and different audiences (ICT)

Geography
How and where do we spend our time?
Link with non-chronological report writing (English) and branching databases / handling data (maths/ICT)

Design and technology / PSHE / Citizenship

Design and technology
Storybooks
Link narrative reading/writing with making storybooks (ICT)

PSHE/citizenship
Living in a diverse world

English

Poetry	Instructions	Narrative Second World War stories	Newspapers	Non-chronological reports	Plays

S/L with group interaction focus

S/L with drama focus
Link with Christmas play

Science

Moving and growing

Habitats

Mathematics

Mathematics Framework
Place value, number operations, money, measures, shape

Religious Education

Celebrations

Celebrations – Christmas journeys
Link with play writing and class orchestra (Christmas play)

Art and design

Portraying relationships

Journeys

Information technology

Within other subjects
Writing for different audiences
Link with book making (D and T) and writing historical narrative (English)

Branching database
Link with geography and maths

Music

Salt, pepper, vinegar, mustard – exploring singing games
Link with history – Opies' collection of oral playground rhymes

The class orchestra – exploring arrangements
Link with Christmas play, English and RE

Physical education

Net/wall games, unit 1
Dance activities, unit 4

Net/wall games, unit 1
Swimming activities and water safety, unit 2: Developing and competence

Source: DfES (2004c: 35).

The principles of cross-curricular teaching and learning

Cross-curricular teaching and learning should be:

- based on individual subjects and their connections through authentic links or through an external theme/dimension;

- characterised and developed by teachers with excellent subject knowledge and a capacity to reconceptualise this within a broader context of learning beyond their subject;

- coherent in maintaining links with pupils' prior learning and experience;

- contextualised effectively, presenting opportunities for explicit links with pupils' learning outside the formal classroom;

- demanding in its use of curriculum time and resources, requiring flexibility and often needing the support of senior managers if collaborative approaches are to be implemented effectively;

- underpinned by a meaningful assessment process that is explicitly linked to, and informed by, the enriched pedagogical framework.

Increased demand for cross-curricular approaches has spread from primary to secondary schools and was strengthened by the proposed Rose Curriculum (DCSF 2009a) and the Cambridge Primary Review (Alexander 2010).

Medium-term plans/units of work

The *Primary Framework for Literacy and Mathematics* (DfES 2006d) provided guidance to show how the specified learning objectives within all twelve literacy strands could be used to plan coherent units of work. Links to a range of resources were also provided. Since the demise of the National Strategies, many of these resources have been held on a national archive site (http://webarchive.nationalarchives.gov.uk). The drawbacks to these detailed units of work (already discussed) notwithstanding, used prudently and flexibly they can provide useful support. Table 15.3 provides an example from the National Strategies of one way of organising Year 3 units across a school year.

TABLE 15.3 Year 3 units of work.

	Unit 1	Unit 2	Unit 3	Unit 4	Unit 5
Narrative block	Stories with familiar settings (3 weeks)	Dialogue and plays (4 weeks)	Myths, legends, fables, traditional tales (4 weeks)	Adventure and mystery (4 weeks)	Authors and letters (3 weeks)
Non-fiction block	Reports (4 weeks)	Instructions (3–4 weeks)	Information texts (4 weeks)		
Poetry block	(4 weeks, which could be spread out)				

Developing units of work

A medium-term plan consists of a series of units of work together with a clear outline of teaching of discrete or continuous word-level skills such as phonics, spelling and handwriting. It is particularly important that during school experience trainees ensure a coherent sequence of lessons that fits within the school's overall long-term plan. Trainees' lesson plans should contain the following:

- the context: number of children, specific needs, allocated time per week, previous linked activities;
- National Curriculum links;
- outline of teaching activities;
- resources to be used, including texts;
- key assessment links.

The following steps in planning units of work need to be considered:

1. Outcomes

Questions to consider include:

- What will the outcome be?
- Will the outcome be written or oral; might it be a performance of some kind?
- Will the outcome be the same for all ability groups?
- Who is the audience for this outcome?
- Is there a real purpose?

2. Teaching sequence

This should consider:

- exciting books, multimodal texts, websites, on-screen texts or films;
- drama strategies;
- use of talk for writing and learning;
- chances for real writing opportunities during each phase of the teaching sequence;
- modelled, shared and supported composition;
- use of reading journals;
- guided reading and writing;
- sentence- and word-level links;
- links to the assessment foci and ongoing assessments, for example using Assessing Pupils' Progress (APP);
- opportunities for incorporating ICT;
- cross-curricular links.

3. Setting objectives and teaching strategies

Ensure that the following points are covered:

■ Objectives need to be reviewed to focus on the learning outcomes for each phase.

■ It should be decided which strategies and activities will help to meet the learning outcomes.

4. Practical constraints

These include:

■ access to resources – especially ICT;
■ additional adult support;
■ timetable constraints.

5. Discrete teaching of certain aspects

For example:

■ Will spelling conventions be taught and investigated?
■ Can independent spelling strategies be taught within the writing process?
■ How and when will sentence-level objectives be taught?
■ Which aspects will require modelled and shared talk, reading or writing?
■ What might guided teaching focus on?
■ How might plenaries be used effectively?

Table 15.4 provides an example of an extract from a unit of work for poetry for Year 5.

Lesson planning

The structure of a literacy lesson has become far more flexible since the introduction of the rigid structure of the literacy hour. Lessons may still follow the structure of the three-part lesson, but teachers may need to vary the use of this structure. In particular, the following should be borne in mind when planning lessons:

■ Phases within lessons should introduce, develop and review learning and should support the overall learning intentions of the lesson.

■ Children should know what they are learning and why.

■ The teacher should orchestrate the structure of the learning but allow children opportunities to explore and question to build their learning.

■ The timings of the parts of lessons should meet the needs of the lesson.

■ Planning across a period of time will be needed, but it should be adapted to meet children's needs.

■ Teachers should ensure that previous learning is built upon.

The following also need to be considered in planning lessons:

- Detail given for the teaching content of the whole-class work with key questions or teaching points.
- Specific planning for a guided session, if included, should show the introduction, focus and follow-up (mini-plenary) as well as the focus for assessment and monitoring.
- Independent work should be clearly outlined with notes for any additional adults.
- Plenary sessions should identify the focus of the lesson, incorporating questions to consolidate learning, build links and provide a range of opportunities for children to review their learning, clarify their understanding and discuss what they have been taught.

Learning objectives

The first step in planning an effective lesson is to decide on a focused objective. Objectives are those things that you expect the children to achieve during the lesson. They are usually set out under phrases such as 'the children will be able to …', 'the children will understand …' or 'the children will know that …'. For example, 'The children will be able to write a poem that includes rhyming couplets.' The objectives for a single lesson should be limited and achievable, and they should be made clear to the children at the beginning of the lesson in child-friendly language.

ACTIVITY: WRITING OBJECTIVES

Look at the objectives in Table 15.5 and decide with colleagues which are achievable objectives with a clear focus. Try also putting those that you feel are achievable in child-friendly language.

TABLE 15.4 Extract from a poetry unit plan for Year 5

W Primary School   **Short-term planning – literacy**

Date: Jan 2012 Year group(s): 5	**Texts:** 'The Highwayman' by Alfred Noyes 'I Saw a Jolly Hunter' by Charles Causley. See daily planning for all other poems used.	
Unit: Additional text-based unit year 5	Outcome: **Phase 1:** To talk about how the poet uses language to create images To reflect on the poem through discussion and making notes **Phase 2:** To explore the meaning of the poem through performance To explore how poets use rhythm and rhyme To discuss ways that different poets present poems on a similar theme **Phase 3:** To explore how figurative language is used to create images and atmosphere To use evidence from the poem to discuss events and ideas To explore the poet's perspective from what is written and is implied To explore how the poet uses language for effect	**Cross-curricular links:** 'Who do you think you are?' topic, starting with the pupil themselves and their senses.
Objectives from strands 1–4 **Speaking and Listening** Understand different ways to take the lead and support others in groups. Use and recognise the impact of theatrical effects in drama. Present a spoken argument, sequencing points logically, defending views with evidence and making use of persuasive language.	Objectives from strands 5–6 **Word** Use a range of appropriate strategies to edit, proofread and correct spelling in their own work, on paper and on screen.	Objectives from strands 7–12 **Reading and Writing** Make notes on and use evidence from across a text to explain events or ideas Infer writers' perspectives from what is written and from what is implied. Explain how writers use figurative and expressive language to create images and atmosphere. Compare how a common theme is presented in poetry, prose and other media. Reflect independently and critically on their own writing and edit and improve it. Use a range of ICT programs to present texts, making informed choices about which electronic tools to use for different purposes

TABLE 15.4 (cont.)

Day	Teaching sequence (phase)	Whole-class teaching (Review, teach, practise, apply, review and evaluate)	Independent and group/guided work (Review, teach, practise, apply, review and evaluate)	Reflection on learning
1 Thurs	**Stand alone day**	Ask the children to get out their literacy target cards and remind themselves of their personal targets. Ask the whole class to think of ways in which we can all 'up-level' our literacy work – jot these down on your whiteboards; feed back suggestions into a whole-class discussion. What are the non-negotiables? (e.g. sentences starting with capital letters, writing being legible, correct punctuation at end of a sentence etc.). Refer to pyramids/classroom displays as reminders of how to achieve this.	Whole class: Discuss the concept of 'new year's resolutions'. Have you made any already? Think about what you need to improve upon this year. This may be something that you need to stop doing! Share your thoughts with the rest of your group. Can you think of two resolutions that you could make that relate to your school work? Can you think of another more general one (e.g. keep my bedroom tidy, stop biting my nails etc.). Decide on three resolutions. In Literacy books, write about your choice of resolutions, stating why you think that these are important for you. *Challenge* – as you do this piece of writing, can you add the things that you need to do in order to meet your literacy targets?	Ask one child at a time to read out their writing to the class. As they read, the rest of us note down any positives that help to up-level the piece (e.g. good openers at the start of sentences, higher-level vocabulary, extended sentences etc.)
2 Fri	**Stand alone day**	**Mental literacy** Discuss how we can all 'up-level' our written work by adding higher-level descriptive words. Teacher then suggests a word, discusses its meaning if necessary, then asks children to have a go at writing a sentence that includes that word. Share sentences and discuss good/incorrect use of the word. Suggestions: devastated, annoyed, astounded, delighted.	Developing Reading Skills reading assessment – persuasion (*Rising Stars* book p. 38) Use this evidence for target cards/APP.	Share new class fiction book, read blurb and discuss. Do you know any other books by this author? Start reading, and discuss story so far if time allows.

TABLE 15.4 (cont.)

Day	Teaching sequence (phase)	Whole-class teaching (Review, teach, practise, apply, review and evaluate)	Independent and group/guided work (Review, teach, practise, apply, review and evaluate)			Reflection on learning
			Less able group	**Middle groups**	**Top group**	
3	1	**Objectives** **Infer writer's perspective from what is written and what is implied.** **To reflect on a poem through discussion.** **To be able to voice opinions in a clear and concise way.** Introduce the poetry unit. Talk about how poets, just like authors, sometimes reveal their own points of view through their work. Read 'I Saw a Jolly Hunter' by Charles Causley. Can you work out the author's point of view on hunting? How do you know this? What gives us clues to his point of view? Encourage children to find the quote from the poem that shows this. Demonstrate how you would set out the quote as part of a written answer.	Read 'Christmas Thank Yous' by Mike Gowar. Can you tell what the poet is thinking as he writes his thank-you letters? How does he really feel about the gifts that he got for Christmas? How do you know what he is thinking? Does the poet want to make you laugh? In literacy books, write a personal response to the poem saying whether you enjoyed it or not and why.	Read 'Absent' by Bernard Young. What do you think the person saying the poem is trying to tell his teacher? How do you think he is feeling? Why do you think this might be? (no right or wrong answer to this!) As LA group - a personal response to the poem. Add quotes to illustrate your thoughts about the poem.	Read 'The Evacuee' by Shirley Tomlinson. Encourage this group to explore the emotions of the child in the poem. Can you imagine what the child must be feeling? How well does the author convey this? Which words or phrases tell you this? Write your personal response to the poem. Include quotes and write about how well the poet conveys the child's emotions.	Ask representatives from each group to come and read their group's poem to the class. For each poem, ask other children in the group to tell everyone what they thought the poet was trying to convey, and to give their own opinions of the poem.

TABLE 15.4 (cont.)

Day	Teaching sequence (phase)	Whole-class teaching (Review, teach, practise, apply, review and evaluate)	Independent and group/guided work (Review, teach, practise, apply, review and evaluate)	Reflection on learning
4	1	**Objectives** **Explain how writers use figurative and expressive language to create images and atmosphere.** Tell the class that the poem we are looking at today is a narrative poem – it tells a story. Read 'The Highwayman' by Alfred Noyes (on interactive whiteboard + paper copy). Stop at suitable intervals and make sure that the children are following the story. Ask the children if they know what 'imagery' is. Give children copies of an extract from the text, one between two. Discuss the extract and how Noyes uses imagery to build a picture in the reader's mind. What else does it add to the poem? Discuss metaphor (e.g. 'The moon was a ghostly galleon…'). How successful is the poet in creating mood/atmosphere in the poem?	Reread the extract and make sure that all children can see a copy. What do you know for sure? E.g. his trousers are brown, his boots go up to his thigh etc. What does the imagery imply? Do you take the metaphors literally, or are they part of an image that the poet wants to plant in your mind? Is the moon really a 'ghostly galleon' or does it just look like one? Ask the children to sketch the image that is conjured up in their minds when they hear this part of the poem. You could re-read it as the children are sketching. May need to finish these sketches for morning work.	Blu-tac sketches to the board. How similar/different are they? Why does the poet go to so much trouble to describe the setting? Encourage children to make a personal response to the poem.

TABLE 15.4 (cont.)

Day	Teaching sequence (phase)	Whole-class teaching (Review, teach, practise, apply, review and evaluate)	Independent and group/guided work (Review, teach, practise, apply, review and evaluate)	Reflection on learning
5	2	**Objectives** **To consider the poet's intentions.** **To be able to compare two poems using the correct terminology.** **To plan and perform confidently as part of a group.** Discuss performance poetry - relate to 5W's poem in our Y5 assembly. Teachers perform a poem of their choice - read the first time in a dull, monotonous voice, and then perform properly. Discuss the difference in the two renditions. Look at 'Ears Hear', 'The Sound Collector' and 'Louder than a Clap of Thunder'. Identify the common theme and compare/contrast. Discuss ways of performing, vary number of voices, add sound effects with body percussion, musical instruments, etc.	See Smart board resources for all of these poems. LA - Practice and perform 'Ears Hear' Middle groups - Practice and perform 'Louder than a Clap of Thunder'. Top - Practice and perform 'The Sound Collector' by Roger McGough. What do you think has happened to the person in the poem? This group has the challenge of the fact that the poem is about silence, so will not be allowed to add sound effects but must hit the right tone of voice when performing	N.B. Allow longer for this! Perform poems in groups Discuss which poem the children preferred and why. Discuss the poet's intentions for each poem

TABLE 15.4 (cont.)

Day	Teaching sequence (phase)	Whole-class teaching (Review, teach, practise, apply, review and evaluate)	Independent and group/guided work (Review, teach, practise, apply, review and evaluate)			Reflection on learning
6	1 N.B. This may take longer than 1 lesson!	**Objectives** **To internalise and recreate the image of a poem.** **To choose words for effect.** 'The Magic of the Brain' (on Smart board) Read poem without revealing title. Ask children to close eyes and run it like a film in their heads. Talk to a partner about their thoughts. Partner to report what they say. Do quick sketch of one image. Describe to class. OPEN-ENDED QUESTIONS. Display text. Read through with children. Which phrases do they like and why? What do you think the title of the poem might be? What would be appropriate? With the whole class, model how to write a version of a verse of the poem (SMELL), thought showering ideas and phrases first, then composing.	LA TASTE Thought shower and then make notes on another of the senses. Together, guided by the teacher, write another verse of the poem.	Middle SIGHT As LA group, but guided by the TA.	Top TOUCH To work together as a group to write their own verse. Working independently.	Listen to what the independent group have written. What works well? When it doesn't 'scan', why not? As a class, compose the final verse (SOUND) of the poem together, then read the whole thing. Evaluate our version of the poem so far - how could we improve it further?
Fri		Spelling Test Word-level work: suffix -ful. Explain rule, work through several examples. Copy rule into literacy books	Support sheet available TA	Copy out list with 2 columns (e.g. beauty, beautiful etc.	As AA but add extra words, use a dictionary to check.	Class story or look at websites on new class author.

TABLE 15.4 (cont.)

Day	Teaching sequence (phase)	Whole-class teaching (Review, teach, practise, apply, review and evaluate)	Independent and group/guided work (Review, teach, practise, apply, review and evaluate)			Reflection on learning
			LA	Middle	Top	
7	2 ML – write a metaphor for feeling sad, feeling happy etc.	**Objectives** **To understand the structure of the poem.** **To write a verse using a given structure.** **To understand imagery.** Reread poem from last lesson – 'The Magic of the Brain' (on Smart board) What images pop into your mind as you listen to the poem? Recap 'imagery' as a device in poetry. Discuss structure – did the independent group for yesterday manage to follow the structure in their verses?	Write out and illustrate the verse composed last lesson. Do this as a handwriting exercise. If time allows, read poetry books, as middle group.	Write out and illustrate the verse composed last time. Do this as a handwriting exercise. Have a selection of poetry books available in the classroom – those who have time can read these/prepare a poem to perform.	Continue with verse started yesterday. Think about suggestions made during the plenary. Can you improve your work further? Read your verses out loud to see if they scan. Make necessary adjustments. Can you compose a final verse of the poem that mentions all the senses (as the original poem does)?	Show children poetry anthologies, all of which have been borrowed from the school library. These will be returned to the library at the end of this week and will be available for you to borrow. (It might be worth reading a few humorous poems to encourage interest!)

TABLE 15.4 (cont.)

Day	Teaching sequence (phase)	Whole-class teaching (Review, teach, practise, apply, review and evaluate)	Independent and group/guided work (Review, teach, practise, apply, review and evaluate)	Reflection on learning
8	3	**Objectives** **To understand and use onomatopoeia.** **To write in the style of the poet.** Look at 'Ears Hear' (on Smart board). Identify the rhyming structure of the poem. Show children how to number the lines and then use numbers to help identify the rhyming scheme (e.g. End of line 2 rhymes with end of line 4, etc.). Identify onomatopoeic words – look at dictionary definition of this word. Teach what this means and ask the children to think of some examples (e.g. buzz, hum, crinkle etc.). Try to find some that rhyme if you can.	Working in mixed ability groupings: 1. Thought shower, then record on a large sheet of paper all the onomatopoeic words that you can think of. 2. Work with a partner to find examples that rhyme and note these down on the sheet (e.g. ring/ding/ping). 3. Write a sound poem for the sounds heard in the classroom. Try to rhyme the last word of each line (as in 'Ears Hear'). e.g. Paper rips Tap drips 4. You have written rhyming couplets, but the poem 'Ears Hear' follows a different structure. Challenge the more able to break up the couplets with another couplet so their verse follows the structure of 'Ears Hear'. Plenary Invite all groups to share today's work with the rest of the class. Teachers help with verse structure if groups have found stage 4 of today's work difficult.	

TABLE 15.4 (cont.)

Day	Teaching sequence (phase)	Whole-class teaching (Review, teach, practise, apply, review and evaluate)	Independent and group/guided work (Review, teach, practise, apply, review and evaluate)	Reflection on learning
9		**Objectives** **Compare how a common theme is presented in poetry, prose and other media.** Explain that all of the poems that we are reading today share a common theme – they are all about friends and friendship. Read: 'Friendship' by VeroniqueTadjo 'Friends' by Elizabeth Jennings 'Harvey' by Judith Vorst 'Shame' by Tracey Blance Discuss each poem in turn comparing and contrasting as you go along. Identify the rhyming structure in those that rhyme. Discuss feelings and the poets' viewpoints. Why is the last poem called 'Shame'?	Give out copies of 'My Brilliant Friend' by Roger McGough. Allow time for the children to read this to themselves, then shared read as a class. Look at the structure of the poem, how each line starts, the length of the lines, the rhyming scheme etc. How does the poem end? Why do you think McGough ends it like this? Chose a title for your poem, e.g.: My Crazy Friend… My Funny Friend… My Lovely Friend… etc. Write your own poem about a real or an imaginary friend, based on 'My Brilliant Friend'. Guided group with T =LA Guided by TA = Middle group Working independently = Top group. <u>Plenary</u> Share good examples of verses written today – possibly make into a class book of poems?	
10		Big writing task – poetry – based on 'The Writer of this Poem' by Roger McGough See separate planning sheet. **N.B. Will need adapting if to be used as a formal assessment piece!**		

TABLE 15.4 (cont.)

Assessment notes	Next steps – new unit
I can talk about how poets use language to create images (+ can use correct vocabulary). AF5 L3 I can reflect on a poem and make a personal response. AF2/AF5 L3 I can perform a poem with appropriate intonation, expression, pace, rhythm etc. AF3 L3 I can identify how a poet has used rhythm and rhyme. I can identify the poet's viewpoint (perspective). AF6 L3 (N.B. Reading AFs!)	**Week 1** **Week 2**
ICT/IWB Poems on IWB	

TABLE 15.5 Learning objectives

Objectives	Comments
1. To be able to use drama techniques to explore issues in a story.	
2. To be able to write a haiku poem.	
3. To be able to use commas in lists.	
4. To know that instructions need to be written in a clear sequence.	
5. To understand how to use conjunctions to join sentences.	
6. To know strategies for spelling new words.	

Timing lessons

Particularly for the less-experienced teacher or trainee, it is important to decide on clear timings for the following:

- an introduction that sets out the learning objective and how children will achieve it through clear success criteria;
- whole-class work (ensuring this is interactive, lively and allows clear modelling of particular aspects);
- guided or independent work, with sufficient time allowed for the children to be able to achieve something of worth;
- plenary sessions to review the work with the children, and where appropriate to help them to self-assess their work and to reiterate teaching points.

Lessons should be lively, with a smooth transition from one aspect to another. However, it is also important that sufficient time is allocated for children to carry out particular activities.

Differentiation

All classes will demonstrate a range of abilities and strengths in different areas. Assessment for learning is therefore the key to effective differentiation, as it provides the vital information needed. Differentiation may involve planning a separate programme of work for one child or a small number of children, as well as preparing different activities or variations on activities for others. This is 'differentiation by task'. Differentiation can also be achieved by support (i.e. with the help of an adult or more able peer), or by outcome where the different levels are shown by the completed piece of work. The key is to provide appropriate support that fits the specific task.

Plenary sessions

Plenary sessions have become widespread practice across the curriculum, perhaps as a result of the introduction of the National Literacy Strategy in 1998. However, the quality of many plenary sessions has been questioned, for example by Ofsted (2002a). One of the common reasons for this is the lack of time allocated for the plenary at the end of the lesson. However, it is crucial for effective learning that pupils review what they have learned and that teachers can not only assess what children have achieved but also reiterate key teaching points. This part of the lesson therefore needs to be planned carefully and should not simply consist of children clearing away or showing their work to others.

Before the lesson:

- take account of the plenary and provide a range of opportunities for children to review their learning, clarify their new understanding and discuss what they have been taught;
- identify questions that will help the children to consolidate and extend their literacy skills and recognise the progress they have made towards meeting the lesson's objectives and any targets that have been set;
- build links between the plenary and other elements of the lesson.

During the plenary:

- challenge children to justify and refine their ideas and findings;
- provide feedback that aims to clarify, refine and extend children's thinking, reasoning and communication skills;
- assess the learning against the lesson objectives and log this information to inform future plans.

After the plenary:

- review the success of the plenary and record briefly information gathered on particular children;
- use the information to inform future plans.

ACTIVITY: EFFECTIVE LESSON PLANNING

Review the checklist of prompts for effective lesson planning below and apply it to a lesson you are planning to teach.

A checklist for lesson planning

1. Objectives

- Is the object achievable in this lesson?
- Is it written in child-friendly language?
- Does it also have linked success criteria?
- Are links provided to the National Curriculum?

2. Introduction

- How will the lesson be introduced?
- How will the children's interest be gained and sustained?

3. Whole-class teaching

- How will links be made to prior learning?
- What visual aids or multisensory teaching will be incorporated?
- What resources will be used?
- In what ways will the learning be modelled?
- What specific questions will be asked?
- How will the lesson be interactive?
- What opportunities for talk amongst pupils will be provided?

4. Guided or independent work

- How will the task be explained?
- How will the task be structured?
- What support will be provided?
- How will the learning be monitored?

5. Plenary session

- Which activities will be included to demonstrate pupils' learning?
- Which key questions will be asked?
- Which teaching points will be reinforced?

Conclusion

Planning for English is undoubtedly complex, but having a clear understanding of the cycle of planning and assessment makes it easier to manage. It is also crucial that practitioners have a clear grasp of the core aspects of teaching speaking, listening, reading and writing. While key skills will require a discrete progression of teaching, many aspects are interrelated. It is also important to bear in mind that talk underpins the learning process and that effective writing should follow plenty of opportunities to plan and talk through the content first. Writing should also be based on having explored good models through reading. One might summarise the process thus:

Good writers talk a lot, read a lot and write a little (but effectively).

Trainee teachers and less-experienced teachers will need to plan in far greater detail for individual lessons, whereas more-experienced teachers can rely on annotations on unit plans devised by the school. Whatever the detail, careful consideration needs to be given to all aspects of the lesson.

Key points

- Understanding the learning process is the key to planning, which must be clearly linked to assessment for learning.
- The core aspects of teaching speaking, listening, reading and writing are fundamental to planning effectively.
- Planning in the EYFS links the areas of learning and should provide first-hand experiences with a balance of teacher-led and child-directed activities.
- Planning for Key Stages 1 and 2 should begin with looking at links across the curriculum.
- Long-term plans will ensure coverage of all areas and, where schools work on a two-yearly cycle, repetition can be avoided.
- Medium-term plans consist of coherent units of work that can be drawn and adapted from a range of published materials.
- Short-term planning requires the teacher to consider clear and focused objectives, timing, and key aspects of the main parts of the lesson.

Further reading

Brien, J. (2012) *Teaching Primary English*. London: Sage.

Cremin, T. (2009) *Teaching English Creatively*. London: Routledge.

Robinson, K. and Aronica, L. (2009) *The Element: how finding your passion changes everything*. London: Continuum.

16

Assessment for learning of English

Purpose of this chapter

This chapter aims to:

- review forms of assessment for English for the Early Years Foundation Stage (EYFS) and Key Stages 1 and 2;
- discuss the characteristics of assessment for learning;
- give examples of involving pupils in the assessment process;
- discuss how to build assessment into curriculum planning;
- explore the assessment of speaking and listening;
- review the assessment of reading and writing.

Forms of assessment

Assessment can be divided into two main types:

- Assessment *of* learning (AoL) or summative assessment. This is a summary of what pupils have learned at a specific point in time. It is a 'snapshot' of what has been learned or achieved.
- Assessment *for* learning (AfL) or formative assessment. This is a process of obtaining information to decide on the point that learners are at in their learning, what the next stage in learning is, where to go next and how to get there (Assessment Reform Group 1999, 2002a, 2002b). It is any assessment activity that informs the next steps to learning.

The following sections discuss the role of each type of assessment in relation to English. The major consideration will be given to the role of AfL to support the effective teaching of English.

Summative assessment or assessment of learning

Summative assessment (or AoL) can be divided into statutory assessment (Standard Attainment Tests) and non-statutory school-based types of assessment. Both of these are usually carried out at the end of a school year or at other key points to provide information to assist in monitoring pupils' overall progress. Statutory assessment at the Early Years Foundation Stage and at Key Stages 1 and 2 consists of the following.

Early Years Foundation Stage profile

The Early Years Foundation Stage profile provides a description of a child's development and progress in relation to the early learning goals contained in the EYFS. The revised EYFS from September 2012 reduces the number of assessment scales and points to seventeen (to reflect the decreased number of early learning goals). There are three prime areas of learning and four specific areas under the revised framework. Of the three prime areas one relates to communication and language, and of the four specific areas one relates to literacy. The revised early learning goals under the prime area of communication and language state (DfE 2012a:7–8):

- *Listening and attention*: children listen attentively in a range of situations. They listen to stories, accurately anticipating key events, and respond to what they hear with relevant comments, questions or actions. They give their attention to what others say and respond appropriately, while engaged in another activity.

- *Understanding*: children follow instructions involving several ideas or actions. They answer 'how' and 'why' questions about their experiences and in response to stories or events.

- *Speaking*: children express themselves effectively, showing awareness of listeners' needs. They use past, present and future forms accurately when talking about events that have happened or are to happen in the future. They develop their own narratives and explanations by connecting ideas or events.

Under the specific area of literacy, the EYFS early learning goals (DfE 2012a: 7–8) set out the following:

- *Reading*: children read and understand simple sentences. They use phonic knowledge to decode regular words and read them aloud accurately. They also read some common irregular words. They demonstrate understanding when talking with others about what they have read.

- *Writing*: children use their phonic knowledge to write words in ways that match their spoken sounds. They also write some irregular common words. They write simple sentences that can be read by themselves and others. Some words are spelled correctly and others are phonetically plausible.

The DfE also sets out the requirement that:

> Year 1 teachers must be given a copy of the Profile report together with a short commentary on each child's skills and abilities in relation to the three key characteristics of effective learning ... These should inform a dialogue between Reception and Year 1 teachers about each child's stage of development and learning needs and assist with the planning of activities in Year 1.
>
> (DfE 2012a: 11)

The key point to bear in mind is that this type of assessment is based on observations made by practitioners throughout the Reception year, and assessments are done in the context of normal activities.

National Curriculum levels

For Key Stages 1 and 2 and above, teachers are required to report children's attainment against National Curriculum levels of attainment and use level descriptors to decide which level a child has achieved. These are broad statements that enable a decision to be made as to a 'best fit' to describe a child's achievement. In English, teachers often meet to moderate judgements about a best fit for each child, particularly for writing. At the end of Key Stage 1, children are expected to achieve level 2, and the expectation at the end of Key Stage 2 is level 4. These levels are further subdivided into three subdivisions within each level (a, b and c, with 'a' denoting the highest) to support teachers' finer judgements. In addition, the DfES provided 'P-scales' (DfES 2002a), which set out statements of achievement for children with special educational needs who are working below level 1.

Standard Attainment Tests (SATs)

Children are required to take SATs at the end of Year 2 and Year 6, in English and mathematics. At Key Stage 1 (Year 2), teachers mark these, but at Key Stage 2 they are externally set and marked. This process has been subject to government review and a report published in 2011 by Lord Bew concluded that external assessment should continue to be carried out, although changes were recommended (DfE 2011c). A stronger emphasis on teacher assessment was a key conclusion. Teacher assessment is the focus at Key Stage 1, with those results superseding any test or task results when appropriate. At the end of Key Stage 2, reading should continue to be externally tested; however, writing composition should be subject only to summative teacher assessment to demonstrate broad range of writing skills over the course of Year 6, and such teacher assessment should be subject to external moderation. The DfE put in place interim arrangements for 2012 for assessing writing, prior to fully adopting the recommendations from Lord Bew in 2013. Tests for speaking and listening will continue to be assessed by teacher judgement.

While these tests provide some information at a specific point of a child's achievement, there are many limitations in relying on them as a means of understanding a child's progress, strengths and weaknesses. The running record conducted at Key Stage 1 is, however, one example of a test that provides some important diagnostic information about a child's reading skills. Many schools also carry out QCA optional tests in mathematics and English every year in Key Stage 2, to provide year-on-year information on a child's progress.

Diagnostic assessment

Diagnostic assessment is a form of test or assessment that provides information about specific difficulties a child may be having. The running record, or miscue analysis, in reading is one example. Another example was provided by the Primary National Strategy in the form of diagnostic marking guidelines for writing (DfES 2001) as an aid to the systematic analysis of children's writing.

Children's progress in phonics is another area that should be carefully tracked and supported by diagnostic assessment. Inevitably, some children will make slower progress, which highlights the vital role of AfL, in which a teacher carefully provides opportunities in all lessons to check children's progress. The *Letters and Sounds* guidance on assessment and tracking includes an example tracking sheet. This framework also identifies a range of opportunities for assessment:

> This can be during the discrete daily phonics session, but will also be apparent during shared guided and independent reading and writing sessions.
>
> Writing samples provide useful evidence of children's phonic knowledge and ability to apply phonic skills, but evidence obtained through observation of children's approaches to reading unfamiliar words is of equal importance.
>
> (DfES 2007a: 3)

The coalition government also introduced a Year 1 phonics screening national assessment from 2012. This assessment framework states that children are expected to (DfE 2011a):

- give the sound when shown any grapheme that has been taught;
- blend phonemes in order to read words;
- know most of the common grapheme–phoneme correspondences;
- read phonically decodable one-syllable and two-syllable words.

The aim of this screening process is to give information about a child's phonic ability at a young age, allowing any necessary intervention to begin at an early stage.

For those children who require additional support, phonics catch-up programmes are also available. One such programme, *Quick Fix for Phonics* (Jolliffe 2012), provides a range of diagnostic assessment activities in order to ascertain how and where to intervene.

Formative assessment or assessment for learning

A considerable amount of research, combined with effective classroom practice, has fused into what is known as assessment for learning (AfL), which has been shown to make a significant difference to children's learning. Black and Wiliam's research found that:

> There is a body of firm evidence that formative assessment is an essential feature of classroom work and development of it can raise standards. We know of no other way of raising standards for which such a strong prima facie case can be made on the basis of evidence of such large learning gains.
>
> (Black and Wiliam 1998: 148)

This research has had a direct impact on government policy and extensive professional development materials were provided by the Primary National Strategy on AfL (DfES 2004a).

The following principles underpin AfL:

- the active involvement of children in their own learning;
- the provision of effective feedback to children;
- a recognition of the profound influence that assessment has on the motivation and self-esteem of children, both of which are crucial influences on learning;
- the need for children to assess themselves and understand how to improve;
- the adjustment of teaching to take account of the results of assessment.

In order for these principles to be put into practice, the following characteristics of AfL are needed:

- use of effective questioning (providing wait time, framing questions and follow-up);
- use of marking and feedback strategies;
- sharing of learning goals;
- peer and self-assessment.

The key change that AfL supports is the active involvement of children in understanding their own learning and how to improve. An effective strategy is to share learning objectives with children in child-friendly language, and also to share the criteria by which they can judge success. Success criteria summarise the key points children need to understand as steps to success in achieving the learning objective. Ideally, children are involved in creating the success criteria with their teachers to ensure they are fully understood. Following is an example of success criteria for Year 2 (DfES 2004b: 33):

Activity: To be able to write instructions

Success criteria:

- Imperative verbs have been used or in child-friendly language: 'Bossy verbs have been used' (e.g. 'Take jelly out of the packet').
- The instructions are in the correct order (e.g. 'Pour boiling water on the jelly. Then stir until the jelly melts').
- The sequence of actions is clear through the use of bullet points, numbers or *first*, *second* etc. Child-friendly version: The order of actions is clear.

Other successful strategies to support AfL include the use of the acronyms WALT, WILF and WINK to involve children in their learning:

- WALT: what are we learning to?
- WILF: what I am looking for?
- WINK: what I now know.

Figure 16.1 and Figure 16.2 provide some examples related to writing.

WALT: What are we learning today?

We are learning to write 'super sentences'.

FIGURE 16.1 Child-friendly objectives

WILF: What am I (the teacher) looking for?

The teacher is looking for interesting and exciting words.

FIGURE 16.2 Child-friendly success criteria

Involving pupils in the assessment process

Schools have developed a range of methods for involving children in assessing their own learning, particularly in plenary sessions, such as 'three stars and a wish', where children share three things they have done well and one thing they would like to improve upon. Another example is the use of 'traffic lights' to show how confident children feel about an aspect of their learning (see Figure 16.3). These can be used in the form of cards that pupils hold up to indicate their level of understanding, or children putting appropriately coloured dots on their work. While these are useful ways of involving pupils in self-assessment, far more rigorous forms of assessment involving pupils need to be developed alongside them that genuinely encourage pupils to reflect on their learning.

RED:
Don't understand

AMBER:
Not sure

GREEN:
Got it!

FIGURE 16.3 Traffic lights: supporting children's self-assessment

ACTIVITY: UNDERSTANDING FITNESS FOR PURPOSE

To ensure understanding of a range of assessments, look at the assessments below and decide on the purpose of each. (There are some suggested answers at the end of the chapter, on page 308.)

Assessment activity	Purpose	Summative or formative
Standardised reading test		
Differentiated questioning		
Phoneme–grapheme correspondence test		
Moderated sample of child's writing		
Running record or miscue analysis of reading		
Guided writing feedback		

Assessment of speaking and listening

Speaking and listening can be difficult to assess due to the fluid nature of talk and the difficulty of using accurate criteria. A key point is to ensure that, in making any summative judgements of National Curriculum levels, a range of observations contributes to an overall level given to provide a 'best fit'.

It is important to link assessment to teaching objectives and to be clear about the nature of the speaking and listening being assessed, to apply agreed criteria and to find efficient ways of recording achievements. Evidence should be collected systematically in the following situations:

- activities that have been specifically set up to teach speaking and listening skills with the criteria for success clearly shared with children;
- planned activities that include substantial oral or group work, which may be related to other aspects of English or other curriculum areas;
- a significant contribution of a child that relates to speaking and listening.

Developing an overall plan for assessing speaking and listening

Developing a plan for assessing speaking and listening should be part of a whole-school policy that

- encourages self and peer assessment;
- collects evidence systematically;
- summarises achievement in order to plan for progression;
- standardises assessment through moderation.

Making and recording assessments

Collecting evidence can take different forms: what is important is to be systematic and to find an approach that is manageable and supports future learning. This may include:

- notes made by the teacher or other adults;
- notes made by the children (e.g. 'talk logs');
- recorded work;
- succinct and accessible records that inform future teaching;
- systems with separate sections for each child.

Building assessment into curriculum-planning

Specifically considering assessment opportunities during planning can help to ensure that assessment takes place systematically. This may include:

- a focus on two or three children each week;
- key objectives for whole-class monitoring that are identified and recorded using a traffic-light system, with coloured dots or ticks (i.e. green for achieved, orange denoting when an aspect needs reinforcement and red for not achieved) – an example for Year 2 is provided in Table 16.1;
- termly checks on children's progress;
- an annual review of progress.

TABLE 16.1 Key objectives recording grid

Pupil's name	Objective 1 Speak with clarity and use intonation when reading and reciting texts	Objective 2 Tell real and imagined stories using the conventions of familiar story language	Objective 3 Explain ideas and processes using language and gestures appropriately

Children's self-assessment

Involving children in assessment is a key part of AfL. It can have profound effects on the learning through enabling children to have an active involvement in their own learning and to understand the means by which they may improve. One example of this is using 'talk diaries' (see Chapter 6).

Assessing against National Curriculum level descriptions

The summary of National Curriculum level descriptions (Table 16.2) from Grugeon *et al.* (2005) can be helpful when it is necessary to find a level that best describes a child's level of achievement. It is important that this judgement is made over a range of activities and over a period of time, so that it accurately summarises a child's achievement.

Assessing pupils' progress in speaking and listening

Assessing Pupils' Progress (APP) is a structured approach to periodic assessment that was introduced following a pilot project in 2006–8 conducted by the Qualifications and Curriculum Development Agency (QCDA) and then rolled out in conjunction with the National Strategies. For English, APP materials were produced for assessment of each attainment target. The approach was widely adopted by schools but has not been promoted by the coalition government since 2010. Due to the number of schools still using this approach, it is helpful to understand its key features:

■ It aims to support judgements of attainment within National Curriculum levels and identify next steps in learning linked to national rates of progress.

■ Information can be used diagnostically to identify information about pupils' strengths and weaknesses to improve planning, teaching and learning.

■ It can help to track pupils' progress over a key stage or longer.

The APP approach is based on assessment focuses (AFs) that underpin National Curriculum assessment and sit between the National Curriculum programmes of study and the level descriptions. Exemplars of pupils' performance at National Curriculum levels of attainment were also provided in the form of 'standards files'. The AFs for speaking and listening are as follows:

■ AF1: talking to others;

■ AF2: talking with others;

■ AF3: talking within role play and drama;

■ AF4: talking about talk.

The assessment guidelines that set out levels of attainment for each AF are available from the National Archives: http://webarchive.nationalarchives.gov.uk/20110809101133/ http://nsonline.org.uk/node/310301?uc=force_uj.

Implementing APP Speaking and Listening involves three phases: planning, reviewing evidence and periodic assessment.

TABLE 16.2 Summary of National Curriculum level descriptions for speaking and listening

	Listening	Talk clarity	Vocabulary
Level 1	Listens to others Usually responds appropriately	Audible	Simple
Level 2	Listens carefully Responds appropriately	Clear	Increasing
Level 3	Listens confidently in more contexts	Confident	More varied
Level 4	Listens carefully in discussions	Confident in more contexts	Developing
Level 5	Can speak and listen in more-formal contexts	Clear in a wide range of contexts	Varied vocabulary and expression
Level 6	Adapts to the demands of different situations	Fluent	Shows variety and fluency

	Discussion	Explanation	Further clarification
Level 1	Conveys meaning	Provides some detail	Beginning to extend ideas
Level 2	Shows awareness of others	Includes some relevant detail	Starting to adapt vocabulary and tone to context
Level 3	Shows understanding of main points	Beginning to adapt talk to the needs of the listener	Some awareness of Standard English. Can explain and communicate ideas
Level 4	Asks questions and responds to the views of others	Talk is adapted to the purpose	Some use of Standard English. Develops ideas thoughtfully and conveys opinions clearly
Level 5	Pays close attention, asks questions and takes account of others	Engages the interest of the listener by inclusion of detail	Beginning to use Standard English appropriately. Responsiveness to ideas
Level 6	Takes an active part; shows understanding and sensitivity	Increasingly interesting through variety of expression	Usually fluent in Standard English in formal situations. Increasingly confident

Source: Grugeon *et al.* (2005).

1　Planning for developing pupils' speaking and listening starts with the curriculum. Teaching should be planned in relation to learning objectives, which will then provide evidence for particular AFs. In turn, evidence from assessment supports more-focused, personalised planning.

2   Evidence for pupils' achievement is built up over time from observations of pupils at work. It should be holistic and draw on a range of sources, including contexts from across and outside the curriculum. Some evidence will come from planned contexts, but it may also arise spontaneously or from pupils' own reflections on their talk.

3   The assessment of speaking and listening therefore requires carefully planned opportunities and ongoing observations of pupils' progress.

Assessment of reading

The two main purposes of assessment in reading are first to assess the child's ability to decode words and second to assess the child's level of comprehension. One of the most effective ways of assessing a child's reading is through the informal process of listening to a child read, looking closely for a child's strengths and weaknesses and any pattern of errors. The running record or 'miscue analysis' is a systematic way of doing this and notes types of errors such as substitution, self-correction, non-response, omission, insertion, hesitation and repetition, as well as reading strategies used to decode words. The resulting analysis can provide useful information for effective remediation and focused teaching.

Miscue analysis

To carry out a miscue analysis with a child, you will need to have a copy of the text the child is reading and then mark it for any errors using symbols. Typical symbols used in miscue analysis are:

- M: meaning (use of context);
- S: structure (use of grammatical knowledge);
- V: visual (use of word recognition and graphic knowledge);
- P: phonic (use of sound–letter correspondences).

The following may also be recorded:

- /: for each word read correctly;
- H: for hesitation;
- T: for a word which the teacher tells the child;
- O: (circle) for an omitted word.

It is important to spend some time with a child carrying out the following procedure before asking him/her to read, in order to make it a non-threatening process:

- Discuss illustrations, cover, author, content etc.
- Read a short section to the child first.
- Ask the child to read from one copy as you record miscues on another.

When analysing a child's reading, for each miscued word ask the following questions:

- Did the miscue look like the text (e.g. 'tiring' for 'trying')?
- Did the miscue sound like the text (e.g. 'sledge' for 'sleigh')?

- Did the word make sense in context (e.g. 'happy' for 'merry')?
- Is the sentence grammatically acceptable (e.g. 'I haven't got a name for him yet' for 'I haven't thought of a name for him yet')?
- Did the child self-correct (e.g. 'would' read as 'want' and then corrected)?
- Was the miscue due to the child being unfamiliar with the idiom used (e.g. 'Last year I received ...' may be an unfamiliar phrasing for the child)?

Reading conferences

Reading conferences or interviews are more-lengthy one-to-one teaching methods. An example of a reading conference prompt sheet is provided below. Conferences are demanding on teachers' time, but conducted periodically (e.g. termly) they can be informative, particularly about the child's attitude to reading, and provide a much fuller picture of strengths and weaknesses and the range and genre of texts read. Harrison (2004) comments that a reading interview can be a much more informative type of assessment than testing, due to the in-depth understanding of the child's attitude and breadth of skills that the interview provides. The example below of questions to support a reading conference would need to be adapted according to the age range of the pupil.

Reading conference prompt sheet

Name: Date:

Self-assessment
- Do you enjoy reading?
- Do you think you are a good reader?
- What makes you think that?
- What do you think you need to do to get even better at reading?

Range of reading
- What makes you choose a book?
- What is your favourite thing to read (fiction, non-fiction or on-screen texts)?
- Do you have a favourite author?
- When do you like reading best?
- What have you enjoyed reading recently?

Skills
- What do you do when you don't know a word?
- If you want to find out about something interesting, what do you do?
- How do you use information books to answer a question?

Current reading

- What are you reading now?
- Tell me about it.
- What do you want to read next?

Guided reading

Guided reading provides an effective way for a teacher to use his/her time to work with a group with matched reading ability on a particular aspect of reading, with the group having copies of the same text. Sessions are usually planned in three parts. First, particular vocabulary and key points about the text are introduced. Second, the pupils are given a particular focus or question to look for as they independently read the prescribed section or pages, with younger children reading aloud to enable the teacher to listen for errors. Finally, the teacher and children talk about the text, with discussion developed to help comprehension of the text. Guided reading also provides an ideal opportunity for the teacher to make a detailed ongoing assessment of children's reading abilities. A record of guided reading linked to the AFs can be a useful resource, particularly if it provides a range of specific questions linked to a particular text. Many examples are available on the internet; for example, see http://education. staffordshire.gov.uk/Curriculum/Subjectareas/EnglishandLiteracy/Primary/assessment.

When listening to children read individually, it is important to note strategies they use and what strategies might support the next steps in developing their reading skills. An example of an individual reading comment sheet is provided in Table 16.3.

TABLE 16.3 Example of an individual reading comment sheet

READING RECORD	Name:
Date:	
Book:	
Known/unknown text Author/genre/contents Prediction of content	
Strategies observed when reading aloud, e.g. use of phonics including blending phonemes	
Child's response Relevant comments on: - the book as a whole, main ideas, main events; - characters, new information, way book is written; - overall impression (e.g. overall independence, accuracy, fluency, sense of meaning, awareness of punctuation, confidence, involvement); - experience and support needed.	

Comprehension skills

The assessment of children's comprehension has, in the past, often been undertaken through comprehension tests or exercises. However, many of these exercises are very limited in demonstrating children's comprehension skills and often are merely exercises in manipulating the syntax of the sentence. For example: 'The glop was nopping the plax.' 'Who was nopping the plax?' A meaningless sentence, but one that nevertheless can be answered correctly ('The glop'!). It is important to bear in mind the different levels of response to text. These consist of:

- *Literal:* this consists of being able to understand the words actually on the page.
- *Inferential:* this requires reading between the lines to ascertain information that is not specifically stated. One example is: 'Peter sheltered beneath his umbrella until the bus came. When he got home his mother hit the roof.' We could make two inferences from this: first, that the weather was wet, and second, why his mother was cross (possibly because he was late).
- *Evaluative:* this involves reading beyond the lines to reflect on aspects such as motive and consequences.
- *Appreciative:* this requires a personal critical response to text. This might include an exploration of the phrase 'hit the roof'.

The Core Position Papers (DfES 2006c) provide detailed discussion of developing comprehension and the important role of inferences in understanding text. Two types of inferences are identified: 'coherence inferences' and 'elaborative inferences'. Coherence inferences range from use of pronouns instead of names in texts to varying vocabulary (such as 'vessel' for 'ship'), both of which improve the style and interest in a text. Elaborative inferences enrich the text, enabling the reader to gain a clear mental image, in some cases through limited but carefully chosen words.

Five specific strategies that have been shown to be particularly effective in developing comprehension skills are prediction, questioning, clarifying, imaging and summarisation (Brown and Palinscar 1985); these are often termed 'reciprocal reading'. Underpinning this is the need for opportunities for meaningful discussion of text through paired, group or guided work.

Another effective means of teaching and improving comprehension skills is through 'directed activities related to texts' (DARTs). These consist broadly of two types: 'text analysis', requiring the reader to locate and organise material, and 'text reconstruction', requiring the reader to sequence text or predict events. These activities are also best carried out when children are organised to work with a partner or in a group, as the resulting discussion requires the children to clarify, expand and explain their ideas.

Periodic assessment of reading

The APP approach, as set out previously, aims to provide a periodic review of children's progress. The seven AFs for reading describe the key elements of performance in reading. They are linked to the National Curriculum programmes of study and the level descriptions, and are designed to give a detailed, analytic view of pupils' attainment across all the key stages and in all types of reading. The AFs aim to provide key areas for assessment across a large area of skills, as shown in Figure 16.4.

Level	Assessment focus
AF1	Use a range of strategies including accurate decoding of text, to read for meaning
AF2	Understand, describe, select, or retrieve information, events, or ideas from texts and use quotation and reference to text
AF3	Deduce, infer, or interpret information, events, or ideas from texts
AF4	Identify and comment on the structure and organisation of texts, including grammatical and presentational features at text level
AF5	Explain and comment on writers' uses of language, including grammatical and literary features at word and sentence level
AF6	Identify and comment on writers' purposes and viewpoints and the overall effect of the text on the reader
AF7	Relate texts to their social, cultural and historical contexts and literary traditions

FIGURE 16.4 Assessment focuses for reading
Source: DCSF and National Strategies (2010) *Assessing Pupils' Progress: a teachers' handbook.* Ref: 00077-2010PDF-EN.

Summative assessment of reading

Formal or summative assessments of reading are carried out throughout a child's schooling, beginning with the Early Learning Goals at the end of the EYFS, and then with Key Stage 1 and Key Stage 2 SATs. The EYFS assessments are made through teacher observation; at the end of Key Stage 1, children carry out a running record that is related to a score and National Curriculum level. They also complete a comprehension booklet based on a short text. At the end of Key Stage 2, assessment is through a reading booklet with a series of different genres and types of questions that aim to test literal, inferential and evaluative comprehension. As mentioned earlier, as a result of the review carried out by Lord Bew (DfE 2011c), some changes in SATs are planned for 2013. The SATs provide standardised scores that can be used to compare a child's progress over a period of time and are used alongside a teacher assessment of a child's ability.

Assessment of writing

One of the most important methods of assessment of children's writing is carried out orally during the process of writing, when the teacher spends time with a child or a group of children and offers advice. This can be done effectively during guided writing sessions, which have a particular focus and group children of a similar ability. Writing conferences can also be carried out on a one-to-one basis, periodically, particularly when a child's lack of progress is causing concern. Here the important features are to note the child's ability to tackle a piece of writing before commencing (through planning orally or in note form); note their response during the writing (including any particular difficulties encountered); and then afterwards review their progress in the completed piece of work.

Opportunities for assessing progress in writing occur in dedicated literacy teaching time and also across the curriculum, where children have the opportunity to practise and apply the skills they have been taught. These opportunities are at times informal as well as formal. They engage children in peer and self-assessment as well as teacher-led assessment.

Involving children

Children can be involved in the assessment process through the sharing of learning objectives and success criteria using, for example WALT, WILF and WINK (as explained earlier in this chapter). Another method is to have children work in pairs and to ask them at strategic points during their writing to stop and discuss with a partner. This of course needs careful guidance, with clear criteria agreed, so that a child understands that a response partner is someone who:

- helps me with my work;
- tells the truth about my work;
- helps me to make my work better.

Using a few prompt questions to guide children is helpful (see pages 292–294).

Marking writing

One of the most common ways in which teachers assess writing is through marking, but this can be ineffective unless it is focused on a specific objective or target. Rather than mark everything that needs correcting, one possible way, recommended as part of AfL, is to identify three successes and one area for improvement. Alternatively, a system could be used that identifies one specific positive comment about the work, one specific point about improvement that relates to the individual child and one that relates to the class target for improving writing.

The Primary National Strategy produced guidance for marking writing, with an overall writing analysis sheet particularly aimed at helping children progress from National Curriculum level 3 to level 4. Such an analysis can be helpful in providing an overall picture of specific strengths and weaknesses and where to target future teaching (see Table 16.4). It is also important to share with children their particular strengths and to enable them to understand how to improve.

Diagnostic assessment

Where a child's progress in writing causes concern, it may be useful to conduct a writing miscue analysis that looks at the process of writing as well as the result. This covers:

- writing behaviour;
- the writing process;
- the purpose for writing;
- form or format;
- text construction;
- vocabulary choice;
- spelling;
- punctuation.

TABLE 16.4 Writing analysis sheet

Grammar	Judgement of effective use		
Significant features at word and sentence level	Yes	No	Partial
Sentence structure simple sentences complex sentences variation within sentences co-ordination subordination			
Word choice noun groups verb choice tense adjectives adverbs pronouns			
Punctuation used to demarcate sentences clauses phrases words in lists direct speech			
Organisation and effect **Significant whole-text features**			
appeal to reader development of topic, content, theme openings and closings organisation and length of paragraphs presentation and layout			

Source: DfES (2001).

Table 16.5 is an example of recording this process. It will need to be adapted so that it is appropriate to the age of the child.

Target-setting

Target statements for writing were provided by the Primary National Strategy in the following areas:

- to audit writing achievement in each year group;
- to set curricular targets for year groups and learning targets for children;
- as a steer for teachers' planning;
- to help focus teaching on key elements of writing;
- as criteria for monitoring teaching and learning.

TABLE 16.5 Writing miscue analysis record

Name:	Date:
1 Writing behaviour (willingness to commence, motivation and engagement with task)	
2 Writing process: (methods used) ■ planning ■ editing ■ independence	
3 Purpose/intention (understanding of reason for writing) ■ awareness shown	
4 Audience (signs of identifying audience for writing) *Awareness of reader* ■ accessibility/clarity ■ register/tone used	
5 Structure/form (suits purpose and audience) *Choice of structure* ■ consistency of form ■ sequence of ideas	
6 Technical features (significant aspects) ■ spelling specific errors or types of errors ■ vocabulary – range ■ punctuation – accuracy ■ syntax: sentence structure ■ other features, e.g. conjunctions	

Source: adapted from Bearne (2002: 498).

It is important that information gained from assessment is used to inform further teaching. The National Strategies' guidance on writing targets can be accessed at http://webarchive. nationalarchives.gov.uk/20101119131802/http://nationalstrategies.standards.dcsf.gov.uk/ node/110239.

The assessment of writing also needs to be summative at specific points to record a child's progress. This requires teachers to give pieces of work at National Curriculum level, which can be problematical. Most schools also make use of sublevels (a, b and c, with 'a' being the highest) to divide each National Curriculum level into three subdivisions. This helps to identify progress within a level and to set focused targets. One effective way of assisting teachers is through moderation of writing with colleagues, where the same piece of work is analysed by different teachers and the results compared. Any such assessments of children should support future teaching and learning.

Assessing pupils' progress in writing

As for reading and also speaking and listening, in the APP approach to writing, teacher assessment judgements draw on the full context of pupils' work, whereas a test can only sample some aspects.

The information gained from the APP approach to periodic review

■ provides diagnostic information on pupils' strengths and weaknesses in relation to specific AFs;

■ enables forward planning based on group and individual pupil needs;

■ makes the most of pupils' learning experiences across the whole curriculum.

The eight AFs for writing describe the key elements of performance in this attainment target (see Figure 16.5). They are linked to the National Curriculum programmes of study and the level descriptions, and are designed give a detailed, analytic view of pupils' attainment across all the key stages and in all types of writing. In each of the eight AF strands, level-related criteria provide the standard of expectation for judging particular aspects of writing. Progression within the strands is shown by differences in the criteria, but also by the use of stems:

■ level 1: in some writing, usually with support;

■ level 2: in some writing;

■ level 3: in most writing;

■ level 4 and above: across a range of writing.

The assessment grids are available in the National Archives; however, the Lancashire Grid for Learning website also has these and has included the EYFS Early Learning Goals and statements relating to handwriting and presentation. These can be found at www.lancsngfl. ac.uk/nationalstrategy/literacy/index.php?category_id=151.

Table of Writing assessment focuses and points to remember, linked to each attainment level	
Level	**Assessment focus**
AF1	Write imaginative, interesting, and thoughtful texts
AF2	Produce texts which are appropriate to task, reader, and purpose
AF3	Organise and present whole texts effectively, sequencing and structuring information, ideas, and events
AF4	Construct paragraphs and use cohesion within and between paragraphs
AF5	Vary sentences for clarity, purpose, and effect
AF6	Write with technical accuracy of syntax and punctuation in phrases, clauses, and sentences
AF7	Select appropriate and effective vocabulary
AF8	Use correct spelling

FIGURE 16. 5 Assessment focuses for writing

Key points

- Summative assessment, or assessment of learning (AoL), provides information about a child's progress at specific points.
- Assessment for learning (AfL) provides valuable information to support the teaching process.
- Involving children in understanding their own learning through sharing learning objectives and success criteria is a powerful strategy to support learning.
- Diagnostic assessment, particularly for reading and writing, can support children with specific difficulties.
- It is important to develop a systematic and manageable process for assessing and recording all aspects of English.

Further reading

Black, P., Harrison, C., Lee, C., Marshall, B. and Wiliam, D. (2002) *Working Inside the Black Box: assessment for learning in the classroom.* London: King's College London, Department of Education and Professional Studies (www.kcl.ac.uk/content/1/c4/73/57/formative.pdf).

Clarke, S. (1998) *Targeting Assessment in the Primary School: strategies for planning, assessment, pupil feedback and target setting.* London: Hodder & Stoughton.

DCSF (2010) 'Assessing Pupils' Progess: a teachers' handbook. London: DCSF Publications. Ref: 00077-2010PDF-EN

For more information on AfL, in particular the ten principles, see www.aaia.org.uk/afl/assessment-reform-group.

For target statements for writing, see www.learninglive.co.uk/teachers/primary/literacy/assessment.

Answers for the activity on understanding fitness for purpose

Assessment activity	Purpose	Summative or formative
Standardised reading test	To provide a standardised reading score as a snapshot of a child's reading ability at that time.	Summative
Differentiated questioning	To provide information during teaching about a child or several children's understanding.	Formative
Phoneme–grapheme correspondence test	To check children's knowledge at a given point in time.	Formative – usually diagnostic and informs future teaching
Moderated sample of child's writing	To provide information about a child's achievement, usually denoted by National Curriculum levels.	Summative
Running record or miscue analysis of reading	To provide information about a child's decoding and overall reading skills.	Formative – diagnostic
Guided writing feedback	To provide feedback at the point of writing during guided sessions.	Formative

Conclusions

This book should be seen as a starting point for further reading as well as for reflection and discussion with fellow professionals. We have attempted to cover a range of key aspects of teaching English to children aged five to eleven, and we hope we have whetted your appetite for more-advanced study.

As we discussed in the Introduction, the curriculum for English and the strategies recommended for teaching and learning are in an almost constant state of change. The first edition, *English 3–11*, was published in the wake of the introduction of the renewed *Primary Framework for Literacy* (DfES 2006b). Some of the key principles for the effective teaching of English had been challenged by the Rose Report (DfES 2006a), which recommended that phonics should play a central role in teaching and learning early reading and writing. Since then the National Strategies, which so dominated many teachers' work, has ceased to exist and a new curriculum is anticipated.

We hope that *English 5–11* has put the frequent changes to the curriculum and the regular pronouncements from the government in the context of good, reflective practice. We hope, too, that the book will help readers to consider how they can be creative in their teaching, find innovative ways of working and be receptive to new ideas.

Developments in technology continue to challenge teachers, many of whom began their careers before computers became a feature of most classrooms and when interactive whiteboards were beyond our conception. Not only do we have to understand how we can maximise our use of the technology that is available now but we also need to be prepared to learn how to use those of which we cannot yet conceive. For it is quite certain that the next few years will continue to see more innovations reaching our schools. If we are to use these discerningly, we will need to develop not only the facility to make the equipment work but also the ability to decide which might benefit our pupils and which would add little to the quality of teaching and learning in our classrooms.

All of which illustrates the size of the task that faces teachers in the twenty-first century. The modern teacher needs to have a broad perspective and a receptivity to change if he or she is to respond to change effectively. Without these, change can be both threatening and unsettling, and teachers' understanding of how they can modify their practice will be limited.

So what can you do, now that you have read this book, to further your development as a teacher of English for children aged five to eleven? We suggest the following:

- Keep up to date on changes to the curriculum and new ideas for teaching by looking regularly at some or even all of the following: the *Times Educational Supplement* (TES), the Guardian weekly educational supplement, professional journals, academic journals, websites and details of the latest publications about English in primary schools.

- Make use of the references in this book to engage in further reading and to gain a different perspective from ours.

- Discuss some of the classroom activities and practices described in this book with fellow professionals, and adapt them to meet the needs of the children you teach.

- Build portfolios of poetry and children's stories that you can draw upon throughout your career.

- Continually look for examples of varied and interesting non-fiction texts to include in your 'literate' classroom.

- Analyse your classroom, asking yourself whether it is language-friendly: is it a good environment for developing speaking and listening, and reading and writing?

- Consider how you cater for children of different abilities and their individual needs.

- Think about how your assessment of pupils' progress impacts upon your planning.

- Reflect regularly upon your own teaching, and look for opportunities to observe that of others, so that you can develop as a teacher of English.

A teacher who does all of the above will be ideally placed to engage with and embrace change while being able to consider its value and relevance to the children he or she teaches, and will, therefore, be a professional. We hope that this book will help you to achieve this.

References

The web addresses for some references were unavailable or unreliable at the time of going to press. It is hoped that they will become available online in the future. In the meantime, information on the publications may be found by searching for their titles.

Adams, M.J. (1990) *Beginning to Read: thinking and learning about print*. Cambridge, MA: MIT Press.

Adams, M.J. and Bruck, M. (1993) 'Word recognition: the interface of educational policies and scientific research', *Reading and Writing: an interdisciplinary journal*, 5, 113–39.

Airs, J., Wright, J., Williams, L. and Adkins, R. (2004) 'The performing arts', in R. Jones and D. Wyse (eds) *Creativity in the Primary Curriculum*. London: David Fulton, 96–113.

Alexander, R. (2000) *Culture and Pedagogy: international comparisons in primary education*. Oxford: Blackwell.

Alexander, R. (2004) *Towards Dialogic Teaching*. Cambridge: Dialogos.

Alexander, R. (2005) 'Culture, dialogue and learning: notes on an emerging pedagogy', Education, Culture and Cognition: intervening for growth: International Association for Cognitive Education and Psychology (IACEP) 10th International Conference, University of Durham, UK, 10–14 July.

Alexander, R. (2010) *Cambridge Primary Review. Primary Review briefing: towards a new primary curriculum*. Cambridge: Cambridge University Press (www.primaryreview.org.uk/downloads/revised_2011-02/CURRICULUM_BRIEFING_REVISED_2_11.pdf).

Alexander, R. (ed.) (2009) *Children, Their World, Their Education: final report and recommendations of the Cambridge Primary Review*. London: Routledge.

Apperley, T. and Beavis, C. (2011) 'Literacy into action: digital games as action and text in the English and literacy classroom', *Pedagogies: an international journal*, 6(2), 130–143.

Arizpe, E. and Styles, M. (2002) *Children Reading Pictures: interpreting visual texts*. London: Routledge Falmer.

Assessment Reform Group (1999) *Assessment for Learning: beyond the black box*. Cambridge: University of Cambridge Faculty of Education (http://assessment-reform-group.org).

Assessment Reform Group (2002a) *Assessment for Learning: ten principles*. Cambridge: University of Cambridge Faculty of Education (http://assessment-reform-group.org).

Assessment Reform Group (2002b) *Testing, Motivation and Learning*. Cambridge: University of Cambridge Faculty of Education.

Australian Government, Department of Education, Science and Training (2005) *Teaching Reading: report and recommendations. National enquiry into the teaching of literacy*. Barton, ACT: Department of Education, Science and Training.

Baldock, P. (2010) *Understanding Cultural Diversity in the Early Years*. London: Sage.

Bandura, A. (1977) *Social Learning Theory*. Englewood Cliffs, NJ: Prentice Hall.

Barber, D. and Cooper, L. (2012) *Using New Web Tools in the Primary Classroom*. Abingdon: Routledge.

Barnes, D., Britton, J. and Rosen, H. (1969) *Language, the Learner and the School*. Harmondsworth: Penguin.

Barnes, D. and Todd, F. (1977) *Communicating and Learning in Small Groups*. London: Routledge Kegan Paul.

Barnes, E. (1997) 'Punctuation signs, symbols and spaces', *Primary English Magazine*, 2(3), 4–6.

Barrs, M. (2000) 'The reader in the writer', *Reading Literacy and Language*, 34(2), 54–60.

BBC (2012) 'Children and TV' (www.bbc.co.uk/health/physical_health/family/family_relationships/you_tv.shtml).

Beals, D. (1997) 'Sources of support for learning words in conversation: evidence from mealtimes', *Child Language*, 24, 673–94.

Beard, R.F. (2000) 'Long overdue? Another look at the National Literacy Strategy', *Journal of Research in Reading*, 23(34), 245–55.

Bearne, E. (2002) *Making Progress in Writing*. London: Routledge Falmer.

Bearne, E., Grainer, T. and Wolstencroft, H. (2004) *Raising Boys' Achievements in Writing*. Baldock: United Kingdom Literacy Association.

Becta (British Educational Communications and Technology Agency) (2003a) *What the Research Says about ICT and Motivation*. Coventry: Becta (www.becta.org).

Becta (2003b) *What the Research Says about Using ICT in English*. Coventry: Becta (www.becta.org).

Becta (2009) *Becta's contribution to the Rose Review*. Coventry: Becta.

Becta (2010) *The 21st century teacher: English – using technology to enhance English teaching*. Coventry: Becta.

Becta NATE (2009) *Primary English with ICT: a pupil's entitlement to ICT in primary English*. Coventry: Becta.

Bennett, R. (2004) *Using ICT in Primary English Teaching*. Exeter: Learning Matters.

Bereiter, C. and Scardamalia, M. (1987) *The Psychology of Written Composition*. Hillsdale, NJ: Lawrence Erlbaum.

Biemiller, A. (2003) 'Vocabulary: needed if more children are to read well', *Reading Psychology*, 24, 323–35.

Black, P., Harrison, C., Lee, C., Marshall, B. and Wiliam, D. (2002) *Working Inside the Black Box: assessment for learning in the classroom*. London: King's College London, Department of Education and Professional Studies (www.kcl.ac.uk/sspp/departments/education/research/crestem/assessment/index.aspx).

Black, P. and Wiliam, D. (1998) 'Assessment and classroom learning', *Assessment in Education: principles, policy and practice*, 5(1), 7–73.

Blackledge, A. (1994) *Teaching Bilingual Children*. Stoke-on-Trent: Trentham Books.

Bloom, B.S. (1956) *Taxonomy of Educational Objectives: the classification of educational goals. Handbook 1: cognitive domain*. New York: Longmans, Green.

Blyton, E. (1968) *The Three Golliwogs*. London: Dean & Son.

Bolton, G. (1986) *Selected Writings on Drama in Education*. Harlow: Longman.

Bourdieu, P. (1977) *Outline of a Theory of Practice*. Cambridge: Cambridge University Press.

Branford, H. (1997) *Fire, Bed and Bone*. London: Walker.

Brent Language Service (2002) *Enriching Literacy: text, talk and tales in today's schools*. Stoke-on-Trent: Trentham Books.

Brien, J. (2012) *Teaching Primary English*. London: Sage.

BFI (British Film Institute) (2003) *Look Again!* Available at: http://www.unicef.org/magic/resources/bfi_Education_LookAgain_TeachingGuide.pdf.

Bromley, H. (2000) 'Never Be Without a *Beano*: comics, children and literacy', in A. Andersen and M. Styles (eds) *Teaching through Texts*. London: Routledge, 29–42.

Brooks, G. (1998) 'Trends in standards of literacy in the United Kingdom, 1948–1996', *Topic*, 19, 1–10.

Brown, A. and Palinscar, A. (1985) *Reciprocal Teaching of Comprehension Strategies: a natural program for enhancing learning.* Urbana-Champaign, IL: University of Illinois.

Browne, A. (1993) *Helping Children to Write.* London: Paul Chapman.

Browne, A. (1998) 'The role of the author/artist: an interview with Anthony Browne', in J. Evans (ed.) *What's in the Picture? Responding to illustrations in picture books.* London: Paul Chapman Publishing Ltd., 192–204.

Browne, A. (2009) *Developing Language and Literacy 3–8, 3rd edn.* London: Sage.

Bruner, J.S. (1985) 'Vygotsky: a historical and conceptual perspective', in J. Wertsch (ed.) *Culture, Communication and Cognition: Vygotskian perspectives.* Cambridge: Cambridge University Press, 21–34.

Bruner, J.S. (1986) *Actual Minds, Possible Worlds.* Cambridge, MA: Harvard University Press.

Bruner, J.S. (1996) *The Culture of Education.* Cambridge, MA: Harvard University Press.

Bryant, P. (1993) 'Phonological aspects of learning to read', in R. Beard (ed.) *Teaching Literacy: balancing perspectives.* London: Hodder & Stoughton, 83–94.

Bryson, B. (1990) *Mother Tongue: the English language.* Harmondsworth: Penguin.

Buckley, B. (2003) *Children's Communication Skills: from birth to five years.* London: Routledge.

Bunting, R. (1997) *Teaching about Language in the Primary Years.* London: David Fulton.

Burnett, C. and Myers, J. (2004) *Teaching English 3–11.* London: Continuum.

Byars, B. (1981) *The Midnight Fox.* London: Puffin.

CACE (Central Advisory Council for Education in England) (1967) *Children and their primary schools. Report of the Central Advisory Council for Education in England (the Plowden Report).* London: HM Stationery Office.

Campbell, R. (1999) *Literacy from Home to School: reading with Alice.* Stoke-on-Trent: Trentham Books.

Canada Council on Learning (2009) *Why Boys Don't Like to Read: gender differences in reading achievement* (www.ccl-cca.ca/pdfs/LessonsInLearning/02_18_09-E.pdf).

Carless, S. (1989) 'Spelling in the primary school curriculum', in P. Pinsent (ed.) *Spotlight on spelling.* Bicester: A B Academic, 14–24.

Carter, D. (2000) *Teaching Fiction in the Primary School.* London: David Fulton.

Cato, V., Fernandes, C., Gorman, T. and Kispal, A. with White, J. (1992) *The Teaching of Initial Literacy: how do teachers do it?* Slough: NFER.

Chall, J.S. (1983) *Learning to Read: the great debate, updated edn.* New York: McGraw-Hill.

Chambers, A. (1993) *Tell Me: children reading and talk.* Stroud: Thimble Press.

Chaney, C. (1992) 'Language development, metalinguistic skills, and print awareness in 3-year-old children', *Applied Psycholinguistics*, 13, 485–514.

Chomsky, N. (1957) *Syntactic Structures.* The Hague: Mouton.

Chomsky, N. (1965) *Aspects of Theory of Syntax.* Cambridge, MA: MIT Press.

Clarke, S. (1998) *Targeting Assessment in the Primary School: strategies for planning, assessment, pupil feedback and target setting.* London: Hodder & Stoughton.

Clay, M.M. (1979) *The Early Detection of Reading Difficulties: a diagnostic survey with reading recovery procedures, 2nd edn.* London: Heinemann.

Clay, M.M. (1993) *Reading Recovery: a guidebook for teachers in training.* London: Heinemann.

Clipson-Boyles, S. (2003) *Drama in Primary English Teaching.* London: David Fulton.

Cohen-Emerique, M. (1999) *Le choc culturel*, 'Revue Antipodes', 145, 11–2.

Comber, B. (1999) TT's *Got Power in It: critical literacies and information technologies in primary schools.* Adelaide, SA: University of South Australia, Language and Literacy Research Centre.

Conteh, J. (2003) *Succeeding in Diversity: culture, language and learning in primary classrooms.* Stoke-on-Trent: Trentham Books.

Cookson, P. (ed.) (2000) *The Works.* London: Pan Macmillan.

Corden, R. (2000) *Literacy and Learning through Talk: strategies for the primary classroom.* Buckingham: Open University Press.

Corden, R. (2004) 'Group work, learning through talk', in T. Grainer (ed.) *The Routledge Falmer Reader in Language and Literacy.* London: Routledge Falmer, 138–59.

Corson, D. (1988) *Oral Language across the Curriculum.* Clevedon, OH: Multilingual Matters.

Cowley, S. (2002) *Getting the Buggers to Behave*. London: Continuum.

Craft, A. (2000) *Creativity across the Primary Curriculum: framing and developing practice*. London: Routledge Falmer.

Craft, A. (2002) *Creativity and Early Years Education: a lifewide foundation*. London: Continuum.

Craft, A. (2005) 'Changes in the landscape for creativity in education', in A. Wilson (ed.) *Creativity in Primary Education*. Exeter: Learning Matters, 7–18.

Cremin, T. (2009) *Teaching English Creatively*. London: Routledge.

Cripps, C.C. (1988) *A Hand for Spelling*. Wisbech: Learning Development Aids.

Cripps, C.C. (1998) *A Hand for Spelling, rev. edn*. Wisbech: Learning Development Aids.

Cropley, A.J. (2001) *Creativity in Education and Learning: a guide for teachers and educators*. London: Kogan Page.

Crystal, D. (1987) *The Cambridge Encyclopaedia of Language*. Cambridge: Cambridge University Press.

Crystal, D. (1990) *The English Language*. London: Penguin.

Crystal, D. (2004a) *Making Sense of Grammar*. London: Longman.

Crystal, D. (2004b) *Rediscover Grammar*. Harlow: Longman.

Crystal, D. (2009) *Txting: the gr8 db8*. Oxford: Oxford University Press.

Csikszentmihalyi, M. (1992) *Flow: the psychology of human happiness*. London: Rider.

Csikszentmihalyi, M. (1996) *Creativity*. New York: HarperCollins.

Cummins, J. (1996) *Negotiating Identities: education for empowerment in a diverse society*. Ontario, CA: California Association for Bilingual Education.

Davies, A. and Ritchie, D. (1998) *THRASS Teacher's Manual*. Chester: THRASS (UK).

Davies, D., Howe, A., Fasciato, M. and Rogers, M. (2004) 'How do trainee primary teachers understand creativity?', in E. Norman, D. Spendlove, P. Grover and A. Mitchell (eds) *Creativity and Innovation: DATA International Research Conference 2004*. Wellesbourne: Design and Technology Association, 41–54.

Davies, J. and Merchant, G. (2009) *Web 2.0 for Schools: learning and social participation*. New York: Peter Lang.

Davis, D. and Byron, K. (1988) 'Drama under fire – the way forward (2)', *2D*, 8(1), 26–27.

Daw, P., Smith, J. and Wilkinson, S. (1997) 'Factors associated with high standards of spelling in Years R–4', *English in Education*, 31(1), 36–47.

Dawes, L. (2002 [2001]) 'Interthinking - the power of productive talk', in P. Goodwin (ed.) *The Articulate Classroom: talking and learning in the primary school*. London: David Fulton, 125–32.

Dawes, L. and Sams, C. (2004) *Talk Box: speaking and listening activities for learning at Key Stage 1*. London: David Fulton.

DCSF (Department for Children Schools and Education) (2008a) *The Bercow Report: a review of services for children and young people (0–19) with speech, language and communication needs*. Nottingham: DCSF.

DCSF (2008b) *Every Child a Talker*. Nottingham: DCSF.

DCSF (2008c) *Talk for Writing*. Nottingham: DCSF.

DCSF (2008d) *Teaching Effective Vocabulary: what can teachers do to increase the vocabulary of children who start education with a limited vocabulary?* Nottingham: DCSF.

DCSF (2008e) *Effective Teaching of Inference Skills for Reading: literature review*. Nottingham: DCSF.

DCSF (2008f) *Safer Children in a Digital World: the report of the Byron Review*. Nottingham: DCSF.

DCSF (2009a) *Independent Review of the Primary Curriculum: final report*. Nottingham: DCSF.

DCSF (2009b) *Support for Spelling*. Nottingham: DCSF.

DCSF (2010) 'Assessing Pupils' Progress: a teachers' handbook. London: DCSF Publications. Ref: 00077-2010PDF-EN.

Dehaene, S. (2009) *Reading in the Brain: the new science of how we read*. New York: Penguin.

DES (Department of Education and Science) (1975) *A Language for Life (Bullock Report)*. London: HM Stationery Office.

DES (1990) *English in the National Curriculum*. London: HM Stationery Office.

DES and WO (Welsh Office) (1989) *Discipline in Schools (Elton Report)*. London: HM Stationery Office.

Devereux, J. and Miller, L. (2003) *Working with Children in the Early Years*. London: David Fulton.

DfE (Department for Education) (2010) *The Importance of Teaching*. London: HM Stationery Office.

DfE (2011a) *Developing a New Year One Phonics Screening Check* (www.education.gov.uk/schools/teachingandlearning/pedagogy/a00197709/developing-a-new-year-1-phonics-screening-check).

DfE (2011b) *The Early Years: foundations for life, health and learning – An Independent Report on the early years foundation stage to Her Majesty's government, Dame Clare Tickell*. DfE.

DfE (2011c) *Independent Review of Key Stage 2 Testing, Assessment and Accountability: final report, Lord Bew*. London: DfE.

DfE (2011d) *Systematic Synthetic Phonics in Initial Teaching Training: guidance and support materials, 2011, notes issued to ITT providers by TDA*. London: DfE.

DfE (2011e) *Teachers' Standards in England from September 2012*. London: DfE.

DfE (2012a) *Statutory Framework for the Early Years Foundation Stage*. Runcorn: DfE.

DfE (2012b) *Development Matters in the EYFS*. Runcorn: DfE.

DfE (2012c) *Review of the National Curriculum Update* (www.education.gov.uk/schools/teachingandlearning/curriculum/nationalcurriculum/b0075667/national-curriculum-review-update).

DfE (2012d) *Review of the National Curriculum in England: what can we learn from the English, mathematics and science curricula of high-performing jurisdictions?* (www.education.gov.uk/publications/RSG/publicationDetail/Page1/DFE-RR178).

DfEE (Department for Education and Employment) (1998) *National Literacy Strategy: framework for teaching*. London: DfEE.

DfEE and QCA (Qualifications and Curriculum Authority) (1999) *English: the national curriculum in England (Key Stages 1–4)*. London: DfEE and QCA.

DfEE (2000) *Curriculum Guidance for the Foundation Stage*. London: QCA.

DfES (Department for Education and Skills) (2001) *Marking Guidelines for Writing* (available online).

DfES (2002a) *Towards the National Curriculum for English: examples of what pupils with special educational needs should be able to do at each P level*. Nottingham: DfES.

DfES (2002b) *Researching Effective Pedagogy in the Early Years*. Norwich: HM Stationery Office.

DfES (2003a) *Excellence and Enjoyment: a strategy for primary schools*. Nottingham: DfES.

DfES (2003b) *The Impact of Parental Involvement on Children's Education*. Nottingham: DfES.

DfES (2003c) *Speaking, Listening, Learning: working with children in Key Stages 1 and 2*. Nottingham: DfES.

DfES (2004a) *Primary National Strategy: excellence and enjoyment: learning and teaching in the primary years. Professional development materials*. London: HM Stationery Office.

DfES (2004b) *Excellence and Enjoyment: learning and teaching in the primary years. Professional development materials*. Nottingham: DfES.

DfES (2004c) *Excellence and Enjoyment: learning and teaching in the primary years. Planning and assessment for learning: designing opportunities for learning*. Nottingham: DfES.

DfES (2004d) *Excellence and Enjoyment: learning to learn. Progression in key aspects of learning*. Nottingham: DfES.

DfES (2004e) *The ICT in schools survey 2004*. London: DfES (www.becta.org).

DfES (2004f) *The Motivational Effect of ICT on Pupils*. Nottingham: DfES.

DfES (2005a) *Communicating Matters: the strands of communication and language*. Nottingham: DfES.

DfES (2005b) *Excellence and Enjoyment: social and emotional aspects of learning* (previously available online).

DfES (2006a) *Independent Review of the Teaching of Early Reading (Final Report by Jim Rose)*. Nottingham: DfES.

DfES (2006b) *Primary National Strategy: primary framework for literacy and mathematics*. London: DfES.

DfES (2006c) *Primary National Strategy: primary framework for literacy and mathematics: core position papers underpinning the renewal of guidance for teaching literacy and mathematics*. Nottingham: DfES.

DfES (2006d) *Primary National Strategy: primary framework for literacy and mathematics* [film]. London: DfES (previously available online).

DfES (2007a) *Letters and Sounds*. London: DfES.

DfES (2007b) *Practice Guidance for the Early Years Foundation Stage*. Nottingham: DfES.

DfES (2008) *Support for Writing*. London: National Strategies.

Dockrell, J.E., Stuart, M. and King, D. (2007) *Talking time: developing language skills in early years settings*. London: Institute of Education.

Duerden, N. (2012) 'The enduring appeal of Enid Blyton', *The Guardian*, 24 March.

Duncan, A. (2010) 'The vision of education reform in the United States: remarks to United Nations Educational, Scientific and Cultural Organization (UNESCO), Paris, France', 4 November (www.ed.gov/news/speeches/vision-education-reform-united-states-secretary-arne-duncans-remarks-united-nations-ed).

Dyson, A.H. (2000) 'On reframing children's words: the perils, promises and pleasures of writing children', *Research in the Teaching of English*, 34, 352–67.

Dyson, A.H. (2001) 'Where are the childhoods in childhood literacy? An exploration in outer (school) space', *Journal of Early Childhood Literacy*, 1(1), 9–39.

Edwards, V. (1998) *The Power of Babel: teaching and learning in multilingual classrooms*. Stoke-on-Trent: Trentham Books.

Ehri, L.C. (1987) 'Learning to read and spell words', *Journal of Reading Behavior*, 19, 5–31.

Essex Writing Project (2003) *Visually Speaking: using multimedia texts to improve boys' writing*. Chelmsford: The English Team, Essex Advisory and Inspection Service.

European Schoolnet (2006) *The ICT Impact Report: a review of studies of ICT impact on schools in Europe* (http://ec.europa.eu/education/pdf/doc254_en.pdf).

Evangelou, M., Sylva, K., Kyriacou, M., Wild, M. and Glenny, G. (2009) *Early Years Learning and Development Literature Review* [DCSF research report]. Oxford: University of Oxford.

Evans, J. (ed.) (2004) *Literacy Moves On*. London: David Fulton.

Ferreiro, E. and Teberosky, A. (1982) *Literacy before Schooling*. London: Heinemann.

FEWG (Film Education Working Group) (1999) *Making Movies Matter: report of the Film Education Working Group*. London: British Film Institute.

Fisher, R. (2002) 'Creative minds: building communities of learning for the creative age', Teaching Qualities Initiative Conference, Hong Kong Baptist University, Hong Kong, China, 2002 (www.pantaneto.co.uk/issue25/fisher.htm).

Fisher, R. (2004) 'What is creativity', in R. Fisher and M. Williams (eds) *Unlocking Creativity: teaching across the curriculum*. London: David Fulton, 6–20.

Fisher, R. and Williams, M. (eds) (2004) *Unlocking Creativity: teaching across the curriculum*. London: David Fulton.

Fitzpatrick, F. (1996) Unpublished notes. Department of Teaching Studies, Bradford and Ilkley Community College.

Fleming, M. (1994) *Starting Drama Teaching, 1st edn*. London: David Fulton.

Fleming, M. (2003) *Starting Drama Teaching, 2nd edn*. London: David Fulton.

Fox, R. (2005) *Teaching and Learning: lessons from psychology*. Oxford: Blackwell.

Frith, U. (1985) 'Developmental dyslexia', in K.E. Patterson, J.C. Marshall and M. Coltheart (eds) *Surface Dyslexia*. Hove: Lawrence Erlbaum, 301–30.

Frith, U. (ed.) (1980) *Cognitive Processes in Spelling*. London: Academic Press.

Galton, M., Hargreaves, L., Comber, C, Wall, D. and Pell, A. (1999) *Inside the Primary Classroom 20 Years On*. London: Routledge.

Gamble, N. and Yates, S. (2002) *Exploring Children's Literature*. London: Paul Chapman.

Gardner, H. (1997) *Extraordinary Minds*. New York: HarperCollins.

Garvis, S. and Pendergast, D. (2011) 'An investigation of early childhood teacher self-efficacy beliefs in the teaching of arts education', *International Journal of Education & the Arts*, 12(9) (http://www.ijea.org/v12n9).

Geekie, P., Cambourne, B. and Fitzsimmons, P. (1999) *Understanding Literacy Development*. Stoke-on-Trent: Trentham Books.

Gentry, J.R. (1987) *Spel ... is a Four-Letter Word*. Leamington Spa: Scholastic.

Goode, and Heathcote, D. (1982) 'Heathcote at the National: drama teacher – facilitator or manipulator?' [NATD's first annual lecture, ed. T. Goode]. Banbury: Kemble in association with the National Association for the Teaching of Drama.

Goodman, K.S. (1967) 'Reading: a psycholinguistic guessing game', *Journal of the Reading Specialist*, 4, 126–35.

Goodman, K.S. (1973) 'Psycholinguistic universals in the reading process', in F. Smith (ed.) *Psycholinguistics and Reading*. New York: Holt, Rinehart & Winston, 177–82.

Goodman, K.S. (1998) *In Defence of Good Teaching: what teachers need to know about reading wars*. York, MA: Stenhouse.

Goodman, Y. (1984) 'The development of initial literacy', in H. Goelman, G. Oberg and F. Smith (eds) *Awakening to Literacy*. Portsmouth, NH: Heinemann, 102–9.

Goodwin, P. (2005) 'Creative young readers', in A. Wilson (ed.) *Creativity in Primary Education*. Exeter: Learning Matters, 44–57.

Goodwin, P. (ed.) (2002) *The Articulate Classroom: talking and learning in the primary classroom*. London: David Fulton.

Goswami, U. (1995) 'Phonological development and reading by analogy: what is analogy and what is not', *Journal of Research in Reading*, 18(2), 139–45.

Goswami, U. and Bryant, P. (1990) *Phonological Skills and Learning to Read*. Hove: Lawrence Erlbaum.

Gough, P.B. and Tunmer, W.E. (1986) 'Decoding, reading and reading disability', *Remedial and Special Education*, 7, 6–10.

Graddol, D., Leith, D. and Swann, J. (1996) *English History, Diversity and Change*. London: Routledge with the Open University.

Graham, J. and Kelly, A. (2003) *Writing Under Control*. London: David Fulton.

Grainger, T. (1997) *Traditional Storytelling in the Primary Classroom*. Leamington Spa: Scholastic.

Grainger, T. (2001) 'Drama and writing: imagination on the page: one', *Primary English Magazine*, April, 6–10.

Grainger, T. (2005) 'Oral artistry: storytelling and drama', in A. Wilson (ed.) *Creativity in Primary Education*. Exeter: Learning Matters, 7–18.

Grainger, T. (ed.) (2004) *The Routledge Falmer Reader in Language and Literacy*. London: Routledge Falmer.

Gravelle, M. (2000) *Planning for Bilingual Learners: an inclusive curriculum*. Stoke-on-Trent: Trentham Books.

Gregory, E. (1997) *Making Sense of a New World*. London: Paul Chapman.

Grugeon, E., Dawes, L., Smith, C. and Hubbard, L. (2005) *Teaching Speaking and Listening in the Primary School, 3rd edn*. London: David Fulton.

Grugeon, E., Hubbard, L., Smith, C. and Dawes, L. (2000) *Teaching Speaking and Listening in the Primary School*. London: David Fulton.

Hall, K. (2003) *Listening to Stephen Read: multiple perspectives on literacy*. Buckingham: Open University Press.

Hall, N. and Robinson, A. (2003) *Exploring Writing and Play in the Early Years*. London: David Fulton.

Halliday, M.A.K., McIntosh, A. and Strevens, P. (1964) *The Linguistic Sciences and Language Teaching*. London: Longman.

Hannon, P. (2000) *Reflecting on Literacy in Education*. London: Routledge Falmer.

Harrison, C. (2004) *Understanding Reading Development*. London: Sage.

Harrison, C. (2010) 'Why do policy-makers find the "simple view of reading" so attractive, and why do I find it so morally repugnant?' in K. Hall, U. Goswami, C. Harrison, S. Ellis and J. Soler (eds) *Interdisciplinary Perspectives on Learning to Read*. London: Routledge, 207–18.

Hatcher, P.J., Hulme, C. and Snowling, M.J. (2004) 'Explicit phoneme training combined with phonic reading instruction helps young children at risk of reading failure', *Journal of Child Psychology and Psychiatry*, 45, 338–58.

Hayes, D. (2000) *The Handbook for Newly Qualified Teachers*. London: David Fulton.

Hayes, D. (2003) *Planning, Teaching and Class Management in Primary Schools, 2nd edn*. London: David Fulton.

Head, C. and Waugh, D. (2007) *50 Shared Non-fiction Texts for Year 1*. Leamington Spa: Scholastic.

Heath, S.B. (1983) *Ways with Words*. Cambridge: Cambridge University Press.

Heathcote, D. (1984 [1969]) 'Dramatic activity', in L. Johnson and C. O'Neill (eds) *Dorothy Heathcote: collected writings on education and drama*. London: Hutchinson, 61–79.

Hetherington, E.M. and Parke, R.D. (1999) *Child Psychology: a contemporary viewpoint, 5th edn*. Boston, MA: McGraw-Hill.

Holdaway, D. (1979) *The Foundations of Literacy*. Sydney: Ashton Scholastic Research.

Holdaway, D. (1982) 'Shared book experience: teaching reading using favourite books', *Theory into Practice*, 21(4), 293–300.

Hoover, W.A. and Gough, P.B. (1990) 'The simple view of reading', *Reading and Writing: an interdisciplinary journal*, 2, 127–60.

Hoover, W.A. and Gough, P.B. (2000) 'The reading acquisition framework', in S. Wren (ed.) *The Cognitive Foundations of Learning to Read: a framework* (www.sedl.org/reading/framework).

House of Commons (Education and Skills Committee) (2005) *Teaching Children to Read*. Norwich: HM Stationery Office.

Howe, A. (1993) 'Perspectives on oracy', in S. Brindley (ed.) *Teaching English*. London: Routledge, 38–47.

Hutchings, J., Bywater, T., Daley, D., Gardner, F., Whitaker, C., Jones, K., Eames, C. and Edwards, R.T. (2007) 'Parenting intervention in Sure Start services for children at risk of developing conduct disorder: pragmatic randomised controlled trial', *British Medical Journal*, doi: 10.1136/bmj.39126.620799.55 (www.bmj.com/content/334/7595/678.full).

Hutt, S.J., Tyler, C., Hutt, C. and Christopherson, H. (1989) *Play, Exploration and Learning*. London: Routledge.

Ireson, J., Blatchford, P. and Joscelyne, T. (1995) 'What do teachers do? Classroom activities in the initial teaching of reading', *Educational Psychology*, 15(3), 245–56.

Johnson, D.W. and Johnson, R.T. (1999) *Learning Together and Alone: cooperation, competitive and individualistic learning, 5th edn*. Boston, MA: Allyn & Bacon.

Johnson, D.W., Johnson, F.P. and Stanne, M. (2001) *Cooperative Learning Methods: a meta-analysis* (www.clcrc.com/pages/cl-methods.html).

Johnson, D.W., Johnson, R.T. and Holubec, E. (1988) *Circles of Learning: cooperation in the classroom, rev. edn*. Edina, MN: Interaction Book Company.

Johnston, P. and Afflerbach, P. (1985) 'The process of constructing main ideas from text', *Cognition and Instruction*, 2, 207–32.

Johnston, R. and Watson, J. (2005) *The Effects of Synthetic Phonics Teaching on Reading and Spelling Attainment: a seven year longitudinal study*. Edinburgh: Scottish Executive.

Jolliffe, W. (2006) *Phonics: a complete synthetic programme*. Leamington Spa: Scholastic.

Jolliffe, W. (2007) *Cooperative Learning in the Classroom: putting it into practice*. London: Paul Chapman.

Jolliffe, W. (2012) *Quick Fix for Phonics*. Witney: Scholastic.

Jolliffe, W., Head, C. and Waugh, D. (2004) *50 Shared Texts for Year 1*. Leamington Spa: Scholastic.

Jolliffe, W. and Waugh, D. with Carss, A. (2012) *Teaching Systematic Synthetic Phonics in Primary Schools*. London: Sage.

Jolliffe, W., Waugh, D. and Taylor, K. (2005) *All New 100 Literacy Hours, Year R*. Leamington Spa: Scholastic.

Jones, R. and Wyse, D. (eds) (2004) *Creativity in the Primary Curriculum*. London: David Fulton.

Kagan, S. (1994) *Cooperative Learning*. San Juan Capistrano, CA: Kagan Cooperative Learning.

Kempe, A. and Lockwood, M. (2000) *Drama In and Out of the Literacy Hour.* Reading: University of Reading, Reading and Language Information Centre.

Kenner, C. (2000) *Home Pages: literacy links for bilingual children.* Stoke-on-Trent: Trentham Books.

Kenner, C. (2004) *Becoming Biliterate: young children learning different writing systems.* Stoke-on-Trent: Trentham Books.

Kerry, T. (2011) *Cross Curricular Teaching in the Primary School.* London: Routledge.

Kirby, J.R. and Savage, R.S. (2008) 'Can the simple view deal with the complexities of reading?' *Literacy,* 42(2), 75–82.

Kress, G. (1982) *Learning to Write.* London: Routledge & Kegan Paul.

Kress, G. (1997) *Before Writing: rethinking the paths to literacy.* London: Routledge.

Kyriacou, C. (1991) *Essential Teaching Skills.* Cheltenham: Stanley Thornes.

Lambirth, A. (2005) *Primary English Reflective Reader.* Exeter: Learning Matters.

Lancet UK Policy Matters (2011) 'Policy summary: sure start', 11 May (http://ukpolicymatters.thelancet.com/?p=975#ref).

Lewis, C.S. (1950) *The Lion, the Witch and the Wardrobe.* Harmondsworth: Penguin.

Littlefair, A. (1991) *Reading All Types of Writing.* Milton Keynes: Open University Press.

Livingstone, S. and Bovill, M. (1999) *Young People, New Media.* London: London School of Economics.

Lloyd, S. (1998) *The Phonics Handbook.* Chigwell: Jolly Learning.

Lucas, B. (2001) 'Creative teaching, teaching creativity and creative learning', in A. Craft, B. Jeffrey and M. Leibling (eds) *Creativity in Education.* London: Continuum, 35–44.

Luke, C. and Roe, K. (1993) 'Introduction to special issues: media and popular cultural studies in the classroom', *Australian Journal of Education, 37(2),* 115–18.

Mackay, D., Thompson, B. and Schaub, P. (1970) *Breakthrough to Literacy.* London: Longman.

Mackey, M. (1999) 'Popular culture and sophisticated reading: *Men in Black*', *English in Education,* 33(1), 47–57.

Malaguzzi, L. (1998) *The Hundred Languages of Children, 2nd edn.* Greenwich, CT: Ablex.

Mallett, M. (2003) *Primary English Encyclopaedia.* London: David.

Marsh, J. and Hallett, E. (1999) *Desirable Literacies.* London: Sage.

Marsh, J. and Millard, E. (2000) *Literacy and Popular Culture: using children's culture in the classroom.* London: Paul Chapman.

Mayer, R.E. and Morina, R. (2002) 'Animation as an aid to multimedia learning', *Educational Psychology Review,* 14(1), 87–99.

McGuinness, D. (2004) *Early Reading Instruction: what science really tells us about how to teach reading.* Cambridge, MA: MIT Press.

Mciver, A. (n.d.) *The New First Aid in English.* Glasgow: Robert Gibson.

McNamara, D. and Waugh, D. (1993) 'Classroom organisation', *School Organization,* 13(1), 41–50.

McWilliam, N. (1998) *What's in a Word? Vocabulary development in multilingual classrooms.* Stoke-on-Trent: Trentham Books.

Medwell, J. and Wray, D. (2007) 'Handwriting: what do we know and what do we need to know?', *Literacy,* 41(1), 10–16.

Medwell, J. and Wray, D. with Moore, G. and Griffiths, V. (2001b) *Primary English: knowledge and understanding.* Exeter: Learning Matters.

Medwell, J., Wray, D., Poulson, L. and Fox, R. (1998) *The Effective Teachers of Literacy Project* [report of a research project commissioned by the Teacher Training Agency]. Exeter: University of Exeter.

Mercer, N. (1995) *The Guided Construction of Knowledge: talk amongst teachers and learners.* Clevedon: Multilingual Matters.

Mercer, N. (2000) *Words and Minds: how we use language to think together.* London: Routledge.

Merchant, G. (2010) 'Virtual worlds as environments for literacy learning', *Educational Research,* 52(2), 135–50.

Merchant, G. and Thomas, H. (eds) (1999) *Picture Books for the Literacy Hour: activities for the primary teacher*. London: David Fulton.

Millard, E. and Marsh, J. (2001) 'Sending Minnie the *Minx* home: comics and reading choices', in *Cambridge Journal of Education*, 31(1), 25–38.

Miskin, R. (2011) *Read Write Inc.: phonics handbook*. Oxford: Oxford University Press.

Montgomery, D. (1997) *Spelling: remedial strategies*. London: Cassell.

Morris, R. (2001) 'Better teaching fosters better classroom control', *Education*, 107(2), 135–8.

Morris, S. and Collins, J. (2002) *Supporting Pupils for whom English is an Additional Language in the Literacy Hour*. Birmingham: Sandwell Literacy Centre.

Moses, B. and Corbett, P. (2002) *Works 2: poems for every subject and occasion*. London: Pan Macmillan.

Mosley, J. (1996) *Quality Circle Time*. Wisbech: Learning Development Aids.

Mudd, N. (1994) Effective Spelling: a practical guide for teachers. London: Hodder & Stoughton.

NACCCE (National Advisory Committee on Creative and Cultural Education) (1999) *All Our Futures: creativity, culture and education (the Robinson Report)*. London: DfEE.

Nation, K. (2010) 'Skills for reading comprehension', in K. Hall, U. Goswami, C. Harrison, S. Ellis and J. Soler, *Interdisciplinary Perspectives on Learning to Read*. London: Routledge, 74–86.

National Writing Project (1989a) *Responding to and Assessing Writing*. Walton-on-Thames: Nelson.

National Writing Project (1989b) *Responding to Written Work*. Walton-on-Thames: Nelson.

National Writing Project (1990) *Children's Perceptions of Writing*. Walton-on-Thames: Nelson.

NICHD (National Institute of Child Health and Human Development) (2000) *Report of the National Reading Panel. Teaching Children to Read: an evidence-based assessment of the scientific research literature on reading and its implications for reading instruction* [NIH publication no. 00–4769]. Washington, DC: U.S. Government Printing Office.

Nickerson, R. (1999) 'Enhancing creativity', in R.J. Sternberg (ed.) *Handbook of Creativity*. Cambridge: Cambridge University Press, 392–430.

Norman, K. (ed.) (1992) *Thinking Voices: the work of the National Oracy Project*. London: Hodder & Stoughton.

O'Neill, C. and Lambert, A. (1982) *Drama Structures*. London: Hutchinson.

Oakhill, J.V., Cain, K., and Bryant, P.E. (2003) 'The dissociation of word reading and text comprehension: evidence from component skills', *Language and Cognitive Processes*, 18, 443–68.

Oakhill, J.V. and Nation, K. (2003) 'The development of comprehension skills', in T. Nunes and P. Bryant (eds) *Handbook of Children's Literacy*. Dordrecht: Kluwer Academic Publishers, 155–80.

Ofsted (1999) *Raising the Attainment of Minority Ethnic Pupils*. London: Ofsted.

Ofsted (2002a) *The Key Stage 3 Strategy: evaluation of the first year of the pilot*. London: Ofsted.

Ofsted (2002b) *The National Literacy Strategy: the first four years, 1998–2002*. London: Ofsted.

Ofsted (2003) *Expecting the Unexpected: developing creativity in primary and secondary schools*. London: Ofsted (www.ofsted.gov.uk/resources/expecting-unexpected).

Ofsted (2009) *English at the Crossroads*. London: Ofsted.

Ofsted (2010a) *Reading by Six*. Manchester: Ofsted.

Ofsted (2010b) *Learning: creative approaches that raise standards*. Manchester: Ofsted.

Palinscar, A.S. and Brown, A.L. (1984) 'Reciprocal teaching of comprehension monitoring activities', *Cognition and Instruction*, 1, 117–75.

Palmer, S. (2006) *The Complete Skeleton Book for Non-Fiction Text Types*. Kirkby-in-Ashfield: TTS.

Perfetti, C.A. (1999) 'Comprehending written language: a blueprint of the reader', in C.M. Brown and P. Hagoort (eds) The neurocognition of language processing. London: Oxford University Press, 167–208.

Perkins, M. (2012) *Observing Primary Literacy*. London: Sage.

Peters, M.L. (1970) *Success in Spelling*. Cambridge: Cambridge Institute of Education.

Peters, M.L. (1975) 'Spelling – further thoughts', *Education 3–13*, 3(1), 36–40.

Peters, M.L. (1985) *Spelling: caught or taught? (A new look)*. London: Routledge & Kegan Paul.

Piaget, J. (1954) *The Construction of Reality in the Child*. New York: Free Press.

Pohan, C. (2003) 'Creating caring and democratic communities in our classrooms and schools', *Childhood Education*, 79(6), 369–73.

Pollard, A. (2002) *Reflective Teaching: effective and evidence-informed professional practice*. London: Continuum.

QCA (Qualifications and Curriculum Authority) (1999) *Teaching Speaking and Listening in Key Stages 1 and 2*. London: QCA.

QCA (2005) *Creativity: find it! Promote it! – Promoting pupils' creative thinking and behaviour across the curriculum at Key Stages 1, 2 and 3 – practical materials for schools*. London: QCA.

QCA and DfES (Department for Education and Skills) (2003) *Speaking, Listening, Learning: working with children in Key Stages 1 and 2*. London: HM Stationery Office.

Robinson, K. (2001) *Out of our Minds: learning to be creative*. Oxford: Capstone.

Robinson, K. and Aronica, L. (2009) *The Element: how finding your passion changes everything*. London: Continuum.

Robinson, M. (1997) *Children Reading Print and Television*. London: Falmer Press.

Rosenblatt, L. (1978) *The Reader, the Text, the Poem: the transactional theory of literacy work*. Carbondale, IL: South Illinois University Press.

Rosenblatt, L. (1989) 'Writing and reading: the transactional theory', in J. Mason (ed.) *Reading and Writing Connections*. Boston, MA: Allyn & Bacon, 153–76.

Ross, A. (1992) *Inspirations for Speaking and Listening*. Leamington Spa: Scholastic.

Rumelhart, D.E. and McClelland, J.L. (eds) (1986) *Parallel Distributed Processing, Vol. 1: foundations*. Cambridge, MA: MIT Press.

Sadoski, M. (2008) 'Dual coding theory: reading comprehension and beyond', in C.C. Block and S.R. Parris (eds) *Comprehension Instruction, 2nd edn*. New York: Guilford Press, 38–49.

Schonell, F.J. (1957) *Essentials in Teaching and Testing Spelling*. London: Macmillan.

Seidenberg, M.S. and McClelland, J.L. (1989) 'A distributed, developmental model of word recognition and naming', *Psychological Review*, 96, 523–68.

Seymour, P.H.K., Aro, M. and Erskine, J.M. (2003) 'Foundation literacy acquisition in European orthographies', *British Journal of Psychology*, 94, 143–74.

Sharan, S. (1990) *Cooperative Learning: theory and research*. Westport, CT: Praeger.

Shaw, B. (1916) *Pygmalion*. New York: Brentano (www.bartleby.com/138).

Siraj-Blatchford, I. (1994) *The Early Years: laying the foundations for racial equality*. Stoke-on-Trent: Trentham Books.

Skinner, B.F. (1957) *Verbal Behavior*. New York: Prentice Hall.

Slavin, R.E. (1983) *Cooperative Learning*. New York: Longman.

Slavin, R.E. (1995) *Cooperative Learning: theory, research, and practice*. Boston, MA: Allyn & Bacon.

Slavin, R.E. and Madden, N.A. (2005) *Fast Track Phonics, Volumes 1–3*. Nottingham: Success for All-UK.

Smith, F. (1971) *Understanding Reading: a psycholinguistic analysis of reading and learning to read*. New York: Holt, Rinehart & Winston.

Smith, F. (1975) *Comprehension and Learning*. New York: Holt, Rinehart and Winston.

Smith, F., Hardman, F., Wall, K. and Mroz, M. (2004) 'Interactive whole class teaching in the National Literacy and Numeracy Strategies', *British Educational Research Journal*, 30, 395–411.

Snow, C.E., Burns, S. and Griffin, P. (1998) *Preventing Reading Difficulties in Young Children*. Washington, DC: National Academy Press (www.nap.edu/readingroom/books/prdyc/execsumm.html).

Stanovich, K.E. (2000) *Progress in Understanding Reading: scientific foundations and new frontiers*. New York: Guildford Press.

Stockard, J. and Mayberry, M. (1992) *Effective Educational Environments*. Newbury Park: Corwin.

Sweeney, J. (1999) *50 Fantastic Poems with Wonderful Writing Prompts*. New York: Scholastic Professional Books.

Sylva, K., Melhuish, E., Sammons, P., Siraj-Blatchford, I. and Taggart, B. (2004) *Effective Pre-school and Primary Education*. London: DfES and Sure Start (http://eppe.ioe.ac.uk/eppe/eppepdfs/RBTec1223sept0412.pdf).

Tann, S. (1991) *Developing Language in the Primary Classroom*. London: Cassell.

Taylor, P. (2000) *The Drama Classroom*. London: Routledge.

Thomas, W. and Collier, V. (1997) *School Effectiveness and Language Minority Students*. Washington, DC: National Clearing House for Bilingual Education.

Tizard, B. and Hughes, M. (1984) *Young Children Learning: talking and thinking at home and at school*. London: Fontana.

Tomkins, G.E. (1994) *Teaching Writing: balancing process and product*. Englewood Cliffs, NJ: Macmillan.

Topping, K. (2001) *Thinking Reading Writing*. London: Continuum.

TTA (Teacher Training Agency) (2000) *Raising the Attainment of Minority Ethnic Pupils: guidance and resource material for providers of initial teacher training*. London: TTA.

UKLA and PNS (United Kingdom Literacy Association and Primary National Strategy) (2004) *Raising Boys' Achievements in Writing*. Royston: UKLA.

Vygotsky, L.S. (1978) *Mind in Society: the development of higher psychological processes*. Cambridge, MA: Harvard University Press.

Vygotsky, L.S. (1986) *Thought and Language* (trans., rev. and ed. A. Kozulin). Cambridge, MA: MIT Press.

Waller, M. (2009) 'Multiliteracies and meaningful learning contexts in the primary classroom', in *Proceedings of the 45th United Kingdom Literacy Association International Conference – making connections: building literate communities in and beyond classrooms, 10th–12th July 2009*. London: University of Greenwich.

Waugh, D. (1998) 'Practical approaches to teaching punctuation in the primary school', *Reading*, 32(2), 14–17.

Waugh, D. (2000a) *Further Curriculum Bank Writing at Key Stage 1*. Leamington Spa: Scholastic.

Waugh, D. (2000b) *Further Curriculum Bank Writing at Key Stage 2*. Leamington Spa: Scholastic.

Waugh, D. (2005) *All New 100 Literacy Hours: Year 2*. Leamington Spa: Scholastic.

Waugh, D., Jolliffe, W. and Taylor, K. (1999) *100 Literacy Hours for Year 2*. Leamington Spa: Scholastic.

Waugh, D. with McGuinn, N. (1996) *Curriculum Bank Writing at Key Stage 2*. Leamington Spa: Scholastic.

Wells, G. (1986) *The Meaning Makers*. London: Heinemann Educational.

Wells, G., Chang, G. and Maher, A. (1990) 'The literate potential of collaborative talk', in M. Maclure, T. Phillips and A. Wilkinson (eds) *Oracy Matters*. Milton Keynes: Open University Press, 95–109.

Welsh Language Board (1999) *Two Languages: twice the choice* [pamphlet]. Cardiff: Welsh Language Board.

Wertham, F. (1953) *Seduction of the Innocent*. New York: Rinehart.

White, T.G., Graves, M.F. and Slater, W.H. (1990) 'Growth of reading vocabulary in diverse elementary schools: decoding and word meaning', *Journal of Educational Psychology*, 82, 281–90.

Whitehead, M. (2002) 'Dylan's routes to literacy: the first three years with picture books', *Journal of Early Childhood Literacy*, 2(3), 269–89.

Whitehead, M. (2004) *Language and Literacy in the Early Years, 3rd edn*. London: Sage.

Whitehead, M. (2010) *Language and Literacy in the Early Years 0–7, 4th edn*. London: Sage.

Wilkinson, A. (1965) *Spoken English* [*Educational Review* occasional publications, no. 2]. Birmingham: University of Birmingham.

Williams, R. (1965) *The Long Revolution*. Harmondsworth: Penguin.

Wilson, A. (2005) *Language Knowledge for Primary Teachers*. London: David Fulton.

Wilson, A. (ed.) (2005) *Creativity in Primary Education*. Exeter: Learning Matters.

Wood, D. (1986) 'Aspects of teaching and learning', in M. Richards and P. Light (eds) *Children of Social Worlds*. Cambridge: Polity Press, 191–212

Wood, D. (1988) *How Children Think and Learn*. Oxford: Blackwell.

Woolland, B. (1993) *The Teaching of Drama in the Primary School*. New York: Longman.

Woolland, B. (2010) *Teaching Primary Drama*. Harlow: Pearson Education.

Wragg, E.C. (1993) *Class Management*. London: Routledge.

Wragg, E.C. (1997) *The Cubic Curriculum*. London: Routledge.

Wragg, E.C., Wragg, C.M., Haynes, G.S. and Chamberlain, R.P. (1998) *Improving Literacy in the Primary School*. London: Routledge.

Wray, D. (1995) *English 7–11*. London: Routledge.

Wray, D. (2004) *Teaching Literacy: using texts to enhance learning*. London: David Fulton.

Wray, D. (2006) *Teaching Literacy across the Primary Curriculum*. Exeter: Learning Matters.

Wray, D., Medwell, J., Poulson, L. and Fox, R. (2002) *Teaching Literacy Effectively*. London: Routledge Falmer.

Wren, S. (2001) *The Cognitive Foundations of Learning to Read: a framework*. Austin, TX: Southwest Educational Development Laboratory (www.sedl.org/cgi-bin/pdfexit.cgi?url=http://www.sedl.org/reading/framework/framework.pdf).

Wyse, D. and Goswami, U. (2008) 'Synthetic phonics and the teaching of reading', *British Educational Research Journal*, 34(6), 691–710.

Yoncheva, Y.N., Blau, V.C., Maurer, U. and McCandliss, B.D. (2006) 'Strategic focus during learning impacts the neural basis of expertise in reading', poster presented at the Association for Psychological Science Convention, New York, US, 25–8 May.

Zar, J.H. (1992) 'Candidate for a pullet surprise' (www.bios.niu.edu/zar/poem.pdf).

Ziegler, J.C. and Goswami, U. (2005) 'Reading acquisition, developmental dyslexia, and skilled reading across languages: a psycholinguistic grain size theory', *Psychological Bulletin*, 131, 3–29.

Index

accents 139, 152
active listening 98, 100, 101, 187, 265
Ahlberg, Allan 30, 43, 153
Aiken, Joan 148, 155, 202
alphabetic code 62, 116, 118-9, 122-3, 128
animation 28, 35, 233, 236, 237
antonyms 174, 218, 222
apostrophes 6, 75-6, 78-9, 81, 82, 150, 218
Assessing pupils' progress (APP) 97, 272, 276, 297,
    302-3, 307
assessment
    for learning 285, 289-90, 308
    formative 289, 292
    of learning 290, 308
    of reading 3, 289, 302, 303
    of speaking and listening 97, 289, 299
    of writing 306
    periodic 297, 302, 307
    summative 289, 291, 295, 303, 306
asylum seekers 184
audience 10, 30, 33, 42, 62, 72, 75, 96, 100, 102, 103,
    140, 170, 172, 197, 202, 205, 210, 211, 226, 233,
    237, 238, 243, 249, 253, 254, 260, 261, 265, 270,
    272, 306
audio recording 236
automaticity 111, 120, 197
Ayres, Pam 153

Bawden, Nina 146, 148
Becta 230, 232, 233, 234, 241
big books 130, 168, 186
bilingual 179, 180, 181, 182, 183, 184, 185, 187
bilingualism 181
Blackadder 174
Blogs 210, 245
Bloom's Taxonomy 93–4, 129
Blume, Judy 148
Blu-ray discs 235, 237

Blyton, Enid 146-7, 155
British Film Institute 32-3
Browne, Eileen 30, 43, 148
Bruner, Jerome 25, 46, 86, 110
Byars, Betsy 144, 150 155

calligrams 245
Carroll, Lewis 78, 151, 155, 217, 256
CD-ROM 172, 173, 236, 241
Chaucer, Geoffrey 79
checking writing 226
children's literature 61, 65, 137, 138, 141, 146, 149,
    155, 199, 237
children's self assessment 294, 297, 303
cinquains 153, 203
circle time 456, 98
class blogs 245
class discussions 15, 21, 22, 60, 94, 159, 276
class management 6, 8, 15, 18, 19, 22, 23, 199, 251
classroom environment 7, 9, 183, 210
cloze 174
cognitive approaches to spelling 221
cognitive development 45, 180
cognitive psychological perspective 108, 109, 136
collaborative puzzle-solving 84
collective nouns 222
comics 30, 36, 38, 42, 78
commas 75, 76, 77, 78, 81, 144, 285
Communicating Matters 47
Communication Language and Literacy 267, 268,
    290
comprehensible misspellings 213
comprehension skills 105, 123, 124, 127, 136, 302
comprehensive reading programme 127- 134
computer games 36, 37, 38, 42, 246
computers 6, 9, 62, 160, 164, 173, 177, 230, 231, 236,
    241, 244, 245, 246, 309
contingent teaching 64, 85

cooperative:
    learning 2, 13, 22, 84, 88, 89, 93, 124, 187, 255,
        262
    work 209
    writing 205, 209
Corbett, Pie 63, 95, 149, 156, 265
core principles of teaching English 263, 265
creative partnerships 26, 88
creativity i, 2, 3, 24, 25-8, 40, 42, 44, 59, 60, 62, 101,
    151, 203, 248, 209, 232
cross-curricular links 28, 149, 269, 271, 272, 150, 161,
    167, 187, 188, 189
culture 24, 28, 30, 32, 35, 36-8, 42, 44, 54, 65, 87,
    110, 148, 153, 179, 181-4, 187-8, 190, 237, 234
curriculum map 269, 270

Dahl, Roald 95, 144, 153, 155, 199, 217
DARTs 302
databases 159, 170, 172, 270
decision-making 2, 4, 5, 8, 9, 12, 14, 85, 89
decoding 109-13, 117, 125, 127-9, 131-2, 136, 265,
    303, 308
descriptive writing 208, 260
Desert Island Discs 176, 177
development of language 2, 11, 51
Dewey, John 165
diagnostic assessment 115, 123, 128, 132, 135, 292
    of writing 30-5
diagrams and charts 174
dialects 66
dialogic teaching 87
dictionaries 21, 152, 153, 159, 168, 169, 171, 173, 174,
    176, 189, 190, 199, 200, 204, 213, 218, 222, 226,
    227, 228, 233, 242
differentiation 123, 225, 234, 285
digital literacy 57, 241
digital recording devices 236
digitised speech 242
digraphs 120-21, 219, 224
discussion texts 164
drafting 73, 81, 165, 194, 197, 203, 206, 209, 226, 241,
    265
drama 2, 3, 7, 16, 18, 26, 33, 34, 38, 39, 40, 42, 54, 56,
    58, 78, 91, 96, 97, 128, 129, 130, 132, 140, 144,
    173, 199, 237, 246, 248-262
DVD 9, 11, 28, 39, 231, 232, 235, 236, 237, 241
dyslexia 7, 107

early writing 58, 62, 77, 192, 197
Early Years Foundation Stage
    Framework 26, 49, 56, 97, 120, 167, 196, 225, 263,
        267, 269, 289, 290
Early Years Foundation Stage profile 290
eBooks 241
editing 72, 73, 197, 201, 209, 237, 241, 243, 244, 265,
    306
educational visits 172
electronic text 238, 240, 241, 244
Elton Report 17

e-mail 28, 29, 37, 162, 172, 210, 232, 241
emergent writing 59
English as an additional language 2, 7, 32, 179, 180,
    191, 251
environment for talk 54
environmental issues 175
environmental print 2, 41, 60, 185, 226
etymology 209, 218, 220, 221
Every Child a Talker (ECAT) 50
Excellence and Enjoyment 26, 27, 28, 92, 98
exclamation marks 75, 76, 78, 253
explanation texts 163

Facebook 29, 245
fiction writing 209
Fields, W.C. 15
film 6, 31, 32, 33, 34, 35, 27, 38, 39, 42, 100, 138, 143,
    148, 176, 237, 252, 272, 280
Fine, Anne 143, 148
flow 25
Foundation Stage profile 290
freeze-framing 33, 35, 39, 130, 255

geography 74, 168, 177, 270
Gibb, Nick 107
Google 172, 242, 247
GoogleEarth 145
grammar i, v, 1, 45, 47, 66, 67, 73, 82, 160, 201, 206,
    222, 305, 314
grammatical rules 72
grapheme cards 224
graphemes 115, 117, 119, 120, 152, 213, 214, 218, 223,
    224, 239
graphic organisers 167
Greek myths 145
group discussion 91, 94, 97, 129, 133, 194
Guardian Education 7
guided reading 20, 31, 94, 105, 129, 132, 171, 272, 301
guided writing 95, 142, 194, 196, 295, 303, 308

haiku 153, 156, 203, 205, 285
handwriting 1, 62, 63, 64, 122, 183, 192, 195, 197,
    198, 199, 207, 222, 226, 238, 242, 243, 272, 281,
    307, 319
history ii, 57, 75, 159, 168, 177, 188, 208, 249, 255,
    270, 317
home literacy 56, 183, 186
homonyms 68, 222, 226, 228
homophones 68, 217, 226, 228
Hood, Thomas 150
hot-seating 56, 128, 129, 130, 132, 140, 254
Hughes, Ted 56, 322
hyperlinks 28, 169, 232, 236, 244, 245

ICT 6, 11, 29, 32, 35, 41, 87, 88, 169, 223, 230, 231,
    232, 246, 247, 270, 272, 273, 275, 284, 312, 315,
    316
independent writing 3, 20, 71, 169, 194, 196, 199,
    203, 265, 266

inference 32, 125, 126, 136, 141, 175, 314
information skills 173
instructions 10, 11, 18, 37, 60, 98, 99, 162, 165, 185, 188, 285, 290, 293
interactive whiteboard 6, 9, 80, 169, 208, 230, 231, 234, 238, 239, 243, 278, 309
internet 159, 160, 170, 172, 173, 175, 231, 232, 234, 236, 239, 244, 245, 301
interthinking 86, 87, 314
iPad 231
iPod 9

jigsawing 170
Jolly Phonics 122, 222, 229

Keats, John 153
Kerr, Judith 195
key learning principles (KLP) 47
knowledge about language 2, 6, 66-83, 176, 179, 182, 202, 253, 262

language acquisition device (LAD) 45, 46
language acquisition support system (LASS) 46
language development 10, 44-46, 49-51, 56, 108, 117
language diversity 187
language surveys 183
Lawrence, Caroline 148
left-handedness 198, 199
learning objectives 12, 17, 71, 202, 203, 209, 271, 274, 285, 293, 298, 304, 308
lesson-planning ii, 11, 18, 56, 273, 286
Letters and Sounds 1, 62, 107, 113, 122, 123, 292, 316
letter strings 216, 220, 225
level descriptions 297, 298, 302, 307
Lewis, Clive Staples 155, 319
libraries 165, 176
library skills 165
limericks 153, 203
linguistic comprehension 111, 112, 115
literacy environment 179, 185
Literacy Framework 6, 68, 203, 248, 261
literacy hour 167, 170, 187, 193, 203, 273
literate environment 196, 197
Lofting, Hugh 147
long-term planning 268, 272, 288
look, say, cover, write, check 220, 228, 239

Magorian, Michelle 145, 148
Malaguzzi, Loris 319
marking 202, 207, 238, 292, 293, 304
mathematics 6, 50, 74, 91, 106, 173, 211, 223, 249, 267, 291, 315, 316
McGough, Roger 153, 279, 283
McKee, David 142
medium term plans 271, 288
metacognition 96
metrophobia 148
MFL (modern foreign languages) ii, 68, 237
Milligan, Spike 70, 153

mindmaps 244
miscue analysis 135, 292, 295, 299, 304, 306, 308
mnemonics 123, 152, 221
modelling writing 63, 195, 196
morphology 112, 218, 220
Morpurgo, Michael 100, 145, 146, 155, 201
Moses, Brian 149, 156, 320
mother tongue 82, 180, 313
multilingual i, v, vii, 179-191, 313, 316, 319
Multimap 172
multimedia 35, 124, 131, 233, 236, 237, 239, 241, 243-246, 316, 319
multimodal texts 24, 28, 30, 42, 232, 236, 246
Murphy, Jill 142, 156

narrative 30, 33, 34, 36, 37, 40, 50, 51, 58, 63, 101, 149, 153, 166, 171, 172, 195, 200, 250, 260, 270, 278
narrative writing 63, 270
National Curriculum 1, 2, 5, 26, 27, 42, 68, 76, 81, 90, 91, 106, 146, 159, 193, 197, 232, 247, 248, 263, 272, 286, 291, 295, 297, 298, 302-308, 314, 315
National Curriculum levels 291, 297, 298, 303, 304, 306, 308
National Literacy Strategy 1, 13, 76, 91, 106, 111, 177, 193, 264, 285, 312, 315, 320
National Writing Project 95, 227, 320
newspapers 9, 79, 161, 162, 171-174, 176, 188, 225, 241
non-fiction i, 2, 39, 73, 127, 130, 158, 159, 161, 162, 165-169, 171, 177, 178, 200, 236, 244, 247, 300, 310, 318, 320
nonsense:
    poems 153
    sentences 70, 74, 82
note-making 165, 209
nursery rhymes 152, 158, 235

Ofsted 6, 26, 88, 106, 111, 116, 117, 181, 229
Open Source software 245
Oracy 88, 90, 92, 318, 320, 322
oral language 47, 50, 90, 116, 123, 127, 251, 313
over-articulation 221

painting 31, 40. 144, 208
parents 2, 7, 12, 35, 38, 45-6, 48, 50, 56-59, 61, 100, 142, 177, 181, 183-6, 197, 218, 225, 231-2, 245, 261, 268
parts of speech 6, 68-71, 74, 151, 173-4
pedagogical content 5
pedagogy 4, 11, 14, 36
PSHE 138-9, 144, 148, 255, 270
persuasion 98, 100, 162, 164, 171, 276
persuasion texts 164
persuasive writing 171, 209, 255
philosophy for children 88
phoneme-grapheme correspondence 196, 209, 295, 308

phonemes 46, 64, 115, 117-123, 128, 130-131, 152, 170, 213-4, 218, 223-4, 239, 265, 292, 301
phonic knowledge 6, 14, 117-8, 131, 168, 170, 197, 204, 220-221, 229, 290, 292
phonic understanding 153, 221, 223
phonics 1, 2, 6, 14, 63, 105-108, 111-112, 115-120, 122-123, 127-128, 131, 136, 196, 213, 215-216, 220, 222, 225, 228-229, 239, 272, 292, 301, 309
phonological awareness 107, 116-117, 120, 127-128, 130, 239
Piaget, Jean 45, 233
picture books 30-31, 43
planning 3, 5, 9, 11, 13, 16-18, 20, 23, 27, 31, 38-9, 56, 60, 63, 85, 91, 96-7, 104, 124, 143, 161, 177, 183-4, 187, 194, 196-7, 199, 231, 241, 243, 245, 249, 260-1, 263-9, 275, 283, 285-9, 291, 296-8, 303, 305-8, 310
planning process 245, 263-4
play
    epistemic 60
    ludic 60
plenary sessions 22, 274, 285, 294
podcasts 235
poetry 32, 38, 137, 143, 148-157
Poetry Please 149
popular culture 24, 35, 37-8, 42
popular music 37, 42
Powerpoint 172, 234
précis 176
prefixes 174, 209, 216-8
Primary National Strategy 161, 168, 170-1, 174, 177, 193, 207, 292-3, 304-5
programmes of study 158, 297, 302, 307
proof-reading 76, 202, 213
punctuation 1, 6, 66, 71-2, 75-82

QCA 26-7, 76, 91, 97, 159, 235, 291
question marks 75-6, 78, 253
questioning 12-13, 84, 92-4, 103-4, 129, 132, 293, 295, 302, 308

rainbowing 170
raising boys' achievements 39, 96
Read Write Inc. 122, 204, 214, 222, 229
reading:
    aloud 16, 18, 20, 31, 75, 80, 113, 126, 129, 132, 134, 139, 140, 149, 155, 166, 169, 205, 253, 256, 290, 301
    and spelling 118, 120, 122, 222
    beginning 116, 127-8, 131
    bottom up 110-11
    in the early years 300
    logs 140-141, 210
    recovery 107, 135
    silent 113, 129, 132, 199, 205
    to children 47, 137-140
    top down 109-111
    wars 106
reciprocal reading 302

recount texts 98-99, 162
reference areas 159
reference texts 169
reflection 276-283
Renewed Framework for Literacy and Mathematics 1, 6, 68, 91, 111, 162, 203, 248, 261, 266, 271, 309
reorganising text 174
report texts 163
reports 98, 100, 171-2, 176, 203, 236, 270-1
responding to children's work 201-202, 227
response partners 76, 81, 95
response to text 302
revising 73, 193, 197, 201, 209, 265
rich scripting 187, 189-190
root words 209, 218
Rose Review 91-2, 111-112, 116, 263
Rosen, Michael 43, 63, 153
Rowling, J.K. 145, 156, 199
running record 135, 291-2, 295, 299, 303, 308

scaffolding 64, 86, 196, 265
scheme of work 5
scribing 62, 95, 193-4, 266
searchlights model 111
seating arrangements 10
self-assessment 14, 84, 293-4, 297, 300, 303
semantic skills 47, 109, 113-4, 124, 174, 188, 190, 222
Sendak, Maurice 30, 40, 43
sentence:
    level 12, 73, 108, 160, 209, 264, 273, 303, 305
    structure 70, 72-4, 197, 305-6
Shakespeare, William 153, 212
shared:
    imaging 187, 189-190
    reading 12, 19, 31, 37, 71, 128-132, 134, 139, 153, 164, 167, 169, 186-7, 197, 209, 254
    writing 16, 62-4, 72-4, 95-6, 142-5, 152-3, 166, 169, 190, 193-8, 203, 205, 209, 219
Shaw, George Bernard 66
short-term planning 268, 275, 288
similes 152, 222
simple view of reading 111-3, 123, 136
Skype 232, 237
smart phones 231-2
Social and Emotional Aspects of Learning (SEAL) 28, 88, 98
Social networking 29, 232, 237
speaking and listening 2-3, 10, 13, 39, 50, 56, 61, 65, 84, 88, 90-93, 96-7, 102-4, 187, 209, 235-7, 239, 242, 245, 248, 254-5, 262, 264-5, 275, 289, 291, 295, 297-9, 307, 310
special educational needs 181, 233, 291
speech marks 76, 78-9, 81, 138, 202, 253
spellcheckers 226, 239-40
spelling:
    dictionaries 176, 200, 227
    principles 212, 218
    rules, 212, 218-20, 228
spoonerisms 226

SATS 134, 291, 303
Standard English 66, 91, 97, 298
stories 2, 16-17, 29, 34, 37, 49, 56, 58, 63-4, 72-4, 78,
    95, 99, 101-2, 137, 139, 141, 143, 145-8, 154-5,
    167, 185, 189-90, 192, 196, 200, 217, 235-6, 245,
    253-5, 260, 270-1, 290, 296, 310
Storr, Catherine 143, 156
storysacks 31, 55
storytelling 34-5, 38, 49, 56, 58, 63, 101, 104, 185,
    250
Success for All 122
suffixes 174, 209, 216-7, 219
supported composition 95, 194, 196, 266, 272
Support for Spelling 1, 212, 216, 218
Sure Start 57
sustained shared thinking 51, 65
Sutcliff, Rosemary 148, 156
syllabic structure 119
syllables 119, 128, 156-7, 228
synonyms 190, 218, 222
syntactic clues 174
systematic synthetic phonics 1, 6, 107, 116, 222

tablet computers 231, 237, 245
talk and writing 95
talk:
    cumulative 86, 88
    diary 102
    disputational 86
    exploratory 87
    opportunities for 38, 49, 56, 98, 103, 124, 264,
        287
    partner 55, 63, 95, 124
talk for learning 84, 88, 90-1, 97
Talk for Writing 1, 63, 95, 192, 258, 265, 272
talking books 235-6, 239
target statements for writing 305, 308
teacher demonstration 194, 266
teacher scribing 95, 194, 266
teaching:
    assistants 10-11, 183, 205
    comprehension skills 61, 105, 123-4, 127, 136, 302
    strategies 123, 179, 181, 186, 273
text messaging 29
theoretical perspectives on reading 108
theories of language development 44
thesaurus 159, 169, 171, 187, 189-190, 199, 204, 226,
    242
This is Your Life 177
THRASS 122, 204, 214
thought-tracking 39

Times Educational Supplement 7, 234, 310
trigraphs 224
triolets 153-4, 156, 203
Twitter 29, 245

University Challenge 34

virtual learning environments (VLE) 231
visualiser 238, 243
visual texts 30
vocabulary 33-4, 38, 40, 47, 50, 61, 70-71, 74, 86, 101,
    112, 116, 120, 123-129, 131-3, 136, 139, 150,
    160-1, 166, 171, 187-9, 199, 201-3, 208, 217-8,
    222, 251-3, 255, 257, 259, 276, 284, 298, 301-2,
    304, 306-7
VoiceThread 237
Vygotsky, Lev 85-6, 110

Wallace and Gromit 35
WALT 293-4, 304
Web 2.0 29, 231, 246
websites 28-9, 32, 37, 161, 172, 203, 210, 226, 231,
    234-6, 239, 247, 272, 280, 310
Who Wants to be a Millionaire? 34
Wifi 231
Wikis 244-5
WILF 293-4, 304
Wilson, Jacqueline 148
WINK 293, 304
word:
    banks 153, 166, 168, 201, 204, 228
    class mobility 68-9
    clouds 245
    level 14, 127-134, 140, 143, 168, 264, 272, 280
    lists 63, 187, 212, 216-8, 220, 239, 242
    recognition 13, 109-14, 117-8, 123-5, 299
    weaving 187, 189-90
word-processing 169, 242, 244, 246
Wright, Kit 43, 153
writing:
    analysis 265-6, 292, 304-6, 308
    boys and writing 28, 39, 96, 197, 233
    emergent 59, 61-2, 196
    narrative 63
    partners 20, 199, 203, 205
    process 94-5, 193, 195, 201, 205, 227, 233-4,
        241-4, 265, 273, 304, 306

YouTube 11, 35, 236

zone of proximal development (ZPD) 86